To Dick
with best regards

Ross

War and Society in Ancient Mesoamerica

War and Society in Ancient Mesoamerica

Ross Hassig

UNIVERSITY OF CALIFORNIA PRESS
Berkeley · *Los Angeles* · *Oxford*

University of California Press
Berkeley and Los Angeles, California

University of California Press
Oxford, England

Copyright © 1992 by the Regents of the University of California

Library of Congress Cataloging-in-Publication Data

Hassig, Ross, 1945–
    War and society in ancient Mesoamerica / Ross Hassig.
      p.   cm.
    Includes bibliographical references (p.   ) and index.
    ISBN 0-520-07734-2 (cloth : alk. paper)
    1. Indians of Mexico—Wars. 2. Indians of Mexico—History.
  3. Aztecs—Wars. 4. Aztecs—History. 5. Teotihuacán Site (San Juan
  Teotihuacán, Mexico) 6. Mexico—Antiquities. I. Title.
  F1219.3.W37H37   1992
  972'.52—dc20   91-42635
                                                                  CIP

Printed in the United States of America

1 2 3 4 5 6 7 8 9

The paper used in this publication meets the minimum requirements
of American National Standard for Information Sciences—Permanence
of Paper for Printed Library Materials, ANSI Z39.48-1984 ∞

For my wife, Debra Higgs Hassig

*Without whose support, encouragement,
and assistance this book could not have
been written*

Contents

Acknowledgments

Thanks are owed to many people for assistance in the writing of this book—many more than will be named here, because ideas, information, and inspiration need not be major efforts but are frequently conveyed offhandedly and often come from unlikely sources. Although I am thanking only those who directly assisted in this project, my debts spread considerably farther.

Where help has been of a specific nature, I have acknowledged its providers in the notes. There are always some whose help has been more general, and among these, I would like to thank John Justeson of the State University of New York at Albany and Jim Fox of Stanford University for help with Maya archaeology and epigraphy. I also owe thanks to Esther Pasztory of Columbia University and Emily Umberger of Arizona State University for help with various aspects of Mesoamerican art. I am also indebted to Dale Floyd of the U.S. Army Corps of Engineers and Dan Rogers of the Smithsonian Institution for information about fortifications. I have also relied on the expertise of J. Richard Andrews of Vanderbilt University in Nahuatl orthography and have greatly benefited from the general advice of Claudio Lomnitz of New York University. As with my previous work on Aztec warfare, I have also been helped enormously by discussions on military matters with Neil Goldberg of the Dalton School. I would like to thank Christine Schultz for drawing the maps. Most important, I have been greatly aided by the advice, forbearance, and editorial assistance of my wife, Debra, to whom this book is dedicated.

This book would not have been possible without the generous assistance of two summer grants from the John D. and Catherine T. MacArthur Foundation, a fellowship at Dumbarton Oaks, and especially a research grant from the Harry Frank Guggenheim Foundation. My thanks to them all.

CHAPTER 1

The Approach to War

Warfare has greatly shaped the cultures and histories of much of the world, including Mesoamerica.[1] Yet, with few exceptions, military explanations of Mesoamerican prehistory have been either cursory or generalized on data from the era of the Spanish conquest. To redress these shortcomings, this book has three major purposes. The first is to clarify Mesoamerica's military past, which was not a simplified version of Aztec practices but differed in weapons and tactics through time and between societies. The second goal is to explain the role of war in Mesoamerican societies. No single rationale can account for how, when, where, and why wars were fought throughout the roughly three thousand years under consideration here. Yet through focusing more consciously and conscientiously on Mesoamerica's martial past, important features and dynamics emerge that promise a better understanding of what did occur. The third goal is to place military matters in a broader social and historical context to show their role in individual societies and in creating and maintaining Mesoamerica as a culture area, thereby providing the indispensable basis for linking and integrating much of the region.

Warfare studies have frequently excluded broader social history because of their specific military focus and, for the West, the assumption that the general historical outlines are already known. This will be partly true here, for some selectivity is vital to maintain the focus of the study. Because precolumbian Mesoamerica is not as well known, more

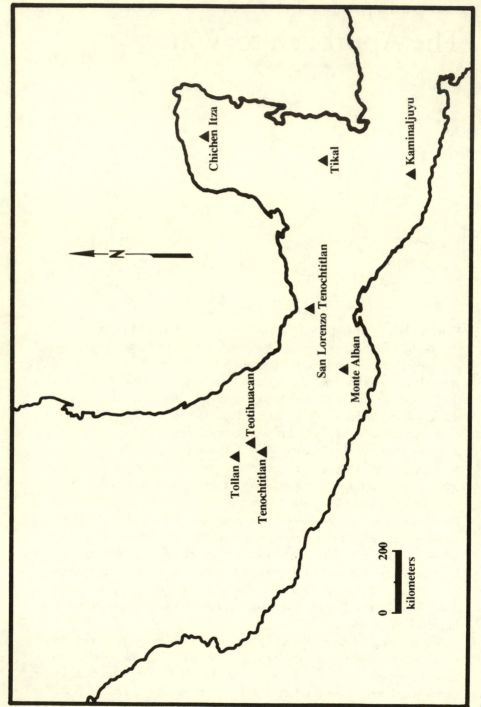

Mesoamerica with major sites discussed in text.

emphasis will be placed on broader social history. The object is not to distort the general picture by eliminating inconvenient data, but to highlight the military aspects so they may be seen more clearly. However, isolated cultures cannot be the primary focus. Military history necessarily concentrates on the relations between societies and emphasizes the importance of relational developments over internal ones.[2] Moreover, as a practical matter, the emphasis will be primarily on the expanding groups which show the military state of the art at that time and on the processes of their expansion: imperialism.[3]

Despite the frequency with which the term is used, imperialism has been defined in various ways.[4] A thorough analysis of these definitions is beyond the scope of this book, but, simply put, an empire is a relationship in which one state controls the effective political sovereignty of another polity, and imperialism is the way in which an empire is established and maintained.[5] Three broad groups of theories purport to explain this phenomenon. The first type sees imperialism as based on an inherent need of the center to expand, as, for instance, capitalism has been viewed as necessarily expanding in search of new markets. Thus, imperialism is seen as arising from a given social structure. The second type sees imperialism as a consequence of the weakness of the periphery where stability cannot be maintained, forcing stronger polities to impose order that allows predictable relations. While social structures are also causal in this view, these lie in the periphery rather than in the center. Although aspects of both of these theories apply, I have adopted the third type as most appropriate, in which expansion is seen as a natural consequence of power differences between polities rather than as arising from a particular social structure.

International relations are basically anarchic, with no guarantee of stability between polities. The greater a society's dependence on others, the weaker it is.[6] Because access to essential external resources cannot be guaranteed, polities expand their domination to bring resource-producing areas within the polity, thus making the costs and benefits of various actions predictable.[7] According to this view, imperialism springs from the existence of competing national sovereignties that expand in relation to their relative power. However, the resources that polities expand to control are culturally determined: some, such as cotton and obsidian, are material improvements, if not necessities, but others, such as cacao and quetzal feathers, are materially nonessential though often highly valued.[8] In the Mesoamerican case, many

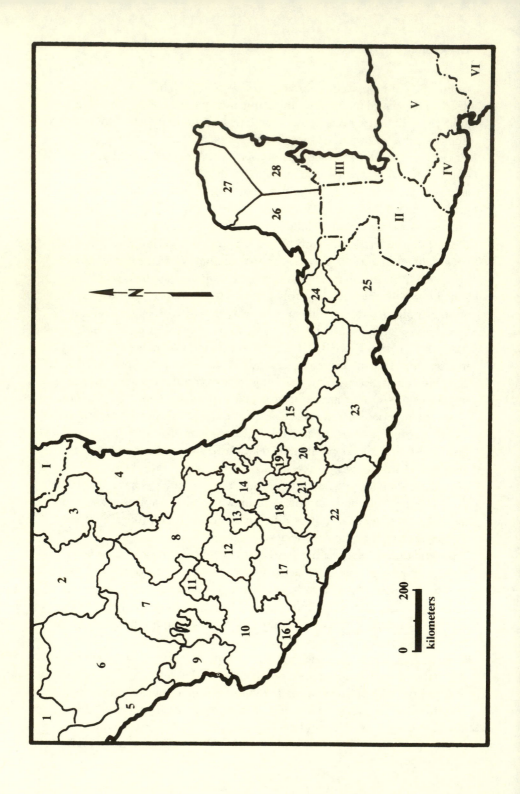

Mesoamerica with modern national and state boundaries:

I—United States of America   IV—El Salvador
II—Guatemala   V—Honduras
III—Belize   VI—Nicaragua

States of Mexico (left to right and top to bottom):

1—Chihuahua   15—Veracruz
2—Coahuila   16—Colima
3—Nuevo Leon   17—Michoacan
4—Tamaulipas   18—Mexico
5—Sinaloa   19—Tlaxcala
6—Durango   20—Puebla
7—Zacatecas   21—Morelos
8—San Luis Potosi   22—Guerrero
9—Nayarit   23—Oaxaca
10—Jalisco   24—Tabasco
11—Aguascaliente   25—Chiapas
12—Guanajuato   26—Campeche
13—Queretaro   27—Yucatan
14—Hidalgo   28—Quintana Roo

The Federal District, bordered by the states of Mexico and Morelos, is unmarked.

political developments can be seen as attempts to gain control over external resources.

ORGANIZATION

There are three major ways to structure a book such as this: thematic, evidentiary, and chronological. The thematic approach focuses on separate topics in isolation, such as arms and armor or tactics, which highlight specific developments, but at the cost of an overall view of societies. The evidentiary approach builds from the strongest data, beginning with the best documented Mesoamerican society—the Aztecs—whose military practices can be discussed with relative certainty, and then modifies this information and interprets earlier cultures in light of it. This puts the most compelling case first but obscures the developmental sequence and risks imposing later practices on earlier societies. The chronological approach—the one adopted here—emphasizes sequential development. The weaknesses of this approach are that it divides thematic topics and begins with some of the poorest data, but I believe these shortcomings are more than offset by the twin advantages of seeing each society as a coherent whole and doing so in a more readable early-to-late temporal sequence.

Reconstructing Mesoamerican societies as coherent wholes from a martial perspective requires an understanding of arms and armor as well as other military technology, such as fortifications and siege machines. Similarly, tactics must also be reconstructed, but because weapons use has remained fairly constant, this can be inferred from the types and proportions of weapons available, as has been demonstrated in the better documented Old World.

It has also been fairly well established that weapons and tactics are closely related to general social structure—not kinship, but the general social nature of the societies in question. Allied with this is army size, which can be based on population figures, at least insofar as maximum army sizes are concerned. Within these limits, more exact estimates can be reached by considering the tactics employed and the nature of the societies involved.

The links between military technology, tactics, and general social and political structure have been firmly established in Old World history and are also substantiated in Mesoamerica for the historically recorded Conquest period. Accordingly, these relationships will serve as a basis for interpreting and linking the available data to achieve the most logical and coherent pattern.

DATA

Most of the direct evidence used in reconstructing the Mesoamerican past is archaeological, including works of art, although even these are limited to the areas and time periods that have received scholarly attention. Site excavations offer the best evidence for population (and hence logistics and imperial structure), site locations, and fortifications. But works of art also provide information on many aspects of warfare that would otherwise remain unknown, frequently offering the only available glimpse of battle tactics, weaponry, combat practices, and various aspects of political rule. However, sculptural and pictorial representations do not always depict practices accurately, because cultural values weigh heavily in what motifs are selected. For example, despite the pivotal importance of the *macuahuitl* (broadsword) in Aztec warfare, as amply attested in Spanish accounts, it is not depicted in precolumbian art even in scenes that show warriors and capture. Moreover, artistic representations are almost always self-depictions, executed at the behest of victors who show themselves as they wish to be seen. For example, on the Stone of Tizoc, the Aztec king emphasizes his ties to the previous empire by wearing Toltec military attire, and a smoking mirror replaces his left foot in the manner of the war god Tezcatlipoca. While such representations are culturally correct—that is, they show elements that are intelligible within that culture—they are not always historically correct.

The extant precolumbian art is also largely elite and urban, which skews depictions toward the powerful, since battles are fought and recorded from the perspective of the rulers. This does not mean such representations are necessarily inaccurate, merely incomplete, omitting much of the perspective of other classes. Thus, the lacunae in the artistic data, the way they have been skewed in their creation and after by the vagaries of preservation and discovery, limit their usefulness as truly comprehensive accounts.

The data that are available often make it difficult to assess the role of the military in precolumbian Mesoamerica in a comprehensive fashion. The period just before the Spanish conquest is relatively well known, thanks to written histories in native, Western, and mixed traditions, as well as archaeological remains and works of art such as sacrificial vessels, commemorative plaques, murals, and so forth. The data are less complete for earlier eras, however, slanting interpretations toward what has survived in the archaeological record.[9] Consequently, much of the Mesoamerican past is reconstructed by comparison and analogy with contact-period groups because, except for a limited corpus of glyphic inscriptions, there are no written accounts for earlier periods.

In my reconstructing a military history, one focus will be on technology, not simply because this has been a traditional approach to the subject elsewhere, but because arms, armor, and fortifications provide perhaps the most complete body of evidence. The history of military technology is enlightening, as new weapons and tactics stimulate each other and engender new responses in the well-known offense-defense cycle.[10] Moreover, military superiority depends, in large part, on which group has the best armaments.[11] However, technology alone does not determine military expansion, especially in a non-industrial society.[12]

Despite its undeniable importance,[13] technology per se does not drive war. It is societal organization that is pivotal, for technology can be used only by groups organized appropriately to take advantage of it.[14] Thus, there is a real connection between weapons and the structure of society:[15] some technology can more readily be adopted by certain types of social organizations than by others without fostering significant, and possibly unacceptable, social change. As a result, technology affects military organization, which in turn influences social and political organization in a reciprocal pattern.[16]

The relationship between technology and organization is not immediate and direct, but is culturally mediated: societal values determine what is, and is not, acceptable weaponry and behavior.[17] There is unquestionably an ideological component to warfare—at a minimum, each culture has its own standards of what weapons and practices are acceptable in warfare[18]—but ideology as reflected in works of art is not my primary focus, as interpretations of it are all too often untestable.[19] Moreover, ideology does not explain the expansion of one group in a situation where the same values are also shared by the conquered societies. But even if ideology can be accurately detected in art, it may not reflect that society's real-world capabilities. Ideology must be reconstructed from behavior: meaning cannot be properly assessed without knowing the real-world consequences of warfare for the people involved. Ideological interpretations of warfare must be based on reconstructions of actual conditions and events—how war affected the people, who participated, what kinds of costs it involved, and so forth. Meaning can be pursued only after the place and impact of warfare in a society have been addressed, not before, and never in isolation.

SOCIETIES

No one doubts the reality of the people behind the artifacts uncovered in Mesoamerica, but identifying specific social groups based on these is often problematic. When historical accounts are lacking, the identification of cultural groupings is typically based on clusters of artistic, architectural, and technological characteristics. This poses few problems where such clusters are spatially or temporally discrete, but the very nature of warfare means contact, expansion, and the spread or merger of archaeologically recoverable artifacts. In such circumstances, how can a specific group that has expanded over large areas be distinguished from different groups sharing widely distributed common characteristics? Historical linguistics can help, but language divisions do not necessarily correlate with cultural ones, and while it is a valuable adjunct, it cannot be the sole basis for tracing cultural groups.

In principle, archaeology should be able to discern and distinguish between cultural groupings, if not political entities, but in practice the fragmentary nature of the data and the poor temporal control that results in aggregating broad time spans make it difficult to differentiate between a widely shared cultural tradition and the relatively rapid intrusion of a culture over decades or even centuries. This is especially true for early periods. Unable to pinpoint groups and distinguish them adequately, we often question the existence of contacting groups, and the spread of new cultural patterns is frequently explained as reflecting pan-Mesoamerican traditions.

Certainly technologies can spread rapidly, especially simple ones that do not require major technological support for adoption, and ideological changes can sweep vast areas, spreading common or similar symbols across cultural boundaries. But even these are not borne on the wind; they require some person-to-person contact, especially in the case of military technology. Arms and armor are not simple technologies readily adopted for their utility. They are closely related to cultural values concerning war and politics and intimately connected with a society's social structure. They do not spread as easily and perhaps as unaltered as, say, pottery forms and motifs. The ideas they reflect may well spread, but not the physical implement; rather, arms and armor are differentially adopted and adapted to local needs, styles, and preferences. Such resistance and partial adoption can easily be seen in the Crusades, in which two major military technologies and styles—Western European Christian and Middle Eastern Islamic— came into prolonged contact without effecting massive adoptions of the other's technology in either case. The few that were adopted, such as Islamic defensive architecture used in European fortifications, were incorporated in a distinctly Western style. Different social structures, if not cultural preferences, pattern the adoption of different military technologies. And where it is difficult to draw major distinctions between societies within a broad cultural tradition, such as medieval Western Europe, it is because these similarities arose in areas of similar social structures.

Thus, while societies are difficult to trace in Mesoamerica on the basis of such relatively simple cultural artifacts as ceramics and lithics, military technologies do provide a basis. Because these tend to form coherent albeit evolving systems and are not readily adoptable into other societies on a wholesale basis, their presence or absence can frequently be used, at least in part, to trace the movement of identifiable groups. Consequently, my focus is on cultures and often specific societies within those traditions because it is people, and not diffuse cultural traditions, who expand militarily.

EXPANSION

Thus far, only tactical matters have been considered, but strategic concerns are clearly evident in the expansion of Mesoamerican empires. Among other things, the ability to wage effective war depends on how a given society copes with the problems of recruitment and logistical support. Who directly participates in war differs according to the organization of society, typically varying by age, sex, social class, and the cost of equipment. Consequently, states with comparable populations may nevertheless field numerically dissimilar forces.[20] Thus, while military power supports the state, internal needs do not always translate into the ability to wage effective war, especially at a distance.[21] Distance translates into time and, more important, food for troops in the field and most polities are limited in the distances they can expand and hold under existing conditions.[22] What a polity can impose close to home is not usually feasible at great distances. Empires may expand quickly and easily into adjacent areas, but they often require some technological or organizational breakthrough to hold distant areas, for large forces cannot be sent great distances and maintained there indefinitely. Moreover, the costs of control increase over time because contacted areas develop in response to imperial influence, often becoming more formidable.[23] This pattern of stimulated development of the periphery provides one of the basic dynamics of Mesoamerican empires. Although such empires faced few major competitors initially, their own expansion stimulated competition in distant areas to the point that the empires could no longer effectively or efficiently enforce their wills. In Mesoamerica, this created a cycle that involved expansion into relative political vacuums, the development of an internal infrastructure dependent on servicing those colonial areas, the development of stronger polities in the periphery that became locally dominant competitors that could not be militarily dominated at such distances, and the ultimate withdrawal from the more distant areas, leading to internal difficulties in the empire as its overexpanded infrastructure collapsed.[24] Mesoamerica experienced cycles of growth and cultural integration, followed by collapse and imperial contraction.[25]

CHAPTER 2

The Rise of Warfare in Mesoamerica

THE EARLY FORMATIVE SETTING

The earliest Mesoamericans[1] were hunter-gatherers organized in relatively small extended families, although exchange, mutual assistance, and marriage required contact with similar groups elsewhere.[2] Because they lacked significant resources to plunder, their warfare was probably limited to occasional raids[3] and, though encroachment would have been resisted, land was not defended to the death. Weaker groups typically yielded to stronger ones and moved elsewhere.

Seasonal abundance encouraged temporary gatherings of nomadic or seminomadic groups, and the first settled communities arose in Mesoamerica between 2500 and 1400 B.C. as more stable agricultural resources enabled increasingly larger groups to settle permanently in a single location.[4] The emergence of settled communities led to economic and social differentiation, increased the importance of territorial control, and encouraged the rise of formal leaders.[5] Occasional raids gave way to more serious conflicts, and settlement defense became increasingly important; people could no longer simply flee, knowing they could secure their sustenance as easily in the next valley. Warfare rose with the creation of fixed assets that could be seized, destroyed, or defended. Permanent dwellings and agricultural fields, not simply the inhabitants and their portable goods, became targets of outside aggression.[6]

Little is known about warfare in Mesoamerica before the Middle Formative because many sources of information, such as paintings, sculpture, and public architecture have not survived from this period. However, tools that could double as weapons, including handheld spears and spearthrowers (atlatls) used to throw smaller spears or darts, have been found as early as 4000 B.C.,[7] suggesting that warfare was relatively unorganized, conducted by small groups armed with unspecialized tool-weapons, and aimed not at conquest but at raiding, for glory as much as for booty.[8] Even with expansion, the goal was not to conquer and dominate indigenous populations, but physically to exclude them. Organized warfare and domination by foreign groups did not truly begin in Mesoamerica until the rise of the Olmecs.

THE OLMECS

The area of greatest cultural complexity during the Middle Formative was the tropical lowland stretching from the Tabasco/Veracruz Gulf coast to the Chiapas/Guatemala Pacific coast.[9] By 1500 B.C., the rich soils and nearly year-round rainfall of the coastal lowlands permitted two harvests a year of crops such as maize, yielding the greatest surplus and supporting the densest population in Mesoamerica. Occupied by Mixe-Zoquean speakers since about 1500 B.C.,[10] the Gulf coast of Veracruz/Tabasco saw the emergence of the Olmecs, Mesoamerica's first sophisticated culture. The best-known settlements are San Lorenzo Tenochtitlan, the most important Olmec center from 1150 to 900 B.C., and its successor site of La Venta, which flourished from 900 to 400 B.C. The Gulf coast was linked to central Mexico, Oaxaca, and Pacific coastal Guatemala by exchange networks, but more than being mere trading partners, the Olmecs expanded out of their heartland into other regions of Mesoamerica. This apparently occurred in two major phases. In the first, dominated by San Lorenzo Tenochtitlan, Oaxaca was the main object of Olmec attention, while during the second, dominated by La Venta, central Mexico and Pacific coastal Guatemala had the most Olmec contact.

Trade, colonization, and religious diffusion have all been suggested to explain the widespread Olmec presence throughout Mesoamerica,[11] but a primarily military expansion is implausible:[12] the Olmecs were few, their centers far from sources of desired materials, and their logistics poor. The most likely explanation for expansion is trade, albeit armed trade, which required relatively few participants and was feasible even under the prevailing limitations of long-distance movement.[13]

Olmec expenditures on public works and elite art objects required a sizable artisan group serving the emerging elites, yet not all Olmec needs could be met locally. Informal trading networks already funneled some goods throughout Mesoamerica, but the existing exchange system was too sporadic and unreliable to meet the growing Olmec demands. The artisans depended on an emerging merchant group both to trade their wares and to secure the exotic raw materials they needed,[14] although this institutionalized trade was limited by the inefficiency of Mesoamerican transportation. All land transportation was by foot, which meant that the cost of transport was linear—the farther the distance, the greater the cost. Thus, only the highest value, lowest bulk goods could be transported for any significant distance, and certainly not foodstuffs.[15] Rare minerals, precious stones, and ceramics have left ample evidence in the archaeological record, but the trade in perishable goods such as cacao, cotton textiles, and rare feathers can only be surmised. Although probably not significant to ordinary Olmecs, this trade was vital to the elites and the artisans they sustained, and if it was to be reliable, trade in an insecure environment demanded armed protection, either by the merchants themselves or by armed auxiliaries.

The most sophisticated Mesoamerican culture of their day, the Olmecs specially trained their soldiers and could send armed forces well beyond their homeland. Although this is debated, the Olmecs were most likely a state,[16] as suggested by monumental construction works involving the transport of large quantities of basalt from the Tuxtla Mountains sixty to one hundred kilometers distant to the various Olmec sites and the planning evident in their layouts. These indicate centralized direction and a labor investment available only to an organization with great coercive power or economic resources.[17] Moreover, the artistry evident in Olmec stone sculptures, jade carvings, and ceramics implies complex occupational specialization, and elite burials of infants provide evidence that status was not simply achieved by virtue of deeds or merit, but as ascribed by parentage. Whatever the importance of religious, political, and economic control,[18] there is monumental evidence that military leadership played a major role in the rise of the Olmec elites.

The emergence of the first major Olmec center, San Lorenzo Tenochtitlan, was tied to the influx of exotic goods from distant sources which began at the same time as major construction,[19] especially of monuments reflecting the exercise of military power. These include monumental basalt sculpture, such as giant heads, commemorative stelae, and altars[20] depicting rulers,[21] frequently in martial contexts. For example, the rulers often bear weapons[22] and are shown with naked, bound prisoners,[23] testifying to the emergence of an unmistakable elite exercising military power by 1150 B.C.,[24] and to the probability that these leaders directly led their forces in combat.[25] Direct evidence of warfare is harder to find, however, because the Olmecs left neither chronicles of war nor fortifications. However, burned bones of adults found in refuse pits along with food remains suggest cannibalism, but because the Olmecs buried their own dead, these bones were presumably of outsiders and, because they were adults, they were probably war captives.[26] Nevertheless, the best information about Olmec warfare comes from their weapons, which for the first time in Mesoamerica were specialized military arms rather than tools put to military use.

The clearest example of new weaponry was the adoption of stone projectile points. Only fire-hardened wooden spears were used at early San Lorenzo Tenochtitlan,[27] and these were probably tools for hunting rather than for war. Though absent from the Olmec area, obsidian was imported from Guatemala and the Orizaba region of Veracruz during the Ojochi phase (1500–1350 B.C.),[28] but obsidian projectile points were adopted only after 1150 B.C., at the same time the Olmecs began their major expansion. These large obsidian points produced spears superior to wooden ones in that both points and long cutting edges could be used to slash and puncture rather than simply be thrown. Other Olmec weapons have not survived, but sculptures depict clubs, maces, and spears.[29] Atlatls, although known, were apparently unimportant as weapons, for they were rarely, if ever, depicted in sculpture.[30] For the first time, military weapons were not simple adaptions of utilitarian tools. They were neither hunting weapons used to fight, such as the bows and arrows of the Plains Indians of North America, nor agricultural tools turned to war, such as the bills of the medieval English peasant.[31] The sole purpose of Olmec weapons was martial.

There is little direct evidence of how Olmec arms were used. However, because similar weapons often give rise to similar tactics,[32] their military potential can be assessed, and, in that the area of Olmec expansion is known, both tactics and strategy can be discussed from this relatively firm foundation. One major shift from earlier times was the Olmec emphasis on shock weapons, hand-to-hand arms such as spears that were meant for thrusting and slashing rather than throwing, as well as crushers such as clubs and maces. Shock weapons won the battles in pre-gunpowder wars,[33] in large part because they were deadlier than projectiles that were relatively easy to dodge or deflect if thrown from a distance. The primacy of shock weapons in combat did not eliminate projectiles, but they were a major improvement, for the hand-thrown spears or atlatl-propelled darts available in Mesoamerica at the time were quickly exhausted in combat and demanded constant resupply, greatly complicating the army's logistics. Thus, beyond their homeland, the Olmecs probably did not rely on the atlatl as a weapon because of its relatively short range and the supply problems it created. But even more important, the atlatl was not very effective against the raiders the Olmecs were likely to encounter. Atlatls became major weapons only after the rise of massed armies, when volleys became important.

Defensive armor was rare among the Olmecs: neither shields nor body armor were depicted in carvings or frescoes.[34] Headgear was worn, but the only helmets that seem protective are found on large three-dimensional stone carvings.[35] In murals, bas-relief carvings, and ceramics, where greater detail is feasible, more elaborate headgear is shown, suggesting that the form-fitting helmets reflect technological limitations in three-dimensional carving rather being accurate depictions of the headgear.[36] Thus, Olmec "helmets" were probably status markers rather than functional protectors, especially since some denote animals like those of later military orders.[37] The lack of body armor may have been a practical matter. Most armor of later periods was made of quilted cotton, and while the Olmecs did weave textiles— cotton cultivation and processing dates to some time after 1500 B.C.[38]— they had not yet been adapted to military use. Moreover, armor is primarily useful against conventional forces fighting set-piece battles, whereas the Olmecs' likeliest opponents would have been hit-and-run fighters. Although armor offers substantial protection, it also reduces mobility, seriously disadvantaging shock-weapon fighters seeking to close with the enemy. This may also explain the lack of shields, for the freedom from encumberment by a shield may well have offset the protection it offered from raiders' weapons.

How the Olmecs used their weapons at a group level, rather than individually, is less certain, although some general possibilities can be suggested. Shock weapons require soldiers to close with the enemy, either individually or in cohesive formations. Formations permit soldiers to concentrate frontally, leaving the protection of their sides and backs to their fellow soldiers who prevent the enemy from attacking exposed flanks and rear. However, there is no compelling evidence of formations being used. Moreover, because they already enjoyed technological and tactical superiority, the Olmecs would have benefited little from the organizational advantages of formations, in that their opponents were not organized armies. Thus, Olmec battles probably devolved into battles between pairs of adversaries.

The Olmecs also stand out from earlier groups by the evident professionalism of their military.[39] Specialized weapons required specialized training because, for the first time, military skills could not be adapted directly from utilitarian pursuits because these weapons had no peaceful use. This training was probably carried out by military societies because Olmec populations were too small to support formal schools. This would also have concentrated military expertise in the hands of the elite, and indeed the available evidence indicates that military ability formed much of the basis for classes and rulership among the Olmecs. Lacking access to specialized training, commoners would have been less skilled militarily and, because they engaged in subsistence activities during much of the year, they most likely played a secondary role in war at best.

How many Olmecs were actually soldiers is uncertain. Virtually the entire male population capable of bearing arms is generally thought to take part in war among preindustrial populations.[40] Though perhaps true of non-state societies, state-level societies reached this degree of mobilization only defensively in emergencies. In states, offensive wars are fought not by the total male populace, but by organized armies of trained soldiers, either full-time professionals or conscripted soldiers who serve for limited periods. Moreover, as warfare becomes more sophisticated, arms, armor, and training all become more costly, increasing the wisdom of deploying relatively fewer but better equipped soldiers who have a distinct advantage over equal numbers of non-state warriors or over defensive forces in which everyone has been impressed into service.[41]

Population estimates offer some basis for assessing military participation, but there are no definite figures for most of the settlements and societies discussed here. Except for the immediate postconquest period, the only population figures available are archaeological estimates that are subject to the vagaries of discovery, differing interpretations, and varying bases of assessment. I am adopting a population model that best approximates the Mexican postconquest situation, despite the fact that many of the groups to be considered do not meet the model's assumption of a stable, non-growing population.[42] However, this procedure does ease the difficulties of comparing diverse societies and is thus justified on that basis.[43] The net result of applying this population model is that 34.24 percent of the males are definitely too young to be soldiers (ages 0–14), 9.82 percent (ages 15–19) are probably too young to have been trained for a professional army (for example, men below twenty usually did not fight in the Aztec army, although they probably participated in non-state societies), and 12.87 percent are probably too old (those fifty and over). Most soldiers are drawn from the remaining pool (ages 20–49, 43.08 percent of the male population) and probably cluster in the 20–34 ages (25.25 percent of the males), although the proportions probably differ by society.

The Olmecs had denser populations than those in the surrounding areas, but even major Olmec centers had only about a thousand residents, with perhaps a few thousand more in the immediate hinterlands.[44] Although the total Olmec heartland population of about 350,000 people[45] could have produced a sizable army for its day—up to 7,648 soldiers, drawing on all elite males between twenty and fifty years of age, or 4,527 if the cutoff age was thirty-five—they probably did not. It is unlikely that the Olmec culture area was politically integrated and thus capable of mustering such a force. During much of the year, heavy rains and rising water seriously limited large-scale contacts between even the most important Olmec centers, making tightly coordinated control between the various sites impossible, and instead encouraging the emergence of multiple competing political centers, each balancing the others and creating real limits on sustainable expansion. Under these conditions, offensive armies raised by individual centers would have been relatively small—twenty-six to forty-four soldiers—if, as the weaponry suggests, they were primarily drawn from the elites.

Larger armies could well have been raised within the Olmec heartland, but there is little evidence of military conflict. Olmec settlements show no obvious concern with security, their locations apparently being dictated by agricultural rather than defensive considerations. This assessment is not definitive, however, as defensive works, such as barriers of living cactus or wooden palisades, could have existed that now remain undetected archaeologically; moreover, the location of Olmec centers in swampy areas provided relative security even without specialized defensive structures such as walls, towers, or moats. Nevertheless, the available evidence indicates that no one threatened the Olmec homelands. The relatively sophisticated groups elsewhere in Mesoamerica were too distant to pose a significant threat, and the Olmecs' closest neighbors were simple horticulturalists. Internal disruptions may have occurred, but defensive fortifications play little role against these. Whatever their domestic concerns, it was the Olmecs' ability to project force well beyond their homeland that made them a major influence in Mesoamerica. The Olmecs were the first to master long-distance operations, overcoming the inertia of timing, speed, and logistics. The timing of military movements was dependent not only on work schedules but also on ecology, for geographical and climatic factors are major determinants of warfare patterns.

Geographically, Mesoamerica begins at the desert in the north of Mexico and extends through Guatemala, Belize, and into Honduras and El Salvador. The coastal areas are low, tropical areas; mountains run along the Pacific portion of the region; and the central plateau encompasses areas of subtropical to temperate climates. The area is generally divided by altitude into three basic zones: the *tierra caliente*, or hot lands (0–1,000 meters), the *tierra templada*, or temperate lands (1,000–2,000 meters), and the *tierra fria*, or cold lands (2,000–2,800 meters). Mesoamerica is enormously varied, with many ecozones yielding different flora, fauna, and mineral products. These conditions fostered considerable trade and interdependence and were major factors in patterning political and military relations. Each altitude zone is further divisible by amount of rainfall,[46] which is distinctly seasonal. Rainfall is generally heaviest in the lowlands and declines with altitude, but more significant than the amount of rain is its timing. The rainy season usually extends from May through September, with a dry season during the rest of the year, but some areas, notably the eastern escarpment of southern Mexico and the Caribbean slope of Central America, receive rain the year round. The eastern coast gets considerably more rain than the western coast, and the interior valleys and plateaus receive only moderate amounts.[47]

The Gulf coastal rainy season extends from late May through November and again from December through March: the dry season extends only through April and May. This would have channeled any large-scale movement of men and supplies to short periods in late November–early December and in April and May, because mass movements are significantly more difficult during and shortly after the rainy season, when dirt roads turn into quagmires and normally fordable streams become impassable rivers. However, once the army was out of the lowlands, the campaign season extended from December to late April/early May. These rainy periods also patterned the two agricultural seasons. In the first, field preparation and cultivation took place between November and February, followed by a May–June harvest; in the second, cultivation ran from April to late May or early June, with

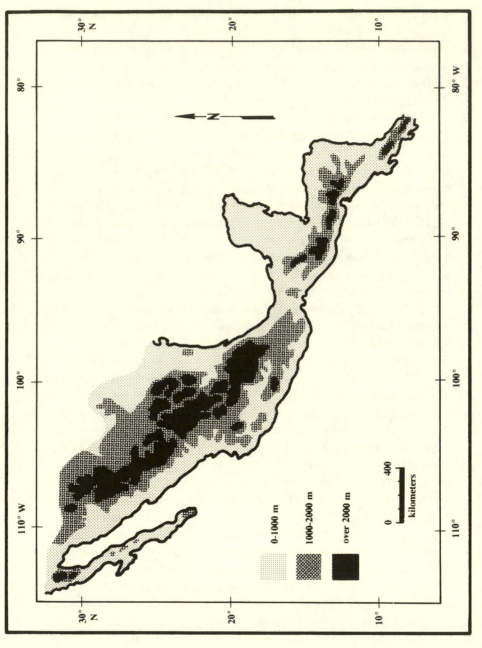

Altitude map of Mesoamerica.

the harvest completed by November.[48] As a consequence, crops needed to sustain troops were most available after June and again after November, with supplies declining thereafter. Thus, from the perspective of supplies, military campaigns were most feasible in December–January and July–August.

It is precisely this ability to feed the forces that largely determined the feasibility of long-distance campaigns. Probable estimates for food consumption are available, based on sixteenth-century records of Indian food consumption: daily adult male rates were .95 kg of maize[49] and half a gallon of water.[50] This does not amount to much individually, but when multiplied by an army, the logistical difficulties become obvious. Provisions had to be carried either by individual soldiers or by specialized porters,[51] and at the standard load of twenty-three kilograms for day-after-day portage, this provided 24 man/days of food.[52] But such a load was well beyond the capacity of individual soldiers already burdened with arms and other equipment, and every kilogram of equipment a soldier carried reduced his food supplies by one day.

The availability of food is the major constraint on conquest because it determined how long an army can march, not just for the Olmecs but for all societies in Mesoamerica. What this time means in terms of distance depends on how fast an army can march which, for preindustrial armies, was 8–32 kilometers a day,[53] a march rate in accord with modern practice. A modern army marches 4 kilometers per hour on roads. This pace decreases to 2.4 kilometers when marching over hills, requiring approximately 20 percent more time than marching on level terrain. Night marches are even slower, averaging only 3.2 kilometers per hour on roads and 1.6 kilometers cross-country.[54] Although it is possible to cover more territory with forced marches, these do not add speed to the march, merely additional time, and they impair the fighting efficiency of the army.[55] Given the scarcity of formal roads, 2.4 kilometers per hour more closely approximates the march rate of Mesoamerican armies. Speed was also affected by march configurations. Although most early armies did not formally march, some discipline had to be observed to keep them together and moving, and march figures offer some basis for calculating the minimum space needed for the movement of troops. Typically, each soldier occupies a square meter with an additional two meters front and back and one meter on each side.[56] Thus, even a small force marching in single file would stretch out for a considerable distance. Lengthy columns can be minimized by increasing the number of files, but this is limited by the size of the roads that would

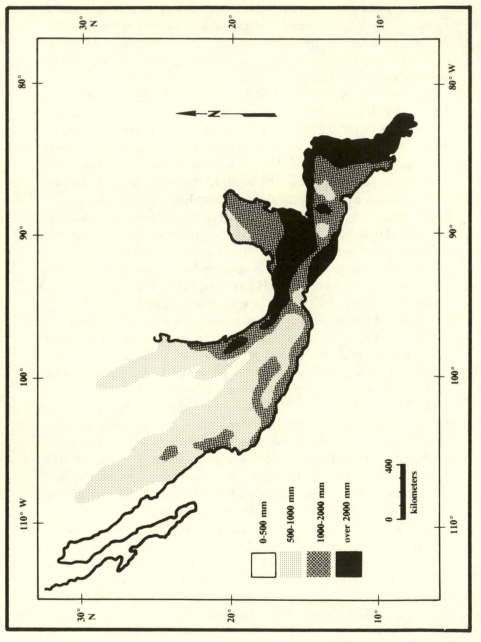

Rainfall map of Mesoamerica.

have been used. In any event, they were faster, safer, and less costly than marching cross-country.

Both the army's size and speed of march affected its logistical requirements. Individual soldiers may have carried all their own food and accepted the limits this placed on their movements, but the Aztecs later turned to professional porters, at a ratio of one for every two soldiers.[57] This permitted the army to travel about eight days, yielding a combat radius of three days, given one day of combat and the following day for rest.[58] Greater efficiency was not feasible, because with the development of the tumpline for carrying loads by Olmec times, land transport had essentially reached the efficiency it was to hold until the Spanish conquest.[59]

The sole alternative to increased range was local resupply, which was feasible within the Olmec area. Beyond, however, supplies en route were unreliable because of the low populations in most of Mesoamerica at that time, the relatively low productivity even among agriculturalists, and the lack of political development that hindered centralized collection and storage of foodstuffs. Many of the groups encountered by the Olmecs were hunter-gatherers offering no significant food surpluses or small agricultural villages in which fields and farmers were dispersed, requiring great effort to accumulate the needed supplies, if this was possible at all. Lacking the organizational or technological skills to overcome these logistical constraints, the Olmecs could only dispatch small forces for long distances. The farther the distance traveled, the greater the logistical demands, and the smaller the numbers that could be sent, making it much likelier that the Olmec presence beyond their homeland was associated with trade, albeit armed, rather than conquest.

The military enterprise was not a simple one. The constraints of political organization, population, and technology were all too real, and the physical setting often played a determining role in whether and when people went to war, how far they went, and how many they were. How these constraints were dealt with figured prominently in the success or failure of states and empires in Mesoamerica.

OLMEC EXPANSION IN THE SAN LORENZO TENOCHTITLAN PHASE

During San Lorenzo Tenochtitlan's dominance, Olmec influence spread throughout Mesoamerica, linking that site to networks exchanging obsidian and other goods with central Oaxaca, highland and Pacific

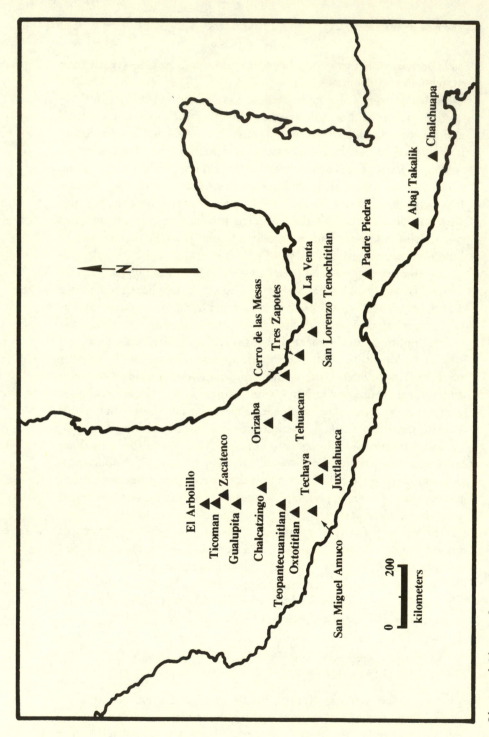

Olmec and Olmec-influenced sites.

coastal Guatemala, and central Mexico.[60] Most notably, there were major Olmec influences in the Valley of Oaxaca during this early period (1150–850 B.C.), but not conquest.[61]

Rather than rely on the intermittent trade that had characterized exchange previously, the Olmecs sought to control the trade in external goods for their own security. But trade, as it existed, had inherent risks and limitations, for it involved passage through and between potentially hostile areas. Military domination of large portions of Mesoamerica was beyond the ability of any group at this time. There were limits to the number of soldiers the Olmecs could send beyond their homeland but they could dispatch armed trading parties. Merchants could trade more safely and reliably over longer distances by being armed or by traveling with small groups of soldiers.

The Olmecs did not directly exploit distant resources; instead, they traded with local groups capable of extracting and processing raw materials in exchange for Olmec goods.[62] When the Olmecs expanded, their greater sophistication was an inducement for local cultures to adopt their practices and values, laying the groundwork for Olmec cultural domination. The system was economical—by using their own merchants, the Olmecs exercised considerably greater control over this exchange than they had under the earlier informal network—but it depended on local demand: the Olmecs could not compel trade. Moreover, because of the great distances they had to transport trade goods, the Olmecs needed very favorable exchange rates to prosper. Central Oaxaca fit this pattern initially,[63] but Olmec influence diminished as the local cultures adopted and adapted Gulf coast elements and the Olmecs' relative superiority eroded. Settlements in the Valley of Oaxaca increased and were organized into a single political hierarchy,[64] with a significant role being played by intervillage conquest,[65] as suggested by the carving of a slain victim from the Rosario Phase (700–650 to 500–450 B.C.) that is strongly reminiscent of later conquest monuments at Monte Alban. Local elites now competed with the Olmecs for these same wares; although they were less prosperous and lacked goods of comparable sophistication to exchange, they also lacked the Olmecs' enormous expense of shipping goods long distance. The local elites became very effective competitors and the rise of Oaxaca diminished Olmec economic interests in the area.[66]

San Lorenzo traded with other sophisticated cultures, but, as with Oaxaca, the local elites were not clients primarily dependent on the Olmecs for their positions. But because the Olmecs were unable to force compliance, once local elites began competing for the same goods, the Olmecs' favored exchange rate eroded, and with the increased costs of transporting the goods to San Lorenzo the Olmecs could no longer compete.

OLMEC EXPANSION IN THE LA VENTA PHASE

The demise of the Oaxaca trade had significant repercussions in the Olmec area. San Lorenzo Tenochtitlan's local dominance rested in large part on its unrivaled ability to import elite goods. But its importance eroded with the Oaxaca trade connection and the discovery of closer sources for the same materials, such as ilmenite and hematite used for mirrors and mosaics.[67] This economic upheaval caused political changes at San Lorenzo, signaled by the deliberate defacement of political monuments around 900 B.C.[68] Previously dependent centers could now tap these closer sources directly. San Lorenzo's pivotal importance as an entrepôt controlling the distribution of elite goods from Oaxaca became irrelevant and the center declined. San Lorenzo's loss of monopoly provided an opening for new competitors and La Venta emerged as the main Olmec center around 900 B.C. La Venta also depended on trade, but in different, and increasingly important, products from the Pacific coast and central Mexico rather than from Oaxaca.[69] Jade, which was not found at San Lorenzo at all, became prominent at La Venta,[70] and the site's importance rested on its control of various materials and the craftsmen working them.[71]

During La Venta's dominance, decorative motifs found in sites throughout Mesoamerica bore unmistakable evidence of an Olmec presence, except in central Oaxaca. There Gulf coast motifs continued as locally perpetuated adaptations of earlier influences but did not reflect a continued Olmec presence.[72] Excluded from central Oaxaca as a result of internal developments, the Olmecs did not reestablish settlements in or significant contact with that area.

During the La Venta phase, trade underwent a number of changes, both in type of goods and method of procurement. Olmec benefits declined as other societies became more sophisticated and trade grew increasingly equal, so that developed areas such as central Oaxaca and Kaminaljuyu were bypassed and effectively excluded from their new trading networks.[73] Instead, the Olmecs created new and dependent trade networks,[74] primarily in central Mexico and Guatemala, avoiding stronger, more sophisticated groups, such as those in Oaxaca, and instead focusing on weaker ones. A series of centers was created or co-opted, dominating trade in elite goods in their respective areas: across central Mexico, the sites of Chalcatzingo, Juxtlahuaca, Oxtotitlan, San Miguel Amuco, Techaya, and Teopantecuanitlan formed part of a mineral route, including jade,[75] while another series stretched from the Isthmus of Tehuantepec to western El Salvador, including Padre Piedra, Abaj Takalik, and Chalchuapa, forming part of the cacao and Motagua jade route.[76] Thus, Chalcatzingo, in central Mexico, became an important Olmec center from 700 to 500 B.C., as was Chalchuapa on the Pacific coast from 900 to 500 B.C.[77]

Contact with the Olmecs still promoted cultural development among less sophisticated groups, but with a difference. Although spurred to greater cultural development, the Olmecs' earlier trading partners were already the nuclei of established exchange networks serving local needs. The Olmecs increased the volume of trade in these exchange systems, but did not fundamentally alter them; they persisted after Olmec withdrawal, which probably freed more materials for the use of local elites. However, the newly emergent elites of the La Venta phase remained dependent because there was relatively little indigenous demand for the local raw materials the Olmecs sought. The wealth and positions of local elites were tied directly to the success of the Olmecs: if the latter withdrew, there was little local infrastructure to sustain the trade on which the local elites now depended.

The Olmec concern in establishing sites in resource-rich areas and funneling these goods back to their heartland is evident in the distribution of Olmec-influenced sites throughout Mesoamerica: the sites were established at strategic passes that channeled the trade.[78] These passes did not control trade, for many were not narrow enough to police all the traffic, nor were they the sole conduits into various areas. But they did offer safety for Olmec traders, food, and a known location that allowed travelers to gauge their supply requirements en route. Moreover, the distribution of these sites clearly shows that their importance lay in a larger trading pattern quite unlike that expected for indigenously important autonomous centers. The La Venta phase sites were not important sites that were coopted, but sites the Olmecs made important. This system was costlier than the previous one because it involved longer distances and greater investment in local development that may well have been beyond the ability of the San Lorenzo Olmecs. But two major military developments allowed the La Venta Olmecs to implement this system.

The development that greatly enhanced Olmec logistical capability and correlated with the La Venta expansion was the tortilla. To this point, maize could not be prepared to yield a portable, nonperishable food for long journeys, and what was available required time-consuming daily preparation. Moreover, this was usually women's work, yet there is little evidence that women accompanied Olmec travelers.[79] The invention of tortillas changed this situation: retoasted tortillas could be easily transported, required no preparation time on the trek, and remained palatable for several days, greatly increasing the Olmecs' logistical capabilities.[80] The evidence of this innovation rests not with the development of tortillas themselves, but with that of the ceramic griddles (comales) on which they are cooked. These are scarce in the Olmec area; there are none at San Lorenzo Tenochtitlan, although some were found later at Cerro de las Mesas.[81] But during the La Venta phase, comales are unexpectedly found in a variety of Olmec-influenced sites, including Tehuacan, Chalcatzingo, Chalchuapa, and in Tlaxcala,[82] suggesting that they were disseminated, if not invented, by the Olmecs. Moreover, comales were not common even where found and thus were not used for everyday food preparation. Rather, tortillas were a special-purpose food used for travel, reducing the time or personnel needed to prepare meals, greatly increasing the distance that could be traveled, minimizing dependence on intervening populations, and adding enormously to the Olmecs' ability to link distant areas of Mesoamerica.[83]

Although the Olmecs could now travel farther or in larger parties, they were less able to deal with the intervening groups militarily. Olmec weapons and tactics were well suited to deal with the conventional threats of relatively advanced societies with which they traded during the San Lorenzo phase. But in the La Venta phase, the Olmecs dealt with less sophisticated societies lacking reliable political hierarchies or fixed assets, and conventional Olmec tactics were markedly less effective against the hit-and-run raiding they were likely to encounter.

The development that allowed the Olmecs to cope militarily with these less sophisticated groups was the invention of a new weapon—the sling.[84] The first evidence of slings is from around 900 B.C., precisely when La Venta was expanding.[85] There are no surviving examples because they were made of leather or vegetable fibers such as yucca, maguey, or cotton,[86] nor are they depicted in Olmec art.[87] What does remain are slingstones; in this case, solid, fired clay spheres ranging from 2 to 4.2 centimeters in diameter.[88] Stone examples are found elsewhere in Mesoamerica; most are between 20 and 40 centimeters in diameter, weigh between 25 and 50 grams, and have a smooth surface,[89] which accords nicely with examples elsewhere in the world.[90]

As with comales, slings may not have originated with the Olmecs, but the distribution of slingstones at Olmec-influenced sites during the La Venta period, including Tehuacan, Chalcatzingo, Zacatenco, Ticoman, Gualupita, El Arbolillo, and Chalchuapa, suggests that the Olmecs spread this technology.[91] The sling's high rate of fire, great range (up to five hundred meters has been reported elsewhere in the world),[92] and effectiveness gave the Olmecs both an offensive and a defensive capability unmatched elsewhere at that time and permitted the expansion of their merchants into areas that had been too hazardous under previous conditions.

Nevertheless, the role of the Olmec military remained protective rather than expansionistic.[93] Local elites apparently voluntary participated in the Olmec cultural sphere, adopting Olmec goods, artistic iconography, and, probably, belief systems.[94] The most plausible type of sustained Olmec control over distant sites was through marital alliances, as may have been the case at Chalcatzingo,[95] although that alone would have provided little basis for any real control. These emergent local elites were not militarily subjugated, nor did they overthrow the Olmecs.[96] They remained dependent on the Olmecs and so maintained the trading system.[97] The demise of these centers was not caused by internal dissension, but by increasing competition from other centers. As local nonallied groups developed their own elites, they created independent trading networks that cut into the Olmecs' networks. In part, this was the result of increasing agricultural productivity that put greater wealth into the hands of the local elites and allowed them to compete effectively with the Olmecs for exotic goods.[98] Growing local wealth, coupled with the great distance the Olmecs had to transport goods, made local elites effective competitors and gradually impoverished the Olmecs, leading to their withdrawal and ultimate demise. The Olmecs did not fight to maintain their position—they lacked the manpower and logistical capability to do so—but simply withdrew when they could no longer sustain mercantile relations.

CHAPTER 3

Warfare and the Spread of States

THE LATE FORMATIVE SITUATION

Following the Olmec decline around 400 B.C., there was no dominant power for almost five hundred years. Mesoamerica reverted to a series of regional cultures, although these were markedly less isolated and shared cultural patterns largely reflecting areas of previous Olmec interaction. This spread of traits between societies fostered a degree of cultural equalization, bringing increasing numbers of peoples into the greater Mesoamerican civilization. Yet despite the lack of expansionistic empires, this was not a period of tranquility. State-level societies developed throughout Mesoamerica during this transitional period, and the basic social and technological groundwork was laid for political and military practices that were to dominate the Classic. However, low populations, difficulties in long-distance travel, and a rough military parity were important in keeping conflicts local. When some centers grew powerful, they nevertheless remained only locally dominant.

The Olmec aftermath was a period of increasing military professionalism among local elites, and specialized arms now dominated warfare. The weapons pioneered by the Olmecs continued into this period, though with some changes in emphasis. Thrusting spears became the primary combat weapons as they spread throughout Mesoamerica. Clubs persisted, but declined in importance in major armies although they remained significant in less sophisticated groups. The use of maces also declined, probably as a result of the adoption of better protection and the advent of more effective and lighter alternative weapons.[1]

Among the best evidence of warfare during this period are carvings from the Gulf coast. Stela D at Tres Zapotes depicts a political scene set within the open mouth of an animal, in which two figures stand, one holds a spear, and a third kneels.[2] Stela A shows a similar scene in which one figure holds a knife and the other apparently holds a trophy head.[3] But the most graphic depiction of warfare is on Monument C: a number of men wear helmets (some in the form of animal heads), carry large rectangular shields, and wield spears and clubs or maces, and one has been stabbed through the knee.[4]

Slings do not appear in works of art and were probably low-status weapons, as they were in medieval Europe,[5] because of the utilitarian skills they demanded. Nevertheless, the distribution of slingstones throughout Mesoamerica indicates the continued use of this effective and inexpensive projectile weapon. Standardizing the slingstones by sizing pottery or grinding stones made slings more effective, in that each slinger would then know with relative certainty how far and accurately he could throw. However, their weight limited the number of sling-stones that could be carried long distance, so unless they could be retrieved for reuse—and the prevalence of fragments suggests that the ceramic ones were relatively fragile—slings were probably used primarily to defend settlements where transport was not an issue.

Perhaps in reaction to slings, shields were widely adopted in the Late Formative, especially large rectangular ones that protected most of the body.[6] Their construction is uncertain, but the shields were probably made of leather, woven materials of various weights, or solid wood, as were later examples, although wood and woven reeds are particularly suited to rectangular forms. These shields appear very sturdy and, if made of solid wood, could directly block weapon thrusts. Lighter materials, such as leather or woven reeds, could not absorb the force of a blow that might break the shieldman's arm—the notorious parry fracture[7]—but they could deflect them, block projectiles, and defend against the cutting effect of blades. The protection these large shields afforded the trunk and limbs was, however, achieved at the price of mobility, suggesting a more set-piece style of combat. In fact, the heavy shield may have been rested on the ground where it could still provide considerable protection from projectiles and, in conjunction with thrusting spears, would have been a formidable deterrent to an enemy charge.

These changes in arms and armor reflect the general Late Formative shift away from guerrilla warriors relying on stealth and weapons that could be used from concealment and toward soldiers formally trained in military skills. Increasingly, wars were fought by professionals wielding specialized arms rather than by warriors with weapons adapted from mundane pursuits. Moreover, there was a greater emphasis on individual protection and an increasing preponderance of shock weapons over projectiles. As specialized arms and armor spread, power differences between cultures grew smaller and fleeting, and no longer resulted in the great superiority the Olmecs had enjoyed over their early contemporaries.

With population growth and the adoption of settled agricultural life, flight in the face of conquest became less feasible. As states slowly emerged, local groups were increasingly thrown into conflicts they could not escape, and the spread of specialized weapons and training raised the level of violence. One response to the emergence of a professional military and the increasing levels of violence was the development of fortifications.

FORTIFICATIONS

As elsewhere,[8] the rise of powerful armies also spurred the development of defensive architecture, although this is not always easy to identify archaeologically in Mesoamerica. While the military nature of the Tower of London or the Château of Angers is apparent, the evidence of fortifications in Mesoamerica is far more ambiguous because of both construction techniques that were common to civil and military structures and the ruin into which most sites have fallen, especially because they were not generally constructed to provide telltale overlapping fields of fire (perhaps because they faced few projectiles). Freestanding walls and accompanying moats provide good evidence of defensive works, but what appear as walled forts from the bottom of a hilltop site are seen as terrace retaining walls from the top. Is the movement of a town to the side or top of a hill defensive or merely designed to relinquish precious bottomland to agricultural use? And if the very nature of sites can be debated, how much more can their function?

Nevertheless, numerous Mesoamerican sites were convincingly fortified,[9] but interpreting these depends on the weaponry they were designed to counter, and, perhaps even more important, on the nature of the regional political situation. Mesoamerican fortifications cannot be easily traced in a single developmental line from earliest to latest. They do not arise at particular times, but rather under particular circumstances. What kinds of fortification are built is a technical decision, taking into account manpower limitations, material availability, site potential, and threats to be countered. *When* fortifications are built is a political decision. They are erected for many different reasons, and not necessarily in response to a single factor. Fortifications are special structures designed with these variables in mind, so comparisons of the efficiency of fortifications in different places and times in Mesoamerica cannot be based exclusively, or even primarily, on their physical attributes. Small walls in a relatively placid area may protect the populace better than large walls in a turbulent one; similarly, a simple wall and moat built to withstand a shock-weapon attack may be far better than large concentric walls in an era of massed projectile fire.

The presence of fortifications does not necessarily indicate rampant warfare, and neither does their absence indicate peace. A disproportionately large city may have little or no need for fortifications, even though lesser cities have them. But even vulnerable centers may be unfortified where the role of defense has been taken over by a state so that lesser sites do not need, or are not allowed, fortifications. Thus, an unfortified zone may well mark the extent of a state's political influence, with the protection of unfortified dependencies coming from political incorporation rather than from bricks and mortar. Similarly, fortifications may not arise simply in response to an outside threat, but may be constructed for political purposes, to dominate other centers.

Because of the high costs of travel and transport—the friction of distance—most war was relatively local. A "placid" area was quite likely to border areas that had fortified in response to large, expanding "placid" polities, producing a patchwork quilt of unfortified zones surrounded by fortified areas. For example, Tehuacan Valley sites began fortifying around A.D. 700,[10] while the fortified sites of the nearby Valley of Oaxaca were abandoned. Instead of marking the moving frontier of imperial systems, fortifications arise in the areas being encroached upon, as a defense. Nevertheless, once an area fortifies, even defensively, it may well threaten adjacent areas.

The size of fortified sites is a key element in assessing their significance. Small fortified sites may deter minor or random threats such as raids, but not major ones.[11] Small fortifications are not intended for any offensive purpose and cannot effectively dominate a sizable hinterland. Large fortifications, however, can have offensive as well as defensive

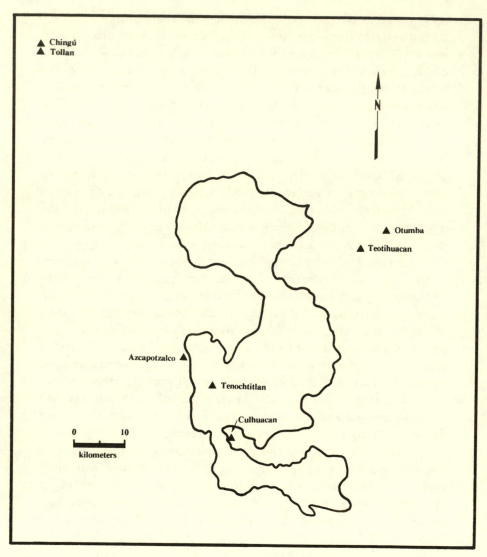

Valley of Mexico and adjacent area.

functions and may politically dominate adjacent areas. But size, too, must be examined regionally. If all the sites are of approximately equal size, a small fortified site is most likely defensive. Fortifications effectively compensate for small populations by substituting labor for soldiers, doing so without increasing the logistical requirements that additional soldiers would entail.[12] Confronted with fortifications, armies had five basic options: they could scale them, breach the walls or gates, tunnel beneath them, lay siege to them, or enter by ruse.[13] Because a successful assault normally requires three attackers for each defender,[14] even a relatively small fortified site could maintain its independence from larger centers, yet be too small to threaten others beyond its immediate hinterland. However, this type of assessment is complicated by the persistence of some fortified sites far longer than the circumstances that led to their construction.

CENTRAL MEXICO

Despite intersite conflicts, there were no major fortifications in the Valley of Mexico during the Late Formative.[15] But from 600 to 300 B.C., the previous pattern of relatively autonomous dispersed settlements was replaced by larger integrated sociopolitical groupings oriented on regional centers, and then by a single center at Teotihuacan.[16] Warfare was localized and relatively minor at this time, but there was resistance to Teotihuacan, as evidenced by the growth of hilltop sites south of that city.[17] Though poorly understood, these sites were too small to threaten others and probably fortified to resist incorporation into the emerging city-state, an effort that was ultimately unsuccessful.

Along with most of the Valley of Mexico, Teotihuacan absorbed much of the adjacent Puebla-Tlaxcala area, whose impressive cultural developments may have predated those in the Valley of Mexico. From 600 to 300 B.C., the Puebla-Tlaxcala towns relocated on fortified hilltops, and during the next four hundred years, small villages virtually disappeared as the population was concentrated in larger centers.[18] Major fortifications were built, possibly owing to internal dynamics[19] but more likely in response to the growing threat from the Valley of Mexico.[20]

Settling atop hills and promontories greatly complicated life—food and usually water had to be hauled up at great cost, and resident farmers had to journey down to their fields daily—and was undertaken only for compelling reasons. However, such locations did benefit from early warnings of approaching threats, a rugged ascent that made assault difficult, and the aid of gravity in throwing missiles and stones down on attackers. But perhaps just as significant were its construction advantages. With Mesoamerican building techniques, a freestanding wall had to be very thick to achieve significant height, but by using the slope of the hill, high walls could be built as part of terraces, forming sheer façades from the outside while elevating the defenders and increasing the internal area.

Despite their apparently defensive purpose, the Tlaxcala fortifications may also have served as centers of militarily dominated hinterlands, much as medieval European castles dominated large surrounding areas.[21] However, strongholds also have limitations: they can dominate surrounding settlements by virtue of superior position and might, but they cannot keep these settlements secure against powerful outsiders or guarantee themselves access as needed. But as long as the strongholds are not conquered, their presence denies their enemies secure control of the area.

In contrast to isolated defensive sites, strongholds are often found in clusters because the creation of a counterbalancing fortification is the only effective way to limit the expansion of the first. Thus, clusters of strongholds may not show political linkage to a larger unit so the fall of an autonomous stronghold would have no effect on the others; without political linkage, the conquest of any single stronghold did not mean the fall of an entire system.

MAYA LOWLANDS

One area with early fortifications was the Maya lowlands, which were populated as early as 1000 B.C. by people who later developed connections with Kaminaljuyu and Izapa.[22] There was considerable conflict and warfare over resources in the lowlands, stimulating the rise of hierarchical political offices and elites.[23] Clubs and knives were used,[24] but the primary weapons were spears that were probably simply tools turned to military purposes.[25] Hit-and-run raids dominated warfare, but they were serious enough to give rise to occasional fortifications.[26]

Rare among the highland Maya,[27] two lowland sites show evidence of significant, permanent fortifications during the Late Formative period. Between 800 and 400 B.C., a 1,300-meter ditch and embankment was built along the eastern side of the site of Los Naranjos, extending from a swamp on the north to a lake on the south. Requiring little architectural sophistication, the ditch was approximately ten meters wide and seven meters deep, as measured from the top of the adjacent embankment, protecting both the site and a considerable sustaining area from an attack from the east. Between 400 B.C. and A.D. 550, a second set of earthworks 3,200 meters long was built farther east.[28]

Fortifications were also built at Becan between A.D. 100 and 250.[29] Located on an outcrop ten meters above the surrounding area, Becan was encircled by a 1,890-meter, kidney-shaped dry ditch spanned by seven causeways.[30] Earth from the ditch was used to build a ten-meter-wide embankment along the inner edge.[31] Ranging from twelve to twenty-seven meters wide (averaging sixteen), and 1.2 to 5.7 meters deep (averaging 2.5),[32] the ditch and embankment confronted the attacker with a combined vertical face some 11.6 meters high.[33] Although the surrounding population may have fled to the site in times of danger,[34] its low resident population (only 400–500) suggests that Becan's fortifications were defensive. Moreover, the fortification did not permit overlapping fields of fire,[35] although this was relatively unimportant since projectile weapons were minor or nonexistent at the time. Providing a reliable defense for those inside, the wall and ditch system was an effective deterrent against the clubs and thrusting spears of the day, especially if the encircling earthen walls also served as elaborate footers for additional wooden palisades.[36]

Located in relatively flat terrain, the lowland sites lacked the defensive and construction advantages of hilltop forts. Nevertheless, care was taken in their siting to incorporate rock outcrops, swamps, and water features into their defenses.[37] The small size of these sites, the lack of extensive screening areas,[38] and the absence of other nearby fortifications strongly suggest that they were for self-protection, as they lacked the offensive menace to intimidate their neighbors. They also lacked storage facilities to provision the inhabitants during an extended assault; their primary use was therefore against raids.[39] Nevertheless, even these small fortifications offered significant advantages. First, many more attackers are required to overcome defenders behind fortifications than in the open, so building defensive works effectively increases the military strength of a center without adding soldiers by using labor during slack periods to build defenses.[40] Building fortifications effectively reduces the need for more defenders by substituting labor that is available throughout the year. Second, almost everyone could aid in the defense, including women and children who could throw stones as well as arms and supplies, giving the defenders an effective combatant force

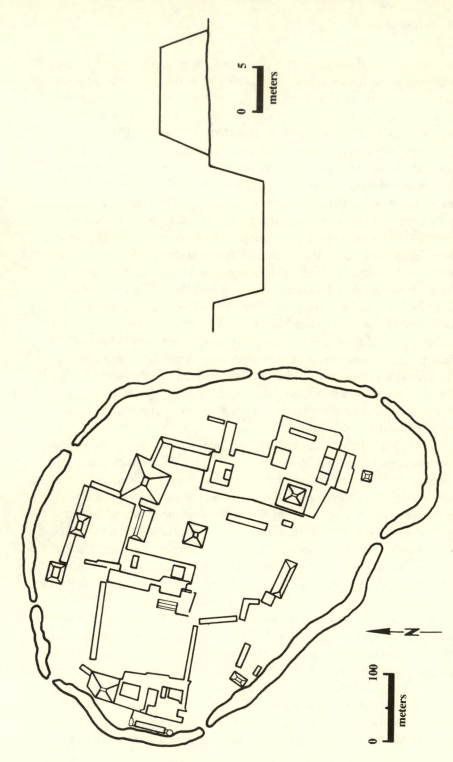

Becan, showing fortifications and simplified interior structures, and wall and moat cross-section. (Adapted from Webster 1976a.)

numerically, if not qualitatively, equal to the forces a city several times its size could dispatch for any distance.

VALLEY OF OAXACA

Probably the most sophisticated culture in Mesoamerica at this time arose in the Valley of Oaxaca. Whether it was a true state as early as 700–650 to 500–450 B.C. (the Rosario phase), there were nevertheless clear elites.[41] Armed conflict is evident from the carvings of slain or sacrificed captives,[42] who were typically shown nude or scantily clad, as among the Olmecs and later Mayas. San José Mogote was the most important settlement, serving as the ceremonial and political center for nearby villages.[43] However, the dominance of these valley-floor sites was fleeting. After 500 B.C., the new political and religious center of Monte Alban arose on a series of hills 300–400 meters above the juncture of three valleys.[44] Gradually, the earlier centers lost their dominance and became Monte Alban-centered, supplying that city through a valley-wide tribute system.[45] At this time, the city had a population of some five thousand, about half the valley's total, but by 300–200 B.C., the population had tripled in the valley, growing to sixteen thousand in Monte Alban.[46]

Why Monte Alban was created is debated,[47] for it was relatively inaccessible and did not have easy access to agricultural lands. It is fairly clear, however, that groups from throughout the Valley of Oaxaca joined in its creation, which was undertaken for reasons unrelated to subsistence. Monte Alban has been interpreted as a confederated "disembedded capital" created to meet a threat from the southern highlands.[48] Whether it was the capital of a confederacy of settlements,[49] Monte Alban's political and military significance is attested by the many carved monuments depicting conquests.[50]

These representations mark a significant change in the treatment of conquered areas. Unlike the previous carved depictions of nude and seminude figures, these captives are well clad, even regally so. These monuments clearly depict conquests; the personages remain bound, but humiliation as signified through nudity is no longer a factor. This respectful treatment of the vanquished is found in most Mesoamerican empires[51] whereas nude depictions are found among non-empires, such as the Olmecs, early Zapotecs, and, usually, the Maya, suggesting that more respectful depictions of conquests were employed in polities seeking to incorporate vanquished areas where at least some degree of local

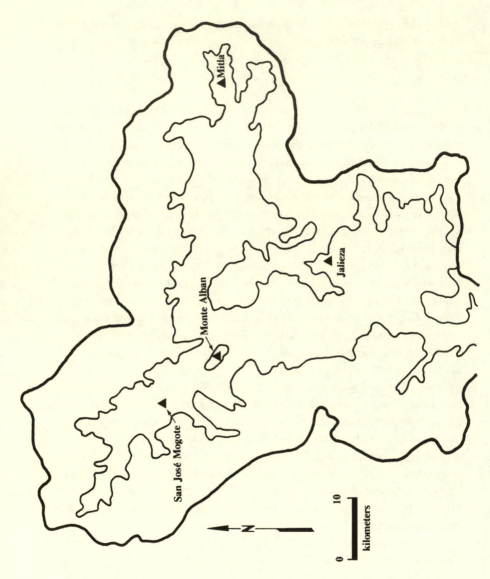

Valley of Oaxaca. (Adapted from Spencer 1982.)

cooperation was desirable. By contrast, nude depictions are found where the goal was to elevate the victorious ruler and to despoil the conquered area rather than to absorb it politically or culturally.

Monte Alban was soon fortified. Around 200 B.C., an earthen wall was built running three kilometers along the north to west portions of the city proper; 3–4 meters high, the wall had a maximum width of twenty meters and had gatehouses to control entry.[52] A reservoir was also built that could hold up to 67,500 cubic meters of water,[53] enough to sustain all the residents of Monte Alban for years and virtually eliminating siege as a threat.

As already noted, the role of fortifications cannot be assessed simply from architecture. Fortifications are not always built for primarily defensive purposes[54] and, though hypothesized, no external threat has been identified to account for Monte Alban's construction in defense. Moreover, no major groups were close enough to be serious threats to the populous Valley of Oaxaca. There was no plausible external threat that might account for the creation of Monte Alban as a defensive reaction: if anything, it was a threat to others. Thus, the construction of Monte Alban can be better seen as a response to an internal dynamic; some consideration of its political organization is therefore in order.

Monte Alban exercised direct political control over its dependencies.[55] In such a territorial system, conquered areas are typically consolidated by replacing local leaders and defeated troops with imperial governors and garrisons, which also requires the creation and maintenance of border fortifications to guard against external encroachment as well as internal flight.[56] This direct exercise of political control permits the extraction of large quantities of goods from the conquered areas, but the cost in terms of administration and security are high. Moreover, because territorial systems rely primarily on direct force,[57] resources are depleted quickly, which slows expansion to a halt as available manpower is absorbed in the control of conquered areas.

Not all areas of potential expansion by Monte Alban have been explored archaeologically,[58] but at least one ethnically distinct area beyond the Valley of Oaxaca has been—the Cuicatlan Cañada to the north.[59] The Zapotecs of Monte Alban invaded the region after 200 B.C., apparently to control trade in vital tierra caliente goods.[60] Occupying the Cuicatlan Cañada also blocked incursions from outside.[61]

When the Zapotecs conquered the Cuicatlan Cañada, they burned the villages and moved their inhabitants to nonarable ground.[62] This could indicate an attempt to maximize agricultural production,[63] but

several considerations suggest otherwise. First, the more accessible ara-
ble lands of the Valley of Oaxaca were not completely occupied. Second, a fortified garrison was constructed at Quiotepec[64] and local agricultural production would have been more beneficial for them than for
Monte Alban, some two days' distance on foot.[65] Third, the earliest
known Mesoamerican skullrack, containing sixty-one human heads,
was erected at the village of La Coyotera as part of Zapotec control by
draconian means.[66] If all the skulls came from La Coyotera, slightly
more than one person was taken from each household—as much as 20
percent of the total population,[67] and a considerable part of the work-
force. Had controlling the economy been the Zapotecs' primary concern, they could easily have expanded farther; the local inhabitants
posed little military obstacle and the additional areas could easily have
supplied Zapotec sites in the region, if not Monte Alban. Despite gaining access to more diverse products, the Zapotecs were primarily concerned with preventing outsider encroachment rather than controlling
the local economy; wealth could have easily been drained from the area
in tribute through indirect rule at significantly lower cost. Instead, the
Zapotecs relocated existing settlements and built, manned, and supplied
a fort that commanded the entry from the Tehuacan Valley area to the
north[68] as well as a major eastward route to the Gulf coast. The fortified
site of Quiotepec marked the northern limits of Zapotec expansion,[69]
and although further expansion was militarily feasible, it would have
required the construction of at least two fortified sites to block outside
incursions because the valley split just above Quiotepec, forming natural passages to both the Tehuacan Valley to the north and the Gulf coast
to the east. Quiotepec offered the most economical military solution,
but it was intended primarily to control the internal population and to
thwart relatively small external threats because it had to do so with the
local garrison and could not be quickly reinforced from Monte Alban,
some two days' march away.

The Cuicatlan Cañada incursion strongly indicates the territorial nature of Monte Alban's expansion,[70] and also suggests a reassessment of
Monte Alban's own fortifications. Its fortified hilltop location gave
Monte Alban clear military superiority over all other towns in the Valley of Oaxaca, the only significant threats it faced. This local dominance
was the goal of Monte Alban's creation and fortification: no outside
threat need be invoked to explain that city's rise. In contrast to the
fortified sites elsewhere in Mesoamerica at this time, Monte Alban's
fortifications were not primarily defensive. All settlements within the

Valley of Oaxaca were potentially at risk from raids by other towns. But Monte Alban's location and fortifications made it essentially invulnerable to threats by any one site or confederacy of sites for several reasons. First, possessing the only significant fortifications in the Valley of Oaxaca, it enjoyed the 3:1 defensive advantage, which meant that any attacker would have to greatly outnumber Monte Alban's defenders. Second, Monte Alban's defenders could remain behind their walls, enabling most of its inhabitants to participate in its defense, raising further the number of attackers required to conquer it. Third, because it was an elite site, a greater proportion of its combatants were highly skilled and trained, further increasing its military advantage. Thus, while Monte Alban may not have removed all local rulers, its fortifications and strong defensive position allowed it to treat them as subordinates within its directly controlled, expanded hinterland.

Monte Alban housed many of the local nobles from throughout the Valley of Oaxaca, concentrating the elite warriors in one location. By fortifying itself, Monte Alban could control its territorial area without expensive garrisoning of every major town,[71] which may have been impossible given its limited population. Direct control entails enormous administrative costs, but by creating an impregnable redoubt overlooking the juncture of the three arms of the Valley of Oaxaca, Monte Alban could exercise relatively direct control at substantially lower cost. With its fortifications, the city was not threatened by any of its tributaries and, in the event of rebellion, the army could bide its time and launch an attack at the most opportune moment. This is not to say that the Valley of Oaxaca was integrated solely on the basis of conquest. Military might allowed Monte Alban to dominate the region, but the relatively homogeneous Zapotec culture provided much of the basis for this integration.

Despite the relative efficiency of Monte Alban's control, the growth of its empire was restricted to a comparatively small area because of its limited population and the technological constraints of Mesoamerica. That Monte Alban was able to create a territorial empire at all is a tribute to its location. Maintenance of fortified boundaries is essential to territorial control, but this lays heavy demands on the tributary populations and was beyond the ability of centers such as Los Naranjos and Becan. Located in flat regions, the cost of building border fortifications at any distance from their centers would have been prohibitive. In the Oaxaca case, however, Monte Alban was fortuitously located in a valley system whose mountainous boundaries formed natural barriers. These geographical features allowed it to fortify only a few passes, effectively seal off the entire region, and subject it to territorial control at a cost in manpower significantly lower than that for comparable non-mountainous areas. Defensive fortifications pose no threat to an enemy who can simply bypass them, but the Zapotec defenses confronted potential enemies with a novel situation. Monte Alban's imperial fortifications were designed to block passage and thus confronted any potential enemy with both defensive strength and offensive threat.

In sum, during the Late Formative, the general sophistication of warfare in Mesoamerica increased. Unlike the Olmec era in which one group held a distinct advantage over the others, professional weapons (and presumably tactics) had now spread to most advanced societies in Mesoamerica. War became a significant factor in creating larger political units, and the nature of those polities was fashioned by what was militarily feasible for the aggressor societies and the recourse of their potential victims. This period lay the foundations for the increasingly sophisticated nature and greater extent of warfare throughout the Classic period.

CHAPTER 4

Teotihuacan and the Integration of Mesoamerica

Teotihuacan emerged as the first great empire in Mesoamerica,[1] dominating areas adjacent to the Valley of Mexico and incorporating them into the city's economic hinterland. Teotihuacan also penetrated far north into the desert and south into the Maya area, exploiting their resources, colonizing many sites, and linking much of Mesoamerica. Yet despite Teotihuacan's enormous impact, little is known of its military, particularly in the early years since most of the information about the army at that time comes from elsewhere in Mesoamerica and not from the city itself.[2]

By A.D. 100, Teotihuacan was the largest city in the Valley of Mexico, and probably in Mesoamerica. As a result of major migration into the site and the state's policy of concentrating rural populations in the city, Teotihuacan was ethnically heterogeneous.[3] Individual households were replaced by apartment compounds between A.D. 300 and 400, about the same time craft production in the city underwent a major increase and state expansion reached beyond the Valley of Mexico.[4] The city owed much of its dominance to the production and distribution of obsidian:[5] obsidian had been worked in the area for centuries,[6] but the lithic industry was now greatly accelerated, involving over four hundred obsidian workshops at the city's height.[7] Centered on its large marketplace,[8] Teotihuacan's economy penetrated much of Mesoamerica and, as a cosmopolitan center, drew in ethnic foreigners, including Zapotecs, people from Veracruz, and perhaps two other, as yet unidenti-

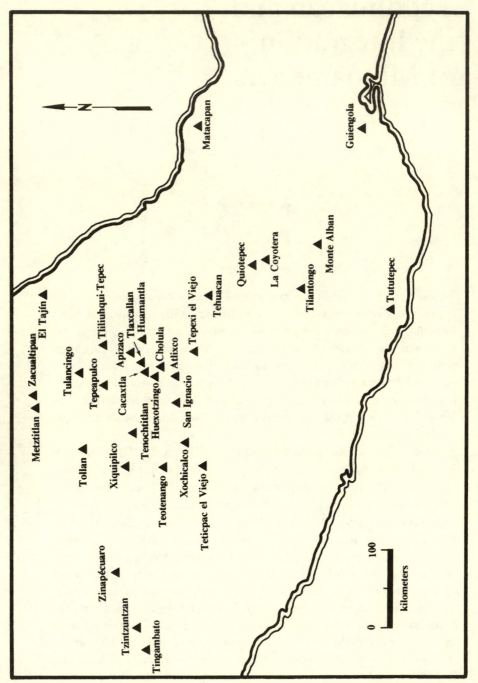

Mexican sites.

fied, groups[9] who occupied distinct compounds within the city over hundreds of years. Although Teotihuacan possessed a powerful domestic industry, economic penetration of foreign areas does not follow naturally. Rather, it frequently entails domination and, at a minimum, a peaceful trading area that, in the context of competing states, requires an armed presence.[10]

Arms and armor offer perhaps the best data about Teotihuacan's military.[11] Part of Teotihuacan's weaponry was inherited from earlier times, especially the thrusting spear.[12] Spears remained dominant on the battlefield but were augmented by atlatls and darts, which became major weapons in the Early and Middle Classic.[13] Atlatls do not have enormous range—not much greater than seventy meters, with an effective limit of around forty-six meters—but they add almost 60 percent more thrust over hand-thrown spears, giving their darts considerably greater penetrating power.[14] Atlatls had been used for hunting for millennia and proved to be effective military weapons because of their great stopping power. Moreover, they allowed Teotihuacan soldiers to pour effective fire into their enemies and disrupt their ranks even before the two sides fully closed for hand-to-hand combat. Atlatls were certainly elite weapons and were probably concentrated in the front ranks in battle, but using them requires both hands. Teotihuacan warriors therefore carried shields, but no other offensive weapons.

Slings continued to be used[15] but, as commoner weapons, they were not depicted in Teotihuacan art. Their longer range and arched trajectory made them formidable weapons, but since weight limited the number of slingstones that could be carried for any distance, their primary role was probably defensive. Axes were present, but if used, they must have been of secondary importance in that they did not compare well with other weapons: they were shorter than thrusting spears and even most clubs and were too poorly balanced and had too short a range to be effective throwing weapons.[16]

Knives are primarily depicted in mural scenes with impaled hearts, suggesting a ritual use,[17] but they were doubtless used in combat as auxiliary weapons, as was the case with subsequent Mesoamerican groups. All combatants may have carried them, although representations show them being carried alone or by atlatlists,[18] which suggests that these troops followed the spearmen to dispatch captured or wounded soldiers. In any case, they played a secondary role. Bows and arrows were still unknown,[19] and blowguns, employed in bird hunting, were not used as military weapons at Teotihuacan or by any subsequent group in Mesoamerica.[20]

There was little armor during the Early Classic, with the primary Teotihuacan innovation being the use of protective helmets of quilted cotton. The only other armor was the shield, which was now smaller. The large shields of the Late Formative offered more protection, but with the adoption of helmets, the defensive role of shields diminished and they could now be made smaller and lighter to increase mobility. The shield's reduced protection was also partly offset by the addition of feather fringes to the bottom and left side, leaving the top and right sides free of obstructions so that the soldiers could wield their weapons without hindrance. Although largely ineffective against direct blows, the hanging feather curtain could deflect spent projectiles and soften direct blows with a negligible increase in weight.[21] This trend toward lighter shields suggests they were made of woven cane or leather and were used to parry blows. Larger shields remained in use beyond the empire,[22] but the lighter Teotihuacan shields made their use at longer distances markedly more feasible.

The shields were held by a single strap at the top, perhaps because they were flexible and had to hang once they were unrolled, or perhaps simply as a carryover from earlier shields. But in either case, this top grip did not permit effective use of the shield *and* the atlatl, given that the latter required two hands, which suggests at least two combat alternatives for the Teotihuacanos. They could have had separate, specialized shieldsmen,[23] but this effectively halves the number of combatants fielded and could only have been used on a limited basis. More likely, atlatlists did not need shields at a distance or during advances while they were still beyond the reach of shock weapons and probably carried them until needed, perhaps tied to their belts.

Taken together, these arms and armor suggest a major shift in combat tactics, not deliberately deemphasizing shock weapons such as clubs and thrusting spears, but elevating the role of projectiles such as atlatls. Atlatls had not been significant in warfare previously, so their prominence at Teotihuacan reflects a major change in wars and how they were fought in Mesoamerica. For the first time, conventional armies dominated the battlefield: instead of conflicts between small groups of hit-and-run raiders, at least one side, if not both, mustered large armies with new formations and massed, effective atlatl fire.[24] Slings had provided projectile fire previously, but slingers require considerable space to wind up and throw. Thus, sling fire was difficult to concentrate and had mostly harassment value against helmeted, shielded soldiers. At-latls, however, could be concentrated, delivering massed fire that was particularly effective against large concentrations of men, penetrating rather than merely pounding them, although atlatlists' vulnerability to thrusting spears and clubs required that they be functionally integrated with protective shock-weapons specialists. Thus, the development of larger armies and battle formations created the necessary conditions for the use of this long-known but neglected weapon and led to the fielding of integrated but heterogeneous weapons offering marked superiority over more homogeneous armies. However, military technology alone was not decisive; Teotihuacan's advantage rested on the integration of technology with superior social-cum-military organization.[25]

Teotihuacan was a stratified society with powerful leaders,[26] but the general absence of dedicatory monuments[27] differs greatly from societies such as the Zapotecs of Monte Alban or to an even greater extent the Maya, in which glorification of rulers was common. One characteristic that may account for this difference at Teotihuacan was its heterogeneity: it lacked the common cultural base of ethnically homogeneous societies,[28] yet its social organization was sufficiently flexible and adaptive to incorporate outsiders, emphasizing residence over kin links in citizenship.[29] Indeed, this may well account for the massive, and apparently voluntary, influx of outsiders that was largely responsible for the city's meteoric rise. Such an influx would have affected the city's political structure as well, suggesting that not all leadership positions were defined by kinship. As population increases, although kinship remains important, especially at the local level, it becomes increasingly inadequate as a political organizational principle, and residence, abetted by kin ties, probably became a key political construct in Teotihuacan, facilitating foreign incorporation and lessening internal unrest. No doubt the Teotihuacan elite dominated the army as well as other aspects of society, but military monuments at Teotihuacan reflect offices or types of warriors rather than specific individuals.[30] This general lack of commemorative monuments reflects a society that stressed types and classes rather than individuals, suggesting that it was not rigidly hierarchical and was open to at least some advancement based on achievement,[31] as it was among the Aztecs.[32] That this was the case is also suggested by the breadth and depth of the military demands on society.

Teotihuacan's imperial accomplishments required too large an army to have been drawn exclusively or even primarily from the nobility. If we calculate the nobility at 10 percent of the population,[33] Teotihuacan could have fielded an offensive army of only 2,550 men at its height, and an effective maximum army of just over 4,300 men if only nobles participated—far too small to have threatened and dominated distant cities. Because cities, especially fortified ones, can draw on virtually everyone for defense,[34] an aggressor must be significantly larger to prevail. For example, if 90 percent of the males can aid in defense, supplemented by women bringing weapons, caring for the wounded, and so forth, a town of one thousand can muster 450 combatants and repel the attacks of a town of five thousand where only the elite are combatants, because the latter could field no more than 250. Under these conditions, a would-be conqueror needs a residential numerical superiority approaching 10:1 or be able to draw on a larger segment of its population for soldiers.

To accomplish its expansion, Teotihuacan fielded a large army that necessarily drew on much of its population, not simply for the Mesoamerican equivalent of cannon fodder, but to serve as well-trained elite troops in a military system I label meritocratic.[35] Evidence of large-scale military mobilization that encouraged commoner participation comes from both the weapons and tactics employed by the Teotihuacan army. The minimal division of troops into spearmen and atlatlists indicates that the army possessed functionally complementary units that were mutually reinforcing and generally superior to homogeneous ones.[36]

The ability to field a large conventional army gave Teotihuacan significant military advantages, but warfare at this scale also caused new problems, even in such seemingly simple matters as giving orders. The confusion and noise of battle made audible commands difficult and unreliable in combat, as did the voice-muffling jawpiece of Teotihuacan helmets; yet some control was essential, at least within units if not armies. Large armies cannot operate on the face-to-face basis of small forces: more formal means of exercising control therefore became crucial. Audible signals and commands probably launched attacks but were unreliable once combat was joined. This difficulty may have been minimized by adopting an overall plan prior to battle, but some coordinated control was essential, at least within combat units. The solution adopted by the Teotihuacanos was the invention of battle standards.[37] These serve as visual rallying points and signal unit movements when oral commands are unreliable. By watching the progress of the standard, any soldier in the unit can tell whether to advance, fall back, or stand his ground.[38] This was at least part of the function of the elaborate feather devices worn on the backs and heads of Teotihuacan military leaders.[39]

These standards both reflect and are essential for the effective use of mass-coordinated battle tactics, as suggested by the presence of complementary tactical units.[40] Such tactics are likelier in a meritocratic society where the repeated drilling this demands is more feasible, because hierarchical differences among combatants permit an effective chain of command, and where there are rewards for the resulting mass tactics.[41] In an army composed of nobles, which I label aristocratic, soldiers are less likely to accept the harsh discipline necessary or the diminution of their individual contributions.[42]

Teotihuacan could field a formidable army, but this did not mean universal expansion from the center. Warfare is a localized affair of taking forces where and when they are needed to meet an opponent. Even an overwhelming force is helpless if it is not where it is needed, and so intelligence is crucial. Political expansion required the timely receipt of information, and while this was easily obtained for adjacent areas, it was often difficult at the great distances at which Teotihuacan operated. Undoubtedly, intelligence was supplied by colonists, but merchants were probably a major, if not the major, source of foreign intelligence, giving Teotihuacan a decisive advantage over other cities lacking a network of far-flung traders.

By A.D. 100, Teotihuacan had grown to at least sixty thousand inhabitants,[43] giving it a potential offensive army of 7,650 men of 20–34 years of age, or an effective maximum of almost 13,000 if the age limit was extended to fifty. There was little or no local opposition to Teotihuacan, for the rest of the Valley of Mexico held no more than fifteen thousand people[44] and no local center or group of centers presented a serious threat to its domination. In all likelihood, Teotihuacan drew on these settlements to augment its own armies, bringing its offensive army to just under 9,600 and its effective maximum to slightly more than 16,000.

The proliferation of specialized military equipment also increased the need for specialized training as simple father-to-son instruction grew increasingly inadequate. As in other empires,[45] Mesoamerican warfare had ceased to be an individual or ad hoc matter and had become a state function, with professional training. This was also reflected in Teotihuacan's arms inventory, with weapons types becoming more restricted and conventionalized, as group training and tactics relied more heavily on predictable combat capabilities. Moreover, this suggests state ownership of weapons, as is common in centralized states.[46] Not everyone in Mesoamerican armies was a professional soldier, of course: many participants were merely fulfilling their tributary obligations. Though all combatants may have had some military training, most were probably militia. Although militia are typically more numerous than professional soldiers, they are not generally as well armed or trained, are usually tied to their home city, and are available for service only for limited periods.[47] Nevertheless, these lower-level units were probably organized on kin and residential bases which, tied as they were to Teotihuacan's economic organization, would have minimized desertions.

Gathering large groups is only half the solution to creating a large army: motivating them is of equal importance.[48] Both pay and booty are significant motivators, but they depend on military success and are probably inadequate by themselves. However, a meritocratic army is also motivated by the prospects of social advancement. Commoners in all Mesoamerican states could benefit from warfare by having their own tribute assessments lessened, by sharing in new tribute, and by generally profiting from the influx of new wealth, but beyond these immediate economic gains, which could not be guaranteed, the lower classes in aristocratic systems stood to gain little from war. Individual gains in meritocratic systems, however, were a major impetus for war, and such societies would have devoted a larger percentage of their resources, which were increased through conquest, to this end and may well have engaged in more warfare.[49]

Personal goals in warfare, such as security or economic gain, require little explanation. In nonstate societies, the goals of warfare are frequently booty, revenge, or glory, and when the warrior's personal objectives cannot be met, the battle is often ended: one's death is neither required nor desired.[50] With the rise of the state, however, its objectives become primary and professionalization involves the rise and enforcement of state objectives. Soldiers still have individual motivations, of course, but state goals are paramount and are imposed on the combatants, and suffering heavy casualties to conquer an objective becomes acceptable. Fighting takes on altogether different characteristics. There may be widespread participation in warfare at the local level by people willing to fight for their own interests (e.g., in defense of their town) but the farther away the war, the more professionalized the combatants, and the greater the subordination of their interests to the longer-term, strategic goals of the state. Thus, imperial expansion often results in both a military and ideological mismatch between contending sides.

The acceptance of state goals is particularly associated with the devel-

opment of a meritocratic military that offers commoner soldiers potential access to gains brought about by these wars.[51] Whereas a meritocratic military system draws its populace into the reward structure, an
aristocratic one does not and actively resists doing so. At Teotihuacan, a
meritocratic system may have been necessary because the heterogeneous
population was not controlled through kin-based elites. Alternatively,
this system may have arisen as a way of attracting and integrating
foreigners into the system. Whatever the origins of its social system,
Teotihuacan offered a degree of social mobility that was impossible in
most Mesoamerican societies.

Teotihuacan could muster a large army, but mass movement brought
constraints of its own. Without any major improvements in roads or
transport technology, Teotihuacan's armies most likely marched at
roughly 2.4 kilometers an hour, or just over nineteen kilometers per
eight-hour day, which virtually ruled out surprise attacks.[52] Any military expansion by Teotihuacan was also constrained by the same seasonal considerations that affected the better-known Aztecs.[53] Planting
began in the spring (usually in late April or May), with harvest in the
late summer or fall (as late as October or early November). Occupied in
crucial agricultural activities, most commoners (approximately two-
thirds of Teotihuacan's population[54]) were unavailable for military service during the summer and early autumn. But even had they been, the
necessary food supplies were not available until after harvest.

Weather was also a constraining factor, especially since Teotihuacan
did not build sophisticated roads between cities, relying instead on existing dirt ones. Stretching from mid May to September,[55] central Mexico's rainy season (which overlapped the agricultural season) quickly
rendered the dirt roads impassable through the churning of thousands
of marching feet, swelled small streams to impassable sizes, and made
travel generally uncomfortable for the people involved. Small groups of
elite soldiers could be dispatched at virtually any time because they were
not farmers, and smaller numbers greatly diminished the logistical and
transit difficulties. But large armies could only be gathered, supplied,
and dispatched on major expeditions during the dry season, creating
distinctly seasonal military campaign periods stretching from late autumn through the following spring, and doing so when much of the
labor pool was unoccupied, so that warfare had minimal adverse effect
on the local economy, a pattern that held true for all three central
Mexican empires.

The limited warfare and raiding typical of earlier polities involved

short distances, usually within the same ecosystem where conditions
were largely the same. But with the growth of its empire, Teotihuacan
expanded into different ecosystems whose local variations required considerable preplanning, which suggests that the reasons for expansion
were sufficiently important to justify overcoming the difficulties of contending with multiple ecological limitations.

Teotihuacan controlled its immediate area, an inner hinterland that
included the Valley of Mexico and adjoining areas of western Tlaxcala
and southern Hidalgo.[56] The city drew in rural populations as early as
the first century A.D., nearly stripping the valley of rural settlements,
leaving only small settlements, minor administrative centers, and the
larger town of Azcapotzalco on the western side of the lakes that administered this less accessible area.[57] Portions of the Puebla-Tlaxcala area
were also within this inner hinterland, and much of its population was
siphoned off into Teotihuacan.[58]

Although most of the city's subsistence needs came from within a
radius of twenty kilometers,[59] Teotihuacan also exercised control over
agricultural areas of a more distant outer hinterland, which included the
Amatzinac River valley, central and northwestern Morelos, and portions of Toluca, Puebla, Tlaxcala, Hidalgo, and Guerrero.[60] By A.D.
300, Teotihuacan expanded into the Tula region, which it closely administered, settling and maintaining the site of Chingú some ten kilometers
east of the later Toltec capital of Tollan.[61] Laid out in a Teotihuacan-
style grid, Chingú covered 200–250 hectares and was established by
people from Teotihuacan who dominated a larger, non-Teotihuacan
population.[62] Before its century-long decline and abandonment by A.D.
700–750, Chingú served as a collection point for locally mined lime
exported to Teotihuacan.[63]

Cholula was also a target, and its proximity to Teotihuacan led to an
inevitable subservient relationship. Located in the Puebla Valley east of
Teotihuacan, Cholula was the center of a culture region that, as early as
200 B.C., was similar to the Valley of Mexico.[64] Cholula adopted some
Teotihuacan traits but was sufficiently independent to remain one of the
three distinct cultures in the Puebla-Tlaxcala area from A.D. 100–650.[65]
However, Cholula itself was part of the Teotihuacan corridor, a narrow
band encompassing numerous cities that ran from Teotihuacan through
the Puebla-Tlaxcala area, through Apizaco to Huamantla, before splitting into routes going toward the Gulf coast, the Puebla Valley in the
direction of Tehuacan and Oaxaca, northeast through Tepeapulco and
Tulancingo, and perhaps on to the Gulf coast and El Tajín.[66] A similar

corridor may have run from Guerrero via the Balsas River, through western Morelos, into the Valley of Mexico.[67]

Cholula was important because of its position on this crucial trade route, but because of its size, confronting Cholula militarily bore substantial risks for Teotihuacan: the chance of failure was significant, as were the negative effects this might have had on other tributary centers. This does not mean that Teotihuacan necessarily avoided war with Cholula; but rather, if it was already engaged in some profitable relationship with Cholula through peaceful means, such as trade—and the archaeological data indicate a longstanding relationship of some sort— conquest might have been unnecessary. Instead, Teotihuacan apparently incorporated Cholula into its economic network and expanded around it as it probably did with other problem areas, dominating it culturally, economically and, most likely, politically.[68]

Archaeologically, the best known area of this outer hinterland is the Amatzinac region of eastern Morelos, where Teotihuacan influence began during the period between 200 B.C. and A.D. 200, increasing markedly until A.D. 600.[69] Teotihuacan locally administered the region from the large center of San Ignacio and reorganized it for intensified agricultural production of such tropical products as cotton, mamey, zapotes, avocados, and cacao.[70]

Teotihuacan's power and control extended only as far as its armies could march, but the primary limitation on the movement of armies was the availability of food.[71] As early as 200 B.C.,[72] comales were found at Teotihuacan in small numbers, suggesting that, as with the Olmecs, they were used for special-purpose foods—most likely to make tortillas for retoasting to be eaten during travel. This preparation yielded a better food on the trek, but did not alter the total amounts needed (.95 kg of maize per day), a logistical problem that grew with the size of the army. Teotihuacan's logistical limitations could be overcome only through local resupply. This, however, depended on the political reliability of the people along their routes, which Teotihuacan ensured by creating dependent areas. Aside from the economic gains of political domination, this strategy had the added advantage of hindering hostile intrusions in that these dependent areas deprived invading armies of logistical support, making Teotihuacan doubly secure.[73]

Control of major obsidian deposits doubtless made Teotihuacan merchants important throughout much of Mesoamerica. But the city's status was further raised by the dynamics of long-distance travel. Distance imposed severe constraints and was a social filter, skewing class representation. Because food supply was the limiting factor in projecting force, the increasing costs of travel with distance reduced the number of nonessential personnel. For armies, greater effectiveness is achieved at the same cost by sending more elite soldiers, and the same may have been true for merchants. The net result is that the farther away a site is from center, the higher the percentage of elites in the contacting party, which may partially account for the exalted image of Teotihuacan throughout Mesoamerica. Generally, foreign Teotihuacan sites were located in resource-rich areas at great distances from the Valley of Mexico.[74] Teotihuacan did not expand out uniformly, nor did it dominate all adjacent regions. For example, the cultures of northern Tlaxcala had little or no contact with Teotihuacan.[75] Teotihuacan influence was highly discontinuous, with zones of influence sandwiched between areas showing little impact.

Perhaps the most famous Teotihuacan-influenced center is Kaminaljuyu, located in highland Guatemala at the site of modern-day Guatemala City.[76] People from Teotihuacan apparently dominated Kaminaljuyu from A.D. 400 to 650–700, with at least part of their presence being tied to the greatly expanded exploitation of major obsidian sources during this period.[77] Teotihuacan's interest was not simply in Kaminaljuyu, but in controlling the goods flowing through its existing trading network.[78] Teotihuacan's relationship with Kaminaljuyu developed gradually, with initial contacts reflecting interregional exchange at an elite level from A.D. 400 to 500, to domination by Teotihuacan elites controlling the obsidian trade and using local labor to construct Teotihuacan-style buildings from A.D. 500 to 550.[79] Kaminaljuyu probably did not pay tribute to distant Teotihuacan, but this may well have been a factor in supporting the Mexican colony. Trade, however, was the rationale of the colony but, as imperial trade, this was not free exchange. Colonies are established not only to ensure access to distant goods, but also to control the market itself. Empires control distant markets by maintaining exclusive rights to trade there, denying access to others, so that, limited to a single trading partner, colonial trade is inherently unequal, working to the advantage of the empire.[80]

Teotihuacan's influence was dramatic at Kaminaljuyu, as its gods were adopted as public figures, though not in Maya residences.[81] This suggests that Teotihuacan dominated a local populace that only partially adopted the elite foreign traits.[82] With a population perhaps as high as twenty thousand in Kaminaljuyu, Teotihuacan exercised its control through political and economic means, by coopting or supporting the increased centralization of the local political elite, rather than through military domination.[83] However, stelae ceased to be erected in the highlands at this time,[84] suggesting the demise of an aristocratic orientation and the dominance of Teotihuacan ideology. Between A.D. 550 and 650, Teotihuacan influence at Kaminaljuyu waned as it withdrew support from the local elite, and withdrew completely in the A.D. 650–750 phase.[85]

Another distant Teotihuacan site was Matacapan on the Gulf coast, which had buildings in pure Teotihuacan style.[86] In contrast to Kaminaljuyu, where Teotihuacan pottery was found only in the Teotihuacan-style residential area and there were no Teotihuacan religious artifacts in households,[87] Teotihuacan household gods were present at Matacapan,[88] indicating the actual residence of Teotihuacanos. Given its location on the Gulf coast, midway between Teotihuacan and Kaminaljuyu, the city was probably an important way station between the two.[89]

Other less-known centers were also influenced by Teotihuacan. For example, the Classic site of Teticpac el Viejo, Guerrero, had Teotihuacan-style talud-tablero construction, suggesting a significant connection with Teotihuacan by way of the Balsas River valley.[90] Tingambato, Michoacan, also adopted Teotihuacan-style talud-tablero construction by A.D. 600.[91] And between A.D. 250 and 500, Teotihuacan influenced, and probably controlled, mineral mining at Chalchihuites, Zacatecas.[92]

Despite Teotihuacan's expansion and the importance of its army, neither the city nor its hinterlands bear much evidence of militarization. The city itself was not fortified, although there were walled areas,[93] such as the apartment compounds,[94] that may have served defensive purposes if the need arose, and natural barriers such as barrancas would have impeded entry.[95] However, Teotihuacan did not need fortifications because of its size and political system. In marked contrast to Monte Alban, which was located in an area of restricted mountainous valleys that could be defended by building a few forts at key points, the center of Teotihuacan's empire lay in a largely open area with too much easily traversable land to seal off through fortifications. Moreover, in a hegemonic system such as Teotihuacan's, fortifications were unnecessary, as can be seen by examining this political system.

A major key to the functioning of hegemonic versus territorial empires is their relative reliance on force versus power. Force is direct physical action—typically military might—that is depleted as it is used. Power is not necessarily force, operates indirectly, and is not consumed in use because it is psychological, the perception of the possessor's ability to achieve its ends. The ability to wield force is a necessary element of power, although a single demonstration, rather than its continued application, may be sufficient to compel compliance. Relying on power is more efficient than force because the costs are paid by the subordinates, thus conserving the dominant polity's force. Moreover, the likelihood of compliance increases with the subordinate's perception that the benefits are greater than the costs. But because a hegemonic system does not rely on local administrative change and bureaucratic integration, its limitations arise from different perceptions of power. As costs rise and benefits decline, compliance becomes increasingly unreliable: the more exploitative a political system is perceived to be, the more it must rely on force rather than on power.

Characteristic political systems and distinctly different ways of exercising control over dependent areas arise from relying more heavily on force or power. Territorial empires must maintain border and control troops in its dependencies year-round, so the cost is high and their empires tend to be relatively small. Hegemonic empires, by contrast, do not generally have these expenses because control is maintained by local forces at local expense, although there is a constant potential for rebellion in that local forces and leadership remain intact. What keeps these tributary centers loyal is the ability of the center to achieve local compliance. Often, as in the case of Teotihuacan, this arises from a disproportionately large population, and it typically involves meritocratic organization allowing more of the populace to participate. Such systems typically lacked fortifications: the capital did not need them because of its overwhelming size and power and tributaries could not have them because they would threaten imperial control. Except at the periphery of the empire, tributaries enjoyed imperial protection and needed no fortifications to deter external aggression.

Beyond the differences in tactical postures, another factor encouraging fortifications in territorial, but not in hegemonic, empires was their respective social organizations. Territorial systems were typically aristocratic, which limited the number of elite soldiers they could muster.[96] This shifted, rather than excused, military service by the bulk of the populace. Relatively untrained and of little value in combat, their labor could be turned to military advantage through the construction of fortifications that magnified the effects of the few elite soldiers such systems could muster. Hegemonic systems, however, were typically meritocratic.[97] As a result, their military labor was relatively skilled and better used in combat and thus was not absorbed in the construction of fortifications.

These two political systems produce distinctive patterns of imperial integrity. Contiguous conquest is a major concern for territorial systems because this creates smaller, more defensible borders, and internal control is easier if refuge regions or potentially hostile groups are removed. By contrast, since hegemonic polities control through power rather than the presence of controlling force, there is no compelling reason to conquer every polity within a prescribed radius of the center. Many "internal" groups may well remain independent because hegemonic control is directed primarily toward areas of concern to the state.

Teotihuacan could have expanded equally in all directions, but many areas of Mesoamerica were unsophisticated, held little interest, and would have been difficult to control hegemonically. Unless they had much-needed raw materials, less developed areas offered little potential for material gain, especially considering the enormous expense of transporting these modest goods over long distances. Bulk goods, such as agricultural produce, could only be brought from adjacent areas. Teotihuacan was large enough to dominate any of its potential competitors, but controlling a vast area was beyond its means. The logistical costs of centralized control were enormous, entailing the army's initial trek to and from the site and an equal expense every time the tributary balked. Any major expansion under these conditions would have soon stretched Teotihuacan's forces beyond their limits. But selective targeting of valuable sites was feasible, and Teotihuacan opted for colonial control in which permanent or semipermanent groups of Teotihuacanos coopted distant sites. Teotihuacan established colonies in distant lands to exercise direct military power; these entered into local alliances, multiplying their own power by that of their local allies. But establishing colonies testifies as much to Teotihuacan's limits as to its power.

Colonial control had several advantages that complemented the limitations of Teotihuacan expansion. Long-term colonists—whether soldiers, merchants, or political elites—were much less expensive than soldiers and administrators dispatched as needed from the capital. Where the local population was too small to sustain continuous travel, or the distances were too great, colonies were cheaper than armies because colonists went only one way and thus needed only half the logistical support. Even if the goal was to establish a sizable colonial group, they did not have to be sent en masse as an army did: instead, they could move in small groups over periods of years until the desired complement was reached. Moreover, sending colonists abroad was less expensive than keeping them in Teotihuacan and drawing in elite goods: people settled in colonies were essentially self-supporting from the perspective of the capital and also generated a flow of exotic goods. Once in place, colonists could exercise control over the surrounding area more consistently and cheaply than an army operating from a central location. And if increased forces were necessary, colonies provided firm bases of support, offering refuge, logistical support, auxiliary troops, and detailed local political and geographical knowledge ordinarily unavailable to a centralized army. In short, a colonial policy was ideally suited to the constraints under which Teotihuacan expanded.

Teotihuacan's control varied greatly in space. Near the capital (within a day's round-trip walk), control was direct, as witnessed by the forced resettlement of rural populations inside the city itself. Within two or three days' walk, not all areas were controlled by Teotihuacan. The increased expense of control at these distances meant some places—typically poor areas or those where settlements were dispersed in rugged terrain—remained independent. But for places offering resources, typically agricultural produce, control was less direct: local populations were often reorganized and relocated for purposes of better production, administered indirectly by regional centers that were in turn responsible to Teotihuacan. Beyond two or three days' walk, areas of control thinned out markedly. As the cost of transport increased, the relatively desirability of most areas declined. Only those with important resources—typically minerals—Teotihuacan lacked and that could bear the costs of transport were taken over.[98] Under the prevailing conditions, a colonial strategy worked best.

Was there a Pax Teotihuacana? Probably not, despite the traditional view of the Classic as a time of peace and a heavy concentration of military imagery at Teotihuacan only after A.D. 600.[99] There was warfare throughout the city's history. The best evidence of Teotihuacan's military expansion comes from foreign areas,[100] but early evidence has also been uncovered in the city itself. Sacrificed soldiers were buried beneath the Pyramid of Quetzalcoatl around A.D. 150. Men eighteen to fifty-five years of age, hands tied behind their backs, were executed and buried with numerous spear points, human mandible and shell-replica necklaces, and slate back disks typically worn by soldiers.[101] The mounting evidence indicates that the military played a major role in the life and growth of Teotihuacan from the outset. Teotihuacan conquered the adjacent areas of the Valley of Mexico, Tlaxcala, Hidalgo, and Morelos, which was feasible because all were very close and relatively backward. But Teotihuacan did not directly conquer larger cities such as Cholula or Monte Alban, which were farther away, much more populous, and accordingly more difficult to subdue. Instead, it entered into other types of economic alliances and maintained trade corridors connecting these areas. Imposing peace everywhere would have been very costly and the benefits would not have accrued exclusively to Teotihuacan's merchants. Rather, other, competing cities' merchants would have benefited as well, at Teotihuacan's expense. Instead, Teotihuacan imposed peace only within its restricted inner hinterland: beyond, it protected only corridors connecting distant trading cities. Thus, Teotihuacan protected merchants rather than places, which was a less expensive strategy, at least initially.

The corridor system sped the travel of Teotihuacan traders and, probably, of military forces, and although these corridors were too small to serve as buffers, the areas through which they stretched apparently posed few threats. Despite creating connections between Teotihuacan and more distant areas, the corridors were not equally accessible to foreign groups. The corridors did not provide quicker transit through any physical property of the routes themselves, but rather in the welcome, security, and logistical support offered by allied towns en route—advantages that would not be available to hostile groups. Thus, the Teotihuacan corridor sped transit to distant areas without simultaneously opening Teotihuacan up to threats returning along the same conduit.

Teotihuacan did not control all of Mesoamerica. Many places were too undeveloped to merit attention, and some places were too far away even for a colonial approach. Other places were simply too strong in relation to their distance to conquer, and still others existed under ecological conditions that made their exploitation difficult at best. Within these limitations, Teotihuacan's approach to imperial domination and expansion served it well, resulting in the greatest degree of political integration yet achieved in Mesoamerica.

CHAPTER 5

The Impact Beyond the Empire

There is no single course of imperialism. Expansion is easier, may extend farther, and requires fewer troops if there is no serious opposition, but relatively unopposed expansion may also bring vulnerabilities. If there is no opposition because there are no strong polities, the conquerors must then rule directly rather than exercising indirect control through an indigenous political organization. Even if indirect control is feasible, these conquered areas may be vulnerable to external threats unless an adequate imperial garrison remains in place. Moreover, the rise of external competitors could force serious changes in the empire, including withdrawal or costly retrenchment. Expansion into contested areas, by contrast, is more difficult, usually yields less imperial gain, and requires political or military consolidation. But once having defeated the opposition, conquerors are at less risk of attack, defeat, or forced withdrawal. In short, all things being equal, an empire that expands in the face of competition is likely to be smaller but stronger and less vulnerable than one that overexpands because it meets no opposition.

Teotihuacan did not overthrow other empires, but dominated largely in the absence of other significant Mesoamerican powers. Teotihuacan exercised power and honed its military skills locally, but expanded in a partial political vacuum and its fate depended as much on its own actions as on what others did. It expanded great distances, largely by following a course of least resistance and did not uniformly conquer everyone. The result was a territorially discontinuous, hegemonic empire. Some sites were simply too large to be conquered relative to their distance from Teotihuacan. The more distant the city, the fewer men Teotihuacan could send against it because of logistical constraints. Thus, a nearby city that posed little difficulty could be virtually unconquerable at a distance and, unless it was on a major trade route, there was no compelling reason to try. Instead, Teotihuacan concentrated its efforts against centers of particular interest, some of which may have already formed economic and possibly political links to Teotihuacan making military conquest unnecessary. Besides, combat is always a risk, especially in a hegemonic system; defeat could lead to resistance elsewhere in the empire, and so targets were not chosen casually.[1] These factors helped determine which major centers Teotihuacan did not conquer, including Monte Alban in the Valley of Oaxaca and the lowland Maya cities. Yet Teotihuacan had some sort of relationship with both areas, and understanding Teotihuacan's impact in either area demands initial consideration of indigenous developments.

MONTE ALBAN

Warfare was prevalent in the Valley of Oaxaca during the Late Formative and Early Classic. Zapotec monuments from A.D. 200–450 emphasize capture and conquest: of the fifteen surviving examples, six depict bound, high-status captives standing atop hill glyphs indicating their places of origin, and two others portray elegantly dressed men wielding lances, presumably Zapotec nobles.[2]

Monte Alban brought more areas under its domination at this time, but in a markedly different way from Teotihuacan.[3] Control was primarily exercised from the elite site of Monte Alban, which was reflected in their military. There was greater conservatism and more continuity in weaponry in Oaxaca than at Teotihuacan, possibly because, having been successful very early, the Zapotecs lacked a compelling reason to change. Zapotec weaponry remained largely unchanged from the Late Formative and consisted primarily of thrusting spears, although clubs— often with stone heads—were used as well.[4] Slings and atlatls were known but not depicted and were probably not elite weapons.[5] Instead of rectangular shields, relatively small, circular shields were worn on the forearm, leaving both hands free and giving spearmen great combat mobility.[6]

Commoner soldiers were not depicted and were probably not significant at Monte Alban. Elaborate military outfits depicting such animals as eagles, jaguars, and coatimundis indicate elite military orders, and it was these elite warriors who formed the basic units of the army.[7] There is little evidence of battle standards, suggesting a lack of formal combat units.[8] Elite warriors used shock weapons for which specialized training was required, rather than projectiles.

The Classic Zapotec military system was primarily aristocratic.[9] In meritocratic systems, the ideology is egalitarian, whatever the reality. Accordingly, warriors are depicted as generalized types rather than as specific individuals. In aristocratic military systems, by contrast, the ideology is elitist. In these systems, individuals—usually kings—are glorified, and are typically named in glyphs. That is, the monuments are erected to glorify kings and nobles in aristocratic systems but not in meritocratic ones where classes or types of warriors are commemorated.

Monte Alban's elite orientation is also apparent in the valley organization. With the most important nobles located in Monte Alban and those of the various valley towns doubtless connected through kin and other ties, the primary concern was maintaining this vertical control. What happened between villages was of little consequence to Monte Alban, and the valley underwent numerous shifts in local connections. What was important was the vertical integration of the valley, the flow up and down the system that maintained Monte Alban and its economic and political control.

Another factor indicating an aristocratic military system was Monte Alban's social organization. Aristocratic systems do not readily accommodate migrants: they are usually strongly kin-based—often with lineage systems, as suggested by Monte Alban's ancestor worship—and exclude foreigners. Despite differences within the Valley of Oaxaca, the region was essentially ethnically homogeneous.[10] Because Monte Alban did not encourage warfare after its initial expansion, large numbers of soldiers were not needed. The nobility supplied enough soldiers that more—necessarily drawn from the commoners—would have been disruptive and dangerous to the existing social hierarchy. Drawing soldiers only from the nobility had operational consequences, deemphasizing projectiles in favor of shock weapons which favored highly trained, individual prowess rather than mass tactics. There is no evidence that Monte Alban's army was divided into complementary arms groups, and indeed its small size made this unlikely. The high degree of training necessary with specialized shock weapons was probably overseen by the military orders. With little formal training, commoners would have been markedly less effective than nobles in combat, and their military obligations were probably met in other ways, such as constructing fortifications, the classic way of converting a capital investment into military superiority.[11]

During the Late Formative/Early Classic, Monte Alban controlled a territorial empire that was necessarily small, given the technological constraints and limited population of Mesoamerica. By building fortifications in the Late Formative, Monte Alban could control its territorial area without expensive garrisoning of every major town, a strategy fostered by the topography that allowed it to seal off the region with a minimal number of fortifications and to govern with relatively few internal alterations as well. There is little evidence that the local leaders were replaced or that subordinate towns were garrisoned, as expected of a territorial empire, because of the role played by Monte Alban itself. The Valley of Oaxaca cities were effectively an expanded local hinterland dominated by and from Monte Alban, just as they had each dominated their own local hinterlands previously. Rather than overtake independent cities that had to be conquered, garrisoned, and governed, because of its size, strength, and territorial strategy, Monte Alban could consolidate control over a much larger area than possible otherwise.

Ethnic differences beyond the Valley of Oaxaca made expansion more difficult and demanded greater use of force, most notably in the form of local fortifications and garrisons. Movement into areas such as the Cuicatlan Cañada was not inevitable, but its long valleys invited conquest from either end, so Monte Alban's expansion may have been preemptive, keeping out invaders from the north who could have then fortified the southern end against the Zapotecs.[12]

During the Early Classic, Monte Alban expanded and consolidated its control, with many military conquests commemorated by carved stones on public buildings in the center of Monte Alban that depict slain or sacrificed captives representing conquered towns.[13] However, Monte Alban's territorial expansion beyond the Valley of Oaxaca was not lasting. Part of the difficulty may have stemmed from the population decline in Monte Alban and its surrounding area in the two centuries following the conquest of the Cuicatlan Cañada, which may have been the result of increased military manpower demands there and elsewhere.[14]

Monte Alban's population fell to 14,500 and the valley's to 20,000 by A.D. 200, leaving a vacant zone around the city that may have been farmed by Monte Alban's residents,[15] and hilltop sites increased, suggesting an increased threat.[16] Throughout its history, Monte Alban was dependent on the rest of the Valley of Oaxaca for food, and the distribution systems became increasingly elite-dominated, although the valley economy remained poorly integrated.[17] For instance, elaborate ceramic goods increased in number, but their production was decentralized and apparently was placed under the control of various Zapotec lords throughout the valley. The three major subregions of the valley were largely autonomous economically and were not integrated at a valley-wide level or by Monte Alban. Local elites were linked to Monte Alban but controlled their own areas without significant exchange with other centers.[18] Instead of being a functionally integrated polity, the Zapotec empire was essentially a series of locally organized and largely autonomous segments over which Monte Alban exercised imperial political control but little else.[19]

In any case, Monte Alban was not prospering: increased manpower demands raised the costs of its empire enormously, although it is not clear whether this was because of foreign threats or increased internal resistance. This threat did not come from Teotihuacan, which early in its development had little impact on Monte Alban, although the Zapotec capital was doubtless aware of this giant to the north.[20] But when Teotihuacan did enter the area, it presented Monte Alban with a major military challenge.[21] Although there is no evidence of an actual military clash, Zapotec border fortifications could not cope with the forces Teotihuacan could throw against it, especially because reinforcements required at least two days to march from Monte Alban.

To this point, Monte Alban's farthest fortifications were at the periphery of its political system, at natural choke points where relatively few defenders could hold off numerous attackers who could bring only a small number of their troops to bear at any one time, until their supplies were exhausted. While the territorial system's defenses were more than adequate against the low-intensity threats against which it was erected, Teotihuacan was a major power and not so easily blocked. Unlike adjacent threats, Teotihuacan was some distance from Monte Alban and could select from any of a number of routes, circumventing the strongest of these local defenses. However successful the Zapotecs' territorial approach may have been initially, maintaining it under these altered circumstances was a major drain on resources and, given its inadequacy in the face of current threats, Monte Alban withdrew from the Cuicatlan Cañada region around A.D. 200.[22] This does not mean Monte Alban was now open to military conquest: the city and region were still formidable and the logistical constraints of the day made its conquest difficult, even for Teotihuacan.

Once the Zapotecs withdrew to the Valley of Oaxaca, they abandoned their territorial strategy[23] and made no attempt to fortify the periphery of a smaller imperial core or passes into the valley.[24] Its ethnic homogeneity and cultural cohesiveness made the Valley of Oaxaca an unlikely beachhead for outsiders, just as the surrounding less sophisticated and ethnically distinct groups helped keep the Zapotecs in place.[25] Instead, Monte Alban concentrated its forces in the capital from which it dominated the region but also protected itself from external incursions by rendering assistance to valley sites. Even if Monte Alban could not have kept Teotihuacan forces out of the valley entirely, it could force them back when climate and labor demands made reinforcement from Teotihuacan difficult.[26] Nevertheless, Teotihuacan was a power to be reckoned with, and the Zapotecs entered into some sort of relationship with it that accelerated and strengthened Monte Alban's more hegemonic style of political and economic control of the surrounding area.

Teotihuacan did not conquer Monte Alban, probably because of the difficulty of doing so rather than any disinclination. Teotihuacan had a larger army, although logistical constraints doubtless kept its army from enjoying numerical superiority in the Valley of Oaxaca. But the army's atlatlists gave it a significant advantage over the Zapotecs who neither gave projectiles pride of place nor were armored against them. The Teotihuacanos also enjoyed a marked advantage in maneuvering formations and tactical reinforcement by complementary weapons units. However, the matchup was not entirely one-sided, and, one-on-one, the Zapotec spearmen may well have been superior to the Teotihuacanos. Their small round shields, worn on the forearm, freed both hands to use their spears more effectively than Teotihuacan spearmen could using the less mobile top-grip rectangular shield. How they actually compared is unknown, but the Zapotecs did not adopt Teotihuacan armaments, perhaps because Zapotec society was conservative or Monte Alban's army was not large enough to make use of complementary atlatl and spear units without drawing on commoners. Most likely, the Zapotec army was already competitive as armed.

As noted, the distance to Monte Alban meant that Teotihuacan would have had difficulty in sending and supporting enough troops to conquer the region, especially since Monte Alban held a strong defensive position behind walls atop a hill that could withstand any siege Teotihuacan could mount. And more to the point, Monte Alban was not an isolated site, but was the head of an empire—the only one

Teotihuacan encountered in its expansion—and could draw on a wide area for support.

The Valley of Oaxaca was dotted with fortifications. Too small to mount a direct attack, these hilltop sites served as refuges to which the defenseless inhabitants of endangered cities fled until the attacking army left. Nevertheless, the sites did have significant military advantages. Atop a hill, they benefited by the 3:1 defensive advantage and could also bring 90 percent of their population into the fight, in contrast to the much smaller forces available offensively. Because of these advantages, a stronghold of a thousand people might fend off an attacking force double that size. However, these fortifications were not mutually reinforcing, for leaving the site's security reduced its armed force from nine hundred defensively to about two hundred offensively, which would make an insignificant difference against the attacking army. Rather, the people remained in their refuges and let the attacker pass unmolested, though the strongholds' very presence could endanger the attackers' supply lines, communications, and possibly the army itself.

All the advantages did not go to the defenders, however. By erecting field fortifications such as ditches, embankments, and walls, and by taking advantage of any defensible terrain features, such as ravines, as few as a hundred men at each site could contain the stronghold by reversing the 3:1 defensive advantage. The townspeople could either remain in place or attack, although their offensive forces would be too few to guarantee success against the entrenched containment force. This strategy, however, was probably not practical in reality in that few attackers would have enough men to leave containing forces at each stronghold. Even the passive presence of numerous strongholds was a major deterrent to invaders.

As formidable as Monte Alban was, Teotihuacan did not simply ignore this prosperous valley empire. During Monte Alban IIIA (A.D. 200–450), the Valley of Oaxaca came under strong Teotihuacan influence as Monte Alban's previous connections with the south and southeast were displaced by Teotihuacan influences, including Teotihuacan ceramics and figurines, as well as Teotihuacan motifs and figures in murals and on stone monuments at Monte Alban.[27] However, Teotihuacan's influence was confined almost exclusively to Monte Alban, with little impact in the valley below.[28]

The timing of Teotihuacan's influence in the area and the changes that the Zapotec empire underwent were not coincidental. Certainly, Monte Alban was not a Teotihuacan colony, nor did it have a Mexican compound analogous to the Zapotec barrio at Teotihuacan.[29] Although Monte Alban was only a third as far away as Kaminaljuyu, Teotihuacan's impact was markedly less, leaving only a tenth the number of Teotihuacan vessels found at the more distant center.[30] However, the nature of Monte Alban's relationship to Teotihuacan is not altogether clear. Although there are carvings of people from Teotihuacan at Monte Alban, none of these are armed, in contrast to their depictions in the Maya area.[31] Instead, a special relationship has been suggested to explain this nonmilitary, noncolonial contact, based on the carvings of Teotihuacan dignitaries found at Monte Alban.[32] Carvings on the South Platform depict eight elite Teotihuacanos visiting Monte Alban; these and other carvings at the site are taken as recording some sort of agreement between representatives of Teotihuacan and Monte Alban at an ambassadorial level.[33]

By A.D. 400 Monte Alban had reached about 16,500 inhabitants, with the valley growing even more, doubling the number of sites and swelling its population to 75,000.[34] Monte Alban exerted even greater control over the valley's economy: ceramic production was simplified, brought into large administrative centers, and fell to plebian status. Lithic production was also administratively controlled, becoming more standardized as the economic system became more centralized, and an integrated, valley-wide exchange system emerged for basic commodities, though there is little evidence of market exchange or marketplaces.[35]

These economic and political changes were most likely the result of Teotihuacan influence. However Teotihuacan influenced the situation—through diplomacy, threats, or intimidation—there was a radical change in Monte Alban's external relationships, as evidenced by the concentration of Teotihuacan goods at Monte Alban.[36] The influx of high status goods, ritual materials, and utilitarian products from Teotihuacan, as well as other goods from throughout Mesoamerica that were available from Teotihuacan merchants, gave Monte Alban a renewed source of local power; these goods did not enter the Valley of Oaxaca in ordinary trade available to everyone, but flowed exclusively to Monte Alban, which controlled their subsequent distribution.[37] Several factors suggest that Monte Alban controlled the flow of outside goods through administered trade, including the lack of marketplaces, the generally vertical flow of goods within the valley, the increasingly centralized and directed production, and the apparent lack of Zapotec merchants, all of which eased foreign economic incorporation.[38] By controlling and restricting the flow of Teotihuacan goods in the Valley of Oaxaca, Monte Alban perpetuated their scarcity, elevated their value, and used them to underwrite its own control. Previously, Monte Alban had depended on goods flowing in from its dependencies for its support, returning political and religious direction. Now, the influx of Teotihuacan goods was a visible measure of Monte Alban's new source of wealth and prestige, and provided a basis for political control largely independent of local support.

Monte Alban's direct control of foreign trade may also explain both the sustained Zapotec presence in Teotihuacan and perhaps the carvings of Teotihuacanos at Monte Alban. Probably without merchants, and certainly without the ability to protect them beyond the Valley of Oaxaca, Monte Alban faced three fundamental options if it wanted to trade with Teotihuacan.[39] First, it could allow all trade in both directions to be carried by Teotihuacan merchants, but this would have ceded the Teotihuacanos considerable economic power. Once granted carte blanche within the Valley of Oaxaca, the Teotihuacanos could have traded with other towns, undermining the economic basis of Monte Alban's control. Second, Monte Alban might have encouraged the growth of its own merchants, but this too would have undermined the control of foreign goods and thus the nobility. Third, without creating a merchant class, Monte Alban could establish a barrio of Zapotec craftsmen in Teotihuacan to supply those goods in exchange and then permit the Teotihuacanos to convey their own wares to Monte Alban. Under this system, the reciprocal trade would take place within Teotihuacan itself and not endanger Monte Alban's control of the Valley of Oaxaca.[40]

There was, however, another military aspect to this exchange. Presumably the Teotihuacan merchants also performed an intelligence function, as they later did among the Aztecs, learning of social and physical conditions elsewhere incidentally if not deliberately. Without merchants, Monte Alban lacked this intelligence beyond its borders. Thus, the Zapotec state controlled internal affairs adequately but was ill-suited for expansion because of the ethnic heterodoxy of neighboring populations, limited manpower, and intelligence inadequacies.

LOWLAND MAYA

The lowland Maya area also experienced extensive Teotihuacan contact, but no conquest, partly because of the jungle terrain that made military control difficult.[41] However, warfare was widespread among the Classic Maya themselves.[42] Rulers' claims of conquests are recorded on numerous stelae erected in their home cities, and arms and armor are commonly depicted in sculptural, mural, and ceramic representations.[43] Yet despite the prevalence of war, there are reasons to believe that it was not as destructive as suggested by the claims of Maya rulers. First, there were relatively few fortifications around or near Early Classic Maya cities despite their obvious defensive benefits. Second, there is little evidence of mass destruction of cities such as one might expect from wars of conquest.[44] Portions of some cities were destroyed, but this was usually limited to the centers, appears ritual, and was probably self-inflicted. Third, large expansionary polities did not develop in the lowlands. Various city-states did, from time to time, conquer other cities, but the prevailing political pattern was one of independent city-states with spatially limited surrounding dependencies.[45] Much of this pattern can be understood by examining the Maya military.

The Classic Maya elite used a wide array of arms and armor, including spears, a variety of bladed and unbladed clubs, shields, and helmets, although during the Early Classic this inventory was simpler. Early Classic Maya spears were primarily used to thrust and slash.[46] Stone points were not excessively large at this time, so that spears could have been used as javelins, although throwing them disarms the soldier.[47] The only part of a throwing spear that is brought to bear is the point, typically made of stone, although fire-hardening the pointed wooden end can also serve.[48]

The Maya less commonly used clubs, some of wood or bone, meant to crush the opponent, while others had single or multiple inset blades.[49] The blades were inserted through holes in the wooden handles, rather than being lashed to the side, and were probably made of flint, which was widely available in the lowlands. These were significantly thicker than obsidian blades, but the latter were scarce imports and, in any case, thickness was necessary to withstand the shock of use as crushers. However, thick blades added weight, requiring a stout handle and producing a relatively short weapon that relied more on mass than on cutting surfaces for effect. Long clubs were feasible but had to be used with two hands, leaving the soldier unable to hold a shield. The shock advantage of these clubs was offset by their shortness and relatively great weight, which suggests that they may not have been primarily military weapons. They may actually have been more important for ceremonial purposes or as execution devices; they may have been used by commanders engaged in directing battle for personal protection rather than as offensive weapons; or they may have served as badges of office.[50]

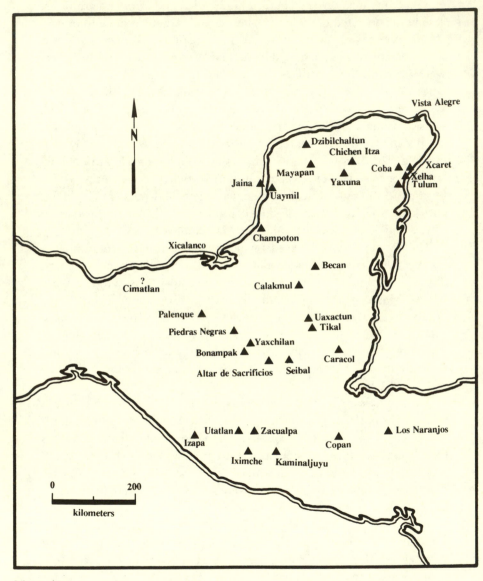

Maya sites.

Slings were known among the Maya but were not elite weapons.[51] The only other major projectile weapon available at this time was the atlatl, but atlatls were not effective weapons in the jungle environment, in small armies where a functional division of forces is not practical, or on raids where surprise attacks limited combat time.[52] Under these conditions, atlatlists had neither enough time to throw a significant number of darts nor an adequate distance to ensure their own safety from enemy fighters. But even more to the point, raiders avoid conventional armies that are the atlatls' best targets, and the Maya did not operate in formations that could effectively mass atlatl fire. In any case, it is fairly certain that atlatls were not integrated into a functioning Maya military complex but were depicted primarily as symbols of power associated with central Mexico, not as functional weapons.[53] Moreover, when atlatls are depicted, the Maya are shown holding the atlatl improperly for casting darts.[54]

Armor was not depicted in Maya sculpture at this time and was not well developed during the Classic, if it was used at all. Shields were not depicted either,[55] but their usefulness, relative technological simplicity, and common occurrence among the Late Classic Maya suggest that they were used in some form, although the added inconvenience of carrying them through jungle growth may have restricted their use.[56] This reliance on shock weapons and lack of armor suggest that the Maya were primarily raiders,[57] sending small armies relatively short distances to strike enemy towns and peoples before hastily withdrawing, rather than fighting conventional armies in set-piece battles. Where opposition is met, raiders typically withdraw because defenders close to home have a significant advantage.

That the Maya did not have large empires,[58] despite widespread warfare, suggests that they were unable to do so. The Maya could have recruited armies capable of subduing other Maya cities by drawing on their entire populace, but they apparently did not. One possibility is that Maya warfare did not aim at conquest; therefore, recruiting, training, and equipping large armies was unnecessary, although Maya conquest claims suggest that this was not the case. A likelier possibility is that Maya armies were small because they were largely restricted to members of the nobility,[59] an interpretation that is supported by several considerations. The first of these considerations is the overlapping pattern of labor demands and ecological conditions that restricted warfare to a short period during the winter and spring.

Although there is considerable environmental variation in the Maya lowlands, the area experiences virtually year-round rainfall, with the maximum from September to November and the minimum from December through May, with the last two months receiving the least.[60] Although the intensity of rainfall varied, agriculture was year-round.[61] Rainfall and agricultural cycles seriously constrained warfare in the Maya lowlands. Although agricultural laborers were free for only a couple of months during the winter, these commoners appear to have played little direct role in Maya warfare except as victims. The agricultural seasons did, however, dictate when food would be available although large supplies were unnecessary under the limited Maya military system. However, the Maya lacked a good, transportable food. Comales were not used by the Classic lowland Maya,[62] thus durable retoasted tortillas were not available, making long-distance forays into areas without reliable logistical support difficult.[63] More disabling was the effect of rain on trails, quickly turning them into quagmires and swelling streams to formidable barriers until well after the rains ended. Thus, passage of large numbers of men along jungle trails was generally not feasible from June until well after November.[64] Moreover, marshaling such large forces would have been economically disadvantageous because, unlike central Mexico, the Maya lowlands lacked a significant agricultural hiatus during which laborers could be diverted to military purposes without compromising the local economy.

Second, the evidence of conflicts and conquests also suggests that large-scale warfare was not typical of the Classic Maya. Instead, Maya warriors were drawn from the nobility who, though somewhat hindered by the rainy season, were not limited by labor demands and could carry out campaigns from January through May. But even had large numbers of soldiers been available, the prevailing paths restricted them to single-file formations, at least at choke points if not everywhere. The Maya soldiers would have marched as fast as armies elsewhere in Mesoamerica—nineteen kilometers a day—but paths limited passage to single file, and stretched out the armed party; the larger the army, the greater its travel time. Being strung out in single file also increased both the likelihood of discovery and their vulnerability: even inferior forces could attack and divide them at any point without fear that troops could be brought up quickly to reinforce those under attack. It also endangered the army because the longer it took for the entire party to arrive, the greater the chance they would be discovered and subjected to a massive counterattack.

Third, because of the enormous investment in arms, armor, and particularly in specialized training in their use, there is an inevitable differentiation in troops in all societies with professional soldiers. No society can afford to equip and train all its soldiers to the highest possible level.[65] The presence of elaborate military garb suggests military orders which probably trained the elite segments of society, although lineages could also have performed this function.[66] Commoners, if they participated in combat at all, were unlikely to have had formal combat training and would have been relegated to peripheral, support, and defensive roles. Fourth, army size, at least of offensive armies, is directly related to the polities' ability to extract goods and services.[67] In the Maya case, this was apparently limited, with the result that they recruited relatively few soldiers.

A final piece of evidence that supports the characterization of the Maya army as aristocratic is that Maya monuments typically depict only nobles engaged in warfare. Although self-aggrandizement by the elite is common elsewhere, as at Monte Alban, Maya monuments typically name the commemorated noble warrior, reflecting an elitist ideology.[68] Maya monuments depict specific kings and nobles rather than generalized warrior types.

Thus, instead of large-scale battles, Maya warfare consisted primarily of raids involving quick attacks and rapid withdrawals by relatively small groups of better trained and equipped soldiers, who were likely to be nobles. Any attempt to raise large armies would have led to increased centralized hierarchical control that demanded greater subordination of the nobles than was generally acceptable.[69] The Maya did not possess large empires because all Maya cities were comparably organized, and few could achieve more than local dominance.[70] Unlike meritocratic empires where power derives, at least partly, from achieved hierarchy and access to goods, power in aristocratic systems is based on kin control of resources. Trade was important but appears to have been controlled by nobles, probably limiting its role in Maya society and eliminating this as an avenue for social rise by commoners.[71] The potential for social mobility was further reduced by the nature of economic ties between city and hinterland. Goods flowed from dominated areas as tribute, parasitically siphoning off local surpluses, rather than as trade stimulating local production. The lack of a well-developed merchant system also hindered military campaigns by limiting the foreign intelligence available to the local ruler.

The elitist nature of the Maya military reflects other social conditions of these societies. Maya city-states were largely ethnically homogeneous, with their nobility and resultant political system based on status determined by parentage.[72] Providing specialized military training for everyone without offering more equitable possibilities for social advancement would alter the internal power balance and risk undermining the kin-based class structure of that society. The main forces in kin-based armies must remain elite or risk ouster.[73] Other societies train commoners in elite arms and skills, but they avoid the potential for revolt by opening their societies to social ascendancy of skilled individuals, channeling their efforts along socially acceptable paths.[74] This permits meritocratic societies to train more men, field large armies, and assimilate outsiders.

Basing the military on the nobility meant that rewards also went to the elites. Moreover, the great diversity of weapons among the Maya indicates a lack of centralized control, suggesting the existence of a warrior class that owned its own weapons rather than a centralized army.[75] This diversity also suggests that Maya armies did not rely on formations of uniform-arms wielders; such formations require training and group discipline unlikely to have been imposed on the nobility.[76] Instead, greater emphasis was probably placed on individual prowess and less on group combat. Moreover, without the impetus of social mobility, aristocratic military systems were more resistant to the adoption of mass weapons.[77] There was little incentive to adopt them among the elites, and the commoners, who could have gained from their use, could not participate.[78] In such a system, commoners had little motivation for warfare.

Drawing primarily or exclusively on the nobility also limited the size of offensive Maya armies to probably no more than 1.3 to 2.2 percent of the total population (all males twenty to thirty-five years of age, or perhaps up to age fifty, drawn from the noble 10 percent of the population).[79] The inherent limitations of such a system would be apparent only if confronted by a meritocratic system fielding vastly larger armies.

Among others, these features of aristocratic systems have led to warfare that has often been interpreted as ritual in nature. All warfare can be considered ritual to some extent in that it is rarely, if ever, an exercise in total domination.[80] All war is based on cultural assumptions about what is and is not acceptable weaponry and behavior and is never a no-holds-barred affair.[81] Furthermore, most armies have some form of chaplaincy, and major political and military events are often scheduled to coincide with important dates. Yet none of this renders wars any less serious. In the Maya area, the symmetry of military arms, forces, and practices on both sides combined to make warfare seem more ritual.[82] To the extent that conventional wars occurred, both sides fought with basically the same types and numbers of troops, used the same arms and armor, shared common notions of what was acceptable, and often met at mutually agreed locations. Thus, clashes often had the appearance of choreographed or ritualized behavior to a vastly greater degree than wars across cultural boundaries where the same arms and armor, army sizes, and behavioral norms were not shared. Yet Maya wars were deadly serious despite this superficial, and culturally external, appearance of ritual.

What these patterns of recruitment and warfare mean can be seen at Tikal, the largest city in the Maya lowlands, with an estimated peak population of 49,000.[83] If restricted to the nobility,[84] Tikal could have fielded an offensive army no larger than 619 and an effective maximum army no larger than 1,055 soldiers. Of course, additional men could be used in support, such as carrying burdens, but the aristocratic military system severely reduced the ability of any Maya city to wage large-scale or extended war. With the 3:1 defensive advantage and the large resident populations that a besieged city could draw on to counter the relatively small forces that could be arrayed against it, the aristocratic military system ensured the relative security of most Maya cities—not against raids, but certainly against outright conquest.

This Maya raiding pattern is also apparent in the dearth of fortified sites in the lowlands. Most Early Classic sites were not fortified,[85] possibly because as a city grows, need declines while costs increase, although some sites were defensively situated near terrain features that funneled passage. For example, both Becan and Tikal were flanked by swamps that limited the areas that could be attacked or required defense, and these reduced the role of surprise and deception. Formal defensive works were found at some Late Formative sites, but with the growth of large polities, these were drawn into even larger polities in which defense concerns focused on complete political systems rather than on isolated sites.

A notable exception to the lack of defensive works at Early Classic sites was Tikal, which had an earthen wall and ditch fortification,[86] a simple type of construction found in the lowland Maya area from the Late Formative through the Classic.[87] However, these fortifications did not encircle and protect just the city, but lay 4.5 kilometers north of Tikal's center, between that city and nearby Uaxactun. The wall and dry ditch stretched 9.5 kilometers, disappearing into swamps at either end.[88] The ditch was on the far side of the wall and was cut three meters deep and four wide into the limestone bedrock, which, combined with the rubble wall, presented intruders with a nearly vertical wall.[89] This was a major construction entailing the removal of approximately 126,000 cubic meters of fill. It may have been used to repel organized bands of invaders from Uaxactun,[90] but the walls are far from the center and too long to be continuously guarded with enough men to repel a determined assault. The wall was effective, however, in delaying attackers enough to alert the city,[91] and to funnel them along routes where they could be counterattacked en masse.

Fortifications and defensive siting are primarily effective against outright conquest and to protect dependent populations if warning is given in time. Entire sustaining areas could not be defended; where fortifications existed, the Maya strategy was to protect the political centers.[92] But such precautions are virtually useless against hit-and-run raids because these hard points are not the targets. Rather, Maya warfare was circumscribed and was primarily important in legitimating political rule.

Elite status alone was insufficient for many positions and offices, and military success was an important qualifier.[93] The Early Classic saw the beginning of a pattern that grew more elaborated in the Late Classic, of powerful leaders shown standing over captives.[94] Ability undoubtedly played a major role in that there were multiple alternative candidates for king, but primary consideration depended on kin ties, royal lineages that determined leadership positions.[95] However, this system was ill suited to control an empire.

Royal succession was also an important means of creating new centers. Lowland Maya cities typically controlled only the area they could directly reach from the center within a day, because the Classic Maya kept power in the hands of the elite and did not delegate power to a bureaucracy.[96] Unable to exercise military control from the capital year-round, colonization was one of the few available alternatives. However, because subjugated cities retained their local populations, colonizing forces had to be large enough to be self-sufficient, for reinforcements were not always available. Tikal may have been able to do this for one or two smaller cities, but its military resources were quite limited and any significant reliance on colonization would quickly exhaust its available military forces. Thus, neither direct nor colonial control was feasible in most cases. Instead, Tikal exercised indirect control by legitimating the rulers of these dependent cities, which they did through marital alliances or by transplanting rulers from their own noble lineages.[97] However, unless they are reinforced by more tangible supports such as economic, political, or military advantages, the effectiveness of kin ties in keeping a political system together diminishes.[98]

Over time, the interests of colonial nobles diverge from those of their parent city. While the burgeoning nobility at Tikal undoubtedly shared in the economic benefits of the city's expanding dominance, the colonial nobles' share diminished and their income increasingly came from their adopted cities. However effective marital ties were initially in linking dependent cities to Tikal, they disintegrated unless they were materially supported.[99] Repeatedly, Tikal's subordinate cities, though tied by marriage to the center, wrested themselves free of Tikal's rule after two to four generations as the local rulers increasingly saw their own interests as being more aligned with those of their subjects. This political disintegration could have been prevented by the liberal application of force, but Tikal lacked the army necessary to underwrite its control militarily and keep regional rulers in line through threat alone. Though effective in first establishing dependent subordinate centers, marital ties are of themselves inadequate for long-term control. Affective ties alone are insufficient: whatever control may be exercised over subordinate centers through marital ties weakens with time unless reinforced.

The Maya were concerned with the control of hinterlands surrounding their capital cities because they were dependent upon people and resources from these zones to sustain the cities, and the wealth and well-being of Maya cities was primarily tied to the size of their hinterlands.[100] Before all the Classic Maya cities arose, urban hinterlands would have been surrounded by areas too far away to be incorporated by any politically dominant city, so that raiding was directed at the intervening areas and may have led to political growth through annexation that did not conflict with other cities. These hinterlands remained relatively small because transportation constraints rendered the Maya unable to integrate large areas.[101] With the growth of more cities, the political landscape was filled with competing polities, each balancing the others. Once a city had control over its transportationally optimal hinterland, little further expansion could be sustained. Raids into competing areas were possible, but it was difficult to integrate distant regions politically and economically. Without much hope of effecting real political expansion, raids aimed at competing cities or their dependents and sought to disrupt these competitors. The political pattern that arose from these raids was one of city-states, each surrounded by a dependent hinterland adjacent to similar political entities so that all intervening areas were incorporated into one or another of the polities' dependent areas. Competition over surrounding areas continued, but during the Early Classic, these sustaining areas were generally small, with the notable exception of Tikal.

Tikal was the largest lowland Maya center during the Early Classic, dominating the surrounding regions and centers and whether foreign contacts were the cause or consequence of its size, Teotihuacan influence in the city is unmistakable.[102] This influence may have been exercised through Kaminaljuyu, which was the likeliest known source for any sustained relationship,[103] but Teotihuacan had contact with Tikal by at least by A.D. 375 and doubtless earlier, well before it consolidated control over Kaminaljuyu.[104] Tikal was too large and too distant for Teotihuacan to control directly, and certainly the latter's relationship to the lowland cities was markedly different from that with the highland Maya.[105] Its ties were apparently commercial,[106] but Teotihuacan influence was significant—enough to have swayed the balance of power in a succession struggle.[107] The first recognizable ruler at Tikal was Jaguar Paw, mentioned in A.D. 317.[108] The next recorded ruler, Curl Nose, took power in A.D. 379 and was the son of Cauac Shield, who may have been a foreign interloper, possibly from Kaminaljuyu.[109] His son, Stormy Sky, came to power in A.D. 426 and, through his mother, linked his paternal clan with the Jaguar Paw clan, the traditional ruling lineage at Tikal.[110] This is commemorated on Tikal Stela 31, in which Stormy Sky is flanked by two Teotihuacan warriors, strongly suggesting a Teotihuacan interest in this ruler and city.[111] Tikal's local dominance may well have been underwritten by the social and military prestige of Teotihuacan.[112]

Teotihuacan touched virtually everywhere in Mesoamerica, but its impact differed enormously. Possessing a social system that allowed social mobility and encouraged broad-based participation, Teotihuacan grew to become the largest city in the New World and was able to field the largest, most capable armies in Mesoamerica. Such military preponderance was decisive in and around the Valley of Mexico, but the limitations of foot transport severely restricted the distance at which Teotihuacan could impose its will. Although no Mesoamerican city could stand up to Teotihuacan in the abstract, travel costs so eroded the forces it could sustain in the field that even moderate sized cities achieved a rough military parity if they were located at considerable distances. Thus, distance layered Teotihuacan's influence, from a tightly controlled inner hinterland to a reorganized and regionally controlled outer hinterland, to areas still farther away that were spotted with colonized sites and peoples more tenuously connected to the empire.

Teotihuacan's expansion simply reached the limits feasible under existing conditions: it was not thwarted by superior powers. Some groups it encountered were doubtless locally powerful, especially Monte Alban, aided as it was by its geographical setting, but these local powers were (probably) all aristocratic. These posed no offensive threat to Teotihuacan but were ideally suited to the mercantile expansion it offered.

The influx of Teotihuacan goods meant not only connections with the major power in Mesoamerica, readily displayed through its imported wares, but it also strengthened rather than undercut local power structures. Both elite and utilitarian wares now poured into the local polities, and they did so through the nobles who then used their distribution to centralize their wealth and power further. This influx, though stimulating, sometimes altered the traditional system, making local rulers more powerful but also more dependent. These local changes were primarily the result of economic flows, not ideological imports. Although ideology does spread with people, Teotihuacan had little interest in altering existing aristocratic systems in that their aims could be more easily met as they were currently configured. That is, there were fewer people to deal with in aristocratic societies because the rulers dominated what were basically command economies, and imperial merchants faced little competition from local traders. The ideological elements that did penetrate were those associated with power and control, notions that fit well with the aristocratic societies, but not those stressing more egalitarian ideals. Thus, the nature of Teotihuacan's expansion and its relationship to these areas was primarily a function of power, the friction of distance, and the suitability of contacted societies to sustain the sort of asymmetrical trade typical of imperial exchange.

CHAPTER 6

The Fall of Teotihuacan and Its Aftermath

Teotihuacan reached its peak around A.D. 500 with a population of 200,000 people, approximately one-third of whom were economic, political, and religious specialists and not farmers.[1] The city also underwent an increase in militarism, especially in the final century before the city's collapse (A.D. 650–750), when many martial depictions appeared in murals and ceramics.[2] Significant changes took place in Teotihuacan's military, affecting armaments, organization, and tactics. Some of these changes merely reflect lacunae in the data, but others are certain and all indicate increasing military pressures, whether internal or external. There was no significant change in arms—thrusting spears and atlatls continued to dominate—but innovations in armor had broad repercussions.[3]

The most significant change was the introduction of body armor during the Xolalpan phase (A.D. 450–650).[4] Made of quilted cotton, this armor was as much as two or three inches thick and found in two basic types at Teotihuacan: one covered the entire body and limbs like mail, whereas the other was a type of tunic that extended only to the knees.[5] This armor was effective against atlatl darts at a distance and could stop glancing or weak spear thrusts, but was not completely proof against darts cast from close range or powerful spear thrusts. Nevertheless, it was very effective against slingstones which relied on impact rather than penetration, and this protection grew as atlatl fire forced slingers back to greater and less effective distances. However, the armor was too bulky to wear on the march and was used primarily in set-piece battles rather than against ambushes or other guerilla-type actions. The earliest evidence of quilted cotton armor comes from Teotihuacan, but the city is located well above the cotton-growing regions, so the idea may have originated elsewhere even though it was adopted most widely at Teotihuacan. In any case, the use of armor required Teotihuacan to have access to, if not control of, cotton-producing areas, such as the agricultural areas of Morelos.[6]

The armor must have been costly since the cotton had to be imported, spun, woven, and worked into a garment that consumed much more material than ordinary clothes. As a result, not all Teotihuacan soldiers could have been equipped with the costly armor, and most doubtless did without. The armor would have been worn by the troops in front, protecting these advancing elements and defending them against the breakup of combat formations: this was the attire of veterans and the elite who led in battle and bore the initial brunt of any clash. Quilted cotton helmets were also widely used, and elite examples were sumptuously decorated to indicate military rank or social status. Covering the head and nape of the neck, these were proof against slingstones and offered some protection against atlatl darts and shock weapons.[7] The adoption of cotton body armor and helmets had a significant effect on combat practices, seen most clearly in the development of the shield.[8]

By the Early Classic, Teotihuacan soldiers had shifted from the larger rectangular shields of the Late Formative to smaller, lighter, and more mobile rectangular ones, although round shields were also used. The round shields were small, lacked feather fringes, and were probably held in place by a strap across the left forearm.[9] The origin of this shield is unclear. It may have arisen earlier in Teotihuacan without being reflected in the surviving data, or, more probably, it was adopted from Monte Alban, where this type had enjoyed long usage. In any case, the arm-strap round shield gave its user markedly greater mobility, while body armor compensated for the smaller shield's lesser protection.[10]

These two shields were not adopted idiosyncratically, but were found in complementary distribution. Atlatlists retained the larger, rectangular shield while spearmen adopted the smaller, round shield. Because they had a relatively short range and were used to break up opposing formations at the outset of battle, atlatlists were placed at the front of the army, opening the attack with dart barrages while they closed with the enemy. This also meant that atlatlists were the most exposed and bore the brunt of the enemies' projectiles, so they retained the shield that afforded them greater protection. Once the two sides closed, however, projectiles could not be used as effectively, and certainly not in massed barrages, as soldiers intermingled and fought hand to hand. During this part of the battle, the spearmen bore the brunt of combat, facing similarly equipped opponents. They fought with spears and used both those and their smaller shields to parry enemy thrusts: not facing projectiles, they did not need as much shielding and, in fact, benefited by the greater mobility offered by the smaller arm-strap shield. Thus, for the first time, there was a division of forces at the elite level into two complementary types of units: atlatl wielders for projectile fire and spearmen for shock effect.

Apparently facing better and more organized opposition, Teotihuacan soldiers required armor that protected not only the trunk against shock attack, but also such extremities as the legs, which were vulnerable to the indiscriminate fire of projectiles. This adoption of more heavily armored infantry may have occurred, in part, to counter problems in the farthest reaches of the empire. Although costly to armor troops, this was nevertheless an efficient use of funds to preserve far-flung imperial control whose major cost was in dispatching and maintaining soldiers at a distance. Yet because armored troops were more effective in combat than light infantry, sending heavy infantry was more efficient in the long run, providing more bang for the Mesoamerican buck. However, the same was not necessarily true in and around Teotihuacan itself. Instead, the development of costly armor may have caused or exacerbated greater social distinctions within the army than had existed previously. A complete elite military outfit was expensive and, unless underwritten by the state, was probably restricted to the upper echelons of society and to experienced veterans. Most soldiers lacked body armor and helmets, probably only carrying shields for defense, especially by slingers and clubmen.

Added to the materiel evidence of professionalization among Teotihuacan's soldiers was the apparent existence of formal military orders similar to the Aztecs' eagle and jaguar knights.[11] Members of these orders entered battle clad in feather-covered suits (presumably worn over cotton armor) representing eagles, jaguars, coyotes, and so forth. To some extent, these orders may have reflected functional combat divisions: jaguar warriors are most often associated with atlatls and darts whereas eagle warriors favor thrusting spears, but this division was not clearcut in practice and these weapons were used by other military groups as well.[12] Neither is it certain that these orders fought as functional units. They may have served as unit commanders, but since other well-armored soldiers who were not members of these military orders greatly outnumbered the members, the former more likely served in command positions.[13]

How the army was mustered, organized, and controlled is unknown, although the presence of apartment compounds typically housing in excess of a hundred people suggests that these may have been the basic organizational units of Teotihuacan.[14] Teotihuacan's mean population for the period of A.D. 300–750 was 125,000,[15] potentially yielding an offensive army of almost 16,000 and an effective maximum of almost 27,000. By A.D. 500, Teotihuacan may have reached a peak in excess of 200,000,[16] fielding an offensive army of 25,500, or an effective maximum of over 43,000. At the same time, the rest of the Valley of Mexico held an additional 105,000 people,[17] boosting Teotihuacan's maximum offensive army to almost 39,000 men and its effective army to almost 66,000—a force unmatched in Mesoamerica at that time.

Although there is little evidence of conflict within the city during this period of increased militarization, Teotihuacan's trade and colonial network began suffering visibly around A.D. 500, reflecting a progressive withdrawal on all fronts that generally reversed the sequence of its initial expansion.[18] Teotihuacan influence greatly diminished in the Maya lowlands and vanished almost completely from Kaminaljuyu by A.D. 550.[19] The mining area of Chalchihuites in Zacatecas fell idle after A.D. 500.[20] The economically important sites that comprised the Teotihuacan Corridor as early as A.D. 100 continued to flourish but became increasingly autonomous toward the end of the Xolalpan and Metepec phases (A.D. 400–750), and Teotihuacan withdrew from eastern Morelos by A.D. 650.[21]

Teotihuacan fell around A.D. 750, but the city was not totally destroyed; the center was burned—primarily the monumental architecture on the Street of the Dead and its associated buildings and temples—but little else was harmed.[22] Most of the destruction involved burning in front of the staircase, and on both sides, the top and inside of the temples, as well as palaces and some apartment compounds. The arson was apparently an internal act carried out by the city's own inhabitants.[23] Because the destruction was concentrated in symbolically important places and this type of ritual destruction had occurred in Teotihuacan previously, the regime governing Teotihuacan was either a party to its destruction or unable to prevent it as it occurred during a time of internal crisis.[24] Teotihuacan's destruction was only partial, and life in the city continued with a reduced population as high as 30,000–40,000,[25] much smaller than its former size but still the largest city in the central Mexican area.

Why this happened is not entirely clear. The city was not in an obvious state of decline when it was destroyed.[26] Various competitors have been suggested as playing major roles in Teotihuacan's demise, including Cholula and Xochicalco.[27] Military setbacks have been implicated in Teotihuacan's demise, but the danger must have been diffuse and it was less important than the impeded flow of goods into the city.[28] Certainly the fact that its people established other towns in the Valley of Mexico suggests that the city's demise was not due to a military attack, particularly because Teotihuacan was by far the largest city in Mesoamerica, had the largest and most formidable army, and no plausible enemy capable of such a defeat has been identified.

The sketchy data available suggest that Teotihuacan fell of its own weight. It had dominated vast stretches of Mesoamerica but was incapable of militarily incorporating every independent city into a Teotihuacan empire. Although it could mount the largest army, Teotihuacan nevertheless lacked the manpower required to conquer and control all the cities: Mesoamerica's far-flung cities presented a serious logistical obstacle that could not be overcome with the technology of the day, nor did Mesoamerica's relatively low population density permit an organizational solution to this problem.

As discussed, conquests at any significant distance were exceptionally costly and, even if achieved, control was difficult to maintain. Only by garrisoning troops and settling peoples in these distant centers could Teotihuacan exercise any significant and sustained domination over them, yet garrisons were expensive to maintain under the manpower and logistical limitations of the Classic period. Accordingly, Teotihuacan established colonies and military enclaves only in selected centers. Nearby areas could be controlled directly from the capital, but colonies offered the surest way to maintain control in distant areas. From these secure centers, Teotihuacan's influence extended into the surrounding areas, either alone or in alliance with local groups who also benefited by the arrangement. Through this mechanism, Teotihuacan dominated production and trade throughout much of Mesoamerica.

Part of the rationale for Teotihuacan's expansion was to control the production or trade of culturally important items. Teotihuacan did not achieve this position simply because it produced some of these goods (notably obsidian) and consumed others (such as exotic minerals). It expanded its own production to levels far greater than that of other sites, both absolutely and per capita, but to benefit by so doing, control of a stable and predictable market was essential. And this is what it sought, spurred, no doubt, by the insistence of the elites whose elevated welfare depended on the acquisition of wealth and exotic imported goods.

Teotihuacan did not compete with other major empires, but expanded under conditions in which it had no real competitors. The greatest brake on Teotihuacan's expansion was the friction of distance, but expansion also generates its own opposition. Teotihuacan unquestionably benefited from its vast trade network, but so did other centers that were tied into it. Teotihuacan's trading partners received goods that bolstered the positions of their local elites, so that Teotihuacan's economic success also led to the growth of increasingly sophisticated and powerful centers, both allied and independent, which contained emergent elites who increasingly competed for local goods.[29] As a result, the trade network not only produced exotic goods and provided a market for Teotihuacan products, it also created competitors. These competitors were not restricted solely to Teotihuacan's trade partners; as each center grew and extended its influence, it also brought more of the surrounding area and towns under its influence and effectively removed these areas as trade partners for Teotihuacan. This was not a military competition, however. Man to man, Teotihuacan soldiers could probably have defeated any competitor, but the great costs of transportation in Mesoamerica meant that, generally, the farther away the target, the smaller the army that could reach it. While Teotihuacan maintained overall military superiority until its demise, it could not maintain local superiority everywhere and thus could not dominate numerically inferior forces at great distances.

As distant cities achieved local military superiority, especially non-allied cities, their elites usurped local goods that Teotihuacan sought and did so with impunity. Teotihuacan may have been able to defend its colonies and merchants even under these circumstances, but it did not have the military dominance to compel trade. This growth in local power posed no military threat to the city of Teotihuacan, but it did endanger its economic network. As foreign trade declined, there were undoubtedly internal pressures in Teotihuacan to counter this. As the number of Teotihuacan craftsmen increased, external markets for their wares had to be maintained, if not expanded. Once its military advantage slipped, however, Teotihuacan could no longer control trade and ensure that it reached home reliably and cheaply, making its colonies too expensive to maintain in relation to the declining benefits they produced.

As its trade and colonial areas contracted, the military became increasingly prominent in Teotihuacan.[30] Part of this may be explained by the return of colonial troops to Teotihuacan who were now concentrating in closer areas that were more easily reinforced and defended. This made both economic and military sense, but it furthered a process of decline as Teotihuacan's control crumbled at the edges of even closer areas.

Artistic representations of military themes at Teotihuacan differ markedly from those found in aristocratic systems. Among the latter, militaristic themes indicate success, so their incidence is greatest during periods of expansion. In meritocratic systems, however, successful expansion inspires few depictions of militaristic subjects, which are created, instead, during periods of failure and contraction, possibly signaling internal repression and a defensive posture in or near the capital. In Teotihuacan's case, the significant increase in military themes reflected a growing reliance on the military as the costs of foreign trade increased.[31] To compensate, Teotihuacan increased its military presence, which was an effective military response but an economically flawed one. Because Teotihuacan controlled long-distance trade, its merchants bore the costs of transport, which increased along with the additional military protection. As a result, the cost of trade goods rose and the wealth of Teotihuacan's artisans declined.

As distant cities grew more sophisticated, Teotihuacan's traditional military stance grew increasingly inadequate to its political purposes. Though no center could have resisted the full might of Teotihuacan, strong centers located at a distance, such as Monte Alban, were locally dominant and remained independent. Distance reduced the forces Teotihuacan could support logistically and the increasingly frequent shift to hilltop fortifications multiplied the numbers Teotihuacan needed to dispatch to maintain control at the previous level. Teotihuacan continued to dominate relatively weak or accommodating centers by virtue of its economic advantages and its larger army, but as old centers grew larger and new ones were built in defensible locations, Teotihuacan could not intimidate them as easily. Increased competition and newer defenses could be overcome only by larger armies, but these were only available by concentrating existing forces, which meant that, while Teotihuacan control declined throughout Mesoamerica, increased control in some areas could be purchased by its even more rapid decline elsewhere. Teotihuacan was forced to withdraw and consolidate in the city because its forces were too few and too dispersed to continue its control of peripheral areas in the face of foreign competition and resistance.

By concentrating the army in the city, Teotihuacan amassed forces of sufficient size to carry out successful offensive strikes, but this was not a successful solution in the long term. This new strategy of dominating from the center was the only one that was feasible, but, although it was tactically successful, Teotihuacan could no longer dominate an area large enough to sustain its own domestic population or to satisfy their growing social expectations. Teotihuacan may have used its military to extract more goods from adjacent areas to compensate for its growing trade deficit, in that this could have been done at relatively low cost. Although greater extraction would have increased Teotihuacan's income by securing needed goods for its elites, it would have had a negligible effect on the city's craft industries because this influx of wealth would not create a greater demand for those goods. In fact, increased tribute extraction from subjugated areas would have greatly reduced their ability to buy these goods, actually reducing trade.

Teotihuacan's increased militarism may also reflect the need to quell internal difficulties that would have hampered its ability to cope with other problems.[32] These difficulties may have been economic in nature, but class conflict may also have risen. As a military meritocracy, Teotihuacan fielded an exceptionally large, well trained, and highly motivated army that played a pivotal role in its expansion. But as expansion stalled and contraction began, it became increasingly difficult to reward successful warriors expecting social mobility, which may well have led to more rigid class barriers,[33] contraction,[34] and, ultimately, the loss of faith in Teotihuacan's political and religious leadership, followed by the ritual destruction and abandonment of the city.

Following Teotihuacan's demise, Mesoamerica fragmented into numerous semiautonomous areas. Interregional exchange continued, but at lower levels, and no single center rose to take over control of the Mesoamerican exchange system.[35] Those that did were aristocratic. Although these polities were less able to expand and dominate large areas, they were also fairly self-sufficient and hence more stable in a world suffering the disintegration of its sole stabilizing empire. Nevertheless, Teotihuacan's withdrawal and demise signaled a major shakeup of relations throughout Mesoamerica and affected all the societies with which it had contact, some detrimentally and others beneficially.

MONTE ALBAN

Given its earlier relationship with and even dependence on Teotihuacan, that city's decline had a major impact on Monte Alban. Monte Alban arose for internal reasons geared to dominating the Valley of Oaxaca and integrating it politically and economically, which it did through a territorial system of control. After A.D. 200, however, it relaxed control beyond the valley itself for at least three reasons: exercising control at that distance was very costly for a relatively small aristocratic military system such as Monte Alban; the earlier threats from the directions of the Gulf coast and the Tehuacan Valley had subsided; and Monte Alban entered into a mutually beneficial relationship with Teotihuacan, which had emerged as the dominant power in central Mexico.

Although Monte Alban was neither a colony nor a colonial enclave of Teotihuacan, it was tied to that imperial capital in many ways, the most obvious of which was economic.[36] Teotihuacan wares and prestige items entered Monte Alban and from there flowed through a local distribution system geared primarily to political, rather than economic, efficiency. In short, Teotihuacan connections helped support and underwrite Monte Alban's control of its region, a control that it continually strengthened and centralized. Monte Alban's rise can best be understood as internally generated, but its political and economic control changed to take advantage of ties to Teotihuacan that allowed the elites of Monte Alban to expand their power more than their own material and organizational resources permitted, strengthening their control locally in a manner that offered greater returns and was considerably cheaper than the territorial system they employed previously.

At the beginning of phase IIIB (A.D. 400 to 650–700), the economy of the Valley of Oaxaca was centered on Monte Alban, with goods flowing into and out of the center, but with little economic integration between lower-level sites.[37] At this time, Monte Alban, with a population of 24,000, dominated a strongly centralized, valley-wide system,[38] but Teotihuacan's declining influence disrupted this system of economic distribution as its trade diminished and Monte Alban received fewer goods.[39] Monte Alban's fate was tied to Teotihuacan's, and when the latter withdrew, it removed much of the material basis of Monte Alban's power and authority. Elite Teotihuacan goods had become important, even crucial, to Monte Alban's control, and without them, local allegiance declined. One theory of Monte Alban's decline holds that, as the political/administrative center of the valley, the city was crucial in fending off external domination, but once Teotihuacan fell, the people of the Valley of Oaxaca withdrew support from Monte Alban, which was obviously costly, opting for smaller and more autonomous polities.[40] A related, and compounding, hypothesis suggests that population pressure led to Monte Alban's demise.[41]

As a result, Monte Alban's centralized control over the regional economy fragmented during the Early and Middle Classic, leading to an increase in intersite competition in the seventh and eighth centuries.[42] Nobles and commoners alike materially benefited by excluding Monte Alban and focusing on local political units.[43] Because Monte Alban had never been self-supporting, once it lost control of elite goods, it lacked the power to compel continued obedience, and its decline was drastic and nearly complete.[44] The decline was gradual, but Monte Alban was beleaguered, having shrunk to about four thousand people by A.D. 650–700, when a new defensive wall was built.[45] Jalieza, with a population of sixteen thousand, emerged as the largest settlement in a valley of politically balkanized petty kingdoms.[46] This political fragmentation effectively eliminated the Valley of Oaxaca as a military force. Warfare continued, but on a lower level between petty kingdoms, with only occasional conflicts between larger confederacies.

THE LOWLAND MAYA

Relying on ties to central Mexico had benefited many Maya cities, but Teotihuacan's collapse undermined them to an equal extent.[47] Teotihuacan's fall reverberated throughout Mesoamerica as trade networks failed, were abandoned, or were reorganized, and the areas least affected were those that had the least contact with Teotihuacan. Cities tied into the Teotihuacan-dominated trade system, such as Tikal, were seriously injured by its collapse. They could reorganize the network, but with central Mexican goods and demand gone, any reoriented trade network would be significantly smaller and less important than its predecessor.[48]

The demise of the Maya cannot be attributed entirely to Teotihuacan's collapse, however. The same emulation and maturation process that undermined Teotihuacan vis-à-vis its trading partners elsewhere also occurred in the lowland Maya area, reducing the dominance of centers such as Tikal in relation to other cities.

An additional factor affecting the consequences of Teotihuacan's demise on the city-states was the distortion it had engendered in Maya social organization. Normally, no more than 10 percent of a population can be supported as social elites, but as Tikal expanded, it coopted the labor of incorporated areas to sustain its own burgeoning elite. Thus, while Tikal's elite were probably never more than 10 percent of the total population it controlled, they were significantly larger than 10 percent of the city's population, which it supported by drawing surplus from distant producers. But since much of its dominance was based on control of the Teotihuacan-connected trade network, when it collapsed, Tikal's expanded resource base shrank, leaving the city with a social structure that could not be supported by local resources, so it collapsed. Teotihuacan's demise also signaled the emergence of cities and elites elsewhere who struggled to take over local and adjacent resources too far from Tikal for it to dominate either economically or militarily. Once the Teotihuacan trade network broke up, Tikal was left with little more than the military to maintain its earlier position. It was unable to do so.

THE MIDDLE CLASSIC HIATUS

One factor that complicates our understanding of the consequences of Teotihuacan's withdrawal is the Classic Maya hiatus (ca. A.D. 534–593), a period traditionally interpreted as a pause in Maya cultural development.[49] This hiatus is reflected in the cessation of stelae construction and erection and in the impoverishment of buried offerings.[50] One theory holds that the Maya hiatus was caused by the withdrawal of Teotihuacan contact, the timing of the two events being highly suggestive. But the cessation of ritual construction and monument building was probably only an indirect result of this withdrawal.[51] The hiatus overtook Tikal with devastating suddenness, but it was neither inexplicable nor unprecedented. Tikal had already experienced the breaking away of a number of its major dependencies (for example, Yaxchilan in 514 and Copan in 564) which asserted their independence,[52] diminishing Tikal's political and economic significance.

Despite sweeping changes that accompanied shifting power and trade relationships, there was no pan-Maya hiatus. The ultimate cause of Tikal's demise may have been Teotihuacan's withdrawal, but its proximate cause was Tikal's conquest by Caracol in A.D. 562.[53] Conquered cities such as Tikal ceased major construction and monument erection, but conquerors, such as Caracol, in fact expanded construction and continued erecting monuments.[54] Conquest did not mean the occupation of Tikal proper, but it did mean the stripping of tribute and labor from its hinterlands, both of which were essential to Tikal's building campaigns. These resources now accrued to Caracol, which underwent a significant population increase and a major construction boom.[55] These events highlight the fact that the goal of Maya warfare was not to dominate and control competing centers, for distance made this difficult, but to demonstrate political legitimacy and relative power in order to acquire dependent populations as an expanded support base for the successful city.

Most Maya centers resumed major construction and political activity around 600, although Tikal did not do so until 692, but instead of a single major center, there were several: Tikal dominated the Peten region, Yaxchilan dominated the Usumacinta region, Palenque dominated the southwestern region, Calakmul probably dominated the northern Peten, and Copan dominated the southeastern region. During the Late Classic, Yaxchilan stands out as a military power. But the Late Classic Maya were neither politically nor economically unified.[56]

The power and position of rulers of independent polities, such as Monte Alban and Tikal, had grown stronger because of their access to Teotihuacan and Teotihuacan-traded goods. Moreover, they had done so at little cost to themselves because the trade network was externally maintained. But this seeming benefit hid a major liability. Once Teotihuacan withdrew, so too did the economic and military support for the trading system, and creating a new one was beyond the economic means and organizational capability of any surviving center. As a result, the wealth and prestige of local elites fell and their capitals declined.

CHAPTER 7

The Late Classic Interregnum

Following Teotihuacan's decline various Maya cities reasserted themselves, albeit in smaller political groupings, and continued a more limited exchange. Eventually, however, the southern lowlands underwent a period of fragmentation, depopulation, and collapse in the late ninth and tenth centuries.[1] In central Mexico, centers such as Cholula and El Tajín retained importance, and other regional centers grew, taking advantage of the economic and political vacuum left by Teotihuacan's withdrawal.[2] Local powers emerged, but nowhere in Mesoamerica were there large empires or broad-based integration.

THE LATE CLASSIC LOWLAND MAYA

With the disintegration of the Maya lowlands into independent city-states and relatively small polities, warfare increased. The absence of larger political aggregations indicates that there had been no gains in manpower needed to create larger ones which suggests, in turn, that Maya armies were still drawn largely, if not exclusively, from the nobility, despite the fact that most major Maya cities held populations below 20,000. During the Late Classic, Tikal's peak population was 49,000, Dzibilchaltun's was 10,000–20,000,[3] Coba's has been estimated at 40,000–60,000,[4] and even the largest Late Classic Maya political units were on the order of 40,000–60,000 people.[5] Royal lineages determined who was eligible for leadership positions, including that of military leader.[6] But office holders nevertheless owed much of their positions to their success in war because there were multiple eligible candidates, and bound captives are frequently depicted on rulers' monuments.[7]

With small, primarily elite, armies, raiding remained the dominant mode of warfare in the Late Classic,[8] a situation reflected in Maya artistic representations of named, individual, noble warriors rather than generalized groups of warriors, clearly documenting the growth of powerful leaders as conquerors.[9] However, battles did take place between cities that were as much as eighty kilometers apart.[10] A wider array of arms and armor was used by the Late Classic Maya elite, elaborating on those of the Early Classic and increasing the number and types of weapons employed, suggesting the continued absence of centralized control and still reflecting a warrior class whose members owned their own armaments.[11] The primary exception to this was at Piedras Negras, which appears to have organized a conventional army more in the central Mexican mold, although they did not adopt Mexican weapons.[12] This probably did not reflect a major social change—the soldiers were nobles, judging from their attire—but it was a major military change, giving Piedras Negras a significant tactical advantage that may account for its rise and probable conquest of Yaxchilan. However, Piedras Negras remained only a regional center, and this military innovation was apparently not widely copied.

Soldiers' attire may have been protective, but the cotton armor common in the Mexican highlands was rare in the Maya lowlands.[13] For example, in the Bonampak mural battle scene, some warriors are depicted wearing jaguarskin tunics; others wear capes, and still others wear nothing on their upper bodies. None wear armor.[14] Helmets, though occasionally depicted, also were rare. They may have offered some protection, but most Maya warriors did not wear them.[15] However, the elaborate military garb does suggest the presence of military orders.[16] Shields were common, although so few are depicted in works of art that predate the Late Classic that it is uncertain whether these were an indigenous development or an adoption from Teotihuacan.[17] The Maya employed two basic types. Small, rigid shields were used that would not snag easily on the march in dense vegetation, and some of these circular shields, or bucklers, seem to have been made of tortoise shells,[18] which may have been the basis of others constructed of different material, most likely leather. These were typically held on the left forearm by a central strap, although some shields had a second strap held in the left hand.[19] These shields offered little passive defense but because of their solid construction, they could parry blows effectively. A second and widely used type of shield was flexible—the only certain Maya shield innovation—and apparently made of quilted cotton on the exterior and a leather backing on the interior, without feather fringes.[20] Lacking a rigid structure, these shields were held by a strap attached to the top and were allowed to hang.[21] This flexibility was a tradeoff between portability and protection, permitting the shields to be furled for easy carrying yet providing adequate shielding against all but major blows. A third type of shield was a rigid rectangle that may have been made of a variety of materials including wood, leather, cotton, and woven reeds.[22] This shield was a Mexican introduction, and its size and rigidity would have made it difficult to carry through dense vegetation. When they are found, such shields are associated with Mexican weapons, gods, and iconography, and were probably symbols of power rather than functional armor.[23]

Late Classic Maya spears were used to thrust and slash rather than throw, because they typically had large points that would have destabilized them in flight.[24] Large points are better for thrusting than small ones because they have long cutting edges, but the Late Classic Maya improved this by inserting two rows of smaller blades behind the point, increasing the cutting edges at a fraction of the weight of an equivalent cutting surface from a larger point.[25] The primacy of slashing can be seen in the depiction of a spear at Seibal that has no distinctive point at all, the cutting surface being composed entirely of inset serrated blades.[26]

A variety of Maya clubs continued to be used, with single as well as multiple large stone blades inserted in a thick wooden handle or embedded in one side.[27] These short, heavy weapons were nevertheless inferior to the longer thrusting spears and neither they nor axes would have fared well against conventionally armed opponents.[28] When used, clubmen probably complemented spearmen and were used for specialty tasks, although clubs would have been excellent raiding weapons to be used against unarmed or lightly armed opponents.

Certain types of weapons and shields were frequently paired. Spearmen most often carried flexible rectangular shields while clubs and axes were typically used with small circular shields, although clubmen and axemen are also depicted helmeted but without shields.[29] Flexible shields provided protection from projectiles but could not parry blows effectively because of both their flexibility and their top grip, which severely hindered this movement in combat. The shield protected the body while the thrusting spear bore the brunt of both offensive strikes and defensive parrying. The circular shields were small and offered relatively little passive protection to the wielder, but being rigid, they could parry blows actively, which was essential in that the shorter clubs and axes were less effective in parrying blows.[30]

The only other major projectile weapon available at this time was the atlatl, but this was still rarely used because of the jungle environment, the elite nature of Maya warfare, and its unsuitability for raiding, in contrast to thrusting spears.[31] Atlatls remained infrequent among the Maya but continued in use as symbols of power rather than as actual weapons.[32]

The greater reliance on more elaborate arms and armor increased the cost of equipping soldiers, which, coupled with the specialized training demanded for the proper use of these weapons, further emphasized the elite nature of the Maya military. Accordingly, there is little evidence of battle standards, indicating a lack of formations, which would have been difficult to maintain in a jungle environment.[33]

Most Late Classic Maya settlements did not have fortifications, which suggests that cities were rarely attacked, probably because of manpower, logistical, and travel limits on large-scale offensive campaigns and the relatively large defensive forces available even to relatively small cities.[34] The few fortifications that have been found, such as Tikal's, that persisted into the Late Classic were probably erected against relatively close enemies who could mount large and effective surprise attacks.

The pronounced seasonality of warfare also continued, with conquests largely occurring from December to early June.[35] Although small raids by elite warriors could take place at any time without disrupting the local economy, most clustered largely within the dry season when the mass movement of men would have been easiest and larger groups could be dispatched. Capture glyphs, however, primarily cluster into two periods, from late November through March and from August to September;[36] these refer to the capture of individuals and reflect raids requiring far fewer men, capable of being carried out at any time of the year.[37] Thus, the primary military threat to cities arose at broadly predictable times when defensive measures could be most easily taken.

Maya leadership was often supported by marital ties between important centers, suggesting a significant amount of political calculation underlying these royal marriages; but marital ties alone were inadequate to create large polities.[38] The primary Maya failing was not an inability to carry out conquests but an inability to integrate conquered areas.

More men and the ability to delegate power were required for more conquests and greater integration, but both would have threatened Maya aristocratic society. Thus, most Maya polities remained small and conquest was aimed not at incorporation of subjugated areas, but at draining off their tribute and labor.[39] This was accomplished through a variety of techniques, ranging from "voluntary" submission to outright conquest, judging by the wide range of types of subjugated captives depicted in Maya carvings, which range from wealthy and unbound to naked and bound.[40]

The conquest relationship was not, however, entirely one-sided: tributaries were secure against raids, at least from the tribute-receiving city. The basic Maya strategy was to extend tributary areas as far as possible to create relatively secure inner zones, even though border areas might still suffer raids by outsiders. If raids continued, however, these towns hived off to become independent or, more often, tributaries of whichever city had proved dominant in the region. The loss of too many dependencies could lead the city to submit as well, for it became vulnerable once its hinterlands were lost, and negotiating a reduction in its dependencies was the only way to regain peace and stability. Thus, Maya expansion seems to have extended only as far as the city-state could draw tribute and labor, not as far as it might trade. Despite the apparent frequency of Maya warfare during the Late Classic, it was fairly small scale and did not lead to large political aggregations.[41]

Although a certain amount of warfare was needed to retain reliable dependencies by reinforcing the capital's dominance and by protecting its dependencies from outside aggression, much Maya warfare was geared to internal political purposes, such as validating rulers. Rulers of Maya cities claimed to conquer other cities, and outright conquest was possible against nearby competitors because these could be directly controlled, and economic integration between Maya cities increased in the Late Classic, providing a new incentive for exercising control over larger areas.[42] Nevertheless, transport limitations restricted the areas that could be effectively integrated into a single polity.

Cities too distant to be incorporated and indirectly controlled were still occasionally attacked. The goal in these cases may not have been to conquer the target city but to curtail its influence or expansion into areas closer to hand. As a result, competing political systems balanced each other: once each city-state achieved optimum expansion, little further conquest could be sustained. Yet raids remained feasible, and they kept adjacent independent areas unstable by continually disrupting them, lessening any threat. The struggle was between Maya city-states, but it was over their hinterlands.

Late Classic Maya civilization collapsed during the mid eighth to early tenth centuries A.D., especially in the southern lowlands.[43] Although the causes were doubtless complex, the collapse was partly the result of economic difficulties, including the loss of control over trade with the Mexican highlands and the maritime reorientation of trade along the Gulf and Caribbean coasts rather than inland.[44] The net result was a loss of both population and cultural complexity, possibly aggravated by incessant warfare.[45] Whatever initiated the collapse, once it began, the die was cast. As long as the Maya landscape was densely occupied by cities, every town fell into one or another city's zone of influence. But once a political vacuum was created by the fall of a city, adjacent groups moved in from dominated regions, undermining the economic support for those cities, precipitating their demise and starting the next round of collapses.

EL TAJÍN AND THE GULF COAST

The situation was somewhat similar along the Gulf coast, where sites such as El Tajín that had close trade connections with central Mexico continued to flourish after the demise of Teotihuacan.[46] However, warfare played an increasingly public role in the political lives of such centers. Probably the best evidence of Middle to Late Classic central Mexican warfare are the carvings at El Tajín depicting warriors holding bound captives.[47] Human sacrifice also becomes a prominent activity and elite warriors and rulers are commonly depicted.[48] Military orders appear to be represented, as are other elite warriors wearing animal helmets.[49] Neither body armor nor shields are represented, but both are used elsewhere on the Gulf coast and were probably common here too.[50] A wide array of weapons are also depicted, including spears, clubs, atlatls, darts, and unhafted stone knives.[51]

THE EMERGENT CENTERS

As noted, most of the militaristic themes in Mesoamerica arose in the Late Classic, reflecting the disruptions of the time. As older centers' spheres of influence contracted, both internal and external pressures increased as political and economic relationships changed and new centers sought to expand their own influence. No single center was suffi-

ciently powerful to take over Teotihuacan's role. Instead, the Late Classic
was a period of political fragmentation during which regional powers
emerged.

Despite the absence of a dominant power in Mesoamerica, the need
for reliable trade continued. The old trade routes still existed, but new
links had to be established and new merchants had to emerge.[52] In
central Mexico, fortified centers, such as Xochicalco, Cacaxtla, and
perhaps Teotenango, emerged with extensive international contacts.[53]
The demand for new traders or trading institutions appears to have
been filled by groups from regions intermediate between the Mexicans
and Mayas. Merchants from the Gulf lowlands, called the Olmeca-
Xicalanca in historical accounts, expanded into the highlands to fill the
economic vacuum, reversing the flow along the same routes that
Teotihuacan had used.[54]

This did not herald an Olmeca-Xicalanca takeover of central Mexico. Their best-known settlement of Cacaxtla was, in fact, only one of
several fortified regional centers—typically in areas that had not been
directly controlled by Teotihuacan, where their formal trade links were
weakest—from which they, and others, eventually dominated the local
trade. Unlike Teotihuacan, however, these fortified sites had no major
home power to back them up in the event of trouble. The Olmeca-
Xicalanca could not militarily dominate the entire area but, in the absence of serious competitors, they were able to reverse Teotihuacan
practice on a smaller and more transitory scale.

THE OLMECA-XICALANCA AT CHOLULA

The Olmeca-Xicalanca rose to prominence in the Puebla-Tlaxcala
area during the Late Classic.[55] However, determining precisely who
they were is difficult. Linguistic evidence is of little help in this case,[56]
but native historical accounts and modern opinion put their origins in
Tabasco.[57] Ceramic continuities suggest that the Olmeca-Xicalanca
who moved into central Mexico were composed primarily of men who
then married local women.[58] In any case, the Olmeca-Xicalanca and
others developed ethnically distinct kingdoms and fortified their cities
to control trade.[59] Around A.D. 800, the Olmeca-Xicalanca conquered
and occupied at least part of Cholula for the next hundred years, as
evidenced by the introduction of new ceramic traits and a radical shift in
burial practices from the interment of bodies in a seated position facing
east to cremation and burial in vases.[60]

Cholula was the largest but least known Olmeca-Xicalanca site.[61] Ceramics found at Cholula and Xochicalco indicate exchange between the two cities and with Cacaxtla.[62] The influence of these sites extended into the southern Valley of Mexico—not by organizing it politically, but by tying it to this interaction sphere and keeping it free of Toltec domination, at least initially.[63]

The central Mexican Late Classic saw the rise of hilltop fortified sites, suggesting political unrest and the general unsuitability of relatively open cities to these new conditions. Unfortified centers such as Cholula were conquered because they controlled trade networks or important resources that made them worth occupying, and conquering them preempted their reemergence as potential threats. But the intruding groups exercised their control from locations selected for their defensive advantages.

THE OLMECA-XICALANCA AT CACAXTLA

The Puebla-Tlaxcala area was turbulent during the A.D. 650–850 period, when the Olmeca-Xicalanca established themselves at Cacaxtla and controlled much of the Puebla Valley, partly through an alliance with new groups that moved into the area from the south.[64] However, the Valley of Mexico had little influence on the Olmeca-Xicalanca, although families may have entered the Tlaxcala region from Teotihuacan or Cholula.[65] From A.D. 650 to 750, the region was dominated by El Tajín and Gulf coast-affiliated groups, with the Olmeca-Xicalanca becoming dominant from A.D. 750 to 850, possibly with the assistance of the Mixtecs who had moved into southern Puebla.[66]

The best evidence of warfare at Cacaxtla comes from a series of extraordinary murals, especially the battle scene and the politico-religious scene. The dates of the Cacaxtla murals are debated,[67] but the Olmeca-Xicalanca context supports a ninth century dating. The murals are quite eclectic, with Maya, Teotihuacan, Oaxaca, and Veracruz style and iconographic elements,[68] but are executed in a naturalistic narrative style without precedent in the central highlands although it is similar to that of contemporary lowland Maya styles.[69] The scenes are unmistakably Maya and were not a copied style, but were painted by a Maya artist, although none of the nineteen glyphs in the murals are Maya.[70]

The battle scene shows a conflict between two groups, victors wearing jaguar skins and vanquished wearing bird—probably eagle—helmets. According to one interpretation, the scene represents a highland (jaguar) victory over lowland (bird) warriors, but an alternative reading identifies the vanquished as Teotihuacanos, and the mural in the upper palace is interpreted as the resolution of this conflict by a third power.[71] Minimally, the battle scene mural depicts a conflict between jaguar and eagle warriors, with the former emerging victorious. The state portraits, located in upper palace A, are presumed to be more recent, and may reflect some sort of rapprochement achieved after the initial clash; jaguar and eagle figures are presented with apparently equal standing, but with the jaguar warriors enjoying military superiority or control.[72]

Late Classic central Mexico saw some significant changes in weapons use, with the invaders merging elements of both Maya and Mexican arms with innovations of their own as revealed by the Cacaxtla murals.[73] Atlatls and darts were the dominant weapons at Cacaxtla, but the darts differed from earlier types by having barbed points and feather fletching along the back of the shaft.[74] The fletching presumably added to the darts' aerodynamic qualities, and the barbed points could not be readily extracted without cutting the wound wider or pushing the point clear through the body.

Thrusting spears continued in use but were secondary to atlatls. The spears had lanceolet or ovoid points rather than barbs because the spears were designed for continuous use, and the points were shaped for easy removal after slashing or impaling an enemy. These spears also had an extended slashing edge of inset blades on the shaft below the point, better than doubling the length of their cutting edges, a trait brought from the Maya lowlands.[75] Although the Olmeca-Xicalanca used thrusting spears, they relied primarily on atlatls, which were ideal defensive weapons for relatively small groups of travelers; they could keep attackers at bay without having to meet them in hand-to-hand combat. The Olmeca-Xicalancas' reliance on these weapons is also supported by graphic representations of wounds in the murals. Puncture wounds from atlatl darts are depicted, but thrusting spears appear to have inflicted the greatest damage, producing the many slash wounds in the murals. Mural depictions also include unhafted stone knives which were used to dispatch wounded opponents as well as ropes used to tie captives.[76] No other offensive weapons are represented.[77]

There was a significant change in the shields used by the Olmeca-Xicalanca. Both rectangular shields and small bucklers were abandoned and replaced by circular shields with hanging feather fringes. The superiority of this shield rested on two characteristics—weight and grip. Flexible rectangular shields are rarely recorded outside the Maya area[78] and made no headway against the solid rectangular shields of central Mexico in hundreds of years of contact between the two military systems, suggesting that while the former was well adapted to a jungle raiding environment, its flexibility was a liability in open terrain and conventional battles.[79] The Olmeca-Xicalanca round shields were rigid and probably made of woven reeds which were significantly lighter than solid wood, and their protective feather fringe that could deflect or block spent projectiles partly compensated for their smaller defensive surface.

The round shield was also helped by a better grip. Rectangular shields were gripped at the top which suggests they were heavy and certainly meant their movements were relatively restricted.[80] By contrast, the round shields were carried on the forearm by a wide strap which suggests they were fairly light and freed the shield hand for offensive use.[81] The round shields also offered unprecedented tactical flexibility because they were equally effective when held at any angle rather than having to hang down or drape over the forearm for support. There was no body armor at Cacaxtla, although jaguar skins, bird helmets, and other elaborate attire were worn.

Central Mexican armies were unparalleled under Teotihuacan, but their arms and combat style were never adopted in the Maya region despite contact as early as the third century A.D. The smaller population, aristocratic organization, and jungle terrain of the Maya lowlands discouraged large conventional armies and set-piece battles, fostering instead smaller armies, greater emphasis on mobility, and less concern for heavy body armor.[82] But because it was not suited to large-scale warfare, the Maya combination of arms and armor initially posed no real challenge to the central Mexican style. However, after the fall of Teotihuacan, central Mexican armor became heavier and armies became smaller, increasing their vulnerability to more mobile forms of combat as exemplified by the Olmeca-Xicalanca at Cacaxtla.[83]

This lighter, mobile combat style may have been prompted by the rise of guerilla-style fighting during periods of political upheaval which set-piece conventional armies were poorly suited to counter. The Olmeca-Xicalanca retained Maya-style thrusting spears with extended bladed sections below the point but dropped the use of clubs, which, though perhaps effective in jungle terrain, were serious handicaps under highland battle conditions. Instead they emphasized atlatls to meet similarly equipped Mexican armies. This shift in tactics also favored intruder forces, such as the Olmeca-Xicalanca, in their confrontations with conventional central Mexican armies.[84] The lack of protection and more numerous wounds, at least to the legs of lightly armored soldiers, would have been offset by the greater kill ratio effected through greater mobility. Although mobility per se was not decisive, it allowed the Olmeca-Xicalanca to outmaneuver slower, heavier formations and to evade or force conflict at times and places of their own choosing.

Blending those aspects of Mexican warfare that best fit with raider tactics, the Olmeca-Xicalanca presented a formidable threat, striking quickly on the offensive and successfully engaging the heavier, less mobile Mexican forces in defensive contests.[85] The Olmeca-Xicalanca did not generally conquer and dominate areas by force because they were too few and their tactics were more suited to defending a small area while controlling a somewhat larger one from a relatively secure location. Cacaxtla's area of influence was quite limited, suggesting a small army, an interpretation supported by the elite gear and the glyphs naming each warrior in typically aristocratic style.[86] However, the limitations of the aristocratic system were not as apparent at Cacaxtla as elsewhere. The intrusive group was male and elite, not a social cross-section; thus their military capabilities were significantly greater than their numbers would suggest, although this was destined to decline with time, intermarriage, and the creation of a sizable sustaining population.

Cacaxtla was too small to mount significant conventional offensives over great distances, instead striking at targets of opportunity. However, because these lighter soldiers could not prevail against heavy infantry in pitched battle, safety meant withdrawing to secure locations after striking and the Olmeca-Xicalanca period in central Mexico saw a shift to fortified hilltop sites in areas that had previously enjoyed open cities.[87] In addition to its hilltop location, Cacaxtla was fortified with earthworks and moats.[88] But rather than being a defensive ploy in the face of a major external threat such as Teotihuacan, Cacaxtla was selected for offensive purpose, offering security behind its fortifications while the relatively light Olmeca-Xicalanca forces sallied forth to dominate their region. Cacaxtla remained the dominant center of the region until A.D. 850, when it was abandoned and the Olmeca-Xicalanca withdrew.[89]

XOCHICALCO

Another major central Mexican site during this period was Xochicalco, located in Morelos sixty kilometers southwest of modern-day Mex-

ico City. Although occupied as early as the Middle or Late Formative, it
was unimportant until the withdrawal of Teotihuacan influence from
the region, after which it grew rapidly and became a major center until
its abandonment after A.D. 900.[90] Like Cacaxtla, Xochicalco was located on an easily defended, fortified hilltop overlooking an alluvial
plain.[91] Defense and regional control were primary considerations in
locating the city for it was not in the best agricultural area of Morelos
and nonresidential or elite areas occupied 69 percent of the city.[92] The
entire hill was extensively reshaped by its occupants, creating large
terraces that were an integral part of the city's defenses.[93] These terraces
created broad spaces within the site, but movement between them was
limited to a few streets and ramps that bridged their steep facades.[94] The
site also has a series of defensive moats and walls, some more than ten
meters high, and several adjacent areas had their own defenses.[95]

Adding to Xochicalco's defenses were a series of roads three to five
meters wide of roughly cut stone, linking various areas of the site.[96] These
roads funneled attackers through restricted areas between fortifications
where they could be more easily resisted while enabling the defenders to
move men and arms within the city to points of attack significantly more
quickly than an attacker could shift troops outside the walls.[97] Only by
bringing enormous armies to bear could an attacker hope to conquer
Xochicalco. From its virtually impregnable location, Xochicalco could
dominate its hinterland, striking at recalcitrant groups with little fear of
reprisals.

There is little doubt that warfare was a concern at Xochicalco, and
a carving of a decapitated and sacrificed man suggests an emphasis on
taking captives and on human sacrifice.[98] Prominently sculpted military figures on the Pyramid of the Plumed Serpent suggest the presence
of military orders at Xochicalco, and, based on the centralization of
fortifications and military themes, warfare was an elite occupation.[99]
However, with its relatively small population, Xochicalco's conquests
probably did not extend for any significant distance.[100] For instance,
the nearby site of Tlacuatzingo constructed its own fortifications,
which would have been unnecessary had Xochicalco been powerful
enough to deter enemies generally.[101]

As at Cacaxtla, the primary weapon at Xochicalco was the atlatl,
which is depicted prominently with the carved warriors on the Pyramid
of the Plumed Serpent, with thrusting spears playing a secondary role,
as did knives.[102] Early in its history, probably before the rise of the
Olmeca-Xicalanca at Cacaxtla, warriors at Xochicalco used the older

style rectangular shields but not armor, wearing instead a Maya-like cape.[103]

Most of the structures visible at Xochicalco were erected between A.D. 650 and 900, including the Pyramid of the Plumed Serpent, which was built in three stages.[104] At each reconstruction, the people destroyed the earlier pyramid and used its rubble for the subsequent one. The ceramics found in the fill between structures 1 and 2 and between 2 and 3 are related to the Maya, indicating that they were Xochicalco's main trading partners.[105] The carvings on this structure are Maya-like, although perhaps not by Mayas themselves.[106] The architectural emulation of other areas, and especially the prominence of Maya-style carvings for important ritual and political monuments, suggests that Xochicalco had a sustained relationship with some Maya group, as well as with the Gulf coast and Guerrero.[107]

The evidence of an aristocratic military system, though weaker than at Cacaxtla, comes primarily from carvings on the Pyramid of the Plumed Serpent, which was elaborately engraved with three tiers of figures.[108] The bas-relief carvings of the lowest tier depict elaborately headdressed male figures sitting within the undulations of feathered serpents;[109] the middle tier reliefs depict individuals with conquered towns;[110] and the top tier, though largely destroyed, shows a series of warriors. Only the lower two tiers are complete enough for detailed comparison: the figures in the two respective tiers are identical. The figures in the middle tier are each enclosed in a separate frame. They are not generic warriors but are a single conqueror who is repeated with each of his conquests.[111]

Although the Pyramid of the Plumed Serpent commemorated more than political events, the structure was undoubtedly decorated, if not constructed, in one effort to commemorate a single individual.[112] This commemoration of a specific individual in an aristocratic style indicates the presence of strong leaders. Coupled with Xochicalco's limited political expansion and its probable aristocratic military system, leadership was most likely kin-based in that it persisted under conditions that shattered meritocratic systems.

Like Cacaxtla, Xochicalco was an eclectic blend of traditions from throughout Mesoamerica, including ceramics from Cholula, Teotihuacan, Veracruz, and the Puuc Maya, showing an earlier connection with the cultures to the south and a later one with the Gulf coast.[113] Architecturally, Xochicalco bears similarities to Maya sites, Tollan, Hidalgo, El Tajín, Veracruz, and Toluquilla, Queretaro, and it drew on Teotihuacan, Zapotec, Oaxaca or Guerrero, Cacaxtla, and Mixtec or Zapotec glyphs and numbering systems.[114] The carvings on the Pyramid of the Plumed Serpent at Xochicalco are in the Maya style, though they had no forerunners or any known progeny.[115]

There is little skeletal evidence to indicate who occupied Xochicalco, but the sculptures show Maya-like personages, and the few burials found at the site show some cranial deformation, which was common in the Maya area and perhaps on the Gulf coast but not generally in central Mexico.[116] However, as with Cacaxtla, there were continuities between surrounding sites and Xochicalco; thus its consolidation of power was not entirely through the imposition of elites from outside.[117]

Xochicalco was unusual not simply because of its location and eclecticism, but because of its large proportion of elite architecture—31 percent of the total.[118] Regional administration does not explain this pattern, for no other administrative centers such as Teotihuacan, Monte Alban, or Tollan held so large an elite. In relation to its architecture, Xochicalco had a small resident population, yet, at the same time, it was not surrounded by large dependent settlements.[119] Distant and large-scale trade better explains the residential pattern, the artistic eclecticism, and portable objects found at the center. However, Xochicalco's obsidian trade suggests that the site's growth was not simply the result of the local economy.

During the Early and Middle Classic, the vast bulk of the obsidian in the Xochicalco area came from the Valley of Mexico. After A.D. 650, there was a major shift when obsidian began arriving in the area from Zinapécuaro, and by A.D. 750, ceramics and obsidian from the Valley of Mexico disappeared completely. Thereafter, Xochicalco's four main obsidian sources were Zinapécuaro, Michoacan; Zacualtipan, Veracruz; Otumba, Mexico; and El Cerro de las Navajas, near Pachuca, Hidalgo, evidencing a radical shift in trade and, presumably, political relations.[120]

Xochicalco began to decline by around A.D. 800 and was abandoned after A.D. 900.[121] Temple A and its three associated stelae, dating to the end of the site's occupation, were intentionally destroyed by the Xochicalco people: the temple walls were broken and the stelae were painted red and shattered, suggesting a deliberate withdrawal from the site.[122]

THE DEMISE OF THE TRADER CITIES

The political instability that fostered the rise of hilltop fortified sites, such as Cacaxtla and Xochicalco, waned in the tenth century. Fortified centers became increasingly unnecessary as stability increased, and with the growth of formidable opponents, small fortified sites could no longer guarantee the security of their hinterlands from incursions. Though the sites were still formidable defensive bastions, the raider tactics of their occupants were now inadequate to hold their hinterlands. Fortified centers were increasingly ignored and circumnavigated, rendering them irrelevant to the general flow of trade. Hilltop sites offered no transportation advantages that would allow them to integrate tributaries more tightly than competing centers. In fact, their locations may have hindered their attempts to maintain significant hinterlands because such sites had relatively small resident populations from which to draw an army. Increasingly, hilltop fortress cities were unable to compete with more conveniently located competitor city-states.

That these centers were not simply local powers is substantiated by their cosmopolitan character; their relatively small size, defensive nature, and eclectic goods and styles suggest they were primarily trading centers. However, military support was essential to the successful pursuit of this trade. Merchants alone cannot maintain a trading system in the face of competition and political chaos. Thus, both the incursion of foreign groups such as the Olmeca-Xicalanca at Cacaxtla and the rise of other centers such as Xochicalco were primarily economic in purpose, although they were necessarily supported militarily. But such fortified trading entrepôts were transitory creations, operating under the special circumstances of the demise of the only power that could ensure the safety and regularity of long-distance exchange at a time when trade demands were accelerating.

The reemergence of strong central Mexican city-states undermined the need for and economic justification of costly hilltop fortified centers, and as distant areas grew increasingly under the domination of emergent powers, the trader cities lost reliable access to these wares. As the Mexican city-states reasserted their dominance and conventional armies grew large enough to both secure trade routes and threaten raider sites, fortified trade centers withered and their occupants withdrew. In the case of the Olmeca-Xicalanca, the demise of the Late Classic Maya also eroded the support needed to maintain their trading network. They needed support, if not military then certainly mercantile, in the sense of having a series of organized centers in the Maya area where goods were gathered, processed, and readied for shipment, and which received the goods flowing out of the Mexican area in exchange. When that support collapsed, the outposts in the Mexican area could not be sustained. The period of trader cities was a phenomenon of the central Mexican political vacuum. They arose in the absence of competing centers and were fortified because only with such protection could they have existed at all. In its absence, they declined just as quickly.

CHAPTER 8

The Reintegration of Mesoamerica

The population of the Valley of Mexico became more dispersed and ruralized following Teotihuacan's decline, although the northern third of the valley was densely settled, culturally eclipsing the southern area. The Valley of Mexico was divided by a virtually uninhabited east-west strip that marked the boundaries of two different zones of influence.[1] The south lacked a major center and remained politically fragmented, dominated by the cities to the south and east beyond the valley. The north, however, was integrated under the sway of the emergent Toltec capital of Tollan, a city of sixty thousand inhabitants, most of whom were craftsmen or other specialists.[2]

TOLTECS

The Tollan area was settled toward the end of the first millennium B.C. but held no major sites until Chingú was established around A.D. 300. Chingú was a regional center for Teotihuacan until it was abandoned around A.D. 700 after a turbulent century of decline.[3] Various groups migrated into the area over the next century, many coming from the north, adding to the existing population.[4] Tollan grew substantially during this period,[5] and in the next phase (A.D. 950–1150) reached its zenith, covering thirteen to fourteen square kilometers.[6]

According to native accounts, one of Tollan's early rulers, Ce Acatl Topiltzin Quetzalcoatl, became embroiled in a dispute.[7] Some of these state that he disgraced himself while intoxicated, and others emphasize a politico-religious dispute in which his desire to sacrifice snakes and butterflies rather than people was thwarted. Thereafter, he and his followers left Tollan and, by the dominant account, went to the Gulf coast and set sail to the east.

This story is apparently a mythologized account of an internal dispute at Tollan owing little or nothing to the issue of sacrifice. As a priest of the god Quetzalcoatl, who was associated with the priests and nobles, Ce Acatl represented the more traditional Mesoamerican elements of Tollan's populace and was engaged in a political struggle with the priests serving the god Tezcatlipoca, a war deity associated with the military and commoners.[8] This dispute may mark the turn away from the more theocratic rule present at Teotihuacan and toward a more secularized rule such as that found later at Tenochtitlan.[9] In any case, there is archaeological support for this myth. An early and important civic-religious center of the settlement, Tula Chico, was abandoned after A.D. 900 and was largely unoccupied thereafter in the midst of an otherwise crowded city.[10] This may well represent the ascendancy of the Tezcatlipoca faction and signal the exodus of the Quetzalcoatl faction.[11] Moreover, around this time, the northern Yucatan site of Chichen Itza began to bear unmistakable evidence of Toltec art and architecture and was probably the ultimate settlement of Quetzalcoatl and his followers or their descendants.

The Toltecs were a multiethnic society, merging Nahuatl- and Otomí-speaking groups from north and northwest Mexico with established groups from Mesoamerica, probably from the southern Gulf coast.[12] The latter are generally credited with bringing high Mesoamerican culture to Toltec society and may have owed their positions at Tollan to their introduction and dominance of the obsidian industry and its associated trade.[13] The fact that Nahuatl became the dominant language of Toltec society suggests that the northern groups ultimately enjoyed superiority, probably numerically as well as politically.[14]

Tollan had powerful political rulers, as indicated by the city's grid layout, which involved centralized planning and enforcement.[15] The relief carvings on Pyramid B apparently depict an accession scene of a Toltec king, but, as at Teotihuacan, there were no monuments dedicated to specific individuals and the Toltecs were not concerned with recording dynastic succession.[16] Instead, the carvings reflect classes or types of warriors.[17] This lack of concern for the descent of rulers, the focus on generic rather than individualistic depictions, the structure of

their army, the extent of Toltec expansion, and the heterogeneous nature of Toltec society pointing to some mechanism for attracting and
incorporating outsiders suggest a meritocratic system.

Much of Tollan's prominence was the result of warfare, for which
there is ample evidence in the city. In addition to the giant stone warriors, there was a skullrack at the site, as well as freestanding sculptures
of reclining figures known as chac mools, thought to be receptacles for
hearts from human sacrifices.[18] Human bone fragments are also common in the archaeological ruins, suggesting human sacrifice and cannibalism, and death and sacrificial depictions adorn the city.[19]

Known mainly from stone carvings and ceramics, Toltec arms included atlatls and darts, knives, and a curved club that I have labelled a
short sword.[20] Toltec warriors also carried round shields and used body
armor.[21] Atlatls provided primary projectile fire in Toltec armies,[22] although slings may well have been used for greater distance. Earlier in
central Mexico, thrusting spears were used with more protective,
though less mobile, rectangular shields. However, the round, fringed
shield introduced by the Olmeca-Xicalancas was widely adopted in
central Mexico: supported by an arm strap, it freed both hands and
deemphasized spears, for atlatlists were now more mobile than ever.
However, once opposing armies closed with each other, atlatlists were
at a real disadvantage and the use of some shock weapon was essential.
This need was met by the short sword, whose longer cutting surface and
lighter weight greatly added to the offensive capability of Toltec
atlatlists.[23] The short sword was the major Toltec innovation in arms.[24]
Unlike swords developed in metalworking cultures, the short sword was
not merely an extension of knife construction to increasingly larger
forms.[25] Instead, this was a major innovation in Mesoamerican stone-
working cultures, though its conceptual foundations were present in
other arms. The practice of setting small blades into wooden handles
had been developed in the Maya lowlands during the Late Classic and
spread into central Mexico with the Olmeca-Xicalancas. The Toltec
contribution was to use this technique to make longer cutting surfaces
on a light one-handed weapon, which was probably a modification
based on unbladed curved clubs brought from the north.[26] Approximately 50 cm long, these curved clubs were inlaid with blades, most
likely obsidian.[27]

The short sword had significant advantages and largely replaced
bladed clubs and thrusting spears. The clubs used previously had large
blades that bore the brunt of the blow, with the wooden handle merely

serving as a convenient attachment and handhold. Although their size gave them strength, it also made them heavy, which limited both the number that could be usefully inset and the length of the handle. Moreover, they were essentially crushers, their effectiveness being more a function of weight than of cutting edges. Thrusting spears became more efficient by insetting blades along the upper shaft, but retaining a large stone point still limited the weapon as a slasher. Set on the end of the shaft, the point was adequately bound for forward thrusts, but it had no lateral backing and was more easily dislodged when used for slashing. By contrast, the short sword was a major improvement as a slasher over either of the weapons it replaced—it was lighter and carried more cutting surface, and each blade was backed by the wooden base that provided direct support; it was an excellent slasher and yet the forward curve of the sword retained some aspects of a crusher when used curved end forward, as the Toltecs did. Shorter than spears and lighter than clubs, the short sword was considerably more mobile. Its use marked a major shift in singlehanded weapons, away from the weight and crushing power of clubs to the cutting surfaces and lightness of swords.[28]

Knives were used in secondary and sacrificial roles and were carried in the left armband where they were immediately accessible.[29] Unlike simple stone blades, Toltec knives were hafted onto wooden handles. As a result, the bladed portion of Toltec knives was smaller than the entire unhafted knives of Late Classic central Mexico, which made them lighter but without sacrificing usable blade surface.[30]

It was now feasible for a single soldier to carry a short sword, atlatl and darts, knife, and shield supported by an armstrap. Instead of dividing their forces into mutually reinforcing atlatlists and spearmen, Toltec soldiers could now provide their own covering fire with atlatls while they advanced and still engage in hand-to-hand combat with short swords once they closed with the enemy.[31] By shifting from projectiles to shock weapons as needed, the same troops were constantly engaged, simplifying combat by eliminating the insertion and withdrawal of specialized troops as needed; combining arms effectively doubled the size of Toltec armies. This did not eliminate specialist fighters, however, for combining projectile and shock weapons was useful primarily when first engaging (and possibly disengaging) the enemy. Thereafter, specialist soldiers could be brought forward to reinforce the front lines, eliminating the need for atlatls to cover their advance or disrupt enemy formations.

The Toltecs' main forces were mobile light infantry, although there are indications that they also relied on more heavily armored infantry, suggesting functionally integrated combat units.[32] There were two types of armor, full body and left arm, both made of quilted cotton.[33] The carved atlantids at Tollan wear quilted cotton padding on their left arms, whereas ceramic warrior figurines are occasionally depicted with full suits of armor, including leggings.[34] Helmets are also depicted, although their protective value is uncertain.[35] Most soldiers, even the elite, were not fully armored and did not carry shields. This is because short swords could also be used defensively, reducing the need for shields, especially when used in conjunction with armored left sleeves.

As at Teotihuacan, Toltec arms and armor reflect standardized weapons suggestive of state ownership and control, a large army, and complementary weapons and units. The Toltecs' combined use of projectiles and swords also demanded battlefield command and coordination to make most effective use of all weapons and to avoid fire from their own side. Moreover, these mass-coordinated battle tactics required drilling, common in a meritocratic society where a command hierarchy can more easily be imposed.

There were military orders at Tollan, probably coyote and jaguar orders,[36] and military imagery in works of art depict types and classes of warriors rather than individuals, indicative of a meritocratic military system. These factors, coupled with the Toltecs' successful expansion, indicate a large, highly organized, and effective army—larger than could have been mounted drawing primarily on the elites. Tollan's multi-ethnic population adds to the evidence for a meritocratic military system. Much of the military establishment appears to have come from the northern Chichimec peoples rather than from more established Mesoamerican groups.

If Toltec political society was based on kinship, it would not have been satisfactory for long in the face of the growing power of the more egalitarian groups, and the Toltec residential pattern of extended families organized into neighborhoods was probably the basis for both military recruitment and lines of command.[37] In any case, at its height, Tollan appears to have been meritocratically organized, an accomplishment made easier by the general lack of heavy armament that allowed large numbers of men to be equipped. With a peak population of sixty thousand, Tollan proper could field an offensive army of 7,575 men from twenty through thirty-four years of age, or an effective maximum of 12,924 by extending the age limit to fifty. Moreover, by drawing on the additional sixty thousand agriculturalists in the city's immediate hinterland,[38] the army could be doubled to an offensive size of 15,150 or an effective maximum of 25,848, a size commensurate with its area of influence and ten times that of an aristocratic army.

The hilltop sites that typified the area's pre-Toltec settlements were abandoned during the Tollan phase, although this did not necessarily reflect peaceful times.[39] Tollan was not fortified but was well located for defense, being situated on an elongated limestone ridge overlooking the valleys of the Tula and Rosas rivers.[40] Nevertheless, houses and house compounds were defensible. Houses were single-story, multiroomed, square or rectangular structures, with walled courtyards accessible only through easily defended L-shaped openings.[41] Thus, Toltec houses were formidable, but whatever advantages Tollan derived from its architecture, its main defense was its size. With a resident population larger than that of any contemporary central Mexican city, Tollan was in little danger of attack.

Tollan was influenced by the architecture of Xochicalco, but there is little other evidence of contact between the Late Classic centers of central Mexico and the Toltecs, although the timing of the former's demise and the latter's rise is suggestive. At a minimum, Tollan took over the trade network these earlier centers had controlled, but it did so on a much sounder basis, and this organizational advantage marked the Toltec ascendancy as surely as it did the decline of its predecessors. Tollan's success in establishing trade networks was tied to its control of obsidian production. Tollan was a city of occupational specialists, one-third of the population producing ceramics, figurines, and stone tools, much of it for export, which was a major key to that city's rise.[42] Tollan's early obsidian supply came from Zinapécuaro, Michoacan, but this gradually declined as a source and was replaced by Otumba and especially Pachuca, which supplied 80 percent of its needs.[43]

Toltec trade extended throughout most of Mesoamerica and beyond, linking them to Chiapas, Guatemala, and Central America, central Veracruz, the Huaxteca, north and west Mexico, and possibly the American Southwest.[44] But goods from southern Veracruz, Tabasco, and Campeche are conspicuously absent at Tollan, indicating a lack of ties with southern Veracruz and the northern Maya areas.[45] Although no market areas have yet been found at Tollan, they must have existed, just as Toltec merchants, organized in a fashion similar to the later Aztec pochteca, are widely assumed to have been present in central Mexico.[46]

Fueling this trade, probable Toltec exports included obsidian tools and elite craft products such as feather cloaks, headdresses, shields, turquoise mosaics, tecali vessels, jewelry, and other international products.[47] These goods were shipped along major trade routes that extended west through Michoacan to the Lerma-Santiago river drainage northwest to the Pacific coast, north along the Sierra Madre Occidental through Zacatecas, and eastward across the mountains to the tropical lowlands of the Gulf coast.[48] In return, valuable minerals and semiprecious stones such as turquoise, serpentine, quartz, rock crystal, mica, amethyst, and cinnabar were acquired from the north; cloisonné and Pacific coast shells came from the west; and fine ceramics and probably cacao, feathers, cotton, and animal skins were imported from the south.[49] These trade links are relatively easy to establish through archaeology at both ends, although the degree to which politics intruded is harder to assess. The Toltecs may have been imperialists motivated by economic goals,[50] but it is difficult to calculate how large the Toltec empire was, if indeed it was a political empire at all. There are no contemporary written accounts of the empire's territorial extent and very little archaeological investigation of suspected Toltec tributaries.[51]

Although any proposed boundaries are strictly conjectural, it has been suggested that the Toltec polity encompassed much of central Mexico, including all the areas to the north up to the western slopes of the Sierra Madre Oriental, portions of Queretaro, Guanajuato, Zacatecas, and Michoacan, as well as Hidalgo, the Valley of Mexico, the Valley of Toluca, and parts of the Bajío and Morelos. It was circumscribed by the limits of effective agriculture to the north, El Tajín to the east, Cholula to the southeast, Xochicalco to the southwest, and possibly an incipient Tarascan state to the west.[52] However, several of these cities had lost their importance before Tollan's expansion, and the notion that competitor cities blocked the Toltecs assumes they had a territorial empire in which expansion was into contiguous areas, an idea undermined by the evidence of distant and widely scattered areas of Toltec interaction. Instead, the Toltecs were apparently organized hegemonically, expanding where necessary but avoiding and omitting strong sites. Given the Toltecs' relatively short span of power,[53] the nature of other Mesoamerican empires, and the relatively low population in relation to the potential size of their domain, their immediate hinterland probably encompassed the area generally defined as the entire empire. The rest of the Toltec empire was probably a series of ill-defined and rapidly changing relationships with other centers, some subordinate in varying degrees and others virtual partners, but not well reflected archaeologically.[54]

The available evidence suggests not so much a military as a trading empire, one that operated through merchant enclaves and settlements rather than military colonization of outlying areas. Rather than dominate an area and tap into the existing trade, the Toltecs apparently sent traders abroad and entered into mutually beneficial arrangements by establishing (or reestablishing) trade links and offering exchange based not only on goods available from Tollan but on generalized trade throughout the entire region. In support of such a trade network, a series of Toltec enclaves provided links, scattered areas of safety, and local knowledge of trading conditions throughout Mesoamerica under conditions in which the generalized safety of merchants could not otherwise be guaranteed.

Military power was important in protecting merchants, but the Toltecs lacked the manpower and logistical capacity to create and maintain an empire in the Aztec mold. Although it was located in a more arid region than most of central Mexico, Tollan's campaign season was still confined to the dry season, from October to June,[55] concentrating major warfare in the dry season following harvest. The general increase in population throughout Mesoamerica by Toltec times made distant logistical support increasingly feasible. However, the Toltecs did not use this potential by creating a tributary network capable of providing support, perhaps because they were unable to field a big enough army to dominate a large area hegemonically. Without a reliable means of resupply beyond Tollan's hinterland, the Toltecs were probably limited to expeditionary exercises that did not aim at political consolidation into the parent polity. Instead, the Toltecs, or allied Nahuatl-speaking groups, created colonial enclaves throughout much of Mesoamerica during a period in which there was no large competitor, and linked the region through their own people, sent abroad to trade, produce, and colonize.

This trade-colony model is similar to that for Teotihuacan except the Toltecs could not sustain a distant military campaign. Tollan had the logistical support to control a large area from the capital, but not enough soldiers, and so the city probably controlled an area roughly comparable to Teotihuacan's inner hinterland, which had been limited by logistical rather than manpower constraints. Another factor that may account for Tollan's scattered colonies was greater market development based on easier transport. The same population increase that eased logistical constraints also sped the movement of traders throughout the region. Every locale could now trade over greater distances for increasingly common goods because merchants could secure the food they needed en route. For the Toltecs, this meant they did not need colonies as close to their capital as had Teotihuacan, and the goods traded became more basic and more plentiful; as greater areas were linked into common economic exchange zones, they became more interdependent. The Toltec situation encouraged more dispersed and more distant trade colonies than had been feasible previously.

The reasons for the Toltec expansion seem fairly straightforward, at least at the level of the state. Tollan owed its economic position to the far-flung Toltec trade network that supplied the city's craftsmen with needed raw materials and sold the goods they produced. The wealth generated from this expanded trade clearly benefited the elites, and the commoners also profited, at least in terms of created jobs and generally greater wealth. But why would elites decide to expand if they were already well off? Two possibilities suggest themselves. They may simply have wanted more or different goods, but these imported goods were needed for some purpose, such as maintaining an expanding nobility, creating or maintaining monumental works because they were functionally important (such as irrigation works) or politically important (such as pyramids testifying to Toltec might). Or they may have needed more goods simply to support a growing population, achieve greater societal complexity, and continue to maintain an adequate standard of living for the people, who ultimately support the elites.

Adding to the need for this expansion was its increasing feasibility. Interregional trade had been controlled by the Olmeca-Xicalanca and other trader cities, but they lacked the power to support their trade network militarily, which meant that it could be sustained only with difficulty in the Mexican area. Tollan, by contrast, grew into a major economic and military power; it was the largest city in central Mexico and had a meritocratic organization that yielded the largest army in the region. Moreover, Tollan had technological and tactical innovations that gave it military superiority. Adding to their power, the Toltecs had trade relations with northern and western Mexico that other cities were poorly placed to disrupt. Thus, Tollan's emergence as a fledgling trading city was supported by independent economic networks and superior military power. The trader cities simply could not compete against this combination of military and economic power and so declined or withdrew.

Wealth depended on the goods entering Tollan, but power depended on who controlled that trade. Left in the hands of others, Tollan would have been vulnerable; it therefore seized direct control of the trade, although the Toltec merchants may have been as much private entrepreneurs as state functionaries. They did not funnel goods from foreign lands to the capital, but enriched themselves so that their actions were dictated by their own interests rather than the direct economic interests of Tollan. Many undoubtedly did trade with Tollan, but the goods found there do not span the entire range of those the Toltecs had access to, suggesting merchants were going elsewhere.[56]

The Toltecs expanded throughout Mesoamerica and also traded far to the north. The use of the short sword in combination with the atlatl gave the Toltecs a significant advantage over existing conventional armies in Mesoamerica. However, their organizational advantages in size and logistical support were probably more important and were certainly longer lasting, for the relatively simple technology involved in the short sword could easily be adopted elsewhere.[57] In spite of military advantages, however, the Toltec empire collapsed. Its demise was not the result of a withdrawal from the periphery culminating in the collapse of the capital. Rather, Tollan was destroyed first, and its polity disintegrated as a result. The Toltec era ended by A.D. 1179, when Tollan met a violent end as the result of famine, rebellion, and Chichimec invasions from the north, and most of the people moved elsewhere.[58] This was not the result of a single cataclysmic event: the city experienced a long decline.[59] Not all of the reasons for Tollan's demise are known, but one influential theory lays much of the blame on long-term ecological changes.[60]

The high cultures of Mesoamerica were all dependent on agriculture that typically requires at least 700 mm of annual precipitation. This zone extended far into the north during the first millennium A.D., but it shifted south of the Tollan area between the twelfth and fourteenth centuries, bringing social disruption as agriculture became less productive and less reliable.[61] Perhaps more important, the desiccation of the north forced many settled agricultural groups to abandon their homes and migrate into Mesoamerica, bringing social dislocation with them. In the end, however, Tollan did suffer violence: much of the city was untouched but most buildings in the main ceremonial precinct were destroyed.[62]

As previously indicated, Tollan fell during massive Chichimec intrusions into the area.[63] At its height, the city and its army were in little danger from roving Chichimecs. However, the Chichimecs brought with them the bow and arrow. In their hands, the bow was probably used for small game, but it became a significant weapon and had a major impact on Toltec military practices and political strategy.[64] Politically decentralized groups using hit-and-run tactics had always posed difficulties in Mesoamerica, but conventional armies' superior weapons and organization could fend off raiders and deny them any given location. However, the bow altered that relationship by giving nomadic raiders a weapon with greater range than spears and atlatl darts and a considerably higher rate of fire than slings.[65] Chichimecs were still inferior to Toltec armies in conventional battles, but they could remain out of range of most Toltec projectiles and return fire with deadly effect while falling back to avoid direct contact.

The impact of this new weapon could have been lessened by urban fortifications, but these had fallen into disuse with the growth of Toltec hegemonic control. With their large armies, the Toltecs could still defend their unfortified cities, but given the distances involved, they could not maintain safe and secure passage between them. Thus, even though the Chichimecs could neither hold fixed areas nor stand up to mainline Toltec troops, they were able to disrupt tenuously connected sites and wreak economic havoc to the extent that Tollan was dependent on sites such as the Hidalgo obsidian mines for economic survival. Chichimec archery did not destroy Toltec domination, but it did shift the balance of power, drastically raising the cost of maintaining a far-flung empire.

A political system based on an extensive trade network but exercising little or no direct political control depends on the traders' ability to defend themselves, which the Toltecs could do at the time they expanded. But traveling bands were particularly susceptible to roving bands of archers, no matter how well armed they were for hand-to-hand combat. There were two potential responses to this problem. First, the Toltecs could have adopted bows and arrows to neutralize the Chichimecs' advantage and temporarily forestalled the disruption. However, until archery was properly integrated into Toltec tactics, it would have had little effect on hit-and-run attacks. Second, the Toltecs could have withdrawn from their extended economic system into more compact polities where tenuous, long-range ties were less important. However, this also would have forced more autonomy onto other cities, undermining the Toltec system and drastically reducing the trade network upon which Tollan's economy depended and which provided the impetus for expansion in the first place. These responses may have been combined, but either undermined the vulnerable Toltec economic system.

Tollan itself was not immediately attacked and destroyed, but suffered a drastic decline because it could no longer guarantee the economic supply lines upon which it was dependent. Following the disruption of their trade routes, the Toltecs moved away from the vulnerable border areas and relocated in more populous areas where these tenuous connections were less important and where the Chichimecs could not as easily intrude.

Had the Toltec empire been integrated into a single, interdependent political economy, its distant cities would probably have fallen with the capital, but there is no evidence that this happened. Instead, other cities with close ties to Tollan continued to function much as they had previously, as one would expect if they were linked only by a loose imperial affiliation.

OAXACA

Although the Toltecs were the most important power in Mesoamerica at this time, they were not the only power, a notable example being a small empire in Oaxaca. The large Classic mountaintop centers of the Mixteca Alta were abandoned as late as A.D. 900 in favor of valley-floor residential settlements as the threats from Monte Alban and Teotihuacan declined. Many of these new centers shared the eclecticism of the period, with architectural and artistic characteristics that marked such sites as El Tajín, Xochicalco, and the Ñuiñe, although the rise of Tollan appears to have dampened these developments, at least among the Ñuiñe.[66] Most Mixtec and Zapotec states were not highly bureaucratized: the ruler lived in his capital and selected nobles to rule various subject communities.[67] But during the eleventh century, a small conquest empire was established among the Mixtecs of Oaxaca by the legendary king, 8 Deer, who was born in A.D. 1011 and died in 1063.[68] During his reign, nearly all of the towns of the Mixteca Alta and the coastal Mixtecs were brought under unified rule,[69] between seventy-five and one hundred conquests being recorded in Mixtec codices for this king.[70] Centered in Tilantongo in the Mixteca Alta, 8 Deer conquered the south coast site of Tututepec, effecting a temporary consolidation of the Mixtec-speaking peoples through a combination of conquests, political alliances, and marital ties.[71] It has even been suggested that he may have dominated the Ñuiñe, perhaps even Cholula and the Tehuacan Valley, and initiated the Mixtec invasions of the Valley of Oaxaca, although the latter may have been spurred by the disintegration of centralized power in Oaxaca or the collapse of the Toltec empire.[72]

There was some Toltec influence in the Mixteca Alta, including a realignment of the Mixtec calendar in A.D. 983 to approximate the

Toltec version; according to one interpretation of the codices, 8 Deer traveled to Tollan to have the nose ornament inserted that legitimated his accession to the throne.[73] Building on that interpretation, it has further been suggested that 8 Deer may have borrowed the Toltec political model for his own expansion.[74] However, 8 Deer's investiture in Tollan is unlikely.[75] Even though 8 Deer created his empire during the heyday of the Toltecs, his military equipment owed more to centers such as Cacaxtla and Xochicalco than to Tollan, which suggests that connections with the Olmeca-Xicalanca in southern Puebla may have been the more influential ones.

The evidence for military equipment derives almost exclusively from Mixtec pictorial codices, which suggest the presence of military orders during 8 Deer's reign, as witnessed by the depictions of elaborate helmets and other garb of the soldiers, particularly jaguar and eagle costumes.[76] According to the codices, round shields with and without feather fringe were carried,[77] but armor does not appear to have been worn, although its use beneath warrior suits cannot be ruled out. The primary weapons were thrusting spears and atlatls and darts.[78] Hafted and unhafted knives were used for sacrificial purposes, while stone and metal axes appear in combat situations.[79] Some bladed short swords were used and a few bows and arrows are illustrated.[80]

Some of these depictions are apparently anachronisms. Though not impossible, it is unlikely that bows had reached the Mixteca Alta during the first half of the eleventh century, given their absence at Tollan at this same time.[81] The scarcity of illustrations of short swords at a time when they were perhaps the most decisive weapon in the Toltec inventory is odd. Four alternative explanations come to mind. First, status considerations may have altered what was reflected in the manuscripts. Second, manuscript painters may have copied such aspects as dress from earlier manuscripts, resulting in anachronistic depictions, as also happened in medieval European manuscripts.[82] Third, the Mixtecs may have retained an older combat stance based on spears and atlatls that had long served them well. Fourth, they may well have had an aristocratic military system in which the main emphasis was placed on relatively small numbers of noble warriors, which is certainly suggested by the codices; thus large formations of soldiers employing both atlatls and short swords may not have been feasible, the Mixtecs preferring instead to rely on specialized hand-to-hand combat. The Cacaxtla style adopted by the Mixtecs was not static, however, and rather than adopt the new short sword, it appears that the Mixtecs adapted existing weapons into the combined projectile and shock-weapon Toltec style, but did so by doubling up on atlatls and thrusting spears in the hands of single combatants.[83] Atlatls had not been widely used in Oaxaca previously. 8 Deer's integration of them with shock weapons into a combined arms force similar to that of previous empires may have been partly responsible for the Mixtecs' expansionist success.

What these codices do provide is pictorial assurance that bows and arrows had reached central and southern Mexico by at least the thirteenth century. It also suggests that the broadsword that dominated Late Postclassic combat was a truly late innovation, at least late enough that the compilers of even those codices dating from the colonial or late pre-Conquest eras recognized that they were anachronistic, but that the bow was not.

This small empire did not long survive its creator. Why it failed is uncertain, but the ruggedness of the terrain and the dispersion of the centers probably hindered the region's integration, so the empire lasted only as long as it had inspired leadership, disintegrating after the death of 8 Deer. The introduction of bows and arrows may have been even more destabilizing for this empire than it had been for the Toltecs, for their widespread adoption tilted the military advantage in the favor of individual towns and against centralized control.

CHICHEN ITZA

Except for Tollan's, the largest Mesoamerican empire was a related system centered at Chichen Itza on the Yucatan peninsula. This empire was not a major military innovator in Mesoamerica as a whole, but it was on a regional basis, introducing new weapons and tactics to the Maya lowlands and precipitating a clash of existing military systems—Maya and Mexican.

The shift from Classic to Postclassic (A.D. 900 to 1500)[84] in the lowland Maya area was heralded by the emergence of Mexicanized groups, the Putun, in the Tabasco lowlands, although political changes and disintegration had begun as early as the end of the eighth century in the Maya region.[85] Called the Itza by the local Yucatec Maya, the identity of the Putun is debated.[86] Several incursions may have taken place, and rather than being a single coherent group, the Putun may have been made up of several independent groups, including Toltecs.[87] The argument for a Maya identity of the invaders rests heavily on the presence of some Mexican architectural and artistic elements in Yucatan before the Itza intrusion and the survival of only Maya speakers in the region at the time of the Spanish conquest. However, the heavy infusion of Toltec architectural forms and decoration,[88] almost identical depictions of warriors at both Tollan and Chichen Itza,[89] the use of Mexican glyphs, and the presence of Nahuatl in northern Yucatan at this time[90] strongly indicate a Toltec presence, and the iconography and language at Chichen suggest it was a dominant one.[91]

As at Tollan, what happened in Yucatan is uncertain and rests on a blend of archaeological data and native historical accounts and legends.[92] The trade routes throughout the central and southern Maya lowlands during the Classic were riverine and overland, but these became Putun-dominated and shifted to seacoast trade around the Yucatan Peninsula by the tenth century.[93]

The arrival of these Toltec or Toltec-affiliated groups accords well with the Toltec legend of the exodus of Quetzalcoatl from central Mexico.[94] Even the Itza leader was called Quetzalcoatl, and that god dominated Chichen Itza.[95] Moreover, despite trade ties throughout much of Mesoamerica, particularly the southern area, none were maintained between Chichen Itza and Tollan. There is evidence of earlier Mexican influence in northern Yucatan, and so the Itza invasion may have begun gradually,[96] but between A.D. 918 and 987, they conquered and established their capital at Chichen Itza.[97] Probably numerically inferior to the resident Maya, the Itza encountered no centralized polity large or cohesive enough to repel them and they ultimately controlled much of northern Yucatan.[98] However, Toltec architecture was confined primarily to Chichen Itza, suggesting that power was exercised in a hegemonic fashion, from the capital, through local rulers by means of a tributary system.[99] The rest of Chichen Itza's influence was tied to trade.

Although the Toltecs were politically and socially dominant in Chichen Itza, comprising most of the leadership, they probably made up only part of the constituency of the invading group. The Itza were a multiethnic conglomeration, with peoples of Toltec origins at the top, but perhaps including speakers of Chol, Chontal, and Yucatec Maya, the last probably being the original occupants of the area.[100] They apparently brought few Toltec artisans with them, relying on Maya craftsmen to execute Toltec designs.[101] Moreover, they may not have brought women either, which would have led to intermarriage and eventual social absorption.[102] The Itza grafted themselves atop an existing society in a political conquest: they had neither the interest nor the full

range of skills to build a society from scratch.[103] Instead, they conquered but did not totally displace the vanquished.

The presence of powerful leaders is evidenced not only by the evident
imperial success of the city, but also by several accession scenes that are
depicted in works of art throughout Chichen Itza.[104] The most prominent of these are found on the Temple of the Chac Mool, the Temple of
the Warriors, and their respective associated colonnades, in the Lower
and Upper Temple of the Jaguars, and elsewhere in the Great Ball
Court.[105] Many glyphs or glyph elements appear in the sculptures in the
Toltec section of Chichen Itza, but they do not reflect individuals and
are not individual names.[106] They appear on a minority of the carvings—about 20 percent in the Temple of the Warriors, which has the
greatest concentration—and may reflect lineages, clans, offices, or
places.[107] The vast majority of the glyphs in the Toltec section of
Chichen Itza are central Mexican in origin,[108] but the eventual amalgam
of Itza and Maya leadership is also indicated in Maya glyphs in the old
section of the city. Kakupacal, a Maya lord who carried out conquests
on behalf of the Chichen polity, is mentioned fourteen times in the
glyphs.[109] In any event, after a brief period, the use of Classic Maya
inscriptions ceased at Chichen Itza.[110]

Much of the rulers' power derived from military success, as seen from
the substantial evidence of warfare in Chichen's art, which includes
murals of warriors and battle scenes. The battle scenes in the inner
chamber of the Upper Temple of the Jaguars in the Great Ball Court no
longer exist but were recorded in watercolors by Adele Breton around
the turn of the century.[111] The center mural in this inner room depicts
two facing warriors, dividing the six battle scenes into two groups of
three. The north scene apparently depicts the early Toltec intrusion into
the area. All the attackers carry round shields characteristic of the Toltecs while the defenders hold rectangular shields characteristic of the
Maya, although both groups use atlatls.[112] One battle takes place in red
hills which may be the Puuc Maya area. The south scene appears to
depict somewhat later events because all the combatants are similarly
clothed and armed, indicating either an internal war or warfare that
took place after Toltec arms and armor had been assimilated by native
Maya groups.[113] Most of these murals (perhaps all, before they were
destroyed) contain solar disks with seated, armed Toltec figures, probably representing a deceased, deified ruler. These scenes are flanked by
armed Toltec figures emerging from a serpent's mouth or intertwined

with a feathered serpent, probably representing other rulers bearing the Quetzalcoatl title.[114]

Few other battle murals survive at Chichen Itza, although one in the Temple of the Warriors depicts a battle between striped inhabitants and black-painted attackers raging in and around a lakeside village. The attackers are winning and are leading away bound captives.[115] Both sides use round shields, but the inhabitants' shields also have hanging feather fringes, and both sides use the short sword, although only the attackers combine this with atlatls and darts.

Chichen Itza presents an interesting picture of Mesoamerican warfare because it is not only the clash of two different cultures, but of two different weapons complexes as well. The Maya arms generally consisted of either thrusting spears with lanceolet points that would not easily become lodged in a wound, and rectangular flexible shields;[116] or small round shields and bladed clubs. Neither combination required much, if any, body armor.

The lack of quilted cotton armor cannot be attributed simply to the climate, as cotton armor was occasionally found in tropical locations such as the Veracruz coast and Altar de Sacrificios.[117] However, armor had never formed part of Maya military equipment, not only because of its cost, but also because its lack of mobility in a raiding strategy. Projectiles were not used in any significant way, either: atlatls were known but used as symbols of power rather than as military weapons, although slings may have been employed in a limited way.[118]

The major change at Chichen Itza was the massive introduction of central Mexican arms and armor, consisting primarily of atlatls and darts, short swords, and knives.[119] The atlatls and darts at Chichen Itza were the same as those found at Tollan—the atlatls were covered with fur and the darts had barbed points to prevent extraction.[120] The short sword with inset obsidian blades is the same as that found at Tollan.[121] Knives played a decidedly secondary role in combat. Hafted and unhafted knives were typically carried with the thrust handle down in the left arm band, with the blade protruding, as at Tollan.[122] Thrusting spears were used but played a minor role.[123] Armor consisted primarily of the round shield, quilted cotton armor on the left arm, and possibly cotton body armor.[124] Round shields were typical, not the small buckler found among the Maya, but larger shields held by two straps, one crossing the forearm and the other across the palm of the hand.[125] Some, but not all, of the shields had hanging feather fringes.[126]

Atlatls provided the primary projectile fire in Itza armies, but the main technological innovation was the use of the short sword.[127] With the substitution of the more mobile, round shield, the short sword largely displaced the thrusting spear. In combat, these weapons were used in sequence. The atlatl-wielding warriors carried the short sword in the left hand with their darts, and the atlatl in the right hand so the latter could be used first, followed by the short sword in the subsequent hand-to-hand combat, doubling each soldier's effectiveness.[128] The heavy reliance on projectile weapons was much more feasible in this area, where ground cover was significantly lighter than in the dense rainforests to the south.

Atlatls gave the Itza a decided advantage over the Maya who were not used to an opening projectile barrage. The darts would have seriously disrupted any initial Maya formations, reducing the battle to hand-to-hand combat against more mobile opponents wielding a weapon that was considerably handier for close-in fighting. Thus, the Itza dominance of Yucatan is partly explicable in military terms. Toltec weapons and tactics gave their wielders a decisive advantage over local weapons and tactics; in fact, some of these weapons were added to the Maya armories, partly displacing traditional Maya weapons.[129] But more significant than the introduction of a new technology is the fact that Toltec weapons were adopted as part of a functional complex tied to new combat tactics and the use of conventional armies that had not existed in the Maya area previously. The Itza may have introduced an element of naval warfare as well. Whether or not they reached Yucatan by canoe, the Itza were strongly tied to the intercoastal trade carried out by oceangoing canoes and rafts. Itza warriors are depicted in murals using canoes in military contexts.[130] How capable the Itza were in naval warfare is uncertain, but they clearly used canoes for transport and attack and could use them to mount offensive fire.[131]

The same military professionalism that existed at Tollan appears to have been introduced at Chichen Itza, including the Mexican meritocratic military system. The Itza did not settle in Yucatan as a complete society, but even if they had done so, it is unlikely they could have remained independent of the more populous Maya among whom they had settled. Most of Chichen society was composed of Maya, resulting in the ethnic heterogeneity well suited to the meritocratic system, permitting the Itza to expand their military base and dominate most of northern Yucatan. However, fostering social mobility through ability rather than kinship also opened the Toltecs to social penetration as Maya warriors were absorbed into the Itza system.[132] Initially, this occurred with the Maya nobility, for they had a virtual monopoly on martial skills. With time, Maya commoners were apparently also admitted meritocratically.[133] The widespread reliance on commoners in offensive combat was both a social and a technological revolution in the Maya area. The idea of a meritocratic military system came from central Mexico, but the large forces it fostered were particularly feasible in the relatively light ground cover of northern Yucatan.

Chichen Itza's peak population is uncertain. The site covered twenty-five square kilometers, but it had a dispersed urban pattern.[134] Dzibil-chaltun had an estimated population of 10,000–20,000 in its sixteen square kilometers,[135] or 625–1,250 people per square kilometer. At that ratio, Chichen Itza would have had a population ranging from 15,625 to 33,250. What this meant for the city's army is unclear in what must have initially been a very confused social situation, with conflict-ing notions of how armies were to be recruited by the two major ethnic groups—Itza and indigenous Maya.

If the entire population was involved on a fully meritocratic basis, Chichen Itza could have mounted an offensive army of 1,973 to 4,198 soldiers and an effective maximum of 3,366 to 7,162. By contrast, an aristocratic system would have yielded an offensive army of only 197 to 420 soldiers and an effective maximum of 337 to 716. The actual military situation at Chichen Itza probably shifted over time, with the Itza segment participating meritocratically and the Maya segment origi-nally retaining its aristocratic approach and gradually becoming merito-cratic, thus swelling the size of Chichen Itza's army. There were military orders among the Toltecs, and the murals at Chichen Itza reveal what may be depictions of back standards, suggesting organized military units that were hierarchically organized. Itza military orders were readily adopted, perhaps because similar groups may have been found among the Maya as well.[136] But large, organized military units were alien to aristocratic systems, although such units and a command hierar-chy were indispensable to larger meritocratic armies.

Chichen Itza's dominance sprang from the size, arms, and organiza-tion of its army, not from its fortifications. No defensive wall enclosed Chichen Itza; the dispersed city relied instead on its size for protec-tion.[137] There is evidence in mural representations of systematic Itza assaults on buildings, as in scenes that depict fiery spears thrown or cast onto the straw roofs of Maya buildings.[138] But assaults on settlements were apparently an Itza offensive strategy and not a defensive problem.

Fortifications existed from early times in Mesoamerica and some basic siegecraft must have been developed to counter these, but there is little evidence of it. In part, the lack of siegecraft may reflect the unwillingness of defenders to remain behind urban fortifications while their dependent towns and fields remained vulnerable. Thus, walls were useful against small raids, but conventional forces usually had to be met in the open. Yet the decision was sometimes made to resist behind walls and the murals at Chichen Itza offer the only solid evidence of a siege machine in precolumbian Mesoamerica.[139] The mural depicts an assault up the stairway of a pyramid that stands behind three towers reaching three to four stories high.

There are several military explanations for the scaffolds suggested by the battle scene. First, the towers could be used by leaders to oversee the battle and issue directions, but relaying orders from the top of the towers to combatants below over the din of battle seems unlikely. Second, they could be used to breach fortifications, but most Mesoamerican walls were not high enough to require anything more elaborate than ladders to scale them. Pyramids were high enough, but a vertical scaffold was of little use because the pyramids' inward slope would have increased the distance from the upper portions of the building to the scaffold the higher they went. Moreover, there were no bridges leading from the towers. The third and likeliest explanation is that the towers were built for the purpose of pouring fire on the target pyramid according to the following circumstances.

In the scene depicted, only atlatls are used, which have an effective range of about sixty meters on level ground. Uphill, this range is reduced for the attackers and increased for the defenders, who have a significant advantage, especially because the attackers had to attack up a pyramid with limited stairways. This allowed the defenders to concentrate their forces and use their atlatls effectively against the front attackers. Moreover, attackers ascending the pyramid through a hail of darts could carry only a few darts and could not return effective fire. In such circumstances, a fire tower would greatly ease the assault by providing the attackers with effective and multiple vantage points from which to strike the defenders, suppressing the defenders' return fire, providing cover for the attackers, and helping redress the attackers' dart limitations.

Although the Toltecs had a significant tactical advantage, expansion beyond Chichen Itza remained difficult, but by A.D. 1100, it dominated the entire coast from Jaina on the southwest to Vista Alegre on the northeast.[140] The Itza were helped in their expansion by the ecology of the northwest Yucatan peninsula: indeed, their success may not have been possible anywhere else in the Maya lowlands.

Northern Yucatan is subject to essentially the same wet/dry cycles as the rest of the Maya lowlands, but the northwestern corner of Yucatan has the lowest rainfall in the lowlands,[141] permitting a longer campaign season than elsewhere in the lowlands. It was no accident that the Itza established their empire where they could most easily dispatch conventional armies that were limited primarily to the winter/spring dry season. Northern Yucatan, and especially the western portion, also had perhaps the best terrain and climatic conditions for military expansion in the entire Maya region. The land was relatively flat and had less ground cover than most of the lowlands[142] and the least rainfall, all of which eased travel considerably. As a result, Itza armies could probably maintain the 2.4 kilometer per hour rate (over nineteen kilometers per day) with little difficulty. The rainy season still limited campaign seasons, but the lighter precipitation produced fewer difficulties than elsewhere in the Maya area.

Food demands nevertheless remained an obstacle. In central Mexico, this was overcome through a combination of politically enforced resupply en route and the use of retoasted tortillas that could be carried for days and remain edible. Comales, essential to the production of tortillas, were generally absent from the Maya lowlands until quite late, but two vessels that are possibly comales were found at Chichen Itza.[143] As elsewhere, this low incidence suggests that tortillas were not an everyday staple, but they did exist and were probably made for special purposes, such as long-distance travel associated with both trade and warfare.

Despite their military power and logistical advantages, the Itza empire did not conquer all of northern Yucatan. South and southeast of Chichen Itza three small, fortified sites sprang up, perhaps marking a frontier of Itza expansion.[144] These were the sites of Cuca, Chacchob, and Dzonot Ake, and their construction differed markedly from earlier Maya fortifications. Cuca, a Puuc town located in very flat land, had two roughly concentric walls:[145] the outer wall was 2,255 meters long, currently only 1–2 meters high and 6–10 meters wide, enclosing an area of 33 hectares. The more massive inner wall was 828 meters long, currently 1–3 meters high and 10–12 meters wide, enclosing 4.6 hectares and the site's religious and elite structures. In a marked departure from earlier Maya earthen wall and ditch fortifications, Cuca's walls were constructed of two dry masonry walls 1.5–2 meters apart with the interior space then filled with limestone rubble.[146] There are no apparent breaks in the wall that served as a gate but ramps or stairways may have been used.[147] There was a cenote between the inner and outer walls,[148] but the low outer wall would have required a large number of defenders unless there was also a wooden palisade. The inner wall, however, was easily defended.[149] Both walls were later additions to an existing town, indicating that, although Cuca was founded around A.D. 850–900, it was occupied beyond A.D. 1000 in an increasingly competitive political environment.[150]

Chacchob, also located in flat country, was enclosed by a 1,410-meter masonry wall, 5–6 meters wide and 2–3 meters high, containing 13.7 hectares and pierced by three gates less than 2 meters wide.[151] The walls were plastered but mortarless and show no trace of timber breastworks or palisades. With a resident population of under a thousand (and perhaps no more than a few hundred), the wall was an enormous social effort amounting to a fifth of the construction of the entire site. Unlike Cuca, Chacchob's walls were built at the same time as the town or shortly thereafter.[152] The site was occupied for a generation or two and then abruptly abandoned, probably as a result of a military emergency, for the gates were filled in and never reopened.[153] Dzonot Ake, located in flat country, was probably encircled by a wall enclosing about 6 hectares.[154] The wall was one of the latest constructions at the site, and there is some evidence of an associated ditch.[155]

All three sites date to around A.D. 1000 and were small and thus politically and militarily vulnerable.[156] None of these sites were within the Chichen Itza polity, and while Chacchob may have been a fugitive elite center, all were local developments reflecting decreased political stability and increasing conflict,[157] most probably in the face of Itza expansion. These small sites were defensive and presented little obstacle, but Itza expansion ground to a halt at the limits of their ecosystem: the Itza were unable to conquer the eastern Yucatan area. Throughout much of Chichen Itza's dominance, a smaller polity centered on the city of Coba in eastern Yucatan faced the larger Itza empire that extended from Tabasco through western Campeche across northern Yucatan to the northeast coast of Quintana Roo.[158]

COBA

The western area of northern Yucatan, which the Itza entered and dominated, had been composed of a number of polities, but the more homogeneous plain of the eastern area was organized into a single major polity dominated by Coba. At its height during the Itza domination of Yucatan, Coba had a population estimated as high as 40,000–60,000.[159] Allied with centers to the south, Coba's prominence sprang from its control of trade on the central Quintana Roo coast and its intermediary role in the north-south trade.[160]

Coba owed its continued independence to two major factors—an ecosystem that hindered Itza expansion and a road-based infrastructure. Western Yucatan had several small road systems. The eastern area was linked by a single system, the largest, centered on Coba.[161] This type of road has been built in the lowland Maya area since the Late Formative period, although most roads merely connected areas within the same site.[162] The Coba roads were built in sections, probably by separate villages fulfilling their labor obligations. Retaining walls were built first and the interior was filled with stones before large, shaped, and faced rectangular stones were used to make unmortared exterior walls. A cambered surface was formed by placing a thin layer of small stones over the larger fill stones and packing, pounding, and wetting a layer of calcareous sand to produce a cementlike, smooth, and puddle-free surface.[163]

Coba's network was the largest in Mesoamerica, with sixteen known roads connecting a variety of centers, the farthest being Yaxuna, more than a hundred kilometers away.[164] The roads were built in exceptionally straight lines and were elevated,[165] varying in height according to the terrain, but averaging .75 to 1 meter high, with some sections as high as 7 meters. Most Coba roads range from 3 to 19 meters wide, with temples and gateway-type structures built at intervals.[166] These roads may have had ritual, social, and economic purposes, but they also define political domains, as at Coba.[167] However, more to the point, roads had military functions as well. Simple dirt trails in the Maya lowlands were adequate for most travel during the dry season, but these quickly become impassable during heavy rains. The construction of formal roads altered this by permitting year-round travel because cambered roads shed water.[168]

Coba was connected by roads to a number of other sites, including the port of Xcaret through which it controlled the sea trade.[169] At Coba, roads provided excellent political connections, regardless of their other purposes. Running in almost perfectly straight lines and built to uniform levels that smoothed terrain undulations, these roads were not primarily economic in purpose, for the latter tended to maximize connections between various termini.[170] Instead, the roads connected only selected points and fostered the fastest possible travel between them, excellently serving military and administrative purposes.

The military benefits of such a system are apparent.[171] Mesoamerican armies could achieve only relatively slow march rates, primarily the result of poor roads and uncertain logistics. The Maya road system, however, largely overcame these, offering flat, hard surfaces that allowed faster walking. Moreover, their width permitted Coba's soldiers to march in much wider columns than elsewhere in Mesoamerica, up to ten men abreast on the longest road.[172] Thus, travel was not temporally restricted: armies could travel day or night and rain posed no major obstacle because the road surface shed water.

Because exact distances and travel times were known, resupply could be more precisely controlled, offering Coba unusual precision in timing and logistics, and giving it tremendously effective control and defense in areas adjacent to the roads—far greater control than anywhere else in Mesoamerica. This meant that Coba could exercise military control over its dependencies directly from the center and could do so year round. Troops could be mobilized from throughout the system and dispatched when and where they were needed, which gave the Coba polity a significant advantage over attackers who could only reinforce their troops during the dry season and by day.

However, roads run in both directions. If a road-connected dependency was conquered, enemy troops could march as quickly to Coba as Coba could to them. But this danger was more than offset by the advantages of the system. Enemy troops still lacked detailed information of the road system, its routes, travel times, and logistical requirements, and though access allowed rapid enemy movement, they were still constrained as to when additional troops could be brought to the road system. Moreover, the Coba soldiers traveled through friendly territory, whereas enemy forces were vulnerable to ambush. Gaining access to the roads was a benefit to the enemy, but not an overwhelming one. For the defenders, however, the roads allowed all available troops to be rushed from throughout the system to the threatened area.

The roads' real advantage was that they unified the polity in a variation of a territorial system, which meant that most or all of it had to be conquered for an attack to be successful. Even if an attacker seized control of one or two towns and was strong enough to hold them, this advantage could not be maintained. The attackers could be reinforced from outside against a counterattack during the dry season, but the situation was drastically altered during the rains when they were effectively cut off from external reinforcement.[173] Consequently, attackers had to station enough men in the conquered town to withstand the full might of the Coba polity. Yet, barring grossly disproportionate forces, the year-round commitment of adequate troops to defend the conquered town was typically beyond the ability of Mesoamerican empires. To subdue a road-linked polity, all or most of the system had to be conquered at once, which required an enormous investment in time, men, and materiel. Thus, through a combination of their own virtues and the limitations of other systems, road-linked polities were relatively stable and secure.

Largely as a result of its superior road-based political integration, Coba and its dependencies remained independent of Chichen Itza. When Coba ultimately declined, it was not from direct assault; rather, it was encircled by the Itza and cut off from its trade routes to the northwest and south.[174] The Coba system collapsed around A.D. 1100.[175]

The Early Postclassic was a period of reintegration of much of Mesoamerica. In central Mexico, the Toltecs emerged as the rulers of a mercantile empire, strongly buttressed by military innovation and might, that pushed out competing trader groups that had established themselves during the fragmentation of central Mexico after the demise of Teotihuacan. However, they did not dominate Mesoamerica in the same fashion or as extensively as had Teotihuacan, and regionally competing polities emerged elsewhere. A Mexican invasion involving Toltecs was responsible for establishing an empire centered on Chichen Itza in northern Yucatan, but there were no sustained ties between the Tollan and Chichen Itza, suggesting that the latter was founded, in part, by a dissident faction. Here, too, other polities continued, but they were buffeted, and strongly influenced, by these foreign invaders, who introduced Mexican notions of warfare, social organization, and political organization into the Maya area. Their political dominance ensured that these would remain important elements of local society.

CHAPTER 9

The Aztec Era

There has been significant archaeological work in many areas of Late Postclassic Mesoamerica, but most of what is known about this time comes from historic sources compiled after the Spanish conquest of Mexico. One thing this fuller data makes clear is that warfare had a major impact throughout Mesoamerica, even on societies not at war. Although not always deployed, most arms and armor used by the Aztecs were available to other groups, which suggests the presence of a Meso-america-wide military industry.

The relative uniformity of Late Postclassic arms and armor depended on access to their raw materials which were available through trade. Obsidian was essential for blades, as was oak for swords, reeds for arrows, and cotton for armor. Many of these materials were important for utilitarian purposes and were available through ordinary exchange mechanisms. But the increased demand for arms and armor stimulated production so that some towns without hostile relations nevertheless engaged in the war industry, making cotton armor exclusively for external sale.[1] Thus, warfare's impact on the economy went well beyond imperial boundaries to unite the region in a massive military-preindustrial complex.

THE MEXICAN AREA

With the demise of Tollan, central Mexico fragmented politically and the Toltecs dispersed to other cities. New groups also migrated into central Mexico from the north, taking over existing cities and establishing others of their own. In some instances city-states became the centers of small empires, with the Valley of Mexico emerging as the locus of the most powerful of these. Centered on the western side, the Tepanec empire dominated much of the Valley of Mexico and areas to the west into the present-day states of Mexico and Guerrero. But no polity controlled vast areas until the emergence of the Aztecs following their overthrow of the Tepanecs in 1428.[2]

AZTECS

When the Aztecs entered the Valley of Mexico at the end of the twelfth century, they were a relatively backward people by Mesoamerican standards. The valley was divided into city-states and their respective dependencies, and the Aztecs became one of these, gradually adopting the organization and culture of their more sophisticated neighbors. In an effort to secure more reliable economic and political ties, in 1372 the Aztecs accepted Acamapichtli, a nobleman from Culhuacan, as their first king. Married to the daughters of the ward headmen, he founded the Aztec noble dynasty that ruled Tenochtitlan, which became the center of an empire in 1428, dominating central Mexico until the Spanish conquest in 1519–21.

Aztec society was divided into nobles and commoners, but with many variations.[3] At the top were the upper nobles from whom the king was selected. The kings were supported by tribute from commoners and subject towns and income from royal lands, while the rest of the upper nobility were supported by tribute-paying commoners and patrimonial lands. As in other meritocratic societies, artistic depictions of rulers were rare.[4]

The next level was composed of the lower hereditary nobles who were the offspring of the ruling class. The commoners supported the nobility through tribute, although particularly important commoner groups, such as merchants and artisans, were exempt from some types of labor obligations and paid tribute in kind. The commoners were organized into groups or wards—originally kin-based but later residentially based—which were overseen by commoner headmen who represented organizational interests before the government. Nominally, headmen were elected, but the position tended to be hereditary in practice. Other commoners who did not belong to ward organizations were permanent, hereditary, laborers on the patrimonial lands of the nobility. At the bottom of the social hierarchy were slaves, usually commoners who had sold themselves into service, although some had been enslaved as punishment for criminal acts. The rights of their owners were limited, and except for labor, slaves were free, could marry, and could own property, including other slaves.

This social hierarchy was not static, however. The Aztecs had a meritocratic system in which social advancement was possible through three occupations: priest, merchant, or soldier. Of these, a military career was the avenue open to the majority of Aztecs. If a commoner succeeded as a warrior, he could achieve the status of meritocratic noble and enjoy many rights of nobility, which became hereditary. This access to higher social standing was a great motivator for commoners to go to war and most probably was a magnet for the thousands of outsiders who migrated into the city.

Disease was not a major factor in Mesoamerican warfare, nor did chemical and biological weapons play major roles,[5] but the evidence of war is overwhelming. The Aztecs formed an empire based on hegemonic rather than direct control, backed up by the enormous force at their disposal. In effect, they ruled through local kings who carried out Aztec dictates. Aztec demands were usually for tribute and military aid, but generally did not otherwise encroach on the prerogatives of the local rulers or peoples. Neither Aztec troops nor puppet rulers were imposed in most cases, although failure to comply with Aztec demands would bring a vengeful army.

Most Aztec arms had been used by earlier groups, but additional ones included a new projectile weapon (bows and arrows) and a new shock weapon (broadswords).[6] The main Aztec projectile weapons were atlatls, bows, and slings. Late Postclassic atlatls had almost 60 percent more thrust than hand-thrown spears, but their effective range was no more than sixty meters. Made of wood and approximately .6 meters long, atlatls had a central groove along which the dart was laid abutted by a hook at the end, and typically had fingerholes, loops, or pegs about a third of the way up the handle. The darts were made of oak and frequently had feathered butts and a variety of points—fire-hardened, obsidian, fishbone, copper, or flint—although barbed stone points were used in combat. The darts were apparently carried loose in the hand rather than in a quiver.

Slings made of maguey fiber were also used, not with randomly selected rocks, but with hand-shaped, spherical stones, and had a probable range of several hundred meters. The Aztecs used simple, rather than compound, bows with sinew or hide bowstrings, measuring up to 1.5 meters in length. War arrows had the same variety of points as atlatl darts and were carried in quivers holding as many as twenty arrows.[7] Poisoned arrows were not used in Mesoamerica, although fire arrows were. Aztec war arrows of standardized sizes were made of straightened reeds bound with maguey fiber to prevent splitting, then fletched, and had obsidian points glued and tied to them; their range was probably 90 to 180 meters.

The main Aztec shock weapons were thrusting spears, clubs, and broadswords. Thrusting spears were 1.8 to 2.2 meters long, with a third of their length dedicated to a cutting surface made of close-set obsidian blades securely glued into grooves. Although significantly less important, several wooden clubs were also used, some plain and others with a variety of stone blades and wooden knobs. Knives were used as well, but in a decidedly secondary role, and axes appear to have functioned solely as execution devices.

An important innovation in Aztec weaponry was the oak broadsword, which was a little over a meter long with close-set obsidian blades glued into grooves on either side. Broadswords often had thongs through which the soldier could put his hand to secure the weapon during battle. Broadswords were a post-Toltec innovation and also postdate the introduction of bows and arrows. The shift from short sword to broadsword eliminated the former's crushing role entirely but otherwise was probably a natural evolution toward greater size. However, the introduction of archery may also have played a part in this shift; they emphasized the rapid closing of combatants to minimize the effects of the arrow barrage and simultaneously required a more effective close-in weapon, in that both sides sought to establish and maintain close contact to minimize the effect of projectiles.

It is unclear precisely when the broadsword was developed, though its likeliest ancestor was the Toltec short sword. Unfortunately, the broadsword is not depicted in any precolumbian artistic media, perhaps because of some Mesoamerican aesthetic similar to the preference of modern generals to be portrayed on horseback rather than in a tank. Nevertheless, the broadsword had become the main battle weapon and its absence in works of art was probably tied to its newness. Even fairly recent weapons such as bows and arrows are represented, which suggests that the broadsword was a still more recent development— certainly post A.D. 1200, probably post A.D. 1300 and possibly as recent as the latter half of the fifteenth century.[8]

However, the use of bows and arrows gave an altogether new dimension to Mesoamerican warfare. Archery alone could not win battles against a thoroughly integrated combined arms force, but it must have been devastatingly effective when first introduced. Long-distance projectile weapons in the form of slings were ancient in Mesoamerica, but these did not compare with bows and arrows. Slings may have had a longer absolute range, but distance per se was less important than effective range, and in that the two weapons were comparable. Moreover, the arrows were lighter than slingstones, which meant that more could be carried.[9] Perhaps most significant of all, archery allowed fire to be concentrated in ways that slings could not. Slingers required considerable room to wind up and throw their stones, which forced them farther apart and kept their fire from being concentrated.[10] Archers, by contrast, could be packed close together and their fire further concentrated by coordinating their release of the arrows, which was more easily accomplished with bows than with slings.

The advantages enjoyed by arrows were similar to those of atlatl darts, but at even greater distances. This allowed the attacking force to fire and fall back without having to engage the enemy directly, producing highly mobile forces with very effective, long-range killing power. Although certainly not effecting a complete shift, archery's greatest impact was to swing the balance of power more in favor of less sophisticated groups, which readily adopted the bow in part because of its utility in everyday life. This shift was not muted until conventional Mesoamerican armies fully integrated the bow and altered their tactics to take it into account, which they had by Aztec times.[11]

With its light weight and longer cutting surface, the broadsword dominated Late Postclassic hand-to-hand combat more than any prior weapon. Only weapons of equal length could stand up to the broadsword; axes, maces, and short bladed clubs almost completely vanished from the Mesoamerican arsenal. Moreover, the broadsword spread quickly throughout Mesoamerica, although whether this indicates a pre-Aztec origin or dissemination in advance of Aztec expansion is uncertain.

Spurred by the introduction and integration of these weapons, the Aztec military also adopted better defensive protection. The Aztecs used shields, various forms of body armor, warriors' suits, and helmets.[12] Although wooden shields were also used, the Aztec military shield was typically round, made of fire-hardened cane tied with maguey fiber and backed with heavy cotton or leather. These shields were about .75

meters in diameter and usually had hanging feather fringes. The elite
also adopted complete torso armor made of a thick layer of unspun
cotton quilted between two layers of cloth. This was typically worn as
jerkins—jackets covering the torso as far down as waist to the top of the
thigh, but without sleeves. Because archery placed continued stress on
mobility, the limbs remained unarmored, but warriors' suits provided
some protection. These suits covered the arms and legs and were made
of feathers, although similar suits of animal skins were worn by the
meritocratic nobles, and were customarily worn over cotton armor.
Other soldiers wore feather tunics and kilts over cotton armor. Helmets
were made of wood overlaid with feathers. This garb was by no means
universal. Only distinguished warriors were entitled to armor, and war
suits were awarded by merit. Combat novices wore maguey-fiber clothing in battle and undistinguished warriors wore only a loincloth and
body paint.

Despite the changes it spurred, archery remained primarily a non-
elite defense. All Aztec soldiers could use bows, but the ranks of archers
were filled by commoners. Elite soldiers continued to rely primarily on
shock weapons for both effective and status reasons since hand-to-hand
combat, not archery, determined the outcome of battles, making these
soldiers more important. Moreover, shock weapons required greater
formal training, effectively increasing the percentage of nobles in that
category, and it was primarily hand-to-hand combat that allowed participants to lay claim to captives and thus rise socially.

Aztec combat between conventional forces, like that of most central
Mexican city-states at that time, typically began at dawn. The opposing
armies faced each other about fifty to sixty meters apart and the start of
battle was signaled by drums or trumpets. Battle began with a projectile
barrage—mostly arrows and slingstones from the commoner soldiers
who fired from long distance.[13] The barrage lasted no more than a
minute or two as the archers and slingers quickly exhausted their ammunition, while the shock-weapon fighters advanced under its protection.
The advance was not a random clash of all combatants. Aztec military
schools had produced a large body of trained soldiers that could be
thrown against the enemy and the Aztecs also kept large forces in re-
serve for use as needed. Those who entered combat first did so in a
regular sequence. The first soldiers to advance were members of military
orders, followed by veteran soldiers leading organized units.[14] As they
advanced, the soldiers followed the tall battle standards of their respective units, for the sounds of battle quickly masked most audible com-

mands. They advanced and fought in open formations rather than in a tightly packed group because they needed enough space to allow an unencumbered swing of broadswords, and this wider dispersion made them poorer targets for massed enemy arrow barrages.[15]

Because both sides advanced, each had to cover only about thirty meters, and as they did so, they cast darts in an effort to disrupt the enemy's formations with their enormous punching power. Once the two sides met, the covering barrage ended lest one's own soldiers be hit, and the archers and slingers shifted their attention to protecting the flanks, covering withdrawals and harassing enemy troops moving into or out of battle.[16] On closing, hand-to-hand battle was joined and atlatls were dropped in favor of broadswords, spears, and clubs. Only the first two or three ranks could bring their weapons to bear effectively, and soldiers were rotated in and out of battle as needed for rest and rearmament.

The basic strategy in a conventional encounter was to maintain a solid front. This limited each soldier's concern to threats directly ahead, confident that the other members of his unit were protecting his flanks and rear.[17] Consequently, a major goal of each side was to break the enemy's front, disrupting his line and throwing whole units into disarray, allowing more troops to pour through and divide his forces. Because only the first few ranks could be brought to bear,[18] if they could not break through the enemy formations the numerically superior Aztecs frequently committed more troops in an effort to extend the front. If they succeeded, they could turn the ends, envelop the enemy, and attack and disrupt their more vulnerable rear.[19]

The Aztec army owed much of its success to size. By 1519, Tenochtitlan held at least 150,000–200,000 people[20] and estimates of the valley-wide population range from 1,000,000–1,200,000 to 2,200,000–2,650,000.[21] This would have yielded an offensive army of 25,250 from Tenochtitlan, drawing on all males between twenty and thirty, and an effective maximum army of over 43,000, drawing on all males between twenty and fifty. For the Valley of Mexico as a whole, the offensive army would have been 151,500 to 334,563 with a maximum effective army of 258,480 to 570,810. In practice, however, the Aztec mobilization was proportional to the perceived threat. If the threat was small, only the elite troops would be summoned, as they were always available. If the threat was greater, additional men were summoned through the ward headmen. And if the threat was very large, additional forces were drawn from allied towns in the surrounding area.

Beyond greater numbers, the Aztecs also had a fully professional corps of soldiers, the result of a formal educational system. Initially, the Aztecs offered formal military training only to the elite, but within two decades of their emergence as an independent power, King Moteuczomah Ilhuicamina instituted training for all males. This was offered through two separate types of schools, one primarily for nobles and the other primarily for commoners.[22] The nobles' school trained the Aztecs' political and military leaders, primarily the sons of the upper nobility, some lower nobility, but also commoners who were to become priests. Nobles' school training was rigorous, covering the intellectual aspects of Aztec life as well as the military arts. The sons of nobles and warriors were held to be more inclined toward the warrior's life than others, and they probably did excel, for they were also apprenticed to members of the military orders. The commoners' schools, located in each of the city's wards, were responsible for educating all the youths therein between the ages of fifteen and twenty years. The intellectual training was less rigorous, but each commoners' school had a staff of accomplished veteran soldiers who trained the youths in military skills. Youths from both schools accompanied the army on its campaigns to teach them about battle, usually as burden bearers. When they reached the age of twenty, those who wanted to become warriors went to war under the protection of a veteran.

Military success and advancement were achieved primarily by taking captives, for which there were both honors and material rewards.[23] Repeated failure ended an aspirant's career. Each captured enemy led to greater honors and higher rank until, after taking four captives, the soldier became a veteran warrior. For taking more than four captives, honors varied according to the ferocity of the captive. A successful soldier could become a captain and could even achieve the highest ranks of general and commanding general, just below the king, who was the commander in chief.

There were also eagle and jaguar military orders composed of seasoned noble warriors. Noble status alone was insufficient for membership: entry depended upon military prowess in taking more than four captives in battle and commoners could also join if they achieved meritocratic noble status. Ranking above the eagle and jaguar military orders were two other military orders—the Shorn Ones and the Otomies. Of these two higher status orders, the Shorn Ones ranked above the Otomies, and entry required even more captives and brave deeds.

In addition to individual ranks, the Aztec army was organized into hierarchical units. The smallest tactical unit consisted of four or five soldiers under the command of a veteran. These were grouped into squads of perhaps twenty men, and larger units of one hundred, two hundred, and four hundred men, each with their own commanders. Reflecting Aztec social structure, these units were drawn from and organized by wards, which probably resulted in cohesive social, as well as military, units. Up to the level of the ward, each unit marched separately under its own battle standard. Above ward level, the army was organized by city with its banner (allied cities followed the same general organization), and the entire army marched under the standard of the king. Most veteran soldiers were dispersed throughout the army, but the military orders operated as separate units. The standard size of the entire army was 8,000 men,[24] with larger forces being composed of multiples or fractions of this number.

Because it incorporated both nobles and trained commoners, the large Aztec army demanded a system of communication and control, and this was composed of the leaders of the various units. Depending upon a hierarchy that was fundamental to meritocratic systems, the imperial command structure allowed the Aztecs to dictate unified battle plans in a way that confederacies could not. Even against populous allied city-states, the Aztec army enjoyed a significant advantage.

Although size, support, and army organization go a long way toward explaining why the Aztecs were so successful in war, they leave unanswered the question of why they engaged in it in the first place.[25] Part of the impetus for Aztec expansion came from their precarious ecological situation. The Aztecs settled on a barren island in the western portion of brackish Lake Texcoco that could not supply enough foodstuffs to maintain the Aztec population. Because of the simple lack of available land nearby, agricultural intensification was not an adequate solution. Instead, military expansion tied to an extractive tribute system was a compelling option. However, internal social dynamics also played a significant part in the decision to expand the empire. When the Aztecs overthrew the Tepanec empire, for the first time the king gained wealth and resources independent of the commoners or ward heads. As a result, the king and nobles emerged not just as a high status group, but as a wealthy class whose political interests could now be furthered largely without commoner hindrance.

Simultaneously, royal succession shifted away from patrilineal inheritance to selection from a small group of the upper nobility, based primarily on ability. The selection of a competent king was especially important to the nobles because his success enabled them to prosper. A poor king threatened the economic welfare of everyone, especially the nobility whose wealth flowed from tribute and tributary lands and thus depended directly on the king and imperial expansion. Any sustained military failure undermined the Aztecs' reputation and shrank the empire that relied on the perception of Aztec power, with a corresponding reduction in tribute goods and lands. Because these flowed disproportionately to the nobility, failure struck directly at their interests and their support for the king. Inactivity or continued failure threatened the king's position. Thus, the dual dynamics of social stratification and royal succession were major motivators of Aztec expansion and warfare.

Tenochtitlan itself was little threatened by the expansion of others even though it was not especially fortified. However, the city was defensible thanks to its island location: it was connected to the mainland by canoes[26] and a series of causeways that could be cut by removing wooden bridges that were built at intervals. The central precinct of the city, though not formally fortified, was enclosed by a wall and contained, among other buildings, the main arsenal, which was watched over day and night.

But more than its location, Tenochtitlan's protection lay in its great population and the extent of its empire. Although there were threats to Tenochtitlan in its early years, by the time of the Spanish conquest it had become the largest city in the Valley of Mexico by many magnitudes, and no single city had enough soldiers to threaten it. Moreover, because everything within several days' march was in the Aztec domain, no enemy could reliably draw logistical support from the hostile populace. Thus, rather than being fortified by wood and stone, Tenochtitlan's defenses lay primarily in its location and size, coupled with a wide buffer zone of tributary provinces.

The Aztecs did not build formal roads outside major centers, so mass movements were greatly impeded during the rainy season from late May to September, limiting their campaign season to the period between December and May when large armies could be mustered and provisioned after the agricultural season. Aztec armies traveled at roughly the same speed as others in Mesoamerica, but this was complicated by their large size. Restricted to double files on the extant roads, each 8,000-man army stretched out for over 12,000 meters on the trail, expanding an eight-hour march to thirteen for the entire army. To alleviate the problem even larger campaigns would cause, each 8,000-man army began its march on a separate day and often traveled to a common destination by different routes. But any major campaign consumed enormous time and, consequently, food supplies, yet without resupply, the Aztecs could carry only eight days' worth.

To meet their logistical requirements, the Aztecs harnessed their tribute system, demanding food from allied and previously subjugated towns along their march. Because each 8,000-man army consumed 7,600 kilograms of maize per day and an eight-day resupply required over 60,000 kg, this system demanded considerable forethought and planning. As part of its tributary obligation, each major town and its dependencies were required to grow food for the Aztec army, and two days prior to the army's departure, runners were sent to the ruler of each major town en route to tell him to gather the supplies. This gave the local ruler enough time to summon the maize from his outlying villages and have it waiting when the Aztec army arrived. Thus, the Aztec army traveled quickly throughout the expanse of its empire with an ease unrivaled in Mesoamerica.

Despite having overcome most previous logistical limitations, Aztec expansion still faced powerful opponents. Internal Aztec political dynamics placed a premium on success that translated into conquering easier prey. Difficult opponents were avoided unless they posed a particular threat and could not otherwise be coopted. Although individual city-states posed few difficulties for the Aztecs, confederacies and empires could be major obstacles. Whereas battles for single cities could be decisive, those for larger polities were not.

Empires could meet threats at their borders, so that even defeat meant only the loss of the immediate area: their armies could withdraw into the safety of their home territory, secure in the knowledge that without logistical support the Aztecs could not safely follow. As a consequence, the Aztecs could only chip away at the peripheries of empires rather than delivering decisive blows. To deal with such opponents, the Aztecs engaged these enemies in continual, though intermittent, combat in a long-term war of attrition that the numerically superior Aztecs were sure to win. With the enemy thus pinned down, the Aztecs then conquered the adjacent areas, gradually encircling the main opponents. Once this was accomplished, more conquests tightened the noose, reduced logistical support, cut off allies, and eliminated room to retreat until the enemy fell.

One way the Aztecs dealt with difficult opponents was through flower wars.[27] Flower wars appear ritual in nature and, indeed, these clashes took place at agreed-on times and places, with restricted forces, and captives were taken for sacrifice. However, the flower war was only one aspect of a larger military process. If successful, a flower war could persuade an opponent that the Aztecs were militarily superior, leading it to submit voluntarily. If that failed, however, the flower war escalated, increasing in participants and adding projectile weapons, effectively shifting from demonstrations of prowess to wars of attrition. Simultaneously and over decades, the Aztecs expanded around flower-war opponents, conquering the surrounding towns until they were cut off and isolated from support, reinforcements, and room to withdraw. Having thus significantly weakened their opponents, the Aztecs would crush them. The initiation of a ritualized war was an inexpensive way of inducing surrender but, if unsuccessful, it was only the initial stage of a long-term strategy culminating in conquest of difficult opponents at relatively low cost and without curtailing Aztec expansion elsewhere. In this fashion, the Aztecs could isolate and reduce major threats while freeing the bulk of their forces to carry out other conquests vital to the perpetuation of the ruling regime and hence assure the prosperity of the empire. However, sieges remained few and shortlived because they required too much food, despite improved logistical support. Starving out a distant city was not a feasible option. Yet the more sophisticated siege towers used at Chichen Itza had vanished, made unnecessary by the greater range of arrows. Fortified cities were now stormed with the help of ladders built on the spot, or they were not conquered at all.

Earlier empires had placed their military power in the service of the economy, notably trade, but this strategy changed with the Aztecs. Trade remained important and military power was still crucial in maintaining it but, for the first time in Mesoamerican history, superior logistical organization made the creation of a vast tribute empire feasible. However, having created such an empire, the Aztecs were also faced with the difficulty of maintaining it, and this they did through a variety of ties linking tributary centers to Tenochtitlan.

Under hegemonic control, tributaries became political dependents but their rulers typically remained in power, freeing the Aztecs from local administration. As long as they complied with Aztec wishes, retaining local rulers was more efficient than replacing them, but this system was constantly vulnerable to dissolution because it did not shift the loyalty of tributary populations from their traditional rulers to the Aztec kings. Local economic relations remained largely unchanged since Tenochtitlan sought to maintain healthy local economies so they could pay their new tributary obligations. Imperial tribute siphoned off wealth, which was a local net loss. But at the same time, Aztec demands stimulated local production and often expanded trade relationships to secure the goods required. Moreover, tributaries benefited in being linked into an Aztec-dominated trade network dispersing rare and elite goods throughout the empire. The Postclassic saw a general increase in exchange throughout Mesoamerica,[28] partly the result of greater population densities that both created a demand and eased travel, but even more due to Aztec expansion.

Religious integration was not a part of Aztec imperial ideology, however. Religious orthodoxy in Tenochtitlan solidly supported the state and its imperial aspirations, but wars were not primarily religiously motivated, although religious mandates were manipulated by the state in the furtherance of its aims. For example, the Aztec kings occasionally demanded labor and materials from both tributary and independent towns to help in the construction of temples to the gods; failure to comply meant war. The timing of these construction campaigns was decided by the king, not by priests or religious events, and the independent groups then targeted tended to be in the direct line of Aztec existing expansion, strongly indicating the primarily political use of religious mandates rather than the opposite. Moreover, there is no evidence of forced religious conversion of conquered towns, in that there was no spread of Aztec gods beyond the Valley of Mexico except with the occasional migration of Aztec populations. To the extent that Aztec expansion had an ideological basis, it lay in its economic benefits and in the social advancement that war offered commoner and noble soldiers alike.

One link that did connect the empire and its tributaries, albeit incompletely, was elite intermarriage.[29] Alliances between allies were commonly cemented through marriage in Mesoamerica, with the offspring uniting the two ruling lines. This was an effective system when the areas linked by marriage were close enough to be undergirded by economic ties as well. But elite intermarriage had little integrative effect between distant places because there was little economic interdependency. Instead, these marital ties created a political bond based on dependency and the weakening of local polities.

Marital alliances created political ties that helped determine who would be king in many areas of Mesoamerica. The likeliest successor was the king's son by his most politically important wife, not only because of his descent but also because of his external political backing. That is, there were usually several legitimate contenders, all descendants of kings; which one succeeded to the throne was based primarily on power and external political alliances. But the existing local network of alliances was disrupted by Aztec conquest. Even if the local king retained his throne, he often lacked the full political support he enjoyed previously. Unless all of that king's allies were incorporated into the Aztec empire at the same time so that there was no major alteration of existing relationships at that level, which typically did not happen, the previous pattern of alliances that was partly responsible for his succession was shattered. Now, some of his original allies were outside the Aztec empire and could no longer be called on for support. Some allies were part of the empire and relationships could continue with these, but they may well have had more important ties to other royal contenders. This radical change in the local political environment often left royal challengers with more intact political support than the reigning king, who would then depend on Aztec backing to remain in power. Thus, marital ties did in some sense unite a fragmented empire, but not by developing interdependent systems linked into a hierarchical political system. Rather, conquest undermined local power structures and the weakened regimes so they were now bound by marital ties as dependents of Tenochtitlan.[30]

Incorporation into the empire also shifted tributaries' attention from local to imperial enemies and had a major impact on their military organization. Military leadership varied among the Aztec dependencies, both by culture and by political complexity.[31] Military leaders were appointed based on merit in some towns, whereas others elected them.[32] Despite regional differences, many central Mexican armies shared common weapons and adopted others as they were disseminated by, or in advance of, the Aztecs. Commoner soldiers typically wore loincloths and primarily relied on weapons such as bows and slings, whereas the nobles and military leaders wore more elaborate armor, carried shock weapons, and frequently used battle standards and war suits.[33]

The military organization of many Mesoamerican societies shared superficial similarities with that of the Aztecs. However, their order of battle varied widely. Combat units were typically organized into squadrons[34] but, in some places, the youths went first, followed by the older warriors, then the leaders, the ruler and nobles, and the veteran warriors.[35] Other groups claimed to have fought without any order.[36] But no other regional army enjoyed the advantage of mass military training that created truly professional armies.

Although there was general access to Aztec tactics and weapons, whether and how these were incorporated depended on the size and composition of the recipient armies. One striking example of weapons incorporation is the use of the atlatl. In major conventional armies, as in Tlaxcallan, the atlatl was used as it was among the Aztecs—to disrupt opposing formations of conventional armies. But armies too small to train complementary weapons forces discontinued use of the atlatl, replacing it with the bow which, in these forces, was essentially a lower-class tool turned to military use.[37] As a result, atlatls remained important in large conventional armies but they were discarded elsewhere.

OAXACA

Among the areas where professional armies declined was the Valley of Oaxaca, which had politically fragmented during the Postclassic period,[38] due in part to Mixtec intrusions into the valley. The movement of Nochixtlan Valley settlements to hilltops as early as A.D. 900 indicates significant warfare in the Mixtec area.[39] This substantially declined during the Postclassic, although intervillage raiding persisted, and the Mixtecs also found themselves threatened by the Aztecs during the Late Postclassic.[40] The Mixtecs entered the Valley of Oaxaca during the Late Postclassic and probably conquered or pushed out some of the established Zapotec communities. Marital alliances may have eased their entry.[41]

Except for 8 Deer's (A.D. 1011–1063) tributary empire at Tututepec,[42] most Zapotec and Mixtec states of this period were neither large nor bureaucratized. Instead, the Valley of Oaxaca was organized into ten to twenty petty kingdoms of about eight thousand people each.[43] The shift from the centralized Monte Alban polity to a politically balkanized landscape was hastened by the Mixtec entry, which disrupted the homogeneity of the valley and introduced people not tied to the kin-based Zapotec ruling class.[44] However, it also fostered greater economic flexibility and competitiveness, leading to increasing valley-wide economic, though not political, integration.[45] Warfare was also decentralized and, though frequent, was largely a matter of hostilities between different rulers rather than between the two main ethnic groups.[46] Zapotecs fought Zapotecs, Mixtecs fought Mixtecs, Zapotecs fought Mixtecs and, despite the traditional Mixtec/Zapotec enmity, the two groups allied to resist Aztec expansion, though with limited success.[47]

There was some variation in arms and armor in the Oaxaca area. For example, the Mixes and Chontales only fought with lances that were three brazas long.[48] However, the Zapotecs and Mixtecs used essentially the same arms and armor: bows and arrows; obsidian-bladed broadswords; spears, some with obsidian blades and others fire-hardened; slings; clubs; and occasionally small axes. They may have also used atlatls, cotton armor, helmets, and shields made of wooden rods laid horizontal to each other for strength and tied with henequen thread, and sometimes covered with hide.[49]

All classes participated in war, but it was primarily an elite occupation.[50] Both Zapotec and Mixtec nobles were better equipped, with cotton armor, thrusting spears and feather standards being typical.[51] Common soldiers usually fought wearing only loincloths and carrying bows and arrows or slings and perhaps shields.[52] They typically fought in open areas by squadrons under leaders wearing feather standards and were often arrayed in two wings.[53] The Mixtecs had relied heavily on atlatls and darts earlier,[54] but these were replaced by bows and arrows in the Late Postclassic.

Political disturbances led to the erection of fortifications, the best known of which is the Mixtec site of Tepexi el Viejo, founded around A.D. 1300 near the border of the Cholula region.[55] Located on a hilltop, Tepexi el Viejo was naturally fortified by precipitous drops on three sides and by outer walls up to 1.5 meters thick and 15 meters high built of caliche bricks.[56] This was not a unique site, however; no town was secure from attack, and fortifications proliferated. Hilltop fortresses were common in the Late Postclassic Valley of Oaxaca, as at Mitla, typically on naturally defensible hilltops to which dry-masonry walls could be added.[57] Although most of these strongholds protected the population—or at least the political leadership—against an assault of limited duration, they could not sustain a large resident population for long. Some fortifications could, however. The best known is Guiengola, a Zapotec mountaintop administrative center of some 54,000 square meters to which fortifications were added.[58] Guiengola's outer walls were about 1.5 meters thick and averaged 3 meters high with only two known entrances.[59] The site contained two natural wells, both within the walls.[60] Besieged by the Aztecs in 1495, its successful defense laid the foundation for a political alliance between the Aztecs and Zapotecs.[61]

GULF COAST

Some Aztec tributaries, such as the Totonacs of the central Gulf coast, claimed no wars at all.[62] Part of this is attributable to the

Aztecs, who discouraged local wars by imposing governors on the tributary towns, enforced by Aztec garrisons in the region.[63] The Totonac towns were not completely untouched by warfare, however. They did have weapons, including bows and arrows, spears, broadswords, and stones,[64] although atlatls had dropped out in the absence of a large professional army.

The Huaxtec area north of the Totonacs was often ravaged by the Aztecs. Possibly because of their historic connections with the Toltecs, the Huaxtecs had used the short sword, but this weapon was discontinued by the Late Postclassic.[65] Although the Huaxtecs still possessed military orders and used cotton armor and round shields, bows and arrows had become their principle weapons, with axes (possibly primarily tools) and broadswords used on rare occasions.[66]

Despite considerable success, some areas relatively close to Tenochtitlan were neither conquered nor coopted by the Aztecs. One factor that limited Aztec expansion was the social complexity of the groups subject to their encroachment. Beyond Mesoamerica proper were many nomadic and seminomadic groups that were generically labeled Chichimecs, the Mesoamerican equivalent of barbarians.[67] Despite several sorties into the north, this area and its peoples were never brought under Aztec domination because they lacked both fixed assets that could be threatened or seized by a conventional army and a political organization that could be coopted. The Chichimecs fought with great skill and daring, clad only in loincloths and armed with bows and arrows.[68] The simplicity of their social organization and their paucity of material possessions lent themselves well to hit-and-run guerrilla tactics against which conventional armies were ill suited. Consequently, Aztec expansion effectively stopped at the northern boundary of Mesoamerica.

Limits on expansion were not restricted entirely to areas beyond Mesoamerica. Within central Mexico, another area unconquered by the Aztecs was the region inhabited by the relatively uncivilized Yopes.[69] United primarily by language, the Yopes lacked a centralized political system, but, excelling with the bow and arrow, they engaged in constant internecine warfare.[70] They, too, lacked the social mechanisms to permit the sort of indirect rule typical of the Aztec empire. But elsewhere in Mesoamerica, only powerful political opponents and the friction of distance limited Aztec expansion. However, other groups that were suitable for conquest nevertheless remained independent through force of arms. The two major powers confronting the Aztecs in central Mexico were the Tlaxcallan confederacy and the Tarascan empire.

TLAXCALLAN AND ALLIES

The Tlaxcallan confederacy was made up of Nahuatl-speaking city-states in central Mexico that individually were too weak to resist the Aztecs. Thus, these cities and kingdoms joined shifting alliances, variously including Tlaxcallan, Cholula, Huexotzingo, Atlixco, and Tliliuhqui-Tepec.[71] Unlike some of their other adversaries, these and other powerful polities, such as the kingdom of Metztitlan,[72] fought wars the same way as the Aztecs.

These polities used the full complement of Mesoamerican weapons, including bows and arrows, atlatls and darts, slings, clubs, spears, and broadswords; as well as shields and cotton armor.[73] Battles were signaled by trumpets, whistles, and drums, and soldiers were grouped in squadrons of approximately a hundred men each, led by unit commanders wearing feather battle standards.[74] Conventional battles opened with a projectile barrage before the armies closed for hand-to-hand combat.[75] As members of stratified societies similar to that of the Aztecs, commoners wore only loincloths, while nobles donned cotton armor and feather suits suggestive of military orders supported by the formal training received by the sons of the nobility.[76] But there was apparently little formal training of commoners, who probably comprised the bulk of the army and relied more heavily on bows and arrows and slings than did the Aztecs. However, the Tlaxcaltecs were already faced with Aztec power and had been encircled by the time of the Spanish conquest.

TARASCANS

The Tarascan empire, perhaps the most powerful group facing the Aztecs, had not yet been forced as far onto the defensive.[77] Located on the shore of Lake Patzcuaro, their capital, Tzintzuntzan,[78] held only 25,000–30,000 people,[79] yet the Tarascans forged a multiethnic empire that occupied most of the present state of Michoacan and part of Jalisco, and incorporated Tarascan, Otomí, and Nahuatl speakers.[80]

Like most states in Mesoamerica, Tarascan society was divided into upper nobility, lower nobility, and commoners, who were all ruled by a king selected from the previous king's sons and approved by the other nobles.[81] The empire was divided into four parts, each with its own lord, and with a king-appointed (or approved) leader in each village.[82]

Much of the mechanics and underlying strategy of Tarascan warfare was similar to, though less sophisticated than, that of the Aztecs. Despite differences, the Tarascan empire was organized very similarly to the Aztecs' hegemonic system. The Tarascan king reputedly appointed the rulers of each town, apparently validating existing succession practices, but he bound these lords more closely to the empire through marriages to his sisters and daughters.[83] When the king died, the lords selected a successor from the king's relatives who then led a raid for captives before he could be crowned.[84]

Tarascan arms typically included bows and arrows, quivers, broadswords, clubs one and two varas long, and slings, as well as cotton armor and cane shields as wide as four-to-five palmas, some of which were covered with hides.[85] This equipment was not evenly distributed, but varied by location and by the class and experience of the soldiers. The veteran soldiers who led villages and wards carried broadswords or clubs and wore cotton armor, although a strong breastplate of tightly woven maguey threads was also worn in some places.[86] Veterans and nobles also wore feathered war suits, while the commoners were typically unarmored and carried only bows and arrows.[87]

Although most areas of Mesoamerica had access to the major Mesoamerican arms and armor, an undoubtedly underreported supply had to be imported. For example, in the Patzcuaro area, where cotton was not grown, some of the soldiers wore maguey-fiber armor. Maguey was not preferred because cotton yielded a shorter, springy fiber that produced a thick, resilient fabric in contrast to maguey's longer, straighter fiber that, while strong, was heavy and not as absorbent.[88] The use of maguey armor in Patzcuaro may partly be attributed to import costs or Aztec interdiction, which would have made the material more expensive, limiting it to the upper classes.[89]

Tarascan soldiers, including subject ethnic groups,[90] were summoned to the capital and then dispatched on wars after the feast of Hanziuánsquaro.[91] The men carried their own food and arms on the march but were also resupplied by villages en route.[92] The soldiers of each town or ward were led under their own standards by a veteran and under the overall command of the general chosen by the king.[93] The soldiers were arrayed for battle with the veterans from Tzintzuntzan in front. The army was organized into squadrons of four hundred men each which could be divided so that most could hide to lure the enemy into an ambush, or deployed to encircle the town for the attack.[94] Adult captives were taken back to Tzintzuntzan for sacrifice; children were enslaved.[95] Whatever additional motives lay behind the total destruction of enemy towns, one was psychological: the Tarascans sought to intimidate others into joining their empire by a ruthless show of force rather than having to resort to armed conquest.[96]

There are no descriptions of Tarascan battles against conventional forces although they won one major victory against the Aztecs and fought another to a draw. Nevertheless, the Tarascans were not a major military power: they had a relatively small population and made little provision for the specialized military training of commoners. Most Tarascan soldiers were unarmored and fought with bows and arrows, and only the elite used armor and shock weapons, yet their heavy reliance on archery gave the army great defensive strength.[97] Their offensive capability, however, was considerably less formidable because they lacked large numbers of hand-to-hand combatants, hence the absence of the atlatl. The relatively dense population in and around Lake Patzcuaro gave the Tarascans an advantage over most of the adjacent peoples and they successfully forged an empire from the surrounding groups. Nevertheless, Tarascan control was seriously limited, so the king settled whole towns of both Tarascans and ethnic minorities in turbulent border areas to prevent encroachment, and these towns typically paid their tribute in war service.[98]

The Tarascans forged an expansionary empire. However, the best documented Tarascan incursion was an unsuccessful attack on the town of Xiquipilco north of the Valley of Toluca.[99] Further expansion toward the east was thwarted by the Aztecs' preemptive conquest of the area and the offensive weakness of too few hand-to-hand elite soldiers.[100] At the same time, however, their heavy reliance on archers gave them a decisive edge in defending their own territory, where they had ample ammunition and a favorable logistical situation. Moreover, the Tarascans could fall back and pick off the Aztecs, who had to husband the limited number of arrows they could bring with them. Scavenging Tarascan arrows to shoot back was only a partial solution, for many would have been broken, and the Aztecs had proportionately fewer archers in any case.[101] These tactical advantages, coupled with the strategic advantage of operating within a large hinterland that denied aggressors logistical support, combined to thwart Aztec thrusts deep in Tarascan territory.[102]

Nevertheless, the Aztecs remained a real threat and, to counter them, the Tarascans built a series of fortifications on the major routes from Aztec-allied areas.[103] Unlike a territorial empire, however, these fortifications were locally manned, often by ethnic minorities, and were designed to give early warning of Aztec incursions and slow their advance rather than to block them. Moreover, the Tarascans controlled their empire hegemonically and adopted this semiterritorial border strategy only in the face of a superior expansionistic empire. Fortifications were effective against direct incursions and the Aztecs responded in kind, building counter fortifications. But the Aztecs' main thrust bypassed these defenses, expanding around Tarascan territory and conquering and incorporating surrounding groups, presumably intending to strangle the Tarascans—a long-term process cut short by the Spanish conquest.

THE MAYA AREA

The Aztecs had made some inroads in the Maya area, especially along the Pacific coast and adjacent mountain areas of Chiapas and Guatemala. There were also Aztecs garrisoned at Xicalanco and Cimatlan[104] poised to thrust into Yucatan when Cortés's arrival cut this short. Although few, if any, Maya polities posed significant military obstacles to Aztec expansion, most had remained independent because of their great distance from Tenochtitlan.

The Toltecs introduced a meritocratic military system at Chichen Itza, and although this eroded the traditional powers and perquisites of the indigenous nobility, most of the Maya soldiers suitable for incorporation into the Itza army were largely nobles, at least initially. As the Maya nobles rose to higher positions in Itza society and as the Itza themselves were absorbed into the larger Maya society, traditional Maya ruling lineages sought to regain their lost privileges. Itza society was increasingly dominated by Maya kin groups until it was overthrown in A.D. 1221 by Mayapan, a hundred kilometers west of Chichen Itza, which became the new dominant center.[105] Economic and internal political difficulties undoubtedly weakened Chichen Itza, but, as a smaller center, Mayapan could not have fielded a large enough army to conquer it. Instead, the Cocom lineage of Mayapan was helped in its overthrow of Chichen Itza by mercenaries. Mayapan sought a return to the older, aristocratic social system. However, overthrowing Chichen Itza demanded a large army, but using a meritocratic system that would have been able to muster enough men would also have undermined their attempted reversion to aristocracy. Their only feasible alternative was to employ outsiders. These would swell their armies but without disrupting their social system because they were not a part of it and would presumably leave after the war. Moreover, these Mexican mercenaries brought the bow and arrow.[106]

Archery gave the Cocom several advantages over the Itza. First, bows and arrows markedly increased their firepower. Arrows do not go farther than slingstones, but the latter rely on impact for effect whereas arrows rely on penetration.[107] Arrows are also lighter than slingstones, so more can be carried and, though more fragile, they are probably easier to retrieve and reuse than stones, especially against Chichen Itza when only the Cocom and their allies had bows. But the greatest advantage of bow-and-arrow use was that archers could be densely packed, permitting more concentrated fire.

At the same time, quilted cotton armor became more prominent in this region.[108] Its earlier absence from the Maya lowlands is not attributable solely to climatic factors: rather, armor was generally unnecessary in Maya warfare and, though the Toltecs used it, it was not critical to their combat style, which stressed speed and mobility. But armor was adopted at this time, probably as a defense against the newly introduced arrow.

These new arms and armor shifted the balance of power against Chichen Itza by providing an effective weapon that required less training than most existing weapons. Archers could strike from a distance while remaining beyond the effective reach of conventional forces, increasing dependencies' ability to resist and disrupting established political patterns and regional alliances.

Following the overthrow of Chichen Itza, a confederation of Cocom, Xiu, and Canul lineages at Mayapan ruled a fairly unified Yucatan for 250 years through a combination of local alliances and the help of soldiers from central Mexico.[109] Mayapan did not grow to the enormous size one might expect for Chichen Itza's successor because its power did not result from size, but from new military technology and combatants.[110] However, this technology spread throughout the Maya lowlands, and because of its small size Mayapan was more vulnerable to attack than previous capitals and was thus fortified. But the economics of fortifications also demanded that the city be as dense as possible to minimize the size of the enclosing wall, to reduce both construction costs and the area each defender had to guard.

In Postclassic fashion, Mayapan built a stone wall but no encircling moat. The wall was 1.5 to 2.5 meters high and 9.1 kilometers long, encompassing an area of 4.2 square kilometers, and was pierced by seven major and five minor gateways.[111] A second wall enclosed the ceremonial precinct.[112] Adding to its defenses, nearly all the houses had boundary walls averaging .6 to 1 meter high, with some as high as 1.5

meters, and twenty-six cenotes within the city walls made the city resistant to sieges.[113]

Mayapan's overthrow of Chichen Itza was not merely a shift in regime, but a change in the entire system of power. This discontinuity is evident in Mayapan's architecture, which broke with the Chichen Itza style.[114] Mayapan also revived the stela cult, with old-style Maya glyphs[115] signaling a return to pre-Toltec social forms, shifting away from the meritocratic system of the Toltecs and toward the traditional aristocratic system of the Maya.[116]

There had been too many social and technological changes for a return to the earlier Maya social structure to succeed, however. Military power no longer remained a primarily noble skill and the introduction of bows and arrows accelerated this social equalization. Moreover, the Mexicans who aided the Cocom revolt against Chichen Itza remained in Mayapan, but because they were accompanied by their women, they were neither absorbed into the Maya population nor did they fit within the traditional social system.

The dominance of the ruling elites was reduced with the spread of bows and arrows that were mastered by all social classes just as the spatial dominance of Mayapan was diminished by archery's spread to other cities. Mayapan's diminished control was expressed in lineage competition. About A.D. 1440, Ah Xupan, from the Xiu lineage, revolted, attacked, and sacked Mayapan, which was abandoned around A.D. 1450, and northern Yucatan disintegrated into sixteen independent and frequently warring states, some centered on fortified cities.[117] Most prominent among these was Tulum, which was allied with Mayapan in some fashion and shared its internal organization, and architectural and ceramic styles.[118] Tulum arose around A.D. 1200 and was a major port and trading center during the Postclassic.[119] Located on a forty-foot limestone cliff six hundred feet from the Caribbean, Tulum's most salient feature was a massive wall averaging twenty feet thick and ten to fifteen feet high, varying with the terrain.[120]

The longest portion of the three-sided Great Wall ran 1,266 feet with two arms of roughly 550 feet ending roughly 40 feet from the cliff, totaling 2,352 feet.[121] A second, smaller wall, 1,240 feet long, eleven feet wide, and six feet high extended from the southwest corner of the Great Wall to the sea, enclosing an additional triangular space.[122] Constructed of unshaped stones and without mortar, the Great Wall had a series of staircases permitting defenders to climb it.[123] The two inland corners held small buildings that may have been

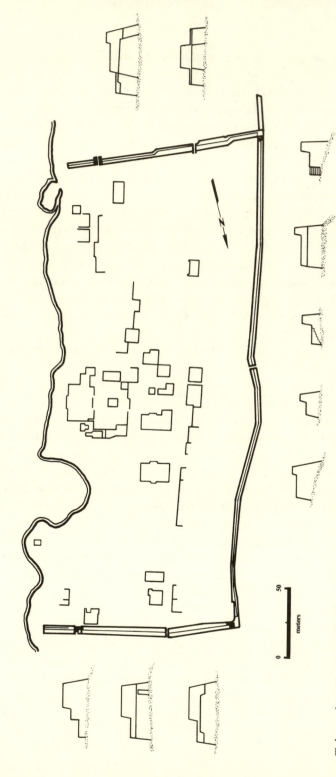

Tulum, showing Great Wall and simplified interior structures. Wall cross-sections not to scale. (Adapted from Hardoy 1973 and Lothrop 1924.)

guard or watch towers, and a cenote within the walls reduced the city's vulnerability to siege.[124]

As with all fortifications, the most vulnerable points were the five gateways, but the passages were narrow, had spaces for defenders, and forced those entering to stoop, placing them at a significant disadvantage.[125] Keeping small and easily defended gates in the walls significantly reduced the fortifications' main weakness, but larger entryways were required for the day-to-day needs of Tulum's populace. These were provided by openings at both ends of the Great Wall, beginning forty feet from the edge of the cliff. Because these openings would have rendered the wall useless, they were probably closed by some perishable material, such as a wooden stockade.[126] Nevertheless, these would have been the weakest points in the city's defenses and logical points of attack. Their placement at the ends forced attackers to funnel their soldiers along the cliff edges, limiting the primary areas to be defended and allowing the defenders' fire to be effectively concentrated. Seaside settlements were particularly vulnerable, and so the nearby peninsular site of Xelha was also fortified.[127]

At the time of the Conquest, northern Yucatan had a population well over 300,000 divided into three social classes: nobles, commoners, and slaves.[128] The nobles occupied all important political and military offices and were the most important merchants, dominating the slave and maritime trades.[129] Commoners made up the majority and held lesser occupations, although wealth increased one's social status; slaves, consisting of debtors, criminals, and commoner captives, occupied the bottom of the social hierarchy.[130] Nevertheless, this system was characterized by a high degree of social and geographic mobility among commoners.[131]

No single polity or society had achieved dominance in northern Yucatan by the time of the Spanish conquest; instead, there were three types of governments operating in the various provinces.[132] One was ruled by a lineally or collaterally hereditary local chief of his own town.[133] His duties included declaring war and exacting military service from his dependent towns. A second type of province was ruled by members of the same name group.[134] The third type of political organization was simply a loose alliance of independent towns.[135] These governmental forms reflect variations on provincial organization, but town organization was similar in all three systems, with the local chief serving as administrative, judicial, and military head. This position could be inherited from father or brother, or it was appointed by the hereditary ruler to whom the local chief was subject as well as the local council, drawn from the leaders of the town's subdivisions.[136]

Late Postclassic Maya weapons were similar to those used elsewhere in Mesoamerica and included a medium-length bow strung with a henequen cord and two quivers of reed arrows with flint or bone points.[137] Atlatls and darts about the size of a man with fire-hardened points were also used, as were both fire-hardened and flint-pointed spears as long as two brazas.[138] Slings were used, as was a wooden broadsword with inset flint blades introduced from central Mexico.[139] Hafted flint knives and axes, usually of stone but sometimes of copper, were also used, although in an ancillary way.[140]

Armor consisted of round shields faced with leather over two layers of wooden rods set at right angles to each other.[141] Quilted cotton jackets that fell to the mid-thigh were also worn, and a few of the lords and captains wore wooden helmets.[142] Elite soldiers wore elaborate garb while commoners wore only loincloths and body paint.[143] Despite the implications of a relatively full complement of arms and armor among the Maya of northern Yucatan, the distribution of armor was in fact highly skewed. Most commoners used bows and some used slings. Spears were not common, atlatls even less so, and broadswords least common, being primarily restricted to nobles and professionals who had access to the necessary training. Similarly, armor and helmets were restricted to the nobility although shields were widely used by commoners as well.

The local chief commanded the men of his town in battle, but a separate war leader who held the position for three years was in charge of formulating strategy.[144] All males owed war service, but paid professionals did most of the fighting.[145] They were paid partly by the war commander and partly by the town, but only in time of war. Other men were also called for service only if there were not enough professionals.[146]

Battles usually took place on forest trails between provinces. Surprise attacks were most common, although not at night, and guards made them difficult. Scouts were sent in front of the army,[147] and an attack was signaled by shouting and whistling, beating turtle-shell drums, and blowing conch-shell trumpets. If the war leader was killed or turned back, everyone returned. Whoever killed an enemy removed his jawbone and cleaned it to wear as an armlet; killing an enemy war leader or local chief was especially honored.[148] Prisoners were bound to a wooden collar or yoke with a rope attached and were taken to their captors' home town, the commoners to be enslaved but the nobles to be sacrificed.[149]

The people of Motul, Yucatan, described their battle formation as composed of two wings made up of the commoners, with a squadron in the middle surrounding their lord and the main priest.[150] Wars were usually short and restricted to October, December, and January, when there was no rain and agricultural demands were low.[151] Moreover, they were fought primarily to acquire slaves, to settle debts or injustices, or to defend their lands rather than for conquest.[152] To defend against enemy raids, some towns were fortified, mostly with wooden constructions such as the ramparts of Champoton and Uaymil.[153] Barricades made of dry stones and timber palisades were also built at strategic points on main roads and were often camouflaged.[154]

The defensive situation was similar among the highland Maya. During the Early Postclassic, open and undefended settlements, such as Zacualpa, were abandoned and relocated to defensible hilltops that were artificially leveled and sometimes fortified, although most of the population continued to live in the surrounding area and used these fortified sites only as refuges in times of war.[155] There was also a shift to more secular control during the period of Mexican migrations into the area, bringing central Mexican, Mixteca-Puebla, and Gulf coast affiliations.[156] Prior to A.D. 1200, there were two or three waves of small, militarized bands that invaded the Quiche region, beginning at the end of the Classic and continuing into the Early Postclassic.[157] These migrants were from the same basic group as the Itza at Chichen Itza, though they were probably originally from the Veracruz/Tabasco Gulf coast region, and spoke Nahua and perhaps Chontal-Maya.[158] Some of these groups claimed Toltec origins, which is supported by the introduction of Toltec-style architecture.[159]

Once in the Quiche area, the invaders established a hilltop defensive center at Hacavitz, then expanded their tribute-based conquest state, settling in strategic, agriculturally productive, warm river basins that were key interchanges for salt, feathers, gems, and obsidian.[160] Combat prowess was no doubt crucial to the invaders' success, but they were advantaged in that the original inhabitants were relatively peaceful and militarily unprepared. Because the invaders were almost exclusively men, they posed a serious military threat to indigenous settlements four or five times their size. Without fortifications, such towns were ill-matched against the professional soldiers of the invaders because even their larger population could have fielded only comparably sized forces of men.[161] The invaders did not bring women with them, but married into the local populations and ultimately adopted the Quiche language.[162] Most of the indigenous Maya were conquered within two generations, the entire Quiche area by A.D. 1350. The Quiche conquest state emerged as the largest ever in highland Guatemala, incorporating roughly 26,000 square kilometers and 1,000,000 inhabitants at its peak in A.D. 1450.[163]

At the time of the Spanish conquest, the highland Maya used a wide range of weapons, including stone-bladed broadswords, fire-hardened spears, slings, and bows and arrows with stone points, as well as shields made of woven wooden rods backed with cotton, and armor of double cotton backstitched with thick cord.[164] This was not the original Quiche complement of weapons, however, for bows and arrows were not used until A.D. 1350, when they displaced the atlatl.[165]

The Quiche social hierarchy was similar to that of other meritocratic societies and was divided into kings, nobles, commoners, and slaves. Nobles achieved their status through patrilineal descent from the original invaders who claimed Toltec heritage.[166] The king was a member of the upper nobility (members of the king's patriline) and was selected from among the previous king's sons, brothers, or close kinsmen.[167] Below the nobles were commoners, mostly from the conquered groups; and below the commoners were slaves, who were war captives, criminals, and the poor who had sold themselves. Late in Quiche history, a serflike class also emerged as expansion created a landless class of conquered people.[168]

The Quiche political system was theoretically a tripartite, and later a quadripartite, confederacy, but it was dominated by the king of Utatlan, whose power derived from his ability as a military leader.[169] Each region of the Quiche confederacy was ruled by a noble who headed the dominant lineage.[170] The ruler or a close relative led that settlement's army, supplemented by soldiers from outlying towns.[171] Most soldiers were commoners, and wars were thus conducted primarily from January through April because the rainy season in the Maya highlands ran from April or May to October, producing forty to eighty inches of rain during that period. Also, labor demands for agriculture were heaviest from May, the main planting season, through December, the main harvest.[172]

The Quiches could reportedly raise an army of 8,000 to 16,000 men, organized into military units marching under their own banners.[173] Nobles and rulers wore feather standards on their heads designed like eagles, jaguars, parrots, and other birds, and cotton armor was also decorated with animals.[174] In battle, the Quiche placed the archers on the right, sometimes with shieldmen in front, or to the rear and the slingers and atlatlists on the left, with the spearmen at the wings.[175]

The Quiches' military success has been attributed to their lineage system,[176] but this did not inevitably result in societal unity.[177] Despite the importance of lineages as territorial units from which military units were organized, the real dynamic in Quiche military success was the rewards that participation offered the individual. As in other meritocratic societies, the Quiche permitted some social mobility; through excellence in war, commoners could achieve meritocratic noble status, which was a great motivator. Among other things, these meritocratic nobles could attend military councils, take up crafts, and exercise greater authority over vassals.[178]

Despite the Quiches' successful domination of a large area, the allied Cakchiquels broke away around 1470 and founded a rival capital at the fortified hilltop site of Iximche.[179] Without Cakchiquel support, Quiche expansion faltered. Utatlan was later dominated by the Aztecs and when the Spaniards arrived, the Cakchiquels were the ascendant power.[180] Despite the military dominance of the Quiche and Cakchiquels, indigenous Maya groups also waged war, primarily to take land and secure tribute, and were organized and armed in a fashion similar to the Quiches, although the Tzutujils apparently did not permit social mobility for accomplished warriors.[181] Even with their seasoned armies, neither they nor the other Mesoamerican empires and city-states were prepared for the arrival of the Spaniards.

SPANISH CONQUEST

Cortés and his men landed in Veracruz in 1519 and, despite clashes with various native groups on their trek toward the Aztec capital and an alliance with the powerful Tlaxcaltecs, the Spaniards and their allies were allowed to enter Tenochtitlan peacefully.[182] A series of circumstances combined to make this possible. The Spaniards did not present themselves as a hostile force, they arrived prior to the harvest when Aztec soldiers were unavailable and unprepared for war, and they were largely oblivious to the perception of Aztec power that was so effective against other Mesoamerican groups. Once in the capital, the Spaniards seized the Aztec king, Moteuczomah Xocoyotl. The battle for Tenochtitlan did not truly begin until he was killed and the Spaniards were driven out, retreating to Tlaxcallan.

The Spaniards brought new military technologies against the Aztecs, including sailing ships, cannons, guns, crossbows, and steel swords and lances, as well as horses and war dogs. However, the Spaniards were so few—numbering in the hundreds—and the Aztecs so adaptable in their responses that most of this technology was not decisive. For example, Spanish lancers were devastating against open formations, so the Aztecs quickly shifted tactics, avoiding open battlefields and shifting to broken terrain where horses could not be used with effect. The Aztecs also relied on passive defenses, such as camouflaged pits and sharpened stakes which effectively curtailed the use of horses.

But the Aztec political disruption was devastating. Moteuczomah's successor, Cuitlahuah, died within eighty days of smallpox introduced by the Spaniards and was succeeded, in turn, by Cuauhtemoc. Customarily, each king began his reign with a show of force to ensure the continued allegiance of his tributaries, but Cuitlahuah had died too soon and Cuauhtemoc, hobbled by the presence of Spaniards, adopted a conciliatory approach. Safe in Tlaxcallan, the Spaniards also made overtures to Aztec tributaries in the east. Disgruntlement at the Aztecs and the Spaniards' military ability drew many former tributaries into the Spanish camp, especially because the Aztecs could not send enough troops to every town to ward off incursions. As defections continued, Aztec forces shrank until they could no longer send an adequate force against the Spaniards without leaving Tenochtitlan vulnerable to attack in the increasingly unstable political situation. The Aztecs adopted a defensive stance, withdrawing to Tenochtitlan to await the erosion of Spanish logistical and political support.

Cortés began a series of campaigns against Aztec allies around the lake shore, most of which the Aztecs countered by using canoe-borne troops. With the disruption of planting and its food supplies dwindling, the Spanish blockaded the city with thirteen sailing ships until famine and pestilence brought Tenochtitlan to its knees. Although Spanish weapons technology did play a role, Cortés's victory was more political than military, disrupting Aztec allegiances through the death of two kings and augmenting his own meager forces with tens of thousands of native troops while undercutting the Aztecs. With the ultimate fall of Tenochtitlan, the rest of Mesoamerica fell to Spanish domination with little or no struggle.

Resistance to Spanish domination continued for decades and even centuries among peripheral groups in the deserts to the north of Mesoamerica and hidden in the jungles to the south. Nevertheless, the Spanish conquest effectively brought large-scale indigenous warfare to an end.

CHAPTER 10

Patterns of Warfare in Mesoamerica

Varying in degree, militarism accompanies the rise of the state. Partly tied to the emergence of new leaders exercising unprecedented powers, militarism is frequently expressed in monuments glorifying conquests and captives, and especially the leaders responsible. The rise of the state typically involves coopting nearby settlements and further expansion often follows, affecting states and non-states alike. But militarism alone is an inadequate explanation of imperial expansion. The mere fact of cultural complexity breeds demand for more and different goods, spurring greater military expansion to meet those demands.

Economic integration of large areas spanning many polities does not necessarily entail political domination by one side; such an exchange system can also be sustained peacefully, based on mutual benefit. But even peaceful exchange requires a military to prevent depredations aimed at traders by groups outside the system or bandits within it. While such exchange systems range from trade imposed by a political power to commerce arising from mutual desire for goods without imperial domination, a military presence is required if it is to be secure. Whether for the relatively benign purpose of creating a secure trading area or for the more probable goal of gaining control over external resources deemed essential to the state, much Mesoamerican trade was political, occurring under the protection of imperial domination.

ARMS AND ECONOMY

There is no economy in isolation, no system of exchanges restrained solely by supply and demand. There are only political economies in which power dictates the conditions of exchange. This does not mean that exchanges are totally divorced from the logic of supply and demand, but rather that the conditions of supply and demand are determined by political structures. These can be harsh, ranging from the imposition of conditions and values of trade on those too weak to resist, to the relatively benign, such as creating secure and favorable trading regions.

No matter how benign, imperial expansion does not create equally favorable conditions for both sides of the exchange. Both trading partners have access to the other's goods, but this cannot be equal, or the empire would be seriously disadvantaged by its added burden of distance and the military protection required to secure the trade. The empire must receive a disproportional benefit and typically does so in the form of unequal exchange exercised through its control of the mechanisms of trade and guaranteed by its military superiority, leaving its trade partners dependent and vulnerable.

Economics may well be a major motive behind imperial expansion, but it is the military that makes empire possible, just as it underwrites a tribute system within the state. Moreover, the relationship between economics and military expansion is frequently reciprocal, with the potential for adequate gain determining whether or not the expansion is undertaken. But the potential profitability of a trade relationship does not determine whether political expansion will take place; military capability does.

Whether a polity expands depends on a variety of factors, including the political context. The known Mesoamerican empires were not inevitable developments. They all expanded into what was essentially an imperial vacuum, facing opposition only from city-states or minor empires. It was this vacant potential that permitted their expansion: they may have remained unimportant polities had there been other major empires. Even without competing polities, the expansion of Mesoamerican empires was also constrained by an ecology that limited the growth of centers capable of producing large, centralized armies, although the social environment played an interconnected and larger role. Aristocratic societies limited military participation to the nobility, producing small armies versed in tactics suited to their military and social aims, but with little expansionist potential. They were wholly inadequate against

Altar 4, La Venta, showing a ruler with a bound captive. (Courtesy of the Instituto Nacional de Antropológico e Historia, Mexico)

Late Postclassic Matlatzinca slingers. (Med. Palat. 220, c. 133; courtesy of the Biblioteca Medicea Laurenziana, Florence)

Drawing of Monument C, Tres Zapotes, showing combat with clubs, spears, and rectangular shield. (From Bernal 1969)

Elaborately carved Postclassic atlatl from Oaxaca, decorated with atlatl- and dart-bearing warriors (specimen 10/8724). (Courtesy of the National Museum of The American Indian/Smithsonian Institution)

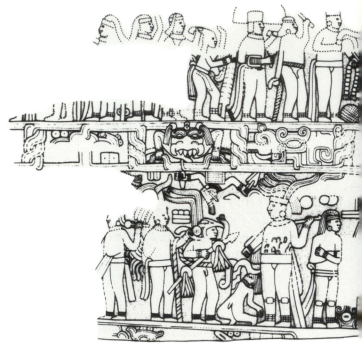

Drawing of building column sculpture 1, El Tajín, showing
warriors wearing suits, bearing atlatls, and holding captives.
(From Kampen 1972: fig. 32a. Courtesy of the University
of Florida Press)

Roll-out of Early Classic vessel 10E-52/2 from Deposit 50, Tikal, showing
Teotihuacan warriors carrying atlatls and darts, approaching a Maya temple.
(Courtesy of the Tikal Project, University Museum, University of Pennsylvania)

Stela 4, Monte Alban, showing an elite warrior symbolizing the conquest of a town by thrusting a spear into its nameglyph. (Courtesy of the Instituto Nacional de Antropología e Historia, Mexico)

Stela Lisa, depicting the presence of unarmed Teotihuacan notables at Monte Alban. (Courtesy of the Museo Nacional de Antropología, Mexico)

Aztec broadsword (macuahuitl) and thrusting spear (tepoztopilli), from an engraving of the Armería Real collection in Madrid. These weapons were destroyed in a fire in the nineteenth century. (From Jubinal 1846: plate 9)

Drawing of right side of Stela 31, Tikal, showing one of two flanking warriors, with a Teotihuacan helmet, shield, and atlatl. (From Jones and Satterthwaite l982. Courtesy of the Tikal Project, University Museum, University of Pennsylvania)

Detail of mural 3, Tepantitla, Patio 9, Teotihuacan, showing a warrior with an atlatl. (Courtesy of the Museo Nacional de Antropología, Mexico)

Room 2, south wall, Bonampak, showing a battle scene depicting clubs, spears, and flexible shields; reconstruction by Antonio Tejeda. (Photograph by Hillel Burger, courtesy of the Peabody Museum of Archaeology and Ethnology, Harvard University)

Drawing of lintel 26, structure 23, Yaxchilan, showing King Shield-Jaguar holding a knife and being presented with his helmet and flexible shield by his wife, Lady Xoc; A.D. 726. (From Graham and von Euw 1977, ©1977 by the President and Fellows of Harvard College. Courtesy of the Peabody Museum of Archaeology and Ethnology, Harvard University)

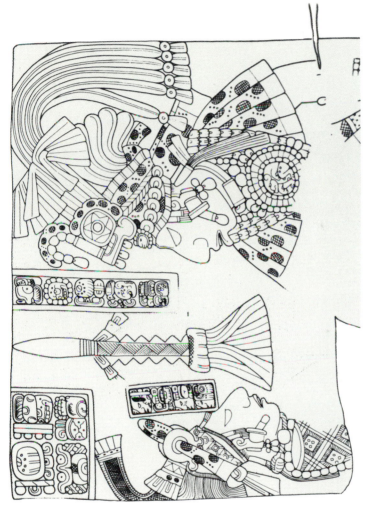

Drawing of lintel 41, structure 42, Yaxchilan, showing King Bird-Jaguar and his wife, Lady 6-Sky-Ahau, separated by a thrusting spear with cutting surfaces of inset blades below the main point; A.D. 755. (From Graham 1979, ©1979 by the President and Fellows of Harvard College. Courtesy of the Peabody Museum of Archaeology and Ethnology, Harvard University)

Portion of the battle mural at Cacaxtla, showing warriors bearing round fringed shields, knives, and atlatls and darts, as well as wounds caused by slashing weapons. (Courtesy of the Instituto Nacional de Antropología e Historia, Mexico)

Detail of right side of a carved warrior at Tollan holding an atlatl. (Courtesy of the Instituto Nacional de Antropología e Historia, Mexico)

Detail of left side of a carved warrior at Tollan holding darts and short sword. (Courtesy of the Instituto Nacional de Antropología e Historia, Mexico)

Mural on south wall of the Upper Temple of the Jaguars, Chichen Itza, showing an attack on a pyramid and two siege towers. (Drawing by Adele Breton; courtesy of the City of Bristol Museum and Art Gallery)

Nezahualcoyotl, king of Texcoco, dressed in a feather tunic and kilt over cotton armor, helmet, shield, and broadsword. (Codex Ixtlilxochitl 106r; courtesy of the Bibliothèque Nationale, Paris)

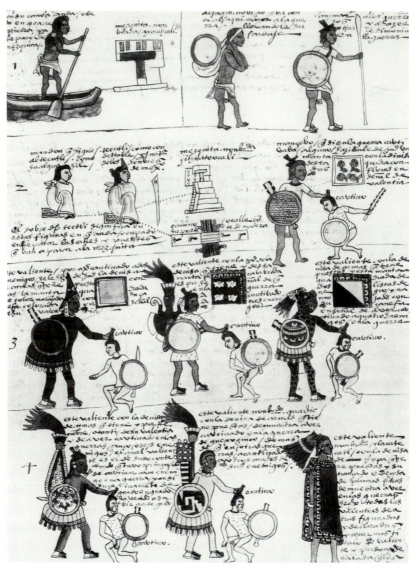

Top row: priests in canoe, carrying goods, and going to war. Second row: lord, youth taking a captive. Third row: warriors taking second, third, and fourth captives, and the attire achieved by these achievements. Fourth row: two knights and a general. (Codex Mendoza, MS Arch. Seld. A 1, fol. 64; courtesy of the Bodleian Library, University of Oxford)

large empires, except when distance or other intervening variables limited any confrontation. By contrast, meritocratic societies offered social
mobility through military success and could raise large, well-trained,
and highly motivated armies, giving them enormous imperial potential.

Hegemonic states and empires predominated in Mesoamerica, but the
differences between these and territorial systems can be overstated. Both
systems relied on intimidation, at least within the immediate hinterlands
that defined their states, and both should be seen as modes of control
rather than concrete entities. Part of the difference between the two
systems was scale. All of the major empires enjoyed disproportionally
large populations and social systems that enabled them to mobilize exceptionally large armies and control vast areas hegemonically beyond a more
directly controlled inner zone. Smaller cities exercised similar hegemonic
control, but over correspondingly small areas, especially where their
social organization discouraged large armies. However, territorial systems were able to take advantage of fortifications to multiply the ability
of relatively small forces to control greater areas. Nevertheless, this was a
limited capability that produced relatively small empires—as in the case
of Monte Alban—and then only where terrain features permitted large
areas to be sealed off by a minimal investment in defensive works. Elsewhere, fortifications could only secure the city proper, although they
could increase its ability to dominate the surrounding area hegemonically. For disproportionally large centers, however, extensive fortifications were wasteful; they are a rational investment only if the center is
weak relative to other external powers. Political systems based on fortified centers are inherently limited in size and power and, though the
defenses add to their strength, such systems are static and cannot adjust
rapidly to new threats.

Beyond each city's immediate hinterland, control becomes more difficult and is sustainable either hegemonically through overwhelming size
and the reliance on compliant local rulers or territorially through the
judicious placement of fortifications, terrain permitting. The latter strategy is more restricted spatially, and has relatively rigid boundaries defined primarily by defensible terrain features. However, this system does
permit relatively fixed hierarchical relationships with subject towns and
a dependable and predictable flow of tribute. Hegemonic systems, by
contrast, depend upon their perceived ability to project force and are
areas of politically and militarily enforced social interaction. But as
such, their areas fluctuate more than those of territorial empires and
their limits are archaeologically difficult to ascertain.

The foregoing are modes of control, and, while topography does affect what is possible, which system is implemented and how depends on internal social organization. A persistent concern of political organizations is maintaining internal control, which generally depends on how goods and benefits are distributed. All states have classes and all those in Mesoamerica had hereditary nobles occupying the upper rungs of society and benefiting accordingly. How rigidly class barriers were maintained varied. Aristocratic societies had insurmountable class barriers while meritocratic societies permitted some mobility, even into the ranks of the nobility.

This mobility was achieved primarily through military success, which led to a greater distribution of rewards throughout society and encouraged broader-based participation in warfare. By contrast, aristocratic societies concentrated wealth and power in the hands of the nobility, offering little incentive for broad-based participation in war and sacrificing greater military potential in favor of preserving its noble-dominated social hierarchy.[1] As a result, meritocratic societies were able to mobilize a much greater proportion of their populace for military service than could aristocratic societies—as much as ten times larger. The more closed a society was to social mobility, the less likely it was to arm and train commoners in elite warfare, the smaller the army it could muster, and the more limited the area it could dominate. In short, the large Mesoamerican empires were all meritocratic, capable of mobilizing large numbers of well trained and motivated soldiers; but because of their limited armies, aristocratic societies remained only city-states except where favorable terrain permitted fortified borders and allowed the creation of territorial empires even with limited forces. Although I am reluctant to place any of these political systems into an evolutionary sequence or developmental hierarchy, aristocratic societies arose first in Mesoamerica, and also where secondary states were stimulated.[2] That is, aristocratic societies are likely to result where imperial contact stimulates or intensifies existing social stratification by channeling goods through the indigenous elite or by supporting them militarily.

Although supernatural sanctions supported all state societies in Mesoamerica, this was probably greater in the case of aristocratic societies than meritocratic ones. To whatever extent social and political legitimacy was tied to divine right, meritocratic societies could count on the added support generated by a somewhat more equitable distribution of benefits and the potential for social mobility, especially when the economy was expanding. Lacking these, aristocratic societies probably relied more heavily on the twin supports of supernatural sanction and armed control.

Aristocratic societies generally lacked the military preponderance needed to ensure hegemonic control over large, competing cities and polities. Nor could they functionally integrate them into the parent polity without threatening their own social order. Placing a local noble on the throne of the conquered city would strike at the legitimacy of the conquered ruling elite and, by implication, the conquering elite as well, risking internal unrest. But even more important, political integration would require the delegation of authority to other nobles who would have at least some presumptive claim to rule, effectively granting them a significant power base too distant to ensure continued control from or fidelity to the parent city. Royal intermarriage or the grafting of noble lineages onto emergent centers provided some control but this was fleeting at best.

Aristocratic hegemonic societies lacked the resources either to conquer large areas or to integrate regions beyond their own urban hinterlands. Territorial systems, however, were able to realize these goals, for they effectively cordoned off their empires from outside influence, leaving local elites little alternative to being incorporated into a larger, regional social hierarchy dominated by the capital. Aristocratic territorial societies lacked the resources for extensive expansion, but because they subordinated without disrupting the local elite hierarchies, the cost of integrating the area cordoned off was relatively low. Lower manpower availability did, however, limit the size of such systems.

Meritocratic hegemonic empires had the greatest territorial expanse, but a considerable degree of delegated authority already existed, as evidenced by the army chain of command, so that further delegation represented a lesser threat in societies already open to broader participation by commoners and nobles alike. With their greater resources in men and materiel and their superior organization, such empires could integrate conquered areas, and this was often done in areas adjacent to the capital, but not farther afield. There, the local hierarchies were generally retained intact. Marital alliances sometimes played a role in this, but here they functioned differently than in aristocratic systems. Empires could back up such newly created marital relationships with force if need be, but typically they did not. Imperial conquest proved that incorporated groups were vulnerable, and this also altered the local ruler's political support by severing its ties to areas yet unconquered. These changes often left other nobles, who also had legitimate claims to the throne, with more support, forcing local rulers to cleave more strongly to the empire or risk overthrow. Thus, meritocratic hegemonic empires could integrate large areas but typically ruled indirectly, retaining local rulers who had good reason to support the system. This produced a more loosely integrated empire, but one that cost little to maintain, freeing imperial resources for further conquest. Nevertheless, if the empire weakened it could no longer guarantee support to all its dependencies. And where local kings' rule depended more on imperial than local support, disruptions and succession struggles could result. Because they depended on the perception of power rather than structural reorganization, once they began to decline, hegemonic empires crumbled rapidly.

By focusing on modes of control (hegemonic versus territorial) and the degree of social participation and mobility (aristocratic versus meritocratic), four ideal societal types emerge: aristocratic hegemonic, aristocratic territorial, meritocratic hegemonic, and meritocratic territorial. These also have spatial correlations: aristocratic-hegemonic societies, such as the Classic Maya, were relatively small and offered little possibility of social mobility; aristocratic-territorial societies, such as Monte Alban, likewise offered little possibility of social mobility but could possess a moderate area delimited by defensive architecture; meritocratic-hegemonic societies, such as Teotihuacan, the Toltecs, and the Aztecs, offered significant social mobility and were responsible for the largest areas; meritocratic-territorial societies are a logical possibility, but the inherent inefficiency of fortifying a region that can be more efficiently controlled from a large, dominant center limits its occurrence to an early stage of a meritocratic hegemonic empire, at best.

Although social organization dictated much about how these societies were structured, ecology also played an important role. As a basic state form, aristocratic societies were viable throughout Mesoamerica, but areas that discouraged large-scale polities, such as the lowland jungles, had virtually no other type of organization. There is nothing inherent in meritocratic societies that would restrict their spatial distribution, but because they could mobilize large forces, they were particularly suited to expansion and the creation of large polities. Consequently, they were typically located in open areas, especially in the Mexican highlands, where control of distant cities was easier. In any case, aristocratic societies had a limited ability to expand and consolidate gains, and then only against other aristocratic societies. Meritocratic societies, by contrast, were well suited to expansion and consolidation. Against other meritocratic societies, size, resources, location, and political alliances undoubtedly dictated the victor, but they enjoyed an almost auto-matic superiority over aristocratic societies.

HISTORICAL TRENDS

Mesoamerican history was not simply a succession of imperial rises and falls or oscillations between social types. Rather, the nature of Mesoamerican empires changed over time. Despite fluctuations and regional variations, there was an overall increase in population through-out Mesoamerica, giving each successive empire access to larger popula-tions which, in turn, permitted larger armies that propelled expansion. For instance, Teotihuacan's direct influence extended into both high-land and lowland Maya zones, but its imperial core, over which it exercised great control, was relatively small, extending only into Morelos. By contrast, the Aztec empire was larger and had better logisti-cal support and, although still centralized, had better control over its tributaries over a much wider area. The Aztec "core" extended into Oaxaca before becoming noticeably less cohesive.

Population growth affected both empires and city-states but it worked more to the advantage of the former because empires were structured to accommodate, and even encourage, population growth, and this permitted a military complexity and sophistication unattain-able by smaller groups. Sometimes innovations in weaponry gave one polity an advantage over others.[3] For example, a projectile advantage enabled relatively small groups to enter new territories because of the tactical advantages this gave them over opposing forces, whereas shock weapons required greater numbers for effect. Weapons were not simply accepted as they appeared. Which weapons were used was largely deter-mined by the nature of that society.[4] As empires grew, they increasingly relied on specialized training of both nobles and commoners unmatched by smaller polities. Moreover, greater size and superior training encour-aged the use of organized combat units, if not formations, and comple-mentary, reinforcing weapons systems that were simply unattainable by smaller polities. The degree of training also fostered the use of special-ized weapons rather than tools turned to martial use.

Specialized weapons requiring formal training were adopted by both aristocratic and meritocratic societies, but egalitarian weapons were not. If a weapon could be used by anyone, either because it required little training or because it adapted existing utilitarian skills, it was less likely to be adopted by aristocratic societies because it was a threat since it promised to place more power in the hands of commoners. This apparently happened at Mayapan. Driven to accept bows and arrows in order to overthrow Chichen Itza, the adoption of this egalitarian weapon undermined the existing social hierarchy and, ultimately, Mayapan's aristocratic rule. That same weapon in a meritocratic society, however, is not socially destabilizing, and in fact increases the power of the empire. At least in Mesoamerica, the major weapons innovations arose in or were quickly adopted by meritocratic societies, giving them an additional advantage. However, not all weapons opened societies: some increased the differences embodied in stratification. An innovation requiring additional training would increase class distance in aristocratic, though not necessarily in meritocratic, societies. Expense, as in the case of cotton armor, favored the elite, but neither greater cost nor specialized training had this effect where arms and armor were controlled by the state, as was typical of meritocratic societies, rather than by individuals, as was the case in aristocratic societies.

Examining types and complexes of weapons can be highly instructive, but a simple analysis based on the presence or absence of certain weapons is often misleading since their role and effectiveness changes over time. This was the case with the atlatl, for example. In Teotihuacan times, it was a specialized weapon and required other troops wielding spears in an integrated system, so only large armies employed it, while smaller ones favored thrusting spears that could be used individually. By Toltec times, however, atlatls and short swords were used in combination, atlatls during the charge and swords thereafter because both were light enough to be carried simultaneously, eliminating the need for specialized troops and effectively doubling their combat strength. It was at this time that atlatls spread throughout lesser armies, such as the Maya, because they were used by elite troops in conjunction with shock weapons. By Aztec times, the superior bow and arrow replaced atlatls in the hands of everyone except the elite troops, who still used them during the charge before shifting to shock weapons. Thus, the atlatl remained important in armies with large elite components but was displaced by the bow in small armies.

One very prominent secular change was the increase in the size and deadliness of the Mesoamerican kill zone—the area between armies in which the opposing weapons were effective. Early in Mesoamerican warfare, the kill zone was relatively small. Because weapons were only deadly close in, opposing forces could avoid contact and, when battle was joined, combatants could close quickly, limiting the effectiveness of projectiles to the time required to reach the opposing forces. But as projectiles, from thrown spears and stones to atlatl darts to bows and arrows, increased their range, the kill zones expanded, making projectiles more important, which in turn made armor more important.

Changes in arms and armor throughout Mesoamerican history presumably reflected increasing effectiveness. However, as a function of weapons and tactics, this assertion rests primarily on common sense; some support can nevertheless be garnered by assessing these changes in terms of the weapons alone. In preindustrial warfare generally, puncture wounds were more serious than cutting or slashing wounds because the former could not be treated as effectively and were likelier to involve internal bleeding.[5] Also, wounds to the abdomen caused the highest mortality rate, closely followed by penetrating chest wounds.[6]

Olmec crushers and slings relied on massive impact for effect, stimulating the development of shields and helmets. Thrusting spears added lethal punctures to the inventory of primary wounds, as did atlatls, and both weapons spurred the adoption of body armor to protect the vulnerable trunk. The short sword combined the slash and puncture of the thrusting spear, and bows and arrows added yet more punctures and increased the distance at which they were effective. Lastly, the broadsword sacrificed punctures for the greater reach of Mesoamerica's paramount slasher. Despite the clear evolution of increasingly efficient weaponry, Aztec arms were illmatched against Spanish armor. Ironically, the crushers of earlier eras would have been more effective against the steel that shielded the Spaniards from Aztec blades.

Fortifications were vulnerable to large armies, and so they were important when they were so far from major centers that large forces could not reach them or when they were built between, rather than during, the heyday of major empires.[7] The size of opposing forces, rather than decisive weapons, undermined fortifications. However, weapons shifts did have collateral consequences for their ability to control their hinterlands. The introduction of new weapons, especially those such as bows and arrows that can be used by large numbers of commoners, does not necessarily shift the balance of power against a fortified center; however, it does tilt it in the dependencies' favor. Even though a fortified city may remain secure from attack, once these new weapons spread, it is more difficult for the center to control its hinterland. The threat is not to the fortified center itself but to the control of its political and economic sustaining area.

Distance remained a major problem in exercising imperial control,

but population growth ensured better logistical support. Sizable populations permitted larger bodies of troops to be sent farther and longer,
changing the overall balance of cost and effectiveness. This shifted the
exploitation of imperial areas from the hands of small groups, such as
traders who were cut off for long periods, to larger bodies of colonists
who could establish better control of distant areas, to indirect control
from centers that could dispatch directives and troops at will.

This growing ability to rule from the center also changed the relationship of the rulers to the ruled. Control through colonization causes
significant changes when imperial administrators try to shift the colonized area to an organizational model patterned on their own because
they are better equipped to exercise control through such a structure.
Moreover, the ability to effect such changes is more important the less
control the empires can exert from the center. Thus, Teotihuacan imposed considerable changes in the areas it colonized. The Aztecs, by
contrast, did not need local colonies to exercise control in most cases.
They were significantly more powerful than Teotihuacan and could
exercise control over their tributaries from the center, and, as deliberate
policy, they effected few changes in dominated areas.

One political tie that spanned the three thousand years of Mesoamerican civilization was marital alliances between ruling elites. However,
what they meant and how they functioned changed over time, relative
once again to the ability to project force. The earliest marital ties were
not militarily supported, so they largely conferred prestige and perhaps
preferential trading privileges. Without the ability to project force over
long distances, marital alliances were ultimately ineffectual for integrating large areas. By Aztec times, however, imperial marital ties could
keep or put someone in power in the dependent polity, because the force
needed to support them could be projected at great distances. Marital
ties shifted from little more than affirmations of allegiance backed up
only by prestige and mutual benefit, to political tools for indirect rule
through now dependent local kings.

In general, each successive empire had greater flexibility in how it
dealt with subjugated regions, and although the military was usually in
service to the economy in Mesoamerica, it was not the prime mover.
This, however, had changed by the rise of the Aztecs. Trade remained
important, but for the first time, logistics and easy transport allowed
tribute to flow from distant areas and permitted troops to ensure that it
did. To the extent this was possible earlier, it happened only with elite
goods, but Aztec power brought that capability to a basic level.

CYCLICAL PATTERNS

There are numerous major secular trends in the history of Mesoamerica, but the cyclical patterns are even more interesting analytically. Perhaps the most prominent cyclical pattern in Mesoamerica is imperial expansion and contraction, rise and collapse. Imperial expansion is readily explicable, but not so contraction or collapse. There are both external and internal theories that purport to explain collapse. External theories focus on such factors as invasions, diseases, and ecological disasters, all of which have been implicated in various collapses. But relying on external factors to explain collapse is relatively unsatisfactory, in that the prime movers are stochastic in nature and generally unpredictable. Internal theories are more satisfying because they typically identify the cause of collapse as some structural element that then allows prediction.

A recent theory sees collapse as an inherent condition of empires: with time, the cost of empire increases as a function of specialization and complexity until it exceeds the benefits of investment.[8] Once this happens, collapse is almost inevitable. Although the rising costs of empire are implicated, collapse is a relational problem, a condition of the international system rather than one inherent in the internal structure of empires. Expansion exacts a cost; however, any increased expense is not inherent in the imperial structure but is the result of the empire's changing relationship to foreign groups, both incorporated and independent. Expansion involves a wide range of cultural contacts that stimulate local developments and thus alters the conditions under which expansion was first initiated. Imperially stimulated local developments, especially social stratification, occur faster than change in the empire itself, making contacted societies more competitive vis-à-vis the empire, at least locally, and raising the costs of control, irrespective of any growth in administration.

Even small competitors cut into the economic flow, forcing the empire to divert resources to control them. Moreover, whether it is successful in controlling trade or not, the empire suffers loss because that same economic flow is achieved only at a greater cost, effectively reducing the return. These competitors do not directly challenge empires' inner zones where control is more direct, but they can challenge imperial outer zones that are integrated more tenuously and hegemonically. The consequences of this are especially pronounced at the periphery where costs are already highest; the empire ultimately adjusts to this additional expense by contracting. The empire requires a constant or expanding economic base, but if it fails to maintain this, shortfalls are either extracted from commoner citizens or from those areas of the empire still fully controlled. Increased extraction from nearer areas can compensate for distant losses, but this also shifts the benefit-to-burden ratio, increasing the likelihood of rebellion, and making this an unsuitable long-term strategy. In short, empires acquire their access to distant goods under relatively easy circumstances, but once a challenge is mounted by competitors who have become more sophisticated through contact, it is much more difficult for the empire to maintain what it has than it was to seize it initially. Increased administrative costs also reduce imperial competitiveness, but such increases are not inherent in empires, although they do become necessary once the effects of cultural stimulation increases the competitiveness of local groups. The cause of collapse is not an inherently increasing administrative expense or some other flaw inherent in imperial structure, but the shift in relational advantage from the empire to the colonized areas. Moreover, these costs increase with both societal complexity and with distance from the imperial capital.

Because costs increase with distance, imperial expansion does not add resources in direct proportion to its size. What can be extracted is directly related to transportation efficiency, which was very low in Mesoamerica. Only exotic goods could be brought from more distant areas. Small empires minimize distance costs and run considerably less risk of collapse than do large empires, yet there need be no significant difference in internal structure. However, the size of the empire's internal structure changes as its domestic organization expands to take advantage of the incorporated areas. These areas become both suppliers of goods for the center and markets for the latter's wares. Thus, when the empire shrinks this does not simply diminish an unearned surplus but causes significant internal disruption. Moreover, an empire cannot easily stabilize itself at a smaller scale, even at the same size it was at an earlier stage, because its imperial hinterland is not simply an area to be milked. Even though that smaller domain could have been maintained had the empire initially expanded to that size and no farther, domestic factors make restabilizing the system at a smaller size difficult.

Withdrawal from these now too-expensive areas could reduce the empire's costs and allow it to reorganize on a smaller scale more in keeping with economic and military realities. Despite the immediate benefits in rationalizing the empire, withdrawing to a smaller area causes internal difficulties. Internal production and trade develop to a scale appropriate to the empire's maximum expansion and cannot easily be reduced to a size appropriate to that the empire reaches following contraction. Because the capital's production and export sectors expand to meet imperial demands, these workers are now dislocated. The impact of imperial contraction was not limited to the commoner classes, but also meant the loss of distant sources of exotic goods, undermining noble status and causing internal competition and social disruption. The development of contact societies is inevitable, as is the rising cost of control, but imperial contraction is not. To avoid this fate, the empire must remain more efficient than its colonies, but superior organization is the only alternative to technological innovations, and the advantage of either erodes as they are adapted and adopted by contacted groups.

As the empire collapses, local states each expand to their fullest natural, though limited, expanse; and eventually another empire begins when one adopts an organizational style that permits administration over larger and larger areas and has the means (possibly new military technology, organization, or tactics) to carry out such an expansion.

In a seminal article, Paul Kirchhoff[9] laid out the basic definition of Mesoamerica as a culture area, founded largely on the widespread adoption of shared culture traits. However, this presents a static view of Mesoamerica. Many of the key traits, such as broadswords, existed no earlier than the fifteenth century, others, such as ballcourts with rings, date back six or seven hundred years, and still others are of undetermined antiquity. In earlier eras, the degree of integration over this broad expanse was significantly less. Rather than a condition, the Mesoamerican culture area was an ongoing process in which traits spread or were rebuffed and areas economically and politically integrated and disintegrated.

Imperial expansion was crucial in creating Mesoamerica as a region. As a culture area, Mesoamerica was a series of overlays—religious, economic, technological, political, and social—resulting from interregional contacts that were often military. A society's ability to enforce its decisions defines the rise and demise of cultures and the spatial and temporal extent of their influence. Moreover, the military enables one group to conquer, colonize, and expropriate the wealth of another, and contact between societies stimulates the spread of ideas, goods, and cultural development. Without the intrusion of various groups into distant areas, the unifying spread of ideas, deities, technologies, and arts would have occurred slowly, haltingly, or not at all. This continual contact explains the adoption of common cultural patterns throughout Mesoamerica, not autochthonous development or the postulation of a pan-Mesoamerican tradition. The vagaries of military expansion fostered the uneven but relatively integrated region defined as Mesoamerica.

Four major expansions—Olmec, Teotihuacano, Toltec, and Aztec, the last three imperial—were crucial in creating the Mesoamerican culture area. Although they varied in their initial rise, each society enjoyed a military advantage in their expansions. First, each was numerically superior. Second, they enjoyed superior weaponry. Third, they enjoyed an organizational advantage, combining their superiority in numbers with both old and new weapons to create larger and better trained, armored, and integrated armies. Fourth, they enjoyed a logistical advantage based first on better foodstuffs—retoasted tortillas—and later on a superior organization that permitted resupply en route. Behind each lay an economy dependent on the export of manufactured goods and the import of exotic goods and raw materials.

Conquests were easiest and most numerous when they were asymmetrical, pitting opponents with major differences in power, military equipment, tactics, and organization. When and where conflicts were relatively symmetrical, little political expansion occurred. Asymmetry was a major factor in imperial expansion, but when this was significantly reduced or eliminated, imperial contraction was the result. To a large extent, these general asymmetrical patterns drove expansion and contraction, producing an imperial cycle in Mesoamerica: a rise to local dominance, expansion, stimulated development in the periphery, and, finally, contraction.

Various idiosyncratic factors doubtless contributed to the rise of a given center to local dominance, but all three empires shared a meritocratic social organization that accounts for much of their expansion into aristocratically organized areas. But despite their expansionist advantage, meritocratic organizations are not as stable as aristocratic ones, which, not having expanded, do not suffer the disruptions of contraction.

The impact of destabilization varies: something that destabilizes the highest organizational level may not destabilize the next level down. City-states are likelier to survive even when empires collapse. City-states can collapse, and probably have the same essential cycles of expansion, contraction, and demise as empires, but the two systems differ in scale, so their growth cycles therefore differ in length.[10] The larger the system, the shorter the cycle because expansion engenders competition that the empire must, but ultimately cannot, meet or overcome in order to maintain the internal social and economic changes resulting from its own expansion. Smaller systems, such as city-states, are typically more successful in assimilating encapsulated populations because, being culturally and ethnically more homogeneous, they usually expand to control a symbiotic city/hinterland area, resulting in internal social and economic systems appropriate to their size. Thus, there are few pressures from competing elites that would favor contraction and cause internal dislocations.

A society based on broadening participation in its reward structure must increase the goods available, hence the vulnerability of meritocratic systems to collapse. The alternative is to close off avenues of advancement, essentially shifting toward a more aristocratic system with its greater stability. Evidence of increasing social stratification at Teotihuacan during its declining years may reflect such an attempt.[11] The Aztecs may also have experienced a similar, though milder, shift. Tizoc sought to erect more rigid class barriers, but given the massive influx of professionally trained commoner warriors, this attempt may have been as significant as his poor military record in bringing about his assassination.[12] The attempt to raise class barriers was apparently repeated two kings later by Moteuczomah. The seeds of destruction are inherent in empires, not as a result of a dynamic internal to imperial organization, but of the inevitable stimulation of competitors at the periphery that fundamentally and adversely alter the costs and benefits of imperial expansion.

These theoretical considerations are not played out with such neatness in the real world, however. The imperial cycle was borne out by the Olmecs and Teotihuacanos, who experienced full expansion and contraction and underwent a natural process of decay. In theory, draconian control could have maintained an empire, but power is subject to the limits of distance, fraying at the edges until the system's fabric is rent. In the case of the Toltecs and Aztecs, however, this cycle was not completed. Instead, both were destroyed at the center by forces extraneous to their imperial structures. The Toltecs expanded successfully but their capital was exposed from the north and ecological changes left them open to hostile incursions, fragmenting their empire before it showed any signs of contraction. A similar fate befell the Aztecs, whose capital was conquered by invaders from outside the Mesoamerican system, leaving the empire without centralized control. During the expansion phase, Mesoamerican empires worked well, but they could not prevail indefinitely against the local developments their very existence promoted.

Notes

CHAPTER 1: THE APPROACH TO WAR

1. The importance of warfare has long been emphasized in military histories, but its importance has been increasingly acknowledged in more general studies of society. See, for example, the recent works of Finer (1975), Giddens (1984:249–56; 1987:53–60, 103–16, 232–35), and Mann (1986:130–76, 231–98).

2. Yadin 1963, 1:1–2.

3. In stressing multisocietal contacts, I am drawing on World Systems theory and allied approaches (Bergesen 1980b:5–7; Bergesen and Schoenberg 1980:231–42; Chase-Dunn 1989:23–26; Davis, Kick, and Kiefer 1989:28; Wallerstein 1974; 1980:21–22; 1984:58). But see Schaeffer (1989b:1) and Thomas and Meyer (1984:466) and the allied approach of Wolf (1982). I am not adopting them wholesale because the Mesoamerican world system was not tied to capitalism in the sense adopted by that school and, despite their importance, neither economics nor class conflict lie at the base of all international relations (Finer 1973:89; Kennedy 1987:xxii–xxiii; Mann 1987:24, 219, 221–23, contra Schaeffer 1989b:2). I see the state as a meaningful actor with its own interests and goals rather than simply an ideological superstructure for an exploitive class-dominated economic system (Kennedy 1987:xxiii–xxiv; Kirby 1989:205; Krasner 1989:70; see Thomas and Meyer [1984:465–66] for a critique of the realist approach). Thus, the role of armies and state expansion requires explanation in its own right. Although I do see trade and exchange as driving forces behind political expansion, I see the locus of the expansion residing in particular types of social organization that offer managerial advantages and in unequal technology that permits this organizational advantage to be used to its fullest.

4. For an overview of theories of imperialism, see Mommsen (1980).

5. Doyle 1986:45. The following summary of theories of empires is also based on Doyle (1986:20–30).

6. This analysis derives largely from Cohen (1973).

7. Cohen 1973:242; Mann 1987:131–32.

8. Cohen 1973:236.

9. See Vencl (1984:121–22) on archaeology's relative neglect of warfare.

10. Dupuy 1984:6, 316; O'Connell 1989:7; Turney-High 1971:7–8; 1981: 135.

11. Cipolla 1965:144.

12. Creveld 1989:19; Dupuy 1984:6.

13. Andreski 1968:81; Cipolla 1965:144; Headrick 1981:3–12; Vayrynen 1989:110.

14. E.g., Lynn 1990. See Finer (1975:91–93) for European examples.

15. O'Connell 1989:34.

16. Finer 1975:90.

17. McNeill 1982:21; Seabury and Codevilla 1989:8, 29.

18. Creveld 1989:72; Jones 1987:182; O'Connell 1989:4.

19. See the examples of interpretations of ideology from works of art from Teotihuacan and Escuintla (Berlo 1983b) and among the lowland Maya (Schele and Miller 1986).

20. Andreski 1968:33.

21. Andreski 1968:85; O'Connell 1989:34.

22. Mann 1987:138; McNeill 1982:8.

23. See Mann (1987:539), Taagapura (1978a), and Tainter (1988:118–23).

24. Contra Boswell, Sweat, and Brueggemann (1989), Mesoamerican empires did not expand to pillage a defenseless periphery and then contract in the face of competitors in the core because such competition did not exist.

25. Similar cyclical dynamics have been noted elsewhere in the world. See, for example, Hart (1948) and Taagepera (1968, 1978a, 1978b, 1979). McNeill (1982:9) has focused explicitly on the military basis of political power.

CHAPTER 2: THE RISE OF WARFARE
IN MESOAMERICA

1. For most Mesoamerican prehistory, precise dates are unavailable. There are exceptions for dated monuments in the Maya area, for the events of the Late Postclassic for which we have written accounts, and for earlier periods where native codical information can be extrapolated backward (as in the case of the Mixtec codices). Nevertheless, few events can be precisely dated so the traditional system of classification will be used which groups general time periods into Formative (or Preclassic), Classic, and Postclassic. These terms do not denote absolute time periods, but developmental ones.

2. Stark 1981:364.

3. O'Connell 1989:25, 31; Stark 1981:353.

4. Boehm de Lameiras 1988:93; Sharer 1989a:4; Stark 1981:345, 353–59.

5. Gamble 1986:26; Stark 1981:363–64, 367–69.

6. Boehm de Lameiras 1988:94; O'Connell 1989:25–26.

7. MacNeish, Nelken-Terner, and Johnson 1967:55, 150–52. Bows and arrows did not exist in Mesoamerica at this time. However, only the projectile points are likely to survive in the archaeological record, and these are subject to various interpretations. Despite attempts to distinguish arrow from atlatl-dart points (Thomas 1978), it is difficult to do so in all cases (Corliss 1980). My assessment of the advent of bows and arrows is based not only on excavated points, but on their depiction in other cultural remains.

8. O'Connell 1989:25.

9. M. Coe 1981:124; Grove 1981a:376.

10. Campbell and Kaufman 1976:80; Diehl 1989b:18; Lowe 1989:39.

11. Bernal 1969:188.

12. Henderson 1979:89, 93.

13. Cobean, Coe, Perry, Turekian, and Kharkar 1971:670–71.

14. M. Coe 1968:110–11; Grove 1968:182–83.

15. Drennan 1984:29–36; Hassig 1985:24–34; 1986.

16. The state interpretation is supported by Bernal (1969:89), Michael Coe (1989:78; Coe and Diehl 1980, 2:147), Drucker (1981:30), and Henderson (1979:90–92), among others. The chiefdom theory is supported by Richard Diehl (Coe and Diehl 1980, 2:147; Diehl 1989d:27–30). See also the discussion by Haas (1982:184–92). For an overview of the differences between chiefdoms and states, see Fried (1967:109–242), Service (1975:14–15, 71–102), and Tainter (1988:24–28).

17. Henderson 1979:92.

18. Coe and Diehl 1980, 1:389; Diehl 1989d:24–26. See Webster (1976d) for a discussion of the suitability of theocracies in the emergence of states.

19. M. Coe 1968:86; Coe and Diehl 1980, 1:387.

20. Thought to depict rulers, each sculpture was destroyed—not wantonly, but systematically over periods of up to six hundred years—in characteristic ways: pits were laboriously bored into the giant heads, the faces on altar figures were cut off, and the stelae and statues were broken to decapitate the people commemorated (Grove 1981b:61–64). Not destroyed by outsiders, Grove (1984:73–74) suggests that this was apparently done by the Olmecs on the death of a ruler, possibly as a symbolic act to neutralize his power, and in one instance, a decapitated stone head was buried with a body in an elite grave. Recently, Porter (1989) has convincingly argued that the giant heads were recarved from the altars.

21. M. Coe 1968:47; 1981:139; 1989:77; Coe and Diehl 1980, 1:392; Lowe 1989:50.

22. Anderson 1978, 1:163. Whether the objects they are holding were actually weapons is not certain. One alternative is that they may be staffs of office.

23. Grove 1981b:61–64. See examples in Bernal (1969: plates 3, 5, 8–11, 13, 14) and Coe and Diehl (1980, 1:figs. 423–28, 443–44, 449). There is also an unusual piece of portable Olmec art that may depict a bound captive (Heizer 1972:74).

24. Coe and Diehl 1980, 2:149.

25. Creveld 1985:17–18.

26. Bernal 1969:88; Coe and Diehl 1980, 1:375, 390, 392.

27. Coe and Diehl 1980, 1:255; M. Coe 1981:128. For fire-hardening, see Cosner (1956) and Evans (1958). The lowland Olmec area lacks suitable stone—obsidian, flint, and chert—but obsidian was imported into the area as early as the Ojochi phase (1500–1350 B.C.) (M. Coe 1981:144), and obsidian blades were manufactured (Coe and Diehl 1980, 1:258). The same was true at other Isthmian sites at that time. For instance, there were no projectile points at the Guatemalan Pacific coastal site of La Victoria from 1500 to 300 B.C., despite compelling evidence that land mammals such as deer were hunted. Fire-hardened spears could have been used, but traps and snares are thought to be more likely (M. Coe 1961:115, 117).

28. M. Coe 1981:144.

29. M. Coe 1965b:764–65; Coe and Diehl 1980, 1:392. Stela C at Tres Zapotes shows shields and spears, though it may postdate the Olmec florescence (Heizer 1967:29; Stirling 1943:20).

A problematic scene is depicted in "The Processional" at Chalcatzingo. This has been interpreted as depicting divine or mythical scenes (Cook de Leonard 1967:57), agricultural rites (Grove 1968), sacrifice (Gay 1972:46), and as a captive scene (M. Coe 1965b:752; 1968:92). The implements held have been considered agricultural tools (Grove 1968), but clubs (M. Coe 1965b:752; 1968:92) or lances (Angulo V. 1987:142) are more likely. Maces also appear (Anderson 1978:158; M. Coe 1965b:764, 766; Stirling 1943:19).

Even more problematic are the so-called "knuckledusters." There are numerous examples of these hand-held devices in sculptures and they have been interpreted as weapons (M. Coe 1965b:764; Flannery 1968:80), but these knuckledusters are also found as decorative motifs—notably on either side of a facial mask (Benson 1971:7–8)—and may have been associated with the ballcourt (Benson 1971:22). None have been found archaeologically, suggesting that they were made of leather or wood and were probably not weapons.

30. The Olmecs did use atlatls, and there are two examples in the Bliss Collection at Dumbarton Oaks in Washington, D.C., one of jadeite (B-32.MJ) and the other of chloromycenite schist (B-33.OS). An atlatl is also depicted on Stela D at Tres Zapotes. Stirling (1943:14–15) claims that the stela is Olmec but acknowledges that the figures appear to be non-Olmec. However, M. Coe (1965b:764) denies that the stela is in bona fide Olmec style.

31. Finer 1975:92; Hogg 1968:25.

32. Creveld 1989:21. However, there is often a lag between the introduction of new weapons and the adoption of appropriate tactics (Dupuy 1984: 303–307).

33. Howard 1990:240; Otterbein 1970:44–49.

34. Later, as depicted in monuments at Tres Zapotes, rectangular shields, like those of the Early and Middle Classic, were used, but when these came into use is unknown.

35. M. Coe 1965b:764; Ekholm-Miller 1973:10–12; Navarrete 1974:6, 8, 12.

36. The relief carvings at Chalchuapa also show "helmets," though of a

slightly more elaborate version than those on the giant heads (Anderson 1978, 1:158).

37. Monument 19 and Stela 3 at La Venta show a figure wearing a head-dress that represents a jaguar head, with the person's face in the mouth (Drucker, Heizer, and Squier 1959:198–99). A painting in a cave at Oxtotitlan shows an Olmec figure with a large headdress and a bound captive (Grove 1970:29–30).

38. King 1979:267.

39. Although, as van Creveld (1989:137–39) notes, there are many forms of professionalism, I see professionalism occurring at the point that specialized training and the use of weapons without utilitarian functions are required. In the Old World, however, Ferrill (1985:11) sees the advent of professionalism as the point at which armies entered battle in formations under a commander.

40. E.g., see Bandelier (1880:98), Cook and Simpson (1948:25–26), and Dobyns (1983:175).

41. Jones 1987:630–34.

42. The data for central Mexico are too poor to assess the model's fit with much accuracy. The model I am using, the West stable population model level 3, at zero percent growth (Coale and Demeny 1966:126), is based on work in Peru where the data are better (N. D. Cook 1981). Because the Peruvian population most closely approximates that of central Mexico—socially, genetically, and epidemiologically—I am using it for that area, as I have done elsewhere (Hassig 1985:178–83; 1988:59–60).

43. The age of soldiers is unknown for most of the societies in question, although they were almost certainly males. The male population breaks down into the following percentages by age group:

age	%	age	%	age	%
0–1	3.35	25–29	8.43	55–59	3.27
1–4	9.74	30–34	7.64	60–64	2.40
5–9	10.84	35–39	6.82	65–69	1.58
10–14	10.31	40–44	5.95	70–74	0.89
15–19	9.82	45–49	5.06	75–80	0.40
20–24	9.18	50–54	4.17	80+	0.16

44. Coe and Diehl (1980, 1:143) estimate the probable regional population for San Lorenzo Tenochtitlan at 5,556, and put the actual resident population of the ceremonial center at 1,000 (Coe and Diehl 1980, 1:147). However, recent work at La Venta suggests a somewhat larger population in the surrounding area (Rust and Sharer 1988).

45. Bernal 1969:24.

46. Sanders and Price 1968:104.

47. Vivó Escoto 1964:200–203; West and Augelli 1976:40–42.

48. Coe and Diehl 1980, 1:19, 2:69.

49. Boletín 1940, 11:16; Borah and Cook 1963:90; Cuevas 1975:52–53; Archivo General de la Nación, Reales Cédulas Duplicadas 3-17-9. These same

documents were the basis for Aztec consumption estimates in Hassig 1988:63–64 and general Mesoamerican rates in Hassig 1985:19–21 where I estimated the caloric value at 3,800. Williams (1989:724) has recently challenged these figures as too high, suggesting instead 2,268 calories per day for light activity, 2,484 for moderate, and 2,916 for heavy, calculating each adult male at 54 kg. I continue to support my figures for several reasons. First, they derive from sixteenth-century sources rather than ex post facto calculations, although I do not contend that the former were always followed or that the latter are without merit. Second, the sources for my figures were for men engaged in heavy labor, not generic calculations for the population as a whole. And third, they conform well to standards used in current armies. For example, the U.S. Army calculates the daily caloric requirements for males seventeen to fifty years of age, at 3,600, which increases by 25 percent to 4,500 calories for heavy work or vigorous training for eight hours (United States Army 1985:2–1, 2–2). The latter figure is, in my opinion, a minimum for packing loads of at least 23 kg over dirt roads in broken terrain or for combat. The U.S. Army does calculate its requirements for a slightly larger individual, however, from 60 to 79 kg (United States Army 1985:Glossary 1). If we use instead the 54 kg figures drawn from the general population as a minimum size and then reduce the army figures proportionally, we would conclude that active men that size would consume from 3,060 to 4,050 calories per day. There remain at least three additional considerations in using these calculations. First, although I cannot assess the actual size of Mesoamerican combat troops, I feel that it is reasonable to assume they were at the upper end for size in their respective populations. Second, active combat troops inevitably fall at the upper end of the caloric requirement scale so that generalized figures that incorporate slack periods do not apply. Third, whatever else may have been going on, there would have been a significant social interest in maintaining their troops in excellent condition. Both of these factors would push the caloric intakes upward, and because the only available sixteenth-century accounts cluster in the 3,800 range—clearly within the range calculated above—I feel they are the best available. These figures also accord well with the military estimates for preindustrial armies in the West. For instance, Parker (1988:75) puts the general ration requirement for European soldiers in the sixteenth and seventeenth centuries at 1.5 pounds of bread, plus 1 pound of meat, cheese, or fish, and 6 pints of beer or 3 pints of wine per soldier per day. The daily ration for sailors in the Spanish armada was 1.59 quarts of water, .71 quarts of wine, 1.5 pounds of biscuits or 2 pounds of fresh bread and, on different days of the week, 6 ounces either of bacon or cheese with beans or peas, or fish with 3 ounces of beans and 1.5 ounces of oil (Rodgers 1939:267–68). The average daily intake of a male in the United States during the last century was 6,000–6,500 calories and for a woman 4,000–4,500 (Engels 1978:123). The ration used by a U.S. soldier during the Civil War weighed 3 pounds—18 oz. hard wheat flour, 20 oz. fresh beef, 2.4 oz. dry beans, 1.6 oz. coffee, .64 oz. salt, .32 gill vinegar, .04 oz. pepper (Engels 1978:125, 125n.14). According to Engels (1978:124), not all calories ideally available can be metabolized by humans. Thus, using more recent estimates of caloric values for maize flour (368 per 100 grams) and maize meal (355 per 100 grams) (Altman and

Dittmer 1968:27), of the .95 kg of maize available, only 82 grams can be absorbed by humans for every 100 ingested (Altman and Dittmer 1968:292). Using these figures to recalculate, .95 kg of maize would yield 3,372.5 calories for maize meal and 3,496 for maize flour, producing only 2,765.5 calories that were actually assimilated for maize meal (figures for maize flour were unavailable). The figures presented for other early army consumption rates all exceed those I have used for Mesoamerica. I have presented my figures so the results can be recalculated by anyone interested so that the final calculations and resultant social consequences can be recalibrated. In any case, my concern centers on the weight that had to be carried, not its caloric value.

50. Engels 1978:18; Jones 1987:52.

51. In contrast to European armies, those in Mesoamerica do not appear to have permitted female camp followers—certainly not during the Late Postclassic and probably not earlier—most likely because of logistical constraints and because their presence was not essential for the typically short duration of Mesoamerican military campaigns.

52. Hassig 1985:32–34.

53. For a sample of march rates for preindustrial armies, see Clausewitz (1943:275–77), Dupuy (1987:150–53), Engels (1978:20), Jones (1987:163, 201), Maurice (1930:212), and Neumann (1971). See also the discussion of various preindustrial examples in Hassig (1988:65–68).

54. United States Army 1971a:11.

55. United States Army 1971a:16.

56. Dupuy and Dupuy 1970:97; Sekunda 1984:23; United States Army 1971b:C–2.

57. Hassig 1988:64.

58. Water was also a serious logistical constraint, for each man needed two quarts per day (Engels 1978:18).

59. Though the existence of tumplines is far from certain, twine suitable for their construction dates from as early as 5,000 B.C. (MacNeish, Nelken-Terner, and Johnson 1967:193, 200, 219). The tumpline, which expedites carrying, was unquestionably in use among the Olmecs at least by La Venta times, based on jade figures (see the example in the Metropolitan Museum of Art, New York). For later examples of tumplines, see Winning (1974b).

60. Agrinier 1984:91–92; Cobean, Coe, Perry, Turekian, and Kharkar 1971: 667–71; Henderson 1979:84; Lowe, Lee, and Martínez Espinosa 1982:121; Marcus 1989:168–69, 191–92; Pires-Ferreira 1975:25, 83; 1978:64–72; Tolstoy 1989.

61. See Caso 1965b:854–55; Flannery, Marcus, and Kowalewski 1981:90. Henderson (1979:93) also questions the feasibility of a military expansion as a prime mover.

62. Acosta 1965:814; Flannery 1968:102, 105–108; Flannery, Marcus, and Kowalewski 1981:90; Henderson 1979:88; Marcus 1983f:356–57.

63. Marcus's (1989:193–94) argument that Oaxaca's social stratification predates Olmec influence in the area does not invalidate this point in that I argue for intensification rather than origins.

64. Flannery, Marcus, and Kowalewski 1981:75–77.

65. Blanton 1983*a*:84; Flannery, Marcus, and Kowalewski 1981: 80, 84–85; Marcus 1976*b;* 1983*a*:107–108.

66. Paddock 1983*a*:98. Kipp and Schortman (1989:374–75, 380) point out that chiefdoms incorporated into state economic networks frequently change as local chiefs attempt to control the new wealth. Moreover, these changes are often associated with increasing warfare (Kipp and Schortman 1989:374–75; Wright 1977:382–83).

67. Pires-Ferreira 1975:84.

68. Grove 1981*b*:61–64; Pires-Ferreira 1975:84.

69. Pires-Ferreira 1978:72–75; Pires-Ferreira and Evans 1978:135–37.

70. M. Coe 1968:103.

71. There was also a marked change in ceramics throughout much of Mesoamerica at this time (Lowe 1989:55).

72. Drennan 1983*a*:49.

73. Kidder 1946:256; Morley, Brainerd, and Sharer 1983:65. However, some Olmec influence appears to have been reasserted at Izapa during this period (Lowe, Lee, and Martínez Espinosa 1982:121–27), although it waned at Mirador, Chiapas (Agrinier 1984:92–93).

74. Pires-Ferreira 1975:29.

75. Grove 1989*b*:142–47; Grove, Hirth, Bugé, and Cyphers 1976:1209; Grove and Paradis 1971:100–101; Sharer 1987*b*:438.

76. Graham 1989:231–35; Grove 1987*b*:439; Morley, Brainerd, and Sharer 1983:64; Sharer 1974:169–70; 1989*b*.

77. Anderson 1978, 1:157–58, 163, 167; Dahlin 1978, 2:176; Henderson 1979:86–87; Sharer 1978*b*, 3:124; 1978*c*, 3:208. Chalcatzingo had shown some Olmec influence as early as 1000 B.C. (Grove 1987*b*:436; Grove, Hirth, Bugé, and Cyphers 1976:1207–1209; Thomson 1987:304).

78. Grove 1968:182–83; 1987*b*:439; Hirth 1978*a*.

79. There is a possible, though improbable, exception at Chalcatzingo, where an Olmec woman may be depicted on a stela (Grove 1984:60–61), although this does not reflect mundane female participation that food preparation entails.

80. Alternative approaches to travel food were feasible. Among North American Indians, both parched maize and baked loaves of boiled maize bread had excellent travel characteristics (Harrington 1908:587; Parker 1968:68). However, parched maize lacks the additional nutritional advantages of having been treated with lime. Gregg (1962:149–50) reported that in the early nineteenth century the Pueblo Indians of the American southwest produced a food that could be used for months on the trail by making a paste of ground maize and cooking it in very thin layers on a hot rock before rolling dozens together to form a roll. There is no evidence that any of these foods was ever used in Mesoamerica.

81. Coe and Diehl 1980, 1:388; Drucker 1943:56–57. The absence of comales is compelling evidence that tortillas were not made at this time. Maize was grown and eaten, but it was probably soaked and prepared as tamales or as hominy.

82. García Cook 1981:250; Grove 1987*b*:437; Grove, Hirth, Bugé, and

Cyphers 1976:1208; Guillén and Grove 1987:52; MacNeish, Peterson, and Flannery 1970:11; Sharer 1978b, 3:125.

83. For a discussion of the time-consuming task of grinding maize and making tortillas, see Bauer (1990).

84. For a brief discussion of the sling elsewhere, see Hogg (1968:28–30) and Korfman (1973).

85. Although slingstones are not found at La Venta, neither are projectile points (Drucker 1952:146), but they were found at San Lorenzo Tenochtitlan (Coe and Diehl 1980, 1:287) and at Tres Zapotes (Weiant 1943:119) and so were known to the Olmecs. Their absence at La Venta is peculiar and may have been an artifact of the relatively hurried excavations (Drucker, Heizer, and Squier 1959:1–2) or it may suggest the exercise of political control that kept such items from the main center. However, the site cannot be considered non-military, given the obvious depictions of captives on altars.

86. Slings were extensively used throughout Andean South America, where superior preservation conditions account for the numerous examples found. They are made of woven fibers, rather than of leather, and usually of cotton. See the examples found at Huaca Prieta (Bird and Hyslop 1985:214). Although their antiquity in Mesoamerica is not supported by surviving examples, a vegetable-fiber sling dating to around 500 B.C. was found in Nevada (Heizer and Johnson 1952).

87. The only examples of slings I have found in precolumbian depictions are in West Mexican ceramic figures (e.g., B. Smith 1968:54–55).

88. These spheres were found at San Lorenzo Tenochtitlan during the San Lorenzo Phase B (ca. 900 B.C.) (Coe and Diehl 1980, 1:287). They were not described as slingstones, but they have been discovered elsewhere and so described (e.g., Sheets 1978, 2:38; Vaillant 1931:305). In the Near East, the earliest slingstones were made of stone or clay and were spherical, beginning in the sixth millennium, then shifting to biconical and becoming ovoid around 4000 B.C. (Korfmann 1973:38). See also Ferrill (1985:24–25).

89. These figures are based on my measurements of slingstones found by George Vaillant at Ticoman, Zacatenco, and El Arbolillo and now housed in the American Museum of Natural History in New York City. Other spherical stones were also found, but these varied substantially in size, degree of sphericality, and surface texture: the most coherent group was composed of very round, relatively polished, or slipped ceramic spheres.

Some of the sample listed below fall either above or below the optimum sizes for slingstones and may have served other functions, but I have retained them in the listing for purposes of comparison. The following list presents the stones' diameters in centimeters and weight in grams:

Stone

cm	gm	cm	gm	cm	gm
4.6	136.1	6.1	323.9	2.6	19.8
3.2	31.7	6.7	325.5	3.0	23.8
4.2	85.8	5.1	184.3	3.2	24.9
3.7	52.2	4.9	204.8	2.9	21.7

3.6	43.9	3.8	47.7	3.1	28.7
3.5	37.5	3.6	68.0	3.3	32.0
3.6	43.3	1.7	4.8	3.4	35.6
3.0	28.2	2.0	9.0	3.4	36.9
3.0	27.0	2.3	10.3	3.6	46.8
3.0	26.7	2.5	12.0	3.8	55.5
2.8	23.4	2.4	15.3	3.5	43.8
2.1	8.3	2.7	19.1	3.4	37.8
3.5	60.9	3.3	30.4		

Ceramic

cm	gm	cm	gm	cm	gm
1.4	3.3	3.0	29.4	3.9	50.0
1.7	5.4	2.9	27.1	3.4	39.1
2.1	9.1	3.3	31.7	3.8	45.8
2.7	19.6	3.4	41.2	3.9	59.2
2.8	21.4	3.6	44.8		

The smallest examples are too little to serve as slingstones and may have been blowgun pellets. The largest are too big to be good slingstones, and the truly large ones (not recorded here) are also crude and do not belong in this same category. The ceramic balls are approximately equal in size and weight to the stone balls.

90. Korfmann 1973:39.

91. Grove 1987c:283; MacNeish, Nelken-Terner, and Johnson 1967:137; Sheets 1978, 2:38; Vaillant 1930:48, 63, 156; 1931:297, 305; 1935:237, 243, 244; Vaillant and Vaillant 1934:98. Slingstones were also found at the Guatemalan site of La Victoria as early as the Conchas I phase (1000–700 B.C.) (M. Coe 1961:106). But with phase dating this broad, it is unclear whether the sling was introduced from outside. It may have formed part of a general Isthmian culture that included the Olmecs.

92. Hassig 1988:80; Hogg 1968:30.

93. Grove 1987b:438; Sharer 1978c, 3:209.

94. Grove 1987b:436; 1989b:132–39. Grove (1989b:130–31) suggests that the art at Chalcatzingo was the work of artists trained on the Gulf coast.

95. Grove 1987b:440.

96. Grove 1984:159.

97. But see the contrary position of Harlan (1979:486), who agrees with the timing of the emergence of Chalcatzingo's elite but suggests that cultural development at Chalcatzingo was independent of outside influences.

98. Grove 1984:164; 1987c:441; 1989b:147. Santley's (1984:604) critique of the feasibility of bulk food transport is well taken, but the Olmecs' original productive superiority did not translate into the export of foodstuffs. Rather, this greater surplus was used locally to support artisans and effectively convert their agricultural surplus into small, elite objects that were then exported.

CHAPTER 3: WARFARE AND THE SPREAD OF STATES

1. Compare the decline of the mace in ancient Near Eastern warfare (Yadin 1963, 1:11).

2. Bernal 1969:88; Stirling 1943:14. Stirling (1943) suggests the animal is a jaguar, while Bernal (1969:113) agrees with Covarrubias that it is some kind of dragon. Stirling (1943:14) describes the spear as a staff.

3. Bernal 1969:88; Stirling 1943:13.

4. Stirling 1943:18–20. The intertwined scrollwork on Monument C suggests that it is post-Olmec (M. Coe 1965b:764; Heizer 1967:29; Stirling 1943:20). The ceramic sequence at Tres Zapotes is well established and dated, but the stone monuments cannot be accurately associated with the ceramics. As noted, Coe maintains that the monument is not in a bona fide Olmec style, and Stirling (1943:30–31) suggests that all the stone carvings belong to the later period of the site's occupation.

5. Edge and Paddock 1988:65.

6. Shield design gradually reflects changing weapons and usage. See, for example, Edge and Paddock (1988:9, 11, 22–24, 46, 61, 83), Hogg (1968: 46–47), Oakeshott (1960:24, 61–65, 175–77, 274–75), and Yadin (1963, 1: 13–14).

7. See the example from Altar de Sacrificios (Willey, Bullard, Glass, and Saul 1972:50).

8. Ferrill 1985:74.

9. Armillas (1948, 1951) and Palerm (1956) discuss a variety of fortifications in Mesoamerica.

10. Drennan 1983b:208.

11. Jones 1987:108–109.

12. Jones 1987:10.

13. Hogg 1981:33–36; Yadin 1963, 1:16–18.

14. Dupuy 1979:5, 11–12; 1987:34.

15. Sanders 1981:176.

16. Sanders, Parsons, and Santley 1979:98. Cuicuilco in the southwest dominated the valley and held 30 percent of its 80,000 people, but Teotihuacan emerged as a rival in the northeast during the 300–100 B.C. phase with the two centers splitting 40–50 percent of the valley population of 140,000 (Sanders 1981:166; Sanders, Parsons, and Santley 1979:98–99, 102). Teotihuacan achieved preeminence when Cuicuilco was largely destroyed by a volcanic eruption around 100 B.C. (Boehm de Lameiras 1988:95–96; Sanders, Parsons, and Santley 1979:106–107).

17. Sanders, Parsons, and Santley 1979:104–105.

18. García Cook 1974:11–12; 1978:175; 1981:253, 256.

19. García Cook and Mora López 1974:23–26. For example, see García Cook and Rodríguez (1975) on the site of Tlalancalequita.

20. The best known Tlaxcala fortification of the Late Formative is Tetepetla (García Cook and Mora López 1974), some 1,000 meters long and 60–120 meters wide (García Cook and Mora López 1974:24). Built atop a hill, partially

protected by walls, and surrounded by ravines over 15 meters deep, access was limited to four entries. The few entryways—always the weakest points in a defensive system (Croix 1972:10; Hogg 1981:9–10; Toy 1985:17, 35)—and the site's hilltop location suggest a primarily defensive purpose, for offensive troops could not be dispatched quickly to seize the initiative (Dupuy 1984:67); the defenders probably remained behind their walls.

21. Jones 1987:127–34.

22. Morley, Brainerd, and Sharer 1983:77–78; Willey 1977:385–86, 401–402.

23. Webster 1977:348–60; Willey 1977:413–14, 419. See Webster's (1977: 343–44, 348–56) analysis of warfare in the rise of lowland Maya civilization in which population pressure plays a crucial role. Human sacrifice is depicted in Izapa sculpture at this time, suggesting a certain level of violence and its association with political rule (Morley, Brainerd, and Sharer 1983:71). See Stela 21 (Norman 1973:plates 31, 32; 1976:122–27).

24. Norman 1976:80–81, 122.

25. Large projectile blades for use on spears—both utilitarian and military—were a Late Formative innovation (Kidder 1985:96–97).

26. Webster 1977:357–58. Settlement location and its relationship to the physical setting is a significant consideration in the nature and number of fortifications. But location alone cannot be taken unadvisedly as a barometer of general political instability or cohesion. The effects of these factors for planned defensive works are enormous, but the earliest permanent Mesoamerican fortifications were of existing centers, not of places located primarily for defensive purposes. Once established, settlements often continue to be occupied regardless of external political circumstances. Only new sites created during the period under threat offer clues to political climate because their builders would have taken security matters into consideration and placed them in the most advantageous locations.

El Mirador's walls probably lacked military purpose (Matheny 1986:25), but what may well have been fortifications occur at Edzna, although they are markedly different from those found elsewhere. Edzna was surround by canals on all four sides. Although they averaged only 1.5 meters deep, the north canal averaged 130 meters wide, the south canal 75 meters wide, and the east and west canals 20 meters wide. The encircled area was connected to the land by a single narrow causeway. Within this moat area was a walled construction that may have been a fortress (Matheny 1986:9–10; Matheny, Gurr, Forsyth, and Hauck 1983:78–79, 169–91). The fortress did not rely primarily on walls for defense; the construction of the encircling canals rendered the site highly defensible.

27. Most Late Formative settlements in the Maya highlands were located in open, undefended valleys or on plateaus (Borhegyi 1965b:62), which suggests either a general absence of warfare or its presence on too small a scale to warrant large settlements taking defensive measures, despite the existence of dominant centers such as Kaminaljuyu, with an estimated dependent population of 50,000. This figure includes the population of Kaminaljuyu plus its satellite villages (Borhegyi 1965b:64). And the drastic decline of the southern highlands at the end of the Late Formative (Borhegyi 1965a:19–20) was the

result not of warfare, but of a volcanic eruption in El Salvador around A.D. 200–250 that drastically reduced agricultural production, leading to massive depopulation and a falloff in trade with other areas (Morley, Brainerd, and Sharer 1983:85).

28. Webster 1976b:361–62, 368.

29. Armillas 1951:78; Webster 1976a:98, 1976b:363. This figure is the result of the reevaluation of the data from an early publication (Webster 1976a:84), where he had estimated the date as A.D. 250–300, or possibly as early as A.D. 100–250.

30. Falkenhausen 1985:118; Thomas 1981:21; Webster 1975:123–25; 1976a:8; 1976b:362.

31. Webster 1976a:12.

32. Webster 1975:123; 1976a:14, 88; 1976b:362. Erosion has reduced the dimensions of the fortifications, and the original ditch averaged 5.3 meters deep while the original wall averaged at least two meters higher than at present (Webster 1976a:88–89).

33. Jones 1987:11; Webster 1975:125; 1976a:89. Webster (1976a:96) estimates that 117,607 cubic meters of earth were removed from the ditch, requiring 352,821 man-days, which could have been accomplished by fewer than ten thousand adult males in forty days of continuous effort.

34. Webster 1976a:93–96.

35. Webster 1979:162.

36. Webster 1976a:89. Rands (1952:44) has suggested that Classic Maya settlements may have been palisaded generally.

37. Webster 1976a:12; 1976b:362.

38. Webster 1976b:367. Matheny (1976:48–51) suggests that the rise of Late Formative fortifications in the Maya lowlands may have been in response to pressure from Teotihuacan.

39. Fortifying centers makes them less vulnerable and substantially reduces the effects of raiding (Jones 1987:108–109).

40. Dupuy 1987:34; Webster 1976b:367.

41. Flannery, Marcus, and Kowalewski 1981:83; Whalen 1988:300–301, 304. Flannery, Marcus, and Kowalewski (1981:84) see no evidence of a state during the Rosario phase, but it does exist during the Monte Alban II phase (200 B.C. to A.D. 200). Data from the Monte Alban I phase (500–450 to 200 B.C.) are too fragmentary to assess with certainty. Sanders and Nichols (1988: 51, 72) dispute the existence of a state this early.

42. Flannery, Marcus, and Kowalewski 1981:80, 87, 90–92; Redmond 1983:4.

43. Flannery, Marcus, and Kowalewski 1981:75–77; Kowalewski, Feinman, Finsten, Blanton, and Nicholas 1989, 1:73.

44. Blanton 1978:1.

45. Kowalewski, Feinman, Finsten, Blanton, and Nicholas 1989, 1:98–99, 145. During Monte Alban Early I, the site of Monte Alban seems to have had virtually no impact on the surrounding communities (Kowalewski, Feinman, Finsten, Blanton, and Nicholas 1989, 1:98).

46. Blanton and Kowalewski 1981:97–99.

47. Blanton 1978; 1983*a*:83–84, 86–87; Sanders and Santley 1978. As Blanton and Kowalewski (1981:113) note, obsidian was not native to the Valley of Oaxaca. Control of that trade may have been one of the major factors in the rise of Monte Alban.

48. Blanton 1978:36–37, 39–40. This thesis was proposed by Blanton (1978:36–37; 1983*a*:84) and is supported by Flannery, Marcus, and Kowalewski (1981:87–88), but it has also been criticized on the basis of both theory (Willey 1979:133–35) and data (Sanders and Nichols 1988:48; Sanders and Santley 1978:303–304).

49. Blanton 1978; Marcus 1983*f*:357.

50. Blanton 1983*a*:84; Flannery and Marcus 1983*b*:89; Flannery, Marcus, and Kowalewski 1981:80, 84–87; Paddock 1966*b*:119, 142; 1966*c*:117–18; Whitecotton 1990:5. Many of these conquest stones are part of Building J, built during Monte Alban II (Marcus 1983*a*:106). Among others, Marcus (1983*a*: 107–108) has identified as conquests the towns of Miahuapan, Cuicatlan, Tututepec, and Ocelotepec, although Whittaker (1980:93–106) questions the accuracy of many of these readings and Sanders and Nichols (1988:50) question their significance.

51. These include Monte Alban, Chichen Itza, and the Aztec empire. However, I know of no examples of either type for Tollan or Teotihuacan, although sacrificed warriors were buried beneath the Pyramid of Quetzalcoatl in elite garb (Sugiyama 1989).

52. Blanton 1978:52, 54; 1983*a*:85; Elam 1989:404.

53. Blanton 1983*a*:85.

54. Elam (1989) discusses the fortifications in the Valley of Oaxaca, but he does so almost exclusively from the perspective of defense against an external threat, and Blanton (1978:54) assumes that the existence of walls at Monte Alban demonstrates a weak or nonexistent dominance over the region.

55. Whitecotton 1977:78–79; Zeitlin 1990:254.

56. The proliferation of defensible hilltop sites suggests greater internal control in territorial systems, in contrast to hegemonic systems where it suggests weakness and greater conflict.

57. This analysis is based on the work of Edward Luttwak 1976. See Hassig (1985:92–103; 1988:17–26) for applications in Mesoamerica.

58. Some archaeological investigation has been undertaken in the southern Isthmus of Tehuantepec seeking to assess its relationship with Monte Alban. Zeitlin (1990:255–59) fails to find evidence for warfare in the area at this time and tentatively notes a weakening of ties between the two regions. He suggests no Monte Alban conquest of the area, at least not on the same model as the Cuicatlan Cañada. See also Marcus (1988:61).

59. The inhabitants of the Cuicatlan Cañada were Cuicatec speakers who were ethnically distinct from the Zapotec speakers of Oaxaca (Spencer and Redmond 1979:201). In a minority view, Sanders and Nichols (1988:73) see this incursion as a Zapotec displacement of the indigenous people. Kowalewski, Feinman, Finsten, Blanton, and Nicolas (1989, 1:193) note the expansion into the Cuicatlan Cañada and suggest potential expansion elsewhere. In the Mixtec

area, however, there is no evidence of a takeover of any valley with a large mountaintop center similar to what occurred in the Cuicatlan Cañada (Marcus 1983*f*:358).

60. Drennan 1989:376; Flannery, Marcus, and Kowalewski 1981:81; Marcus 1983*a*:108; Redmond 1983:26, 143; Redmond and Spencer 1983:117, 119; Spencer 1982:216; Spencer and Redmond 1979:202–205; Zeitlin 1990: 253. Agricultural goods from the area include not only relatively common beans, chile peppers, and husk tomatoes, but also fruits usually available only in the tierra caliente, such as avocados, zapotes, and coyol palms (J. E. Smith 1979:219–26, 236–43).

61. The Cañada is the main artery connecting the Valley of Oaxaca to the Tehuacan and Puebla valleys and is narrowly constricted in places by steep mountains (Redmond 1983:17, 21; Spencer and Redmond 1979:205).

62. Redmond 1983:32–34; Spencer 1982:243; Spencer and Redmond 1979:208.

63. Redmond 1983:31; Spencer 1982:222.

64. Flannery, Marcus, and Kowalewski 1981:81; Redmond 1983:91–120; Redmond and Spencer 1983:119; Spencer 1982:220. The estimated population of the seven settlements supporting Quiotepec was 1,940–2,050, yet the carrying capacity of the area was only 393. This suggests a coercive system in which other settlements are forced to supply this outsized garrison population (Spencer 1982:221).

65. Spencer 1982:222.

66. The skullrack has come to be known by its Aztec name, *tzompantli*. Flannery, Marcus, and Kowalewski 1981:81; Redmond 1983:129; Redmond and Spencer 1983:120; Spencer 1982:236–39; Spencer and Redmond 1979: 211.

67. La Coyotera is estimated to have had fifty-five to sixty households during the period (Spencer 1982:234). The skulls were of various ages and both sexes, which Spencer (1982:239) interprets as indicating that entire families were killed for rebellion.

68. Spencer and Redmond 1979:205. South of this fortification, the pottery was in the Monte Alban style, whereas the pottery to the north of the fortification was in the Tehuacan Valley style, indicating that the main threat came from this direction (Flannery, Marcus, and Kowalewski 1981:87; Marcus 1983*a*:108). These clearcut ceramic styles on both sides of this divide probably account for the tendency of modern writers to ignore the equally significant Gulf coast access. Moreover, Tehuacan does not appear to be a significant threat to Zapotec interests at this time; the former area does not appear to have had a fully stratified state (Spencer 1979:28–36).

69. Redmond and Spencer 1983:119.

70. Kowalewski, Feinman, Finsten, Blanton, and Nicholas (1989, 1:193) note Monte Alban's imperial expansion, but interpret it differently.

71. At this time, Monte Alban did maintain administrative centers in peripheral areas of the Valley of Oaxaca (Kowalewski, Feinman, Finsten, Blanton, and Nicholas 1989, 1:150).

CHAPTER 4: TEOTIHUACAN AND THE
INTEGRATION OF MESOAMERICA

1. Bernal 1965*b*; 1966.
2. Cowgill 1977:188–89; R. Millon 1981:213; 1988*a*:109.
3. R. Millon 1976:228; 1981:208–10; Pasztory 1988*a*:53.
4. R. Millon 1973:54; 1976:215–17; 1981:206–10.
5. Boehm de Lameiras 1980:53.
6. This concentration of the obsidian industry at Teotihuacan was a long-term process and is evident in the changes in procurement patterns beginning as early as the Middle Formative, well before the rise of Teotihuacan (Boksenbaum, Tolstoy, Harbottle, Kimberlin, and Neivens 1987:70–73; Charlton and Spence 1982:50–57).
7. R. Millon 1973:56; 1981:223–25; Spence 1967; 1981:770–74; 1984: 95, 106–107; 1986. Teotihuacan also controlled obsidian working at more distant sites (Charlton 1977:285–87; Charlton and Spence 1982:60–67), as well as its distribution (Charlton and Spence 1982:63–65; Spence 1977:293–97). Drennan (1984:36–39) sees long-distance trade as more feasible during the Classic, despite his reservations about Formative trade. However, see Clark's (1986) critique of the role attributed to Teotihuacan's obsidian industry.
8. R. Millon 1973:46, 53; 1976:241–42. See also Kurtz's (1987) discussion of the role of trade in the rise of Teotihuacan and McNeill's (1982:38, 53–54) consideration of market economies and war.
9. R. Millon 1973:41–42; 1976:234.
10. Andreski 1968:85. By contrast, Hall (1986*b*:161–63) suggests that, at least in Europe, empires impede trade.
11. The military industry of the early Near Eastern empires was relatively small, because bronze arms and armor lasted for generations (McNeill 1982:1). The same was not true of Mesoamerican empires. Relying heavily on obsidian blades that frequently broke in use, the arms industry must have been large, although it was not necessarily distinguished from general obsidian working.
12. See Miller (1973:fig. 363) and Pasztory (1988*c*:168–76) for examples of spears in murals from Teotihuacan. Spear points were also found in grave contexts (Linné 1942:134, 136).
13. For examples of atlatls and darts in Teotihuacan murals, see Miller (1973:figs. 194, 335, 336) and C. Millon (1988*b*:212, 214). See also the two excavated atlatls from this period, both of which measured approximately 50 cm long (Cook de Leonard 1956).
14. Hassig 1988:79; Spencer 1974:52.
15. This assessment is based on the widespread use of slings elsewhere in Mesoamerica at this time and on the archaeological recovery of slingstones at Teotihuacan (Linné 1934:121).
16. Hassig 1988:90–92. One ceramic example shows a Late Classic Quiche Maya figure bearing a rectangular shield in the left hand and an ax in the right hand (Sotheby's 1987:Lot 238). In the Old World, metal axes were used as throwing weapons (Jones 1987:98), but they were not widespread.

17. Pasztory 1974:19n.9; 1976:333–34, 389; Séjourné 1966a:102; 1966b: 294–95, 305; 1966c:91; 1969:172, 262. R. Millon (1988b:106) suggests the murals from the Techinantitla compound celebrate rituals involving bloodletting and heart sacrifice of war captives by military figures. Knives have also been recovered from burials (Linné 1942:136–38).

18. Séjourné 1966b:156–57; 1966c:110–11, lam. 32; 1969:201, 286–87.

19. Tolstoy (1971:281–83) notes the similarity in sizes of projectile points at this time and for later periods when they were unquestionably hafted on arrows, and notes a graffito that may suggest the use of bows. However, this is highly uncertain, as he acknowledges. Many earlier writers (e.g., Linné 1934: 133–35, 143–48) also assumed that bows and arrows were common as early as the Middle Formative in Mesoamerica based on the size of projectile points uncovered. The smaller points, however, were probably for atlatl darts. There is no substantial evidence of bows and arrows at this time. Atlatls have been recovered from this period, but no bows or arrows, nor are there sculptural, mural, or ceramic depictions of them, although there are for spears, atlatls and darts, clubs, and slings.

20. Linné 1934:120–21; 1942:81–82, 187; Riley 1952:302. See also the example of a blowgun hunter on a Teotihuacan ceramic pot (Linné 1942:89). Based on modern examples in Mexico, the blowgun has a short range and is relatively harmless unless poison is used (Linné 1948:117–18). Blowguns become effective military weapons only if used with poison (Hogg 1968:31).

21. Hassig 1988:86.

22. Oddly, perhaps the best known cultures of the Early/Middle Classic, at least in terms of their arms and armor, are those of West Mexico. Less known archaeologically than most of Mesoamerica, West Mexican cultures produced realistic ceramic figures, among which well-accoutered warriors are prominent. The main weapons represented include clubs, often with points or blades at the end, spears, and slings (Gallagher 1983:40–41, 86, 105–106; Kan, Meighan, and Nicholson 1970:figs. 131, 147g; Winning 1974a:27–28). However, some of von Winning's interpretations of these implements are questionable in that he errs in his identification of a spearthrower and in his claim that slings are used only by shamans and are therefore not weapons. Numerous examples exist of slings being used by armored warriors. Shields are not common on warrior figures, but those depicted are typically rectangular. For example, see the large shield in Gallagher (1983:fig. 117). However, small round examples are occasionally shown (Gallagher 1983:fig. 133; Kan, Meighan, and Nicholson 1970: figs. 74, 89; Winning 1974a:29). Frequently, the warriors are shown wearing what is described as "barrel armor" because of its shape, which protects the trunk but not the limbs. Judging by the sewn closures, this armor was constructed of leather or fabric. Helmets woven of wicker or similar material are also common (Gallagher 1983:40–41, 86, 105–106; Kan, Meighan, and Nicholson 1970:figs. 64, 83, 86, 89, 118, 131; Winning 1974a:52, 60–61). Victors are shown grasping their foes by the hair, a conventional depiction of conquest throughout Mesoamerica, and prisoners are bound (Gallagher 1983:43; Winning 1974a:39). Unfortunately, the dating of these ceramic figures is not secure (Bell 1971:697–98). These figures provide an exceptionally large sample of

warrior types, but provenance is often based solely on style, which is attributed to the Late Formative. However, it may well have extended through the Classic, so that the martial traits shown may not be from the Formative era (Gallagher 1983:16, 28, 36; Meighan 1974:1256–58). Nevertheless, these vivid ceramic reminders illustrate how widespread and important warfare had become by this time.

23. This was the case in the ancient Near East (Yadin 1963, 1:14) and was occasionally the practice among the Aztecs (Hassig 1988:150).

24. Weller 1966:19. Formations—the organized use of arms—are perhaps the most decisive element. See the examples from ancient Greece and Rome (Weller 1966:19–20, 23–24).

25. Creveld 1989:19.

26. Cowgill 1983:335–37.

27. Pasztory 1988a:50.

28. Pasztory (1988a:50) suggests that Teotihuacan art commemorated the corporate group rather than individuals. Pasztory (1988b:161) further proposes that Teotihuacan used its iconographic writing system rather than a Maya-style hieroglyphic system precisely because this helped integrate its heterogenous population by presenting glyphs that could be commonly understood because they were not tied to a specific language.

29. R. Millon 1973:54; 1976:223.

30. A seeming exception to this is a series of murals from the Techinantitla compound at Teotihuacan that date to around A.D. 700 and show military figures accompanied with glyphs. René Millon (1988b:80–82, 91, 107) suggests that these murals most plausibly depict a procession of generals and reflect a long military tradition among kinsmen occupying that apartment compound. Clara Millon interprets the glyphs as names—personal, family, or kin-group (C. Millon 1988a:119; R. Millon 1988b:80)—and the figures as military commanders (C. Millon 1988a:124, 131). By contrast, Esther Pasztory (1988a:49–50, 75) suggests that the glyphs depict offices, for Teotihuacan art expressed impersonal and communal values rather than glorifying individuals.

Although the bar-dot numerical system was used at Teotihuacan (Caso 1967:143–48, 162–63), the Techinantitla glyphs lack numbers, yet in the Zapotec depictions of Teotihuacanos at Monte Alban during the Middle Classic, glyphs and accompanying numbers appear (Marcus 1983c:175–76; C. Millon 1988a:125). None of these glyphs bear two sets of numbers and so cannot indicate both month and year, nor are they years alone as not all are yearbearer glyphs (Whittaker [1983:105–108] based on Caso [1947]). Consequently, they are probably not actual dates (Edmonson 1988:16). The likeliest interpretation is that they are calendrical personal names. And if, as seems likely, the Zapotec glyphs were direct translations of these foreigners' names, some Teotihuacanos had calendrical names, even if not all. At Techinantitla, by contrast, none of the glyphs are calendrical, which strongly suggests that they are not name glyphs. However, since the tassel-headdress element is common to all the military figure glyphs (see C. Millon 1973:301–306), they probably reflect titles—most likely military—rather than personal names.

31. Santley 1989b:93–95.

32. Meritocratic advance was a feature of the much better documented Aztec army, although the nobility clearly dominated it (Hassig 1988:39).

33. Sjoberg 1960:110.

34. Hassig 1988:58–60.

35. Similarly, the elimination of aristocratic distinctions in the Roman army led to greater operational flexibility and maneuverability (Dupuy 1984:22).

36. Jones 1987:629.

37. The existence of battle standards is well attested for the Aztecs (Hassig 1988:57–58), where insignias were constructed of feathers over a light wicker frame that was worn on the unit leader's back. Creveld (1989:38–40) discusses the general use of battle standards for command and communications. See also Burne (1955:32–34) for the use of standards in late medieval England.

38. Hogg 1968:177–78.

39. For examples, see C. Millon (1988a:114–21).

40. Creveld 1989:92–93; Weller 1966:19.

41. Andreski 1968:97–98.

42. See Creveld (1985:50) for a similar situation in medieval European armies where the presence of noble knights led to poor or nonexistent chain of command.

43. Sanders, Parsons, and Santley 1979:105–106.

44. Sanders, Parsons, and Santley 1979:107. The population in the rest of the Valley of Mexico could have mounted a total offensive army of just over 1,900 and an effective maximum of over 3,200.

45. Andreski 1968:34.

46. Andreski 1968:87–88; Creveld 1989:12.

47. Jones 1987:57, 645. Although it similarly was not a standing army, that of sixteenth-century England was professional (Jones 1987:171).

48. For an interesting analysis of support for a war policy in terms of economic interests by various factions within a state, see Kiser (1989).

49. Finer 1975:95; Jones 1987:664.

50. For an example of North American Indian deportment in battle, see Calloway (1987:197–98, 231–33).

51. Andreski 1968:99–100, 134.

52. In preindustrial Europe, the slowness of armies virtually guaranteed that they clashed only by mutual agreement, given that neither side had the speed to force battle when the other was at a disadvantage (Creveld 1985:26).

53. Hassig 1988:53–54.

54. R. Millon 1981:220; Sanders, Parsons, and Santley 1979:109–10.

55. Vivó Escoto 1964:200–203; West and Augelli 1976:40–42.

56. Hirth 1978b:331; Hirth and Angulo Villaseñor 1981:137; Sanders, Parsons, and Santley 1979:127–28.

57. R. Millon 1981:220; Sanders, Parsons, and Santley 1979:128.

58. García Cook 1974:13; 1978:176.

59. Sanders, Parsons, and Santley 1979:128.

60. Hirth 1976:34–38; 1978b:325, 331; R. Millon 1981:223.

61. Cobean and Guadalupe Mastache 1989:37; Diehl 1983:42; Healan, Cobean, and Diehl 1989:241; R. Millon 1981:222–23.

62. Cobean and Guadalupe Mastache 1989:37; Healan, Cobean, and Diehl 1989:241; Healan and Stoutamire 1989:234.

63. Cobean and Guadalupe Mastache 1989:37; Diehl 1983:42; Healan, Cobean, and Diehl 1989:241.

64. This is based on the similarity of ceramics between Cholula and the Valley of Mexico (Müller 1970:142). Among the sites sharing Cholula culture are Manzanilla, Flor del Bosque, San Mateo, and Chachapa (García Cook 1981:267).

65. Tenaneyecac culture in the center maintained some contacts with Cholula but not with Teotihuacan; Teotihuacan culture dominated the north and west, and Cholula culture dominated the south (García Cook 1978:176). The recognized similarities and differences between Cholula and Teotihuacan are based primarily on ceramic inventories. Among the Teotihuacan ceramic traits not found at Cholula are frescoed vessels and candeleros, while other items, such as Tlaloc effigy vessels, polished redware, and red-on-buff ceramics, were markedly less common (Dumond and Müller 1972:1209). But differences in pyramid construction also point to variant traditions: Cholula's pyramid had a nucleus of adobe whereas those of Teotihuacan were of clay (Marquina 1970b:39).

66. García Cook 1978:176; 1981:267; Kolb 1986:181; R. Millon 1981:223; Proskouriakoff 1971:563. Among the highly valued Gulf coast products available from the El Tajín area was cacao (see Kampen 1979:93–95, fig. 2).

67. García Cook 1981:267; Lister 1971:625; R. Millon 1981:223.

68. Müller 1970:142; Sanders, Parsons, and Santley 1979:133–34.

69. Hirth 1978b:323; Hirth and Angulo Villaseñor 1981:143, 145, 148; R. Millon 1981:222–23.

70. Hirth 1978b:325, 328; Hirth and Angulo Villaseñor 1981:138.

71. McNeill 1982:9.

72. Rattray 1973:85–86.

73. The buffer effect of the eastern Morelos area was real, but since the existence of logistical/buffer zones on all sides of Teotihuacan is not certain with present knowledge, its defensive usefulness may have been limited.

74. Hirth and Angulo Villaseñor 1981:137.

75. García Cook 1978:176.

76. R. Millon 1973:58; Wauchope 1975:55. Another site, well known artistically though less so archaeologically, is Escuintla, Guatemala, where numerous artifacts testify to a Teotihuacan military presence (Berlo 1983b:83–87; Hellmuth 1975:9–19).

77. Cheek 1976:56–66; 1977:443; Sanders 1978:38–39. See Coe and Flannery (1964) for a discussion of the El Chayal obsidian site.

78. Sanders 1974:112; Santley, Ortiz, Killion, Arnold, and Kerley 1984:1–8. Teotihuacan did not take over the entire highland Maya area. Its interests were apparently in controlling trade and other highland cities, such as Zacualpa, were not politically or economically dominated by Teotihuacan, although central Mexican trade goods were present (Wauchope 1975:35, 39).

79. Borhegyi 1965a:21, 32; Cheek 1976:57–62; 1977:443–49; Sanders 1978:38.

80. Krasner 1989:69–70.

81. Sanders 1974:106. Among others, these Teotihuacan gods include Tlaloc, Xipe Totec, Tlaloques, Ehecatl, Xolotl, Tepeyolotl, Tlalchitonatiuh, Mictlanteuctli, and a butterfly goddess (Borhegyi 1965a:29).

82. Sanders 1978:39. Some Teotihuacan ceramics were imported to Kaminaljuyu (Kidder, Jennings, and Shook 1946:165, 229–38, 255) and others were made locally as the result of intimate contact with Teotihuacan (Borhegyi 1965a:23–24; Kidder, Jennings, and Shook 1946:198, 218–22).

83. Sanders 1974:111–13.

84. Borhegyi 1965a:18.

85. Cheek 1976:65–67; 1977:448–49. In the Late Classic, Kaminaljuyu had ceased to be a major center (Sanders 1974:107–108).

86. M. Coe 1965a:704–705; R. Millon 1981:226; Santley 1989a:135–36; Santley, Ortiz, Killion, Arnold, and Kerley 1984:18; Valenzuela 1945a:93; 1945b:107.

87. Kidder, Jennings, and Shook 1946:256; Parsons 1978:29; Sanders 1978:37.

88. Santley 1989a:136–38; Santley, Ortiz, Killion, Arnold, and Kerley 1984:18–19.

89. M. Coe 1965a:704–705; R. Millon 1981:226; Santley, Ortiz, Killion, Arnold, and Kerley 1984:1–8. By around A.D. 400, there was also a strong Gulf coast influence in Teotihuacan (R. Millon 1973:58), and Santley, Kerley, and Kneebone (1986:118, 124) suggest Matacapan was also a consumer of Teotihuacan-worked obsidian.

90. Arana and Quijada 1984:57–58.

91. Piña Chan 1982:41–46, 91; Siller 1984:61–64.

92. Kelley 1971:777–87; R. Millon 1981:227; Weigand 1978:74–79; 1982:89–92.

93. R. Millon 1973:39.

94. These compounds bear some resemblance to the fortified households in early Greece in which the wealthy had private fortifications prior to the development of city-wide walls (Croix 1972:21). However, the similarity is superficial. Most of Teotihuacan's populace was eventually moved into apartment compounds, all of which had walls.

95. R. Millon (1973:39–40) also notes the potential for cactus walls and the barriers formed by chinampas to the south. However, the last is only hypothesized because there is no direct archaeological evidence for irrigation agriculture at this time (R. Millon 1973:47).

96. A meritocratic territorial system is possible but unlikely, for the defensive posture afforded by fortified borders is unnecessary when large forces are available.

97. An aristocratic hegemonic system is possible but unlikely: it would lack the forces necessary to maintain control over a large and far-flung empire.

98. As with the Olmecs, the Teotihuacanos introduced comales into colonial areas, but they remained rare. Only three were found at Kaminaljuyu (Kidder, Jennings, and Shook 1946:208), suggesting their special purpose—for travel food—rather than everyday use.

99. Barbour 1975:140; R. Millon 1976:239–40; 1981:242n.26; Pasztory 1978b:14; 1978d:133.

100. R. Millon 1988*a*:109–10.
101. Sugiyama 1989:90–98.

CHAPTER 5: THE IMPACT BEYOND THE EMPIRE

1. This was the case with the Aztecs who were also organized hege-monically. See especially the consequences of Tizoc's disastrous rule (Hassig 1988:189–205).

2. Marcus 1983*b*:137, 139.

3. Paddock 1966*b*:151.

4. Linné 1938:63–64, plate 18*c,d*. See the example of a thrusting spear in a mural from Monte Alban tomb 105 (Marcus 1983*c*:142) and another held by a Zapotec warrior on Stela 4 at Monte Alban (Paddock 1966*b*:148). Knives were also used as secondary weapons (Boos 1966*a*:100), but blowguns were not, if they were present at all (Linné 1938:64–65).

5. Linné (1938:64) failed to find solid evidence of the atlatl among the Classic Zapotecs, but does mention some equivocal examples.

6. For examples of these shields, see Boos (1966*a*:63, 100, 325; 1966*b*: 109, lam. XCI, 119, lam. CI) and Linné (1938:plate 18*c,d*).

7. For examples, see Boos (1966*a*:64) and Paddock (1966*b*:146, 171). Redmond (1983:173–76) suggests that the jaguar was a symbol of Zapotec military orders, as perhaps were other animals.

8. The elaborate finery sometimes evident was probably just that. For examples, see Boos (1966*a*:62, 63) and Paddock (1966*b*:148).

9. Wilkinson and Norelli (1981:755–56) suggest that, except for longev-ity, classes were not rigid at Monte Alban, based on analysis of skeletal material at the site, and thus argue for considerable social mobility. This line of reasoning is a powerful argument against class endogamy, but two considerations reduce its applicability here. First, the sample used for the analysis generalizes from the entire history of Monte Alban up to the Spanish conquest and contains a sizable number of skeletons of unknown period, significantly skewing the analysis because the relatively closed class system suggested by the other data is re-stricted to the Late Formative and Early Classic. Second, this analysis does not distinguish between class mingling by intermarriage, most likely of commoner women, or by individual advancement, most likely of commoner men. In any event, the social advancement this suggests may have been completely unrelated to military activity.

10. Paddock 1966*c*:122.

11. Dupuy 1984:35.

12. The Tehuacan Valley appears to have posed no significant threat. There, some fortified hilltop sites were built as early as the Early Palo Blanco phase (150 B.C.–A.D. 250) and occupied until sometime in the Late Palo Blanco phase (A.D. 250–700) (Drennan 1979*b*:169–71). However, the largest of these was at the northern end of the valley, farthest away from the Valley of Oaxaca and presumably built in response to closer threats in Puebla.

13. Blanton 1983*a*:85; Flannery and Marcus 1983*b*:89–90; Flannery, Mar-cus, and Kowalewski 1981:85; Marcus 1983*a*:106–108; Paddock 1966*b*:142.

However, Santley (1989b:95–96) interprets the Monte Alban monuments as reflecting degrees of political control over the surrounding areas.

14. Kowalewski, Feinman, Finsten, Blanton, and Nicholas 1989, 1:158; Spencer 1982:245.

15. Blanton and Kowalewski 1981:100; Kowalewski, Feinman, Finsten, Blanton, and Nicholas 1989, 1:159, 161–62, 164. Although Kowalewski, Feinman, Finsten, Blanton, and Nicholas (1989, 1:198) feel that tribute better explains Monte Alban's economic base, they also suggest that this vacant land was used as farm land by the inhabitants of Monte Alban.

16. Kowalewski, Feinman, Finsten, Blanton, and Nicholas 1989, 1:153. At this time, ballcourts arise in the largest towns of the valley's various subregions. Kowalewski, Feinman, Finsten, Blanton, and Nicholas (1989, 1:193) tentatively suggest these ballcourts may have been associated with military garrisons.

17. Kowalewski, Feinman, Finsten, Blanton, and Nicholas 1989, 1:180–81, 198–99; Kowalewski and Finsten 1983:417; Paddock 1966c:127. This assessment of the pattern of economic flows is based on the distribution of ceramics (Kowalewski, Feinman, Finsten, Blanton, and Nicholas 1989, 1:180).

18. Kowalewski, Feinman, Finsten, Blanton, and Nicholas 1989, 1:162, 180, 185–92, 198–99.

19. Kowalewski, Feinman, Finsten, Blanton, and Nicholas 1989, 1:199.

20. Although rare, some Teotihuacan pottery was found at Monte Alban during this period (Kowalewski, Feinman, Finsten, Blanton, and Nicholas 1989, 1:213).

21. Spencer and Redmond 1979:212.

22. Kowalewski, Feinman, Finsten, Blanton, and Nicholas 1989, 1:213, 510; Redmond 1983:145, 154; Spencer and Redmond 1979:212.

23. But see the contrasting positions of Kowalewski, Feinman, Finsten, Blanton, and Nicholas (1989, 1:199) who interpret the earlier buildup around Monte Alban and its subsequent decline as an imperial-level change in emphasis, a deliberate shift in policy about what areas to develop.

24. For example, there were no fortifications in the mountains between the Valley of Oaxaca and the Cuicatlan Cañada until after the withdrawal of Teotihuacan influence in the region (Drennan 1989:378).

25. Friedman 1977:72, 76.

26. The rainy season in the semiarid Valley of Oaxaca extended from May through September (Smith 1983:14), but the primary climatological obstacle to Teotihuacan's control was in the central highlands.

27. Bernal 1965a:802–803; Blanton and Kowalewski 1981:100; Caso 1965a:856; 1965b:903; Caso and Bernal 1965:881, 887; Kowalewski, Feinman, Finsten, Blanton, and Nicholas 1989, 1:511; Marcus 1983c:175; R. Millon 1973:58; Paddock 1966b:127, 141; 1978:46. Among the Teotihuacan ceramics found at Monte Alban are thin orange ware, cooking pots, floreros, low tripods with covers, ring bases, double cups (candeleros), stucco-coating, and cups (Bernal 1965a:803). Teotihuacan motifs and figures appear in Monte Alban tombs 103, 104, 105, and 112 (Caso 1965a:868). However, see Winter's (1977) position that Teotihuacan influence in Oaxaca was minor.

28. Kowalewski, Feinman, Finsten, Blanton, and Nicholas 1989, 1:249.

This is little evidence of Teotihuacan ceramics in the rest of the Valley of Oaxaca (Kowalewski, Feinman, Finsten, Blanton, and Nicholas 1989, 1:213).

29. Bernal 1965a:802; Marcus 1983c:175, 180; R. Millon 1973:40–41; 1981:210; Redmond 1983:152–53.

30. Monte Alban is 350 km from Teotihuacan, whereas Kaminaljuyu is 1,050 km (Flannery and Marcus 1983c:161).

31. R. Millon 1973:42.

32. Flannery and Marcus 1983c:161–62.

33. Marcus 1983c:175, 179.

34. Kowalewski, Feinman, Finsten, Blanton, and Nicholas 1989, 1:201, 212.

35. Kowalewski, Feinman, Finsten, Blanton, and Nicholas 1989, 1:202, 210, 212, 214–21, 225–26, 250. Flannery and Marcus (1983c:162) find no evidence for a marketplace at Monte Alban, although Blanton and Kowalewski (1981:106) suggest the possibility of a central market near the base of Monte Alban's north slope.

36. Kowalewski, Feinman, Finsten, Blanton, and Nicholas 1989, 1:181, 229, 249; Redmond 1983:153–54.

37. Goody 1971:42–43; Price 1978:174, 180.

38. Kowalewski, Feinman, Finsten, Blanton, and Nicholas 1989, 1:213. Trade administered at the highest levels of the polity best fits the distribution of Teotihuacan products in the region. Goods were also increasingly homogeneous (Kowalewski, Feinman, Finsten, Blanton, and Nicholas 1989, 1:214).

39. Kowalewski, Feinman, Finsten, Blanton, and Nicholas (1989, 1:511) suggest that the Valley of Oaxaca region supplied itself and Teotihuacan with Pacific coast products, including cotton and textiles.

40. The presence of expatriate Zapotec barrios in Cholula and elsewhere suggests that this was a standard practice where exchange relationships were long term (Hirth and Swezey 1976:12–15). The nearby site of Manzanilla was dominated by Teotihuacan, judging by the preponderance of the latter's ceramics and architecture, although the site was within Cholula's political and economic sphere. During the Late Classic, approximately A.D. 500 to 700, Monte Alban IIIB ceramics were recovered from the site and two Oaxacan tombs from that period were also found.

41. E.g., Hammond 1982:358. Whatever the lowland environment may have been later, at this time it was primarily jungle (Wiseman 1978:171).

42. M. Coe 1980:61; Healy and Prikker 1989. Also, note Rands's (1952) dissertation taking this position very early. Based on military architecture alone, Webster (1976b:370) feels that Maya society was characterized by large-scale warfare throughout most, if not all, of its developmental sequence. Gibson (1985:172) contests this on the same grounds, but unconvincingly (Willey 1985:182). Conventionally, the Maya Classic is divided into the Early Classic (A.D. 250–550), the Middle Classic hiatus (A.D. 550–600), the Late Classic (A.D. 600–800), and the Terminal Classic (A.D. 800–900) (Morley, Brainerd, and Sharer 1983:90).

43. Spear points were also occasionally placed in Early Classic elite Maya

men's burials, suggesting the ideological, if not practical, importance of war (Agrinier 1970:38–39, 67).

44. D. Chase (1988:9) states that formal warfare in the Early Classic was quite limited, and Culbert (1988:139–42) notes that during the Early Classic, warfare as reported in hieroglyphic inscriptions was relatively limited.

45. Culbert 1988:136. The presence of multiple power centers works against the emergence of a single authority (Tilly 1975b:28), and in the Maya case, cities' independence from outside political domination was shown by the erection of emblem glyphs, just as their dependence was reflected by their absence.

46. Depictions of spears are rare, as with weapons generally at this time. Two examples of what may be spears are shown on Tikal Stela 9 (9.2.0.0.0) and Stela 13 (9.2.10.0.0), although they are somewhat distorted (Jones and Satterthwaite 1982:24, fig. 13b; 33, fig. 19b), and possibly on Early Classic Yaxha Stela 6 (Proskouriakoff 1950:fig. 40b).

47. However, projectile points were not common in Classic times (W. Coe 1965b:597, 599), which suggests their greater use on reuseable spears. There is no evidence supporting this ethnographically common usage of spears for the Early Classic Maya, but in their utilitarian functions, spears were doubtless thrown. This may have carried over into their military use as well.

48. Large stone points had been in use in the Maya lowlands since the Late Formative, apparently on spears (Kidder 1985:97). Fire-hardening was used among earlier groups and also appears among the Late Classic Maya.

49. A club with three celt-blades extending through the shaft are depicted on Uaxactun Stela 5 (Graham 1986:143; Proskouriakoff 1950:fig. 38a) and on an Early Classic carving at Loltun, Yucatan (Proskouriakoff 1950:fig. 38b). Stone mace heads have also been recovered (Parsons, Carlson, and Joralemon 1988:128).

50. Although not depicted, knives were undoubtedly used, possibly for these same purposes. In the Late Classic murals at Mul-Chic, Yucatan, knives are depicted in what appears to be an execution scene (Piña Chan 1962:111–15).

51. The antiquity of slings is based on linguistic evidence, with the Maya word for sling going back as far as 1,000 B.C. (James A. Fox, personal communication). Blowguns may have been used as well, but not as military weapons (Shook 1946).

52. Use of the atlatl was largely restricted to the Late Classic/Early Postclassic of northern Yucatan (W. Coe 1965b:601). See also Proskouriakoff (1950:99).

53. Schele and Friedel 1990:147. The principal example is on Tikal Stela 31, in which a Maya noble is flanked by two Teotihuacan-style warriors (who Schele and Friedel [1990:155–56] identify as Curl Nose, a Maya king) carrying atlatls (Jones and Satterthwaite 1982:64, figs. 51a, 52a). However, a design on a ballcourt marker at Tikal on Structure Sub 4b, Group 6C-XVI, dated to A.D. 375, and identifying the person as Smoking Frog, an Early Classic ruler at Tikal, uses an emblem of an atlatl over a bird that bears a striking resemblance to those in murals at Teotihuacan (Laporte and Fialko C. 1990:53). Stela 5 at Uaxactun shows another example (Graham 1986:143; O. G. Ricketson 1937:179–80).

Schele and Friedel (1990:152) assert that Tikal used the atlatl in its conquest of Uaxactun in the fourth century, but I find little support for this claim. If the weapon was used, and if it was as decisive as they claim, it is implausible that it would then be abandoned by Tikal and not adopted by others; yet the paucity of atlatl depictions clearly suggest that this weapon played no significant role among the Classic Maya.

54. Schele 1986:15.

55. One possibility is that the Maya actually did not use shields, or that shields were comparatively crude. This suggestion is supported not only by their absence, but also by the erroneous depiction of the Mexican shields. The rectangular Mexican shields had functional feather fringes on the bottoms and outside (left) edges, leaving the top and inside (right) edges around which the soldiers fought unencumbered. On Stela 31 (Jones and Satterthwaite 1982:64, figs. 51*a*, 52*a*), however, the fringe is shown on the inside edge, which would have seriously hindered combat. The excellent detail suggests the artist must have seen the shields, but the erroneous positioning of the fringe indicates that he was unfamiliar with the way they functioned in combat. Occasionally, at Teotihuacan, artistic perspective demands that shields be held in the right hand, but the unfringed portion remains toward the inside (A. G. Miller 1973:109). The only other instances I have found of a feather-fringed rectangular shield being held inappropriately are at Teotihuacan in which a figure holds a jaguar mask in the right hand and a rectangular shield with the inside edge fringed (A. G. Miller 1973:111; Pasztory 1976:235, fig. 112), which may reflect a state of disrobing, and another example in which a human figure holds a shield with the fringe on the bottom and inside, although he is not adorned for war and holds a feathered object (a removed mask) in the other hand (Séjourné 1966a:104, 300–301; 1966b:52; 1969:284–85).

56. Although the Maya lowlands today are largely tropical rainforests, especially in the area that was central during the Classic, it is uncertain whether jungle dominated at this time. Pollen analysis suggests that the lowlands were not covered by jungle during the Classic (Cowgill, Goulden, Hutchinson, Patrick, Racek, and Tsukada 1966:123; Wiseman 1978:176). However, the samples were taken from lake regions that had the heaviest settlement, so the forest reduction that took place there through agricultural and house clearing and other uses may not have been typical elsewhere, and forests may well have dominated much of the lowlands, especially between settlements, as Wiseman (1978:xii) notes. Rainfall in the Tikal area averages 55 inches per year (Willey, Smith, Tourtellot, and Graham 1975:13).

57. Seabury and Codevilla 1989:115.

58. Cowgill 1974:55–56.

59. Based on the Bonampak murals, Thompson (1955a:63) suggests that warriors were drawn exclusively from the upper classes, with the peasantry participating only as victims. Thompson (1955b:51) interprets the scene as a surprise raid since the enemy are unarmed. Baudez and Mathews (1978:33) interpret the nudity of the victims as prefiguring their captive status and, as Rands (1952:79) notes, only captives are shown, not slain soldiers. Miller

(1986:95–96, 113–30) disputes Thompson's interpretation. For a medieval European analogy, see Oman (1982:229–32, 235).

60. Turner 1978:fig. 9.2; Vivó Escoto 1964:201, fig. 11. In addition to this general pattern, relatively wet and dry years tend to alternate in three- to four-year cycles (Willey and Smith 1969:40).

61. Redfield and Villa Rojas 1934:42. The temporal pattern of agricultural activity is based on Redfield and Villa Rojas's (1934:4–8) study of Chan Kom, a village in the northern Maya Lowlands, and on J. Eric Thompson's (1930:41–54) study of San Antonio in southern Belize. In swidden cultivation, most of the brush is felled during the autumn and early winter. This is followed by a period of up to three months before the milpa is burned, an activity that begins in early March, peaks in April, and continues into early May (Higbee 1948:460; Redfield and Villa Rojas 1934:44–45; Thompson 1930:41, 47, 53–54). Sowing begins with the rains in late May or early June, with the maize harvest ripening in late September to November, followed by harvest beginning in November and continuing during the next months (Redfield and Villa Rojas 1934:44–45; Thompson 1930:41, 47, 53). A second, though smaller, crop is planted in November or December and harvested in March or April (Higbee 1948:460; Thompson 1930:54). Because maize keeps better if left on the stalk to dry, the dry month of March is the best time for harvesting (Redfield and Villa Rojas 1934:45).

62. Taube 1989:33.

63. Webster 1976b:367. Riverine Maya could have used canoes and thus been less restricted by transport constraints. However, canoe transport would put the combat season during and immediately after the rainy season, which would directly conflict with the greatest agricultural labor demands.

64. Rain generally favors light forces whereas dry weather favors regulars, and jungles favor defensive rather than offensive actions (Seabury and Codevilla 1989:104–106).

65. See the social and military differentiation in medieval Europe on the basis of cost of arms and armor (Finer 1975:92, 102–103; Weller 1966:42). See also Contamine (1984:96–97) on the high cost of equipping a knight.

66. Although military orders existed among the Maya in the Postclassic period and evidence for them is stronger in the Late Classic, there is no direct evidence for them in the Early Classic. However, Webster (1976c:13) argues for their presence as early as the Late Formative on functional grounds.

67. Finer 1975:95.

68. Santley 1989b:92–93; Tainter 1988:162.

69. Andreski 1968:29; Finer 1975:103; Moskos 1976:59, 61, 64–65; O'Connell 1989:33.

70. Tilly 1975b:28.

71. Schele and Friedel 1990:93. Compare feudal Europe (Finer 1975:87).

72. Schele and Friedel 1990:85–87; Webster 1977:366–67. Political obligations in such systems are man-to-man rather than being a function of territorial location (Finer 1975:86). Friedel and Schele (1988:563) point out the enormous emphasis placed on lineage among the nobility. Based on ethnohistoric, epi-

graphic, and ethnographic lines of evidence, Classic Maya social organization was patrilineal, as was their dynastic succession, and was presumably patrilocal (Hammond 1982*b*:182–83; Hopkins 1988:116–17). This is supported by data from the colonial period, when Yucatan Maya social organization was patrilineal (Haviland 1973:147; Roys 1943:35) and the basic residential pattern was the extended family (Kurjack 1974:92–93; MacKinnon 1981:245).

73. Sinden 1979:303, 314. Based on an analysis of residential structures, it appears that Tikal's political rulers had the ability to build defensive works, but their control did not penetrate to the level of the family, which had considerable autonomy (MacKinnon 1981:246).

74. Goldstone 1982:193. See Brustein (1986:157) on the relationship between societal stability and lower class incorporation into the reward structure.

75. Andreski 1968:88; Creveld 1989:12.

76. Oman 1982:243–46.

77. Compare the resistance of medieval knights in Europe to the adoption of the plebian (and equalizing) crossbow (Finer 1975:93).

78. Crossbows filled this role in the Middle Ages, just as guns did in the sixteenth century, greatly opening up military participation because they required less training than the weapons they replaced, and making their users more potent in relation to their respective elites.

79. See Contamine (1984:88–89, 132–33, 156), Delbrück (1982:234–35, 240), and Oman (1976:63–64) for medieval European examples in which commoners were essentially excluded from military roles. Similar participant percentages are found in most contemporary societies, as well as in medieval England (Contamine 1984:117). Contemporary military participation is far below these figures. The percentage of the military in NATO countries typically falls below 1 percent and that for Warsaw Pact countries falls just above 1 percent (Military Balance 1989:16–78). The United States military was .85 percent of its total population in 1989 while the Soviet Union's military was 1.48 percent (Military Balance 1989:16, 32). Particularly militarized states have somewhat higher participation ratios. For example, Iraq's was 5.4 percent and North Korea's was 4.6 percent, in contrast to South Korea's 1.5 percent (Military Balance 1989:101, 164, 165). On a worldwide basis, approximately .6 percent of the population is in the military (Sivard 1986:32).

80. In acknowledging the ritual aspects of warfare, I do not accept Eliade's (1974:29) extremist position in which all war is ritual and none has rationalistic motives.

81. For example, various forms of behavior that would have been militarily and politically effective were foresworn by the combatants on both sides in World War II. Among these were political assassination, use of poison gas, and economic disruption through counterfeiting the enemy's currency.

82. O'Connell 1989:8.

83. Haviland (1969:430) estimated the population for the Late Classic. Sanders (1972:125), however, puts it at only 32,600 for the same period.

84. Adams 1977*b*:153–54; Demarest 1978:101–102; Webster 1977:365.

85. Gibson (1985:171) estimates that fewer than 1 percent of all Formative and Classic Maya sites had fortifications.

86. Puleston and Callender 1967:40–43; Morley, Brainerd, and Sharer 1983:114. These defensive works are tentatively dated on the basis of an Early Classic potsherd buried in the topsoil beneath the wall rubble (Puleston and Callender 1967:43) although Webster (1976b:363) puts it in the Late Classic. Other possible Early to Middle Classic Maya fortified sites include Dzonot Ake, Edzna, La Victoria and Acatucha in Southern Quintana Roo, and Calakmul (Webster 1976b:364–66). In discussing Uaxactun, O. G. Ricketson (1937:32) notes the lack of fortifications but comments on the use of henequen plants in the highlands as defensive barriers. Another possible candidate for Late Formative/Early Classic fortification is Muralla de León (Rice and Rice 1981). Despite mixed ceramics that could sustain several alternative interpretations, Rice and Rice (1981:281) feel it dates to the Late Formative/Early Classic based on the ratio of early to late ceramic fragments. However, the dry-wall construction (Rice and Rice 1981:272) is markedly different from other well-dated Late Formative/Early Classic Maya fortifications but is typical of Late Classic/Early Postclassic construction techniques. Both Fox (1987:84, 98) and Hammond (1989:666) support a Postclassic date for the site.

87. Webster 1976b:368.

88. Puleston and Callender 1967:43. Another wall was located 8 km south of Tikal's center (Rice and Rice 1981:272).

89. Puleston and Callender 1967:42–43.

90. Puleston and Callender 1967:43; Webster 1976b:363.

91. Webster 1976b:367.

92. Webster 1976b:368–70.

93. Heads were taken in battle (Hellmuth 1987:76), indicating a concern for accountability for deeds and suggesting that Maya warfare had important social consequences.

94. At Tikal, Stelae 5 (9.15.13.0.0) and 10 (9.2.11.10.16) depict rulers standing on bound captives (Jones and Satterthwaite 1982:17, 26, figs. 7b, 14b). Because silent reading is a relatively recent phenomenon—found in Western civilization only since medieval times—it is probable that these stelae were proclaimed aloud by a formal reader on significant occasions (Chaytor 1941–42; Clanchy 1979:2, 214–20; Leclercq 1982:15, 72–73).

95. Closs 1984; Fox and Justeson 1986; Marcus 1987; Mathews 1985; Morley, Brainerd, and Sharer 1983:93–94, 107; Proskouriakoff 1963, 1964; Thompson 1982.

96. Geographically dispersed bodies can maintain cohesion only through a principle of subordination, such as bureaucracy (Andreski 1968:121).

97. Haviland 1977; Morley, Brainerd, and Sharer 1983:95, 113. El Zapote appears to have been tied to Tikal by a marriage between the sister of Tikal's ruler on Stela 31 and the king of El Zapote, as was Uaxactun (Marcus 1976a:39–41; Mathews 1985:44). For a general consideration of Classic Maya marital alliances, see Fox and Justeson (1986) and Mathews (1985).

98. In a study of European royalty, Fleming (1973) found little relationship between marriages and political conditions.

99. Sanders (1990) suggests that the Maya elite practiced polygyny, based on the disproportionate number of females in the graves behind an elite house in

Copan. If so, continued marriages of colonial rulers with the large number of noble offspring polygyny implies may have helped tie colonial areas to the center for longer periods. However, the grave data could also reflect domestic servants or concubines without formal marital status.

100. Prior to the introduction of foreign influences, there was little trade in basic commodities between settlements in the ecologically homogeneous Maya lowlands (Tourtellot and Sabloff 1972:128–32).

101. Some centers controlled hinterlands as small as 1 square kilometer while the largest, Tikal's, was 123 square kilometers (50 square miles). The distance between larger sites averages 20 to 30 kilometers (Morley, Brainerd, and Sharer 1983:211), giving each city a politically dependent area of one day's travel.

102. W. Coe 1965a:35–37; Coggins 1979:251; Hoopes 1985:149; Miller 1978:66–69; Morley, Brainerd, and Sharer 1983:107. Teotihuacan influence, though often tenuous, is found at many Maya sites in both the Maya highlands and lowlands. For instance, Teotihuacan tripod vessels and green obsidian from central Mexico were found at Early Classic Río Bec (Ball 1975:115), green obsidian has been found at Altun Ha, and Teotihuacan figurines have been found at Becan (Hoopes 1985:149–50, 159). Teotihuacan influence is acknowledged throughout Classic Maya Belize (Hammond 1982:358), and Teotihuacan architecture has been found at Dzibilchaltun in northern Yucatan (Andrews 1981:339). For further consideration of Teotihuacan influences at various Classic Maya sites, see R. Millon (1988a).

103. Coggins 1975:143–200; Schele 1986:1. One basis for this relationship would have been the trade of obsidian from the highland to the lowlands where it is not found, in exchange for lowland flint (Thompson 1965:333).

104. As noted earlier, a Tikal ballcourt marker dated to A.D. 375 uses a Teotihuacan bird and an atlatl to identify an Early Classic ruler (Laporte and Fialko C. 1990:53).

105. Webster 1977:362. One striking difference between the two areas is the presence of a few comales in the Maya highlands and their absence in the lowlands. This pattern suggests direct ties between Teotihuacan and the highlands, but it also suggests that the lowland cities dealt with Teotihuacan indirectly, through Kaminaljuyu, a connection that did not require long-distance foodstuffs prepared with comales.

106. Coggins 1975:144; Morley, Brainerd, and Sharer 1983:114; Proskouriakoff 1965:475; Sanders 1978:43; Schele and Friedel 1990:163; Webster 1977:361–62.

107. Teotihuacan warriors are depicted on Stela 31 at Tikal (9.0.10.0.0; A.D. 446) (Jones and Satterthwaite 1982:64, figs. 51a, 52a). For a detailed discussion of the many Teotihuacan elements at Tikal, see Coggins (1975:138–200). William T. Sanders (personal communication) has suggested that Teotihuacan mercenaries may have aided various Maya rulers.

108. Coggins 1975:142; Jones and Satterthwaite 1982:124; Morley, Brainerd, and Sharer 1983:107.

109. Jones and Satterthwaite 1982:126. Coggins (1975:142, 144) suggests that the accession of Curl Nose may have ended the rule of the Jaguar Paw clan,

replacing it with his own. Part of Coggins's (1975:179–80) argument linking Kaminaljuyu and Tikal rests on a Mexican-style cylinder vessel depicting Teotihuacan-style warriors approaching a seemingly Maya priest, and showing Mexican-style pyramids. At the time of her analysis, Kaminaljuyu was the only known Early Classic Maya site with Teotihuacan architecture, but recently this has also been found at Dzibilchaltun in northern Yucatan (Andrews 1981:325).

110. Coggins 1975:187–88.

111. W. Coe 1965a:37; Coggins 1975:143; Jones and Satterthwaite 1982: figs. 51a, 52a; Mahler 1965:582; Morley, Brainerd, and Sharer 1983:111; Proskouriakoff 1965:475. Schele and Friedel (1990:161) interpret these warriors as Curl Nose in Mexican military attire. The Tlaloc figure depicted on the Mexican shields is the type identified by Pasztory (1974:13–14) as his war-deity manifestation.

112. Schele (1986:4, 12, 18; Schele and Friedel 1990:130–31) interprets this as the genesis of a new war cult, which she calls Tlaloc-Venus, associated with sacrifice and astronomy beginning in A.D. 378. See her list of war-related events and astronomically significant days (Schele 1986:9–12).

CHAPTER 6: THE FALL OF TEOTIHUACAN AND
ITS AFTERMATH

1. R. Millon 1973:45; 1976:212; Sanders, Parsons, and Santley 1979:109, 127.

2. R. Millon 1981:242, 240. For example, knightly orders are not depicted in ceramics until the Xolalpan and Metepec phases, becoming common at the end of the Metepec phase (Barbour 1975:140).

3. Weller 1966:19.

4. Figurines with quilted cotton armor appear in the Xolalpan phase (A.D. 450–650) at the earliest (Warren Barbour, personal communications).

5. Warren Barbour, personal communication; R. Millon 1988b:105; Séjourné 1966a:99.

6. Hirth and Angulo Villaseñor 1981:145.

7. Barbour 1975:136; Séjourné 1966a:121.

8. See Burne (1955:36) on the reduction in size of shields in late medieval England as armor increased.

9. For examples of smaller circular shields in the murals at Teotihuacan, see Pasztory (1988c:168, 170–75).

10. Yadin 1963, 1:15, 64.

11. Barbour 1975:140; Séjourné 1966a:99, 101, 116.

12. There are exceptions to this association between weapons and warriors. Pasztory (1976:fig. 122) shows the figure of a bird armed with an atlatl and darts, and Séjourné (1966b:50–51; 1969:102–103) shows a jaguar figure with the small circular shield usually associated with thrusting spears. Other figures such as coyote warriors are also depicted wielding atlatls (Miller 1973:figs. 335, 336; Pasztory 1976:380–81; Séjourné 1966a:201; 1969:129) and human and supernatural figures are also shown both with atlatls (Pasztory 1974:12–13;

1976:327–29, 386) and with spears (Séjourné 1966*b*:124, 276–77; 1969:116–17). They do not carry shields, although the coyote figures are associated with jaguar figures, the former being the upper figures while the latter are the lower in a room mural in the apartment compound of Atetelco. However, the relationship does hold in the mural depicting warriors holding atlatl darts over a lower mural panel showing jaguars (Séjourné 1966*b*:56–57; 1969:104–105).

13. Séjourné 1966*a*:106.

14. R. Millon 1976:216, 225.

15. Sanders, Parsons, and Santley 1979:109.

16. R. Millon 1973:45; 1976:212; 1981:208; Sanders, Parsons, and Santley 1979:109.

17. Sanders, Parsons, and Santley 1979:110–11. The rest of the Valley of Mexico was potentially capable of fielding an offensive army of almost 13,400 and an effective maximum of over 22,600.

18. Diehl 1989*c*:10; Guadalupe Mastache and Cobean 1989:55; Pasztory 1978*b*:7, 10; R. Millon 1973:63.

19. Cheek 1977:448–49; Pasztory 1978*b*:12.

20. Kelley 1971:787; R. Millon 1981:227; Pasztory 1978*b*:14.

21. Hirth 1978*b*:325; R. Millon 1981:223.

22. Diehl 1989*c*:9, 11; Diehl and Berlo 1989:2–3. See Yoffee (1988) for a summary of collapse theories and Tainter (1988:19–20) for an overview of collapse characteristics.

23. R. Millon 1981:236–37. As Millon notes, Batres's possible reference to slaughtered inhabitants found in the House of the Priests (R. Millon 1973:63) provides some slight evidence of invaders. But if invaders were involved in the destruction, they must have been closely associated with Teotihuacan and understood its symbols of power and ritual.

24. R. Millon 1981:236–37. The front and sides of the staircase of the Pyramid of Quetzalcoatl were burned during the Tlamimilolpa phase (ca. A.D. 200–450).

25. Sanders, Parsons, and Santley 1979:130. However, Diehl (1989*c*:11–12) challenges this estimate as too high.

26. R. Millon 1981:235.

27. García Cook 1981:269; R. Millon 1981:235; Pasztory 1978*b*:15; Sanders, Parsons, and Santley 1979:134, 137.

28. R. Millon 1973:63; 1981:235–36; Pasztory 1978*b*:8, 14; Sanders, Parsons, and Santley 1979:137.

29. Vayrynen 1989:123. Wauchope (1975:55) suggests that the non-Teotihuacan-dominated cities of highland Guatemala outstripped Kaminaljuyu because they developed more successfully.

30. Cowgill 1977:189.

31. Pasztory 1978*b*:14.

32. R. Millon 1973:63; Rosenau 1989:23.

33. Pasztory (1988*a*:75) suggests that there was an increase in dynastic-style depictions of elites in Teotihuacan art toward the city's end.

34. The influx of outsiders is likeliest during a period of economic expan-

sion, whereas the opposite is likely during economic contraction (Andreski 1968:133).

35. Diehl and Berlo 1989:4; Pasztory 1978*b*:15.

36. Flannery and Marcus 1983*c*:161–62.

37. Kowalewski, Feinman, Finsten, Blanton, and Nicholas 1989, 1:262–63, 270.

38. Blanton and Kowalewski 1981:105; Kowalewski, Feinman, Finsten, Blanton, and Nicholas 1989, 1:261, 281, 511.

39. Kowalewski, Feinman, Finsten, Blanton, and Nicholas 1989, 1:254, 259; Paddock 1983*b*:187. This is most obvious archaeologically for obsidian. Kowalewski, Feinman, Finsten, Blanton, and Nicholas (1989, 1:511) speculatively suggest that the Valley of Oaxaca region supplied itself and Teotihuacan with Pacific coast products, including cotton and textiles. With the ebb of Teotihuacan's influence generally, Monte Alban received less obsidian.

40. Blanton 1983*b*:186; Blanton and Kowalewski 1981:112; Flannery and Marcus 1983*d*:183–84. See Paddock (1966*b*:151–53) for a brief consideration of the cost of maintaining Monte Alban. An older and now discounted theory tied the collapse of Monte Alban to changes in the Mixteca and indirectly to the Toltecs (Bernal 1965*a*:808–809).

41. Blanton 1983*b*:186.

42. Kowalewski, Feinman, Finsten, Blanton, and Nicholas 1989, 1:270; Whitecotton 1990:7.

43. This reorientation on local polities is also evident in stone monuments that no longer focus on militaristic themes, but concentrate on kinship and marriages (Marcus 1983*d*:191).

44. Blanton 1983*b*:186; Flannery and Marcus 1983*d*:184–85.

45. Blanton and Kowalewski 1981:108; Kowalewski, Feinman, Finsten, Blanton, and Nicholas 1989, 1:251, 253, 305l; Paddock 1983*b*:187.

46. Blanton and Kowalewski 1981:108; Kowalewski, Feinman, Finsten, Blanton, and Nicholas 1989, 1:297, 305.

47. Proskouriakoff 1965:475.

48. See Cowgill's (1974) discussion of the Maya in the wake of Teotihuacan's collapse.

49. Morley, Brainerd, and Sharer 1983:90, 115. Also see Culbert's (1988:143) discussion of the concept.

50. Sharer (Morley, Brainerd, and Sharer 1983:115, 148) suggests that the hiatus resulted from Teotihuacan's withdrawal from the area.

51. A. Chase and D. Chase 1987:18.

52. Morley, Brainerd, and Sharer 1983:111–13.

53. A. Chase and D. Chase 1987:6; A. Chase 1988:2; D. Chase 1988:2; A. Chase and D. Chase n.d.*a*:1, 5; Culbert 1988:143; Schele and Friedel 1990:171–74.

54. A. Chase and D. Chase 1987:17; A. Chase 1988:2–3; A. Chase and D. Chase n.d.*a*:6, 14–16.

55. A. Chase 1988:8–10.

56. Morley, Brainerd, and Sharer 1983:115–18, 128–32.

CHAPTER 7: THE LATE CLASSIC INTERREGNUM

1. The Classic Maya collapse is much debated. However, Webster (1977: 367–68) points to competition over resource areas that led to increased warfare and militarism leading to the collapse.

2. Paddock 1983c:210.

3. This estimate is down from an earlier high of 42,000; see Andrews and Andrews (1980:17) for a discussion of these figures.

4. Kinz and Fletcher 1983:210. This figure seems high and may reflect a difference in perspective between these authors and others working in the Maya area.

5. Webster 1977:366.

6. Fox and Justeson 1986; Marcus 1976a:19, 39–41; 1987; Mathews 1980; 1985; Morley, Brainerd, and Sharer 1983:93–94, 107; William T. Sanders, personal communication.

7. Although Maya nobles appear to have had sexual access to more than one woman (Sanders 1990), they were apparently formally monogamous. Such a restriction on the proliferation of nobles is consistent with an aristocratic system that cannot expand overly much and therefore wants its wealth and privileges to remain intact in the hands of a limited nobility. Bound captives are shown on Piedras Negras Lintel 4 (W. Coe 1959:13), Stelae 12 (A.D. 795) (Greene, Rands, and Graham 1972:44–45), and 35 (Maler 1901:74); on Aguateca Stela 6 (A.D. 771) (Greene, Rands, and Graham 1972:190–91); on Tikal Altars 8, 9, and 10 (Greene, Rands, and Graham 1972:296; Jones and Satterthwaite 1982:figs. 30, 32, 34a, b) and Stelae 4, 10, 11 (Jones and Satterthwaite 1982:figs. 7, 14, 16), 18 (A.D. 731?), and 19 (A.D. 680?) (Greene, Rands, and Graham 1972:126–29); on Yaxchilan Lintel 12 (Graham and Von Euw 1977:33) and Hieroglyphic Stairway 3 (Graham 1982:166, 168, 171); on a Late Classic lintel in the Yaxchilan vicinity (Greene, Rands, and Graham 1972:144–45); on Bonampak Lintels 1, 2, and 3 (A.D. 790) (Greene, Rands, and Graham 1972:156–61) and Stela 3 (A.D. 785?) (Greene, Rands, and Graham 1972:152–53); on Ixkun Stelae 1 and 5 (Graham 1980:138–39, 149); on Ucanal Altars 1 and 3 (Graham 1980:165, 167); and on Tonina Monument 8 (Mathews 1983:27–31). Capture scenes are also depicted on Yaxchilan Lintels 8 and 45 (Graham 1979:99; Graham and Von Euw 1977:27), in submission before a lord at Yaxchilan Lintel 16 (A.D. 770?) (Greene, Rands, and Graham 1972:80–81), bound and being stood over by their captors in Stela 12 at Piedras Negras (W. Coe 1959:12), and being held by the hair by a lord at La Mar Stela 3 (A.D. 795) (Greene, Rands, and Graham 1972:60–61). See also the studies by Baudez and Mathews (1978) and Marcus (1974) of captives.

8. Lowe 1985:202.

9. Maya rulers are depicted standing on other people at Palenque on the Tablet of the Temple of the Sun (A.D. 690) (Greene, Rands, and Graham 1972:30–31), and on the Tablet of the Slaves (A.D. 730) (Greene, Rands, and Graham 1972:38–39); on Dos Pilas Stela 17 (A.D. 810?) (Greene, Rands, and Graham 1972:200–201); on Seibal Stela 11 (A.D. 849) (Greene, Rands, and

Graham 1972:234–35); on Ixkun Stela 1 (A.D. 790) (Greene, Rands, and Graham 1972:346–47); on Naranjo Stelae 13, 14, 19, 21, 23, 24, 29, and 30 (Graham 1978:77, 79; Graham and Von Euw 1975:37, 39, 49, 53, 59, 63); on Ucanal Stela 4 (Graham 1980:159–60); on Ixtutz Stela 1 (Graham 1980:175); on Itzimte Stela 11 (Von Euw 1977:27); on Xultun Stelae 1, 4, 5, 8, 14, 17, 21, 22, 23, 24, and 25 (Von Euw 1978:11, 19, 23, 31, 46, 55; Von Euw and Graham 1984:73–74, 77, 79–80, 83–84, 87–88); on Tikal Stelae 5, 10, and 11 (Jones and Satterthwaite 1982:figs. 7*b*, 14*b*, 16*a*).

10. A. Chase and D. Chase n.d.*b*:14.

11. Andreski 1968:88; Creveld 1989:12. Changes between the Early and Late Classic may reflect the relative scarcity of Early Classic monuments that has skewed the sample. But the developmental sequence from simpler to complex arms and armor between the Early and Late Classic suggests that these depictions generally reflect reality.

12. A military force of six identically armed and clad warriors are depicted before their rulers on Lintel 2 (see Maler 1901, plate XXXI) in A.D. 658.

13. Schele and Miller 1986:214. What may be armor is shown in carvings on Yaxchilan Lintels 16 (ca. A.D. 770) (Graham and Von Euw 1977:41; Greene, Rands, and Graham 1972:80–81), 41, and 45 (Graham and Von Euw 1977:41, 99), covering the torso but not the limbs. What may be a feather tunic is shown on Naranjo Stela 21 (Graham and Von Euw 1975:53). Quilted cotton armor is found on ceramic warrior figurines from Altar de Sacrificios (Willey 1972:37), Seibal (Willey 1978:23), Jaina (Schele and Miller 1986:230), and Palenque (Rands and Rands 1965:fig. 34). See also Rands and Rands (1965:543–46). However, see the examples in Pollock (1980:196, 197, 269, 303, 319, 379, 442, 449).

14. Bonampak 1955; Mahler 1965:585. The Chacmultun murals in building 3 show Maya warriors carrying thrusting spears, but wearing little formal attire (Barrera Rubio 1980:175–76; Thompson 1904:14–17, plate VIII).

15. In the Bonampak murals (Bonampak 1955), a number of soldiers wear headgear representing animals and supernatural figures (Thompson 1955*a*:52). Helmets may appear on the Palenque Tablet of the Slaves (A.D. 730) (Greene, Rands, and Graham 1972:38–39) and on Lacanha Stela 1 (A.D. 593) (Greene, Rands, and Graham 1972:164–65). Maler (1901:59) interprets Piedras Negras Lintel 2 as depicting a richly dressed warrior wearing a great helmet with plumes of feathers. A soldier wears an avian costume on Oxkintok Stela 12 (Proskouriakoff 1950:fig. 88*b*). And at Altar de Sacrificios, a ceramic figurine shows a warrior with a jaguar-head helmet (Willey 1972:37); there is another jaguar helmet on Yaxchilan Lintel 26 (Graham and Von Euw 1977:57), while one at Chama shows an animal-head headdress (Rands and Rands 1965:fig. 34).

16. Military orders existed later and Thompson (1955*a*:63) suggests their presence in the Late Classic based on the attire of the warriors depicted in the Bonampak murals.

17. For example, shields are depicted at Uaxactun (O. G. Ricketson 1937: 178). They are also depicted on figurines from Altar de Sacrificios (Willey 1972: 34, 37, 75) and Seibal (Willey 1978:23), on stelae at Aguateca and Dos Pilas

(Graham 1967:10, 12), and on a ceramic vessel (Kerr 1989–90, 1:57), where shields are larger than usual—possibly a concession to the miniature format. See also Proskouriakoff (1950:93).

18. Examples of small, circular shields are found on El Cayo, Wall Panel 2 (A.D. 700–750) (Greene, Rands, and Graham 1972:58–59); on Yaxchilan Lintel 25 (ca. A.D. 780) and Lintel 42 (ca. A.D. 760) (Greene, Rands, and Graham 1972:86–87, 90–91); on Aguateca Stela 6 (A.D. 771) (Greene, Rands, and Graham 1972:190–91); on Dos Pilas Stelae 1 (A.D. 706) and 17 (A.D. 810?) (Greene, Rands, and Graham 1972:194–95, 200–201); on Tamarindito Stela 3 (Late Classic) (Greene, Rands, and Graham 1972:204); on Tikal Lintel 3, Temple IV (ca. A.D. 750) (Greene, Rands, and Graham 1972:302–303); on Naranjo Stelae 1, 11, 19, and 21 (Graham and Von Euw 1975:11, 33, 49, 53); on Xunantunich Stela 8 (Graham 1978:55) and Lintels 42 and 52 (Graham 1979:93, 113); on Itzimte Stelae 3, 10, and 12 (Von Euw 1977:11, 25, 29); on Tzum Stela 3 (Von Euw 1977:55); on La Honradez Stela 5 (Von Euw and Graham 1984:109–10); on the El Peru Stela (Hellmuth 1987:134); and on Tikal Lintel 3 (Jones and Satterthwaite 1982:fig. 74). These shields also appear on painted ceramics (Robicsek 1981:70–72, 74, 112). Also see the probable turtle-shell shield on Stela 7 at Aguateca (Graham 1967:24).

19. Hellmuth 1987:134.

20. Thompson 1955b:62. Those depicted in the Bonampak murals are 60–90 cm long and 30–50 cm wide. Other examples are shown at Yaxchilan Lintel 16 (ca. A.D. 770) (Graham and Von Euw 1977:41; Greene, Rands, and Graham 1972:80–81), Lintel 45 (ca. A.D. 750) (Graham 1979:99; Greene, Rands, and Graham 1972:92–93), elsewhere in the Yaxchilan vicinity (Greene, Rands, and Graham 1972:144–45), and on La Honradez Stela 3 (Von Euw and Graham 1984:103). Flexible shields are also found on painted ceramics (M. Coe 1978:49–50; 1982:21).

21. See Kerr (1989–90, 2:204) for an inside view of the top grip of a flexible shield. An unusual round shield is depicted on a Maya ceramic vessel (Kerr 1989–90, 1:69). In contrast to most round shields, this example is somewhat larger and is held by a loop attached to the top, suggesting that it is flexible. Adding to the peculiarity of this depiction is the fact that the four figures holding these shields are also armed with axes. Axes are usually paired with small round shields that are used for parrying because the ax is too short to be truly suitable for this defensive maneuver. Another possibility is that this unprovenanced vessel may be fake.

22. Representations of rigid rectangular shields are found on Lacanha Stela 1 (A.D. 593) (Greene, Rands, and Graham 1972:164–65; Proskouriakoff 1950:fig. 44b), Aguateca Stela 2 (A.D. 736) (Greene, Rands, and Graham 1972:186–87), Naranjo Stela 2 (A.D. 716) (Graham and Von Euw 1975:13; Greene, Rands, and Graham 1972:322–23), and Piedras Negras Stelae 26 and 35 (Proskouriakoff 1950:figs. 53a, b).

23. A fourth type, a "keyhole"-shaped shield, was found depicted on a ceramic figurine from Seibal, but is very uncommon (Willey 1978:23).

24. O. G. Ricketson 1937:178. Spears are shown at Palenque, Tablet of the

Temple of the Sun (A.D. 690) (Greene, Rands, and Graham 1972:30–31); on
Piedras Negras Lintel 2 (Maler 1901:59), Lintel 4 (ca. A.D. 700) (Greene,
Rands, and Graham 1972:50–51), and Stela 35 (Maler 1901:74); on La Mar
Stela 3 (A.D. 795) (Greene, Rands, and Graham 1972:60–61); on Yaxchilan
Lintel 12 (Graham and Von Euw 1977:33), Lintel 16 (ca. A.D. 770) (Graham
and Von Euw 1977:41; Greene, Rands, and Graham 1972:80–81), Lintel 25,
(ca. A.D. 780) (Graham and Von Euw 1977:55; Greene, Rands, and Graham
1972:86–87), Lintel 45 (ca. A.D. 750) (Graham 1979:99; Greene, Rands, and
Graham 1972:92–93), Stela 5 (Late Classic) and Stela 20 (ca. A.D. 700)
(Greene, Rands, and Graham 1972:112–13, 130–31); on Aguateca Stela 2
(A.D. 736) and Stela 6 (A.D. 771) (Greene, Rands, and Graham 1972:186–87,
190–91); on Bonampak Lintels 1, 2, and 3 (ca. A.D. 790) (Greene, Rands, and
Graham 1972:156–61); on Tikal Lintel 3, Temple IV (ca. A.D. 750) (Greene,
Rands, and Graham 1972:302–303); on Naranjo Stela 8 (Graham and Von
Euw 1975:27) and Stela 21 (Graham and Von Euw 1975:53); on Xunantuich
Stela 8 (Graham 1978:123) and Stela 9 (Graham 1978:125); on Itzimte Stela 9
(Von Euw 1977:23); and on Tzum Stela 6 (Von Euw 1977:63). Spears are also
depicted in figurines at Altar de Sacrificios (Willey 1972:34), in the graffiti at
Tikal (Trik and Kampen 1983:figs. 9, 15*b*, 16, 26*a*, 32*a*, 47*f*, 47*i*, 47*n*, 55*e*, 58*c*,
75*d*, 76*f*), on painted ceramic vessels (M. Coe 1978:49–50, 65, 67–68, 85–86;
1982:21, 23, 78; Kerr 1989–90, 1:57, 59; Robicsek 1981:70–72, 74, 112) and
in the Bonampak (Thompson 1955*a*:48) and Chacmultun murals (Thompson
1904:14–17, plate VIII). However, portable art, such as ceramic vessels and
figurines, are often without provenance and thus of uncertain date and origin.
Moreover, some of those not unearthed as the result of archaeological excavations are of questionable authenticity and should be used advisedly as corroboration rather than as primary evidence. See also Proskouriakoff (1950:99) and the
discussion in Willey, Bullard, Glass, and Gifford (1965:412) on the suitability of
Classic Maya points as thrusting weapons. Some spears show no points, or only
very small ones, and have no trailing decoration behind the point that might
have hindered its flight, which indicates that they could have been thrown,
unlike the heavier thrusting spears. Also, the spears are held in an overhand way
that suggests they may have been intended to be thrown as javelins (Kerr 1989–
90, 1:14). However, other depictions show spears being used to stab with this
same overhand grip (e.g., Greene, Rands, and Graham 1972:160–61) and the
Bonampak murals also show spears with small points (some with considerable
decoration) used to stab in this overhand manner and often held very far back
on the shaft.

25. Spears with toothed insets below the point are shown at Yaxchilan
Lintels 8 (ca. A.D. 750) and 41 (ca. A.D. 760) (Graham 1979:91; Graham and
Von Euw 1977:27; Greene, Rands, and Graham 1972:72–73, 88–89), and on
Yaxchilan Stelae 18 (A.D. 731?) and 19 (ca. A.D. 680) (Greene, Rands, and
Graham 1972:126–29).

26. Stela 1 (A.D. 869) (Greene, Rands, and Graham 1972:216–17).

27. Pollock 1980:172, 322, 508, 514; O. G. Ricketson 1937:178; Thompson 1955*b*:61–62. Clubs are also depicted in ceramic figurines from Altar de

Sacrificios (Willey 1972:34, 75). Rands and Rands (1965:543–46) also report clubs as diagnostic traits of Classic Maya warrior figurines although they are erroneously labeled macuahuitls (broadswords). A mace is held by a ceramic figure from Chama (Rands and Rands 1965:fig. 34). See also Proskouriakoff (1950:99). Axes are shown on Yaxchilan, Lintels 42, dating to A.D. 760 (Graham 1979:93; Greene, Rands, and Graham 1972:90–91) and 58 (Graham 1979: 125), on Aguas Calientes Stela 1, dating to A.D. 790 (Greene, Rands, and Graham 1972:182–83), on Itzimte Stela 3 (Von Euw 1977:11), on the Dumbarton Oaks Palenque Tablet (Robicsek 1981:230), and on ceramics (M. Coe 1978:35, 37–38, 49–50; 1982:24–25; Hellmuth 1987:104, 305; Kerr 1989–90, 1:69, 121; Robicsek 1981:23, 25, 180). A wooden club inset with stone blades is also shown on Uaxactun Stela 5, tentatively dated A.D. 366 (Greene, Rands, and Graham 1972:308–309). In the Bonampak murals, one figure holds a club with toothlike blades (Thompson 1955b:62) and a similar weapon is shown on Uaxactun Stela 5 (Graham 1986:143) and on a carving at the Hunacab mouth of the cave at Loltun (Proskouriakoff 1950:fig. 38b). Two Palenque figures carry clubs with three and six blades respectively (Rands and Rands 1965:figs. 33, 34). One unusual weapon is a long pole with three inset blades on Tikal Stela 20 (Jones and Satterthwaite 1982:fig. 29). This type also appears on a painted ceramic vessel in a supernatural context (Robicsek 1981:28).

28. Axes were probably executioners' tools (Robicsek 1981:15), as was the case among the Aztecs (Hassig 1988:92). See the elaborate dress of ax-carriers suggesting their noncombatant role (Pollock 1980:449). Metal axes are much superior to stone ones (Ferrill 1985:39). In the Old World, relatively short arms, such as axes and maces, generally declined as armor improved and they were replaced by longer arms, such as swords and halberds (Ferrill 1985:20; Yadin 1963, 1:11).

29. Pollock 1980:172, 319, 442, 508, 514; Kerr 1989–90, 1:69.

30. Slings and blowguns continued in use but not as military weapons (W. Coe 1959:12). See the blowgun scenes on Maya vessels (Hellmuth 1987:205, 212–13, 256; Kerr 1989–90, 1:68; Robicsek 1981:83–84). Slings themselves are not found, but slingstones have been recovered archaeologically. Carefully finished spherical stones that were probably slingstones were found at Classic Uaxactun and at Copan (E. B. Ricketson 1937:191). Similar spheres were found at Tikal, Altar de Sacrificios, and elsewhere (Haviland 1985:167, 175; Willey 1972:95, 138–39). Knives were used only as secondary weapons, primarily to dispatch the wounded and are also shown in sacrificial scenes at Bilbao Monuments 1 and 21 (Greene, Rands, and Graham 1972:396–97, 410–11). Both monuments date from the Middle Classic. Knives are also depicted on Yaxchilan Lintels 4 and 26 (Graham and Von Euw 1977:19, 57), in the murals at Mul-Chic, Yucatan (Piña Chan 1962:111, 113), and on Maya ceramics (Kerr 1989–90, 1:49, 91), but these appear to be for executions and are not weapons. A possible weapon that may fall into the knife category is an eccentric flint similar to the Olmec "knuckle-dusters" and which may or may not have been a weapon. This is shown on Naranjo Stela 30 (Graham 1979:79), Tikal Altar 5 and Lintel 2 (Jones and Satterthwaite 1982:figs. 23, 72), and on painted ceramic vessels (Hellmuth 1987:77). See also Proskouriakoff (1950:99). See the

examples in Pollock (1980:196, 197) of Maya warriors using knives to deliver the coup de grace.

31. Thrusting spears dominate the battle depicted in the Bonampak murals; there are also a few clubs, but atlatls and slings are completely absent (Bonampak 1955).

32. Atlatl darts are depicted on Naranjo Stela 2 (A.D. 716) (Graham and Von Euw 1975:13; Greene, Rands, and Graham 1972:322–23) and on a Maya ceramic vessel (Kerr 1989–90, 1:74), and both atlatls and darts are represented on Ucanal Stela 4 (Graham 1980:159–60). A graffito from Tikal may depict atlatl darts (Trik and Kampen 1983:fig. 64g). See also Pollock (1980:196, 197). An unusual (and possibly unique) depiction of an atlatl being used in combat by a Classic Maya warrior is found on a ceramic vessel (Kerr 1989–90, 2:207). This scene shows a lone atlatlist and several spearmen, suggesting its use simply as an alternative weapon rather than one to be used en masse and from a distance. However, questions of provenance and authenticity render this example problematic.

33. In the Bonampak battle scene (Bonampak 1955), large fanlike devices on staffs are displayed that, if battle standards, would suggest the use of military formations and thus larger armies. However, the fanlike devices appear only to the side of the main activity and are located with the trumpeters, suggesting that they did not serve as combat standards but more likely royal emblems. Moreover, the murals at Chacmultun (Thompson 1904:14–17, plate VIII) and the graffiti at Tikal (Trik and Kampen 1983:figs. 18e, 65i, 68a, 70e, 73) show these same features oriented vertically, which suggests that they may simply have been parasols or fans (Miller 1986:23), although these parasol-like standards are hoisted on spear shafts. See also Kurbjuhn's (1977) discussion of Maya fans as political symbols.

34. The relative absence of fortifications in the Maya lowlands is at least partly the result of not looking for them and because the primary thrust has been to look for earthen and stone walls, leading archaeologists to ignore possible organic remains of such defensive structures as wooden palisades. The large defensive wall and dry moat at Tikal were not recognized as such for years despite being pierced by paths along which archaeologists repeatedly passed between Tikal and Uaxactun. Palisades would leave even fewer traces (Webster 1976a:89; 1979:148).

35. I am indebted to John Justeson for supplying the data for this and the three following notes concerning the timing of Maya warfare. Though not comprehensive, the following claims of warfare and conquests have been found in the Maya lowlands. All dates are Gregorian.

Caracol over Tikal	1 May 562
Caracol over Naranjo	27 Dec 631
Caracol over Naranjo	4 Mar 636
Tortuguero	4 Jun 644
Tortuguero	23 Dec 649
Tortuguero	1 Apr 652
Piedras Negras	16 Feb 662

Piedras Negras	5 Mar 669
Tikal	28 Sep 671
Dos Pilas/Tikal	12 Jan 670
Dos Pilas	11 Dec 672
Dos Pilas	16 Dec 677
Dos Pilas	14 Feb 697
Dos Pilas/Tikal	1 Jun 705
Altar de Sacrificios	8 Dec 713?
Yaxchilan over Lacanha	14 Jul 729
Dos Pilas over Seibal	3 Dec 735
Quirigua over Copan	3 May 738
Yaxchilan	9 May 755
La Mar over Pomona	27 Apr 774
???	28 Mar 780
???	2 Apr 781
??? over Yaxchilan	6 Apr 782
Piedras Negras over Pomona	5 Apr 794
Yaxchilan	16 Mar 808

See Culbert (1988:143–48) for a year-by-year overview of Lowland Maya political history based on inscriptions.

36. Though not comprehensive, the following conquest claims have been found in the Maya lowlands. All dates are Gregorian.

Tikal over Site Q	8 Aug 695
Naranjo over Ucanal	7 Sep 698
Tonina over Palenque	11 Feb 711
Yaxchilan over Lacanha	19 Nov 564
Chinikiha	27 Dec 573
Yaxchilan	1 Jul 594
Yaxchilan	2 Aug 647
Tortuguero	21 Nov 649
Tortuguero	23 Dec 649
Palenque	28 Aug 654
Palenque	2 Aug 659
Dos Pilas	2 Mar 664
Dos Pilas	12 Jan 670
Yaxchilan	24 Feb 681
Yaxchilan	25 Feb 681
Yaxchilan	29 Nov 689
Tikal over Site Q?	8 Aug 695
Yaxchilan	21 Nov 701
Yaxchilan	18 Nov 713
Palenque	19 Sep 723
Yaxchilan	3 Sep 727

Yaxchilan	14 Jul 729
Yaxchilan	18 Apr 732
Bonampak	17 Sep 740
Yaxchilan	10 Feb 752
Yaxchilan	9 May 755
Bonampak	8 Jan 787
Bonampak	12 Jan 787
Yaxchilan subsidiary site?	23 Aug 783
Piedras Negras	27 Aug 787
Copan	9 Mar 793
La Mar	18 Nov 794
Yaxchilan	17 Dec 796
Yaxchilan	29 Dec 796
Yaxchilan	16 Mar 808
Yaxha captures Bat Jaguar	14 Aug 796
Yaxchilan	2 Jan 798
Yaxchilan	30 Jul 798
Yaxchilan	1 Nov 798
Yaxchilan	29 Dec 799
Yaxchilan	30 Jan 800
Yaxchilan	6 Mar 800
Yaxchilan	22 Mar 800

37. The Bonampak murals do not show anyone being killed. Instead, figures are depicted being taken prisoner (Rands 1952:79). Two other types of war-related events—executions and marriages—were recorded, but are not directly tied to combat and exhibit no seasonal clustering.

Ax Events

Altun Ha	6 May 596
Tortuguero	3 Feb 645
Tortuguero	28 Jul 649
Tortuguero	4 Jun 644
Tortuguero	28 Nov 649
Palenque over Site Q	28 Aug 654
Palenque	22 May 729
Dos Pilas over Seibal	4 Dec 735
Quirigua	3 May 738
Ixkun	22 Dec 779
La Mar	1 Apr 792

Marriages

21 Feb 636
21 Nov 686
22 Nov 686

21 Aug 695
17 Mar 714
18 Mar 714
7 May 725
30 Jun 729

38. Adams and Jones 1981:301; Sharer 1978e:63–67. Marital ties alone were unstable, lasting perhaps two to three generations for newly established sites but only one to two for existing cities. See Johnston's (1985:49–56) assessment of marital alliances in the Río Pasión region.

39. Schele and Miller 1986:219. This is particularly apparent at Palenque, where the conquest monuments were carved elsewhere and carried to that city (Baudez and Mathews 1978:36).

40. However, Baudez and Mathews (1978:32) interpret these representations as successive conditions of the same captives.

41. Lowe 1985:203–204.

42. Tourtellot and Sabloff 1972:131–33.

43. Culbert 1973b:16–17; Santley, Killion, and Lycett 1986:125.

44. Lowe 1985:202–203; Sabloff and Rathje 1975. See Adams's (1973:21–34) summary of collapse theories in the Maya area.

45. Lowe 1985:207; Tainter 1988:167, 173, 175.

46. García Payón 1971:527–32; Pasztory 1978b:13.

47. Kampen 1972:fig. 32a; Tuggle 1968. For excellent line drawings of the major sculptures, see Kampen 1972.

48. Kampen 1972:51, 55, 56, 61, 93, 96–98, figs. 20, 23, 32a, 32b, 34d. Artistic representations of military activity at El Tajín appear primarily in carvings on columns that apparently depict the life of a king of that city, named 13 Rabbit, who lived around A.D. 900 (Kampen 1978:121–22; Tuggle 1968:45–46). These monuments, including stelae, commemorate rulers in a fashion that suggests an aristocratic military system (Kampen 1979:101). Kampen (1979) also suggests that many of these representations are in a Maya style.

49. Military orders: Kampen 1972:figs. 32a, 32b; 1979:96; figs. 24 (fish), 32a and 32b (birds), 34c (coyote); Tuggle 1968:41.

50. The best example of armor (Kampen 1972:fig. 32a) shows a man in a bird helmet wearing a suit, but he appears to be a captive rather than a warrior from El Tajín. There is one possible depiction of a shield in an incomplete carving that may show a round shield with a feather fringe (Kampen 1972:fig. 32b).

51. Kampen 1972:figs. 22, 23, 32a; Tuggle 1968:41.

52. Kolb 1986:183.

53. Armillas 1951:78–80; Drennan 1983b:208; Elam 1989:406; Piña Chan 1972:31.

54. There was an increase in per capita obsidian use from Formative to Classic to Late Classic, making regional interdependence increasingly pressing (Santley 1989a:143–44). The existence of a far-flung trade network is supported by the presence of portable goods at Cacaxtla suggesting trade ties with Oaxaca and the Gulf coast (Nagao 1989:93) and by the influence of Teoti-

huacan, Cholula, the southern Gulf coast, and the Maya area on Cacaxtla's ceramic assemblage (López de Molina and Molina Feal 1986:69–70; McVicker 1985:82). Schele and Friedel (1990:163) note the spread of Maya motifs to Cacaxtla. Ball and Taschek (1989:190) maintain that, after Teotihuacan's withdrawal, Maya societies took control of the trade links, especially intermediate Maya groups who Sharer (Morley, Brainerd, and Sharer 1983:159) suggests may have been Putun Maya. The trading hypothesis for Cacaxtla finds significant support (López de Molina 1977b:9), including a recently discovered mural depicting God M (identified by Thompson [1966:165] as the Maya merchant god), and a loaded packframe (Carlson 1989).

55. Armillas (1945:137) suggests the Olmeca-Xicalanca may have spoken Macro-Otomangue, Chocho-Popoloca, or Popoloca-Mixteca, and that they were strongly Nahuatlized. This last conjecture is probably incorrect.

56. There were Maya loanwords in Nahuatl in central Mexico, but this may have been incidental to trade and is not directly relevant to Cacaxtla (Justeson, Norman, Campbell, and Kaufman 1985:70).

57. Berlo 1989a:30; Davies 1977:107–10; Ixtlilxóchitl 1975–77, 2:7–8; Kubler 1980:164; Lombardo de Ruiz, López de Molina, and Molina Feal 1986:503; McVicker 1985:84. But see Nagao (1989:86, 86n.7). See also Lombardo de Ruiz (1986:241–42), who compares the historical accounts of the Olmeca-Xicalanca movements with archaeologically recovered materials at Cacaxtla.

58. However, see the position of García Cook (1981:264, 269) who suggests that the Olmeca-Xicalanca were not simply recent immigrants, but may have had contacts with the Tlaxcala area from as early as A.D. 300.

59. Lombardo de Ruiz, López de Molina, and Molina Feal 1986:503. García Cook (1981:269) suggests that the Olmeca-Xicalanca may have contributed to the downfall of Teotihuacan but, if so, their role was certainly not pivotal.

60. Carrasco 1971:471; Davies 1977:106–15; Dumond and Müller 1972:1210; García Cook 1974:15; 1981:269; Ixtlilxóchitl 1975–77, 2:7–8; Jiménez Moreno 1966:63; Kubler 1980:164; Lagunas Rodríguez, Serrano Sánchez, and López Alonso 1976:82–84; López de Molina and Molina Feal 1986:14–17; Müller 1970:139–42; Muñoz Camargo 1947:35–39. This hundred-year period, from A.D. 800 to 900, is the Cholulteca I phase (Lagunas Rodríguez, Serrano Sánchez, and López Alonso 1976:82–84).

61. Cholula is commonly viewed as controlling Cacaxtla (Foncerrada de Molina 1980:186), but this is probably biased by the vagaries of whose historical chronicles survived.

62. Dumond and Müller 1972:1215; Noguera 1945:139–51; 1960:66; Sáenz 1961:43. Noguera's (1945:139–40) assessment of trade between Cholula and Xochicalco did not take Cacaxtla into account as excavations of that site only began in the late 1970s. There is also an architectural similarity between Cholula, Xochicalco, and El Tajín (Pasztory 1978c:112).

63. Sanders, Parsons, and Santley 1979:149.

64. Armillas 1945:138–40; García Cook 1974:15; 1981:269.

65. García Cook 1978:177; 1981:270, 273; Sanders, Parsons, and Santley 1979:133–37.

66. García Cook 1978:176–77; 1981:270; Molina Feal 1977:3.

67. Kubler (1980:173) puts them at A.D. 700–900, whereas López de Molina (1977a:3) puts them at A.D. 700–800.

68. Foncerrada de Molina 1976:8–20; 1982:23, 27–33; Kubler 1980:164–69, 173; López de Molina 1977a:6; 1977b:7–8. Foncerrada de Molina's (1980:184) claim that the Cacaxtla style was unique to the area underemphasizes the similarities with elements elsewhere, and her later work (Foncerrada de Molina 1987:29–33) makes explicit connections with the Maya area.

69. Baird 1989:106; Foncerrada de Molina 1980:184; Robertson 1985:291, 294–96, 298; Walling 1982:211–13. McVicker (1985:89) feels the style of the Cacaxtla murals is less sophisticated than the murals at Bonampak and resembles that found in the coastal regions northwest of Bonampak. Based on additional newly discovered murals at Cacaxtla, Foncerrada de Molina (1987:30–33) sees strong Maya influences, with possibly ties to the Maya site of Palenque. However, this intrusive style had no long-term impact on central Mexican art (Robertson 1985:301).

70. Berlo 1989a:23; McVicker 1985:82, 89; Robertson 1985:299; Walling 1982:209. Baird (1989:114–15) suggests parallels with Dos Pilas and Aguateca, and Lombardo de Ruiz (1986:227, 234) compares elements from the murals with Teotihuacan and the Maya sites of Bonampak, Yaxchilan, Mulchic, Uaxactun, Copan, Chicanna, and Altun Ha. Despite the absence of clearcut Maya glyphs, Kubler (1980:169) points out two possible exceptions: something that resembles the lily-jaguar glyph in the head of the north panel jaguar-serpent and something that resembles the Tikal Emblem glyph in the south jamb headdress. McVicker (1985:92) suggests that this nonglyphic style of mural was a foreign elite's attempt to communicate with their dominated subjects whereas Foncerrada de Molina (1980:194) suggests that the Maya influences at Cacaxtla reached that site by way of Teotihuacan rather than directly, and Berlo (1989a:29–30) suggests the Cacaxtla glyphs derive from Teotihuacan's experiments in writing, but there is little material evidence of significant Teotihuacan ties (Nagao 1989:92). A third possibility is that Maya artists executed the murals for Mexican patrons who had no need for Maya glyphs (Walling 1982:209). However, a fourth, and I believe the best, possibility is that these peoples were Maya but they came from one of the groups that did not use Maya hieroglyphs or they were heavily influenced by Mixe-Zoquean writing systems (Justeson, Norman, Campbell, and Kaufman 1985:67–68).

71. Foncerrada de Molina 1980:192–93; Kubler 1980:172; McVicker 1985:96–97.

72. Foncerrada de Molina (1980:192) and McVicker (1985:84) claim the politico-religious murals are somewhat later than the battle murals, a position with which I agree, for the two vastly different states of affairs are not likely to have held simultaneously, and the upper structure containing the politico-religious murals partly rests on the lower structure containing the battle scene. However, Kubler (1980:173) feels the two sets of murals are contemporaneous. Foncerrada de Molina (1980:193) interprets this scene as a peace treaty whereas Kubler (1980:172) feels that the seated stucco figure between the jaguarman and birdman figures represents the emergence of a third coastal power

(probably Putun Maya) that resolved the differences between the other two. Alternative interpretations of this changing status include the resolution of insurrection, but this is unlikely. The two sides reflect different military traditions, with one group using rectangular shields and atlatls and the other using round shields and a mix of atlatls and thrusting spears. Interpreting this as the outcome of a marital alliance that fostered political peace is supported only by analogy (Robertson 1985:301). That the Jaguar was superior is suggested by the contrasts between the Eagle and Jaguar warriors in the upper temple. The Eagle warrior holds a crossbar-scepter (Cacaxtla 1987:113), presumably symbolizing political power, whereas the Jaguar warrior holds a bundle of atlatl darts (clearly identified as such by their barbed points) (Cacaxtla 1987:95).

73. No complete record of the Cacaxtla murals has been published because more are being uncovered, but good photographs of most of the murals are available in Cacaxtla (1987).

74. These details may show up better in these murals than in earlier carvings or ceramics and thus may not actually reflect a technological change, although because darts without barbed points are depicted in murals at Teotihuacan I am inclined to see these as real changes. At Cacaxtla, at any rate, archaeologically recovered points confirm the types depicted in the murals (López de Molina and Molina Feal 1986:70–74). Baus de Czitrom (1986:529) also lists one arrow among the weapons shown in the mural, but there is no evidence for bows and arrows in Mesoamerica at this time, nor for any bow in the murals. The object she identifies as an arrow is an atlatl dart. Lombardo de Ruiz (1986:224) also misidentifies darts as arrows at Cacaxtla. An interesting aside suggested by the battle mural is the issue of atlatl dart quivers. Kubler's (1984:83) claim for atlatl dart quivers at Tollan is unsupported (see Hassig 1988:293–94n.29); none have been found archaeologically, nor are any depicted in sculpture or paintings. Rather, atlatlists are consistently shown carrying darts in their hands. This mural at Cacaxtla shows the only certain depiction of atlatl darts in a formal carrier—a bundle rather than a quiver—although one may be depicted in the Mixtec Codex Vienna (1963:20) dating some 500–700 years later. See also Winning's (1980) discussion of ritual cloths used to hold darts at Teotihuacan.

75. These inset blades are functional and not simply a decorative feature (contra Baird 1989:116) so their similarity with spears elsewhere is, perhaps, less meaningful. See Larick (1985) for an analysis of spear changes based on both function and style.

76. Berlo 1989a:28–29; Walling 1982:206.

77. Berlo (1989a:29) suggests that a partial glyph immediately in front of one of the Cacaxtla warriors depicts a fending stick. I do not feel this to be the case for two reasons. First, the initial identification of fending sticks was an erroneous one made by Charlot (1931, 1:252) of depictions of a curved club at Chichen Itza. See also Hassig (1988:294–95n.36). If the glyph is taken to refer to the misidentified weapon, this is its earliest (and highly improbable) appearance. And second, the partial glyph appears remarkably similar to speech glyphs found at Xochicalco (Hirth 1989:figs. 4b, 5).

78. Flexible shields were noted among the Aztecs by Díaz del Castillo (1908–16, 2:65) during the Spanish conquest but were minor.

79. Shield designs are typically functional rather than decorative, and often have a major impact on combat. See Dupuy (1984:43–44).

80. There were also occasional examples of round shields with top grips among the Maya. See the example in Schele and Miller (1986:231).

81. A similar hand-freeing development also occurred in the Byzantine empire (Dupuy 1984:56). Round shields were used earlier in the Maya area, but typically not with center arm loops. Rather, they had round hand loops at the top. See the Jaina example (Schele and Miller 1986:231).

82. Compare Dupuy (1984:66). Although not typical of lowland Maya warfare, heavy armor was found along the Gulf coast during the Late Classic, from Veracruz through Yucatan.

83. Jones 1987:18–20.

84. Ferrill 1985:143–44.

85. Foncerrada de Molina (1980:186–92) sees an essential continuity between Teotihuacan and Cacaxtla based on art styles. By contrast, I see a distinct break in military styles, strategic postures, political systems, and some weaponry between Teotihuacan and Cacaxtla, and far greater continuity between the latter site and the Maya area.

86. Baird 1989:114; Berlo 1989a:29.

87. García Cook 1981:270.

88. Armillas 1945:141–42; 1951:81; Foncerrada de Molina 1980:183; Kubler 1980:173; Lombardo de Ruiz, López de Molina, and Molina Feal 1986:504; McVicker 1985:82.

89. García Cook 1981:271; López de Molina and Molina Feal 1986:18.

90. Hirth 1984a:580, 584; Hirth and Angula Villaseñor 1981:148; Hirth and Cyphers Guillén 1988:13, 16, 19, 110–19, 145. After it was abandoned, Xochicalco dropped from 4.0 square kilometers to only 11.54 hectares (Hirth 1984a:580, 584; Hirth and Cyphers Guillén 1988:121, 139). Although Teotihuacan ceramics have been recovered from Xochicalco, these were mixed with Late Classic ceramics, were probably heirlooms, and their presence does not indicate contact between the two sites (Hirth 1984a:580).

91. Armillas 1951:78–79; Blackiston 1910:300–302; Gonzales Ortega 1938:421, 425; Hirth 1984a:581, 583; 1985:2–3; Hirth and Cyphers Guillén 1988:119–20, 135–39; Noguera 1945:120; 1960:34; Pasztory 1978b:16; Purdie 1912:482, 491; Seler 1888:80. For a dissenting and decidedly minority opinion about Xochicalco's fortifications, see Hardoy (1973:91).

92. Hirth 1984a:579–81.

93. Hirth 1984a:581, 583; 1985:2–3; 1989:70–72; Noguera 1945:120. See also the map of fortifications at Xochicalco in Hirth and Cyphers Guillén (1988:136) or Hirth (1989:71).

94. Hirth 1984a:583.

95. Hirth 1984a:583–84; Hirth and Cyphers Guillén 1988:137.

96. Hirth 1984a:582; Hirth and Cyphers Guillén 1988:132–33, 135; Pasztory 1978b:19.

97. Croix 1972:48–49; Toy 1985:170.

98. Hirth 1985:8; 1989:75–77; Peñafiel 1890, 1:33; Seler 1888:91.

99. Hirth 1985:1; 1989:73, 77. There is no evidence that these military orders are composed of *cuauhpipiltin*, meritocratic nobles.

100. Hirth (1984*a*:581) initially suggested that Xochicalco controlled a region covering much of western Morelos and neighboring portions of Guerrero, but extended this to include the area north to the Ajusco Mountains bordering the Valley of Mexico and south and west into the Mixteca Baja and the Balsas depression (Hirth 1989:77).

101. Hirth 1985:3; 1989:72.

102. Breton 1906:63; Hirth 1977:42; Seler 1888:86. Thrusting spears are not shown held by elite warriors but are represented in town glyphs (see Berlo 1989*a*:fig. 13*a*, p. 33). There are no bows and arrows at Xochicalco (Peñafiel 1890, 1:23). The obsidian projectile points Sáenz (1961:40–43; 1964*a*:70; 1967:10, 14) describes as arrow points are doubtless atlatl points. Weapons with barbed points and fletched shafts superficially resembling arrows are carved on the Xochicalco stelae (Sáenz 1961:49, 55; 1964*a*:73, 75), but they are actually atlatl darts, as they have the same diagnostic traits as the atlatl darts shown in the Cacaxtla murals and on the Pyramid of the Plumed Serpent at Xochicalco (see Hirth 1989:73), and both lack nocks. Although they are not depicted in the sculpture at Xochicalco, obsidian knives have been recovered archaeologically (Sáenz 1967:10, 14).

103. Although not definitively dated, the Pyramid of the Plumed Serpent appears to have been built relatively early in Xochicalco's history (Sáenz 1963:23; 1964*b*:13–14). In contrast, Escalona Robles (1953:364) dates the final construction of this pyramid at A.D. 905, based on the glyphs on its façade, but because the calendar system lacked an absolute starting point, this date is speculative.

104. Hirth and Cyphers Guillén 1988:121; Sáenz 1963:12–13.

105. Sáenz 1963:20.

106. Nagao (1989:94–95) says the Maya-like sculpture on the Pyramid of the Plumed Serpent is stiff, suggesting unfamiliarity with this mode of representation. She further identifies the cross-legged figure motif on the lower platform as a type that frequently appears on portable art in the Maya area, although it also appears on monumental art. She indicates that these depictions may have served as models for the carvings but acknowledges that no such Maya objects have been found at Xochicalco, although other types of Maya carvings have been.

107. Noguera 1961:37. However, I am not convinced by Nagao's (1989:98–100) argument that Xochicalco primarily traded with Oaxaca, Veracruz, and Guerrero and Michoacan, even though these areas had little impact on its monumental art, and that Xochicalco adopted foreign styles to emulate and identify with a superior authority, to express far-flung ties, or to symbolize supremacy and conquest. On the contrary, I take the emulation of Maya styles to indicate a close connection, without which there is little reason for copying.

108. Building E is the largest temple at Xochicalco and was apparently the primary focus of public worship (Hirth 1984*a*:582).

109. Burland (1952:121) interprets these representations as the fire god, whereas Noguera (1960:52) interprets them as lords or chiefs.

110. Hirth 1985:7; 1989:73–75. Burland (1952:122) interprets these figures as priests, possibly of the god Xiuhteuctli, but Berlo's (1989a:30–34) lengthier and more detailed comparative assessment presents a more compelling case for a conquest interpretation.

111. If the repeated person on the Pyramid of the Plumed Serpent is the same individual, why is he not named? Maybe he did not need to be, or perhaps he is named (as Tizoc is on the Stone of Tizoc)—his name may be all or part of the circle, mouth, bag, or part of the headdress, or the speaker glyph. The conqueror glyph element at Xochicalco's Pyramid of the Plumed Serpent may be the double trapezoid hat that also appears worn by a Tlaloc-like figure on Stela 2 and above an atlatl dart. Repeated carvings are also found in later sculptures. Groups on the warrior benches at Tollan and Tenochtitlan and on the Aztec Stone of the Warriors are presented en masse or in a sequence. They thus appear to represent numerous different individuals. Carvings in which the same figure is repeated in multiple distinct scenes—separated either by the completeness of scene or by a formal framing device such as a dividing line—as in the Stone of Tizoc and the recently discovered Aztec cuauhxicalli, depict the same figure repetitively, typically to recount a series of historical acts (see discussion in chapter 9). In the case of the Stone of Tizoc, it relates a series of conquests, and so too does it relate conquests by the same individual in the case of the Pyramid of the Plumed Serpent.

112. The pyramid is noted for its calendrical information (Breton 1906:63; Burland 1952:124–26; Gonzales Ortega 1938:429; Noguera 1960:45–47; Palacios 1948:463–64; Peñafiel 1890, 1:43; Seler 1888:84–85) that may commemorate a shift in the prevailing system (Noguera 1945:136; 1960:47, 52; but see Sáenz's [1964a:79] criticism of this notion). It also has significant religious content, as witnessed by the feathered serpent (Batres 1912:407; Burland 1952:120–21). The Pyramid of the Plumed Serpent went through three different constructions (Sáenz 1963:12–13). The short term of each, coupled with the pyramid's lifespan of less than 150 years (Sáenz 1963:23), supports the notion that the existing façade was constructed in one effort and likely commemorates the exploits of a single individual.

113. Hirth and Cyphers Guillén 1988:14; Nagao 1989:96; Noguera 1945: 139–51, 154; 1960:37; Sáenz 1961:40; 1964a:70, 80; 1967:10–13. However, Hirth (1984a:580) notes that all of the Teotihuacan ceramics are late (Metepec: A.D. 650–750), and they were found mixed with even later goods, suggesting that they were probably heirlooms and that their presence did not represent contemporary contact with Teotihuacan. For a fuller consideration of the ceramic assemblage at Xochicalco, see Hirth and Cyphers Guillén (1988:42–89).

114. Burland 1952:119, 124–25; Caso 1967:146–49, 173–78; López de Molina 1977a:6; Nagao 1989:93; Noguera 1945:154; 1948–49:115–19; 1960:67–68; Sáenz 1964a:78–79; 1967:19.

115. Robertson 1985:301.

116. Burland 1952:122; García Payon 1971:527; Sáenz 1964b:15–17; Steward 1956:137, 141.

117. Hirth and Cyphers Guillén 1988:148.

118. Hirth 1984a:581; Hirth and Cyphers Guillén 1988:147.

119. Hirth 1984a:581.

120. Hirth and Cyphers Guillén 1988:128, 150.

121. The abandonment of Xochicalco after A.D. 900 cannot be identified with certainty, but it may be supposed that it fragmented politically with the arrival of hostile groups (Hirth and Cyphers Guillén 1988:139). Its abandonment around this time is supported by a shift in ceramics, those found at the much-reduced Xochicalco during the following phase (A.D. 900–1250) are unlike those of the Valley of Mexico (Hirth and Cyphers Guillén 1988:139).

122. Sáenz 1961:61–62, 69–70, 78–80.

CHAPTER 8: THE REINTEGRATION OF MESOAMERICA

1. Sanders, Parsons, and Santley (1979:146–49), supported by Diehl (1983:137), interpret this as a division between Toltec and Cholula zones of influence.

2. Tollan is located on the site of modern-day Tula, Hidalgo. See Davies (1977:25–75) for a lengthy consideration of the location of Tollan, and Healan (1989b:5–6) for further discussion of that debate. Population estimates for Tollan vary considerably. Diehl variously estimated Tollan's population at 30,000–40,000 (Diehl 1983:60; Healan, Cobean, and Diehl 1989:245) and 32,000–37,000 (Diehl 1981:284). Stoutamire (1974:13) estimated the population at 65,000 and Yageun at 18,800–34,800 (Diehl 1983:60). Cobean and Guadalupe Mastache (1989:38) put Tollan's population at sixty thousand, an estimate supported by Healan and Stoutamire as a reasonable minimum (1989:235; Healan, Cobean, and Diehl 1989:245). Sanders, Parsons, and Santley (1979:143) also put Tollan's population at sixty thousand. In the face of the more recent estimates and a relatively clear majority opinion, I am using the sixty thousand population estimate.

3. Cobean and Guadalupe Mastache 1989:37–38; Diehl 1983:42; Guadalupe Mastache and Cobean 1989:51–55; Healan, Cobean, and Diehl 1989:241; Healan and Stoutamire 1989:234; Matos Moctezuma 1986:4.

4. Diehl 1981:279; Healan, Cobean, and Diehl 1989:241. The introduction of different ceramic traditions supports native historical accounts of various groups migrating into the area (Diehl 1983:42–43, 49–50).

5. Estimates range from 19,000 to 27,000 inhabitants, but Diehl (1983:43) reduces these by 40–50 percent.

6. Tollan Phase. Diehl 1981:280; 1983:58; Healan 1977:141; Healan, Cobean, and Diehl 1989:239, 245; Stoutamire 1974:13.

7. See Chadwick (1971b:475–76), Feldman (1974a), Mandeville (1970:130–46), and Tozzer (1957, 1:27–30) for summaries of the main accounts.

8. Chadwick 1971b:495–96; Tozzer 1957, 1:29.

9. Gendrop (1987:160) notes that representations of warriors in the art of Tollan occupied places that, until then, had been reserved for depictions of priests.

10. Cobean and Guadalupe Mastache 1989:38; Healan, Cobean, and Diehl

1989:241; Matos Moctezuma 1974b:69. The Prado ceramic complex occurs almost exclusively in Tula Chico and has close ties to the Bajío from which Tollan's founding elite may have originated (Healan, Cobean, and Diehl 1989: 241; Healan and Stoutamire 1989:234–35). Earlier, this area was thought to have remained completely vacant (Diehl 1981:280; 1983:45), but it has since been recognized that, although there was no construction, it was not totally unoccupied (Healan, Cobean, and Diehl 1989:244).

11. Diehl 1981:290.

12. Davies 1977:106, 141; Diehl 1983:14, 48–50; Healan 1989b:3; Healan, Cobean, and Diehl 1989:251; Katz 1972:125. For an overview of native accounts of Tollan, see Feldman (1974b:131–34).

13. Davies 1977:177; Diehl 1983:48–49; Healan, Cobean, and Diehl 1989:251. Archaeological evidence indicates that a foreign group settled in the south periphery of the city and was eventually incorporated into the city. Probably Nonoalca, they may have developed Tollan's obsidian industry, which expanded out from that same peripheral area of the city (Healan, Cobean, and Diehl 1989:251).

14. The Mesoamerican group—the Nonoalca—apparently did not speak Nahuatl when they entered Tollan, for there is little evidence of Nahuatl earlier in Mesoamerica (Justeson, Norman, Campbell, and Kaufman 1985:68), but they did when they left (Davies 1977:169).

15. Diehl 1983:16. This grid is not very pronounced and was recognized only recently (e.g., Diehl 1974b:191; Mastache Flores and Crespo Oviedo 1982:31; Stoutamire 1974:13), perhaps because the orientations changed during three different periods of growth (Healan, Cobean, and Diehl 1989:239, 244–45).

16. Kristan-Graham 1989:302–303, 316.

17. Seven of the column carvings of warriors are accompanied by glyphs, but they appear too abbreviated to be proper names. Kristan-Graham (1989: 202–203) argues that they are not placenames because they lack locative indicators and suggests that they may indicate lineage or clan affiliations, arguing by analogy from the fuller data at Chichen Itza. However, she does interpret the pillars as portraits of historic individuals, even though they are generically rendered (Kristan-Graham 1989:253, 255).

18. Diehl 1983:66, plates 12, 24; 1989b:26; Matos Moctezuma 1986: 18, 31.

19. Diehl 1983:94–95, 98. See examples of death and sacrificial depictions in Diehl (1983:plates 15, 18; 1989b:23), Healan (1989d:127), and Matos Moctezuma (1986:6, 8).

20. Bows and arrows were not used by the Toltecs. No arrow points have been recovered from Tollan (Janet M. Kerley, personal communications), nor are these weapons depicted in Toltec art. The projectile points recovered at Tollan that were reworked for hafting (Benfer 1974:59) were presumably used on atlatl darts. The objects identified as arrows by Matos Moctezuma (1986:24) are atlatl darts. However, the Aztecs thought the Toltecs had bows and arrows, or they were at least described as having them (Kirchhoff, Odena Güemes, and Reyes García 1976:185–86, 204–205; Sahagún 1950–82, 3:27, 35).

21. See the weaponry on the atlantids and carved columns in Fuentes, Trejo, and Gutiérrez Solano (1988:plates 19–22, 60–74).

22. Acosta 1961:226–27. For examples, see the atlatl held by a warrior on a carved frieze on the El Corral pyramid (Acosta 1974:33), the atlantids (Zambrano 1985:54), the façade of Pyramid B (Diehl 1983:plate 16), and in ceramic figurines (Stocker 1983:68).

23. Slashing weapons became dominant in the Old World with the advent of iron (Dupuy 1984:2–3; Ferrill 1985:43), which was markedly more suited to this purpose than bronze. In Mesoamerica, this development did not rest on such a technological breakthrough, but on altering existing weapons to new uses.

24. Acosta 1961:227–28. The short sword is depicted in carvings at Tollan (Zambrano 1985:54) and in the context of atlatls and darts (Diehl 1983:51, 62; Fuentes, Trejo, and Gutiérrez Solano 1988:plates 19*b*, 19*i*). These weapons were unfortunately and inappropriately labeled "fending sticks" at Chichen Itza, where it was thought they were used to bat darts out of the air (Charlot 1931, 1:252) on the erroneous assumption that these were defensive, rather than offensive, arms. The use of obsidian blades in these weapons appears to be a Toltec innovation, but the clubs themselves may have originated in the desert north (Peckham 1965).

25. Hogg 1968:21.

26. See the examples of curved clubs in the American Southwest (Peckham 1965).

27. Zambrano 1985:63. This weapon is depicted at Chichen Itza being used to sacrifice a person (Morris, Charlot, and Morris 1931, 2:plate 145), which strongly suggests it had obsidian blades. The Late Postclassic Codex Borgia (Códice Borgia 1980, 3:13, 49, 63, 64, 70) shows this type of weapon studded with blades and similar bladed examples are depicted in Mixtec examples. Note especially the example in Codex Zouche-Nuttall (1987:66).

28. Dupuy (1984:2–3) notes that thrusters had been more important in the Old World until the advent of iron made slashers more feasible. In the Mesoamerican case, the Toltec short sword was the first true slasher, but it was based on obsidian blades inset in a broad, relatively thin wooden handle.

29. Acosta 1961:227; Zambrano 1985:61; see examples in Fuentes, Trejo, and Gutiérrez Solano (1988:plates 19*i*, 31, 60, 63, 68–70).

30. Compare the examples at El Tajín and at Cacaxtla, discussed earlier.

31. Compare the Roman combined use of its short sword and javelin (Jones 1987:27) and the comparable advantage the development of the bayonet gave seventeenth-century musketeers (Archer 1987:267–69; Finer 1975:108).

32. See Diehl 1983:108–109.

33. See the protective sleeve on the warriors on the El Corral pyramid (Acosta 1974:33) and on the small atlantids (e.g., Fuentes, Trejo, and Gutiérrez Solano 1988:plate 25).

34. Diehl 1983:108–109; Stocker 1974:49, 52.

35. Diehl 1983:109; Fuentes, Trejo, and Gutiérrez Solano 1988:plates 14, 15.

36. The upper frieze of Pyramid B shows collared jaguars and coyotes (Diehl

1983:plate 8; 1989*b*:22) which Diehl (1983:63) feels represent Toltec military orders analogous to the Aztec Eagle and Jaguar knights, and warrior figurines also show coyote masks (Stocker 1974:49, 52; 1983:22). See also the effigy jar of a man's face emerging from a coyote mouth (Diehl 1983:plate 42).

37. The houses were probably of common kin groups, possibly based on ancestor worship judging by the altar burials: the buildings were larger than at Tenochtitlan or Monte Alban and were probably multifamily (Diehl 1981:286; 1983:72; Healan 1977:147, 149; 1982:130–32). The city was laid out on a grid pattern, forming large neighborhoods or barrios six hundred meters on a side, with a concentration of large buildings that were probably temples in one corner (Diehl 1983:89). Thus, the struggle between kin and residential bases of political control, and hence aristocratic and meritocratic military systems, may have been a significant part of the legendary ouster of Quetzalcoatl.

38. Diehl (1983:102) puts the population of Tollan and its hinterland minimally at 100,000. However, since his estimate for Tollan proper is only 40,000, his estimate for Tollan's hinterland is 60,000, the same as that of Sanders (1981:186) and of Sanders, Parsons, and Santley (1979:144).

39. Cobean and Guadalupe Mastache 1989:38.

40. Diehl 1974*b*:191; Healan 1977:140.

41. Diehl 1983:69–70; Healan 1977:143, 148–49; 1982:130; 1989*c*:62.

42. Diehl 1983:110–11; Healan 1986:146–51; Healan, Cobean, and Diehl 1989:248.

43. Diehl 1981:290; 1983:111; Healan, Cobean, and Diehl 1989:248; Healan, Kerley, and Bey 1983:137; Healan and Stoutamire 1989:224.

44. Diehl 1981:289; 1983:89, 115; Healan, Cobean, and Diehl 1989:247; Neff 1989:256. The Toltecs had particularly close ties with the Huaxtec area on the north Gulf coast, perhaps forming a symbiotic region with central Mexico (Diehl 1981:290). These close ties are supported by legends that tell of a Toltec migration through the Huaxteca before settling at Tollan (Stresser-Péan 1971: 586). Several fortified sites in northern Veracruz are considered to be of Toltec origin, including Castillo de Teayo, Tenampulco, Puebla, Tuzapan, and Cachuatenco (García Payon 1971:532–33), and there was a Toltec garrison at Tabuco, near Tuxpan (García Payon 1971:535). See Diehl and Feldman (1974: 105–107) for a list of goods traded between the two areas. There were also Mesoamerican contacts with the American Southwest at this time (Lister 1978: 234–40). Weigand, Harbottle, and Sayre (1977:18, 21–22) suggest colonial exploitation of turquoise by the Toltecs from this area, especially at Chaco Canyon, and it has been suggested that anomalous burials with exotic goods at the Anasazi sites of Pueblo Bonito and Ridge Ruin were those of Mesoamerican merchants (*pochteca*) (Reyman 1978:251, 258).

45. Diehl 1981:289; 1983:115–16; Healan, Cobean, and Diehl 1989:246–47; Neff 1989:256.

46. Acosta Saignes 1945; Diehl 1981:289; 1983:114, 116; Healan, Cobean, and Diehl 1989:247; Neff 1989:256; Reyman 1978:251, 258. Kristan-Graham (1989:268–77) argues that the processional figures carved in the vestibule in front of Pyramid B at Tollan are probably merchants (pochteca).

47. Diehl 1974*b*:193; 1983:117.

48. Diehl 1981:289; 1983:114.

49. Diehl 1981:289; 1983:115–16; Healan, Cobean, and Diehl 1989:246–47; Neff 1989:256.

50. Diehl 1983:140.

51. Diehl 1983:118. Boehm de Lameiras (1980:54–56) feels the Toltecs controlled their territory by dividing it into five administrative provinces, each governed indirectly from a regional capital: Tollan, Tulancingo, Teotenango, Teoculhuacan, and a fifth whose name is not known.

52. Diehl 1974b:194; 1981:290–91; 1983:118–19; Diehl and Feldman 1974:107.

53. Tollan was a political or military power only during the Tollan phase (A.D. 950–1150/1200) (Cobean and Guadalupe Mastache 1989:46).

54. Diehl 1983:118. Sites such as Xochicalco cannot be taken as marking the boundaries of the Toltec empire because such a notion implies a territorial empire based on contiguous expansion and control that is atypical of central Mexican empires. Even if such sites remained important during the Toltecs' reign, hegemonic systems often bypass strong opponents and continue their expansion beyond, leaving politically isolated sites in their wake. Compare the nature of the Aztec empire in Hassig (1985:86–103; 1988:17–26).

55. Diehl 1983:41; 1989a:8. Modern annual precipitation is 612 mm.

56. For example, metal was a notable trade good associated with Toltec merchants, yet none has been found at Tollan (Diehl 1983:116; Lothrop 1952:7).

57. See the examples of the short sword in the Mixtec area (e.g., Codex Selden 1964:13, 17; Codex Vienna 1963:48; Codex Zouche-Nuttall 1987:66, 68) and at Castillo de Teayo (Seler 1960–61, 3:422).

58. Diehl 1974b:194–95; 1983:158, 161; Sanders, Parsons, and Santley 1979:149–50. There is debate over the precise date of Tollan's collapse, although 1179 is traditionally accepted. However, there is no conclusive evidence, ceramic or otherwise, concerning how or when Tollan collapsed (Cobean and Guadalupe Mastache 1989:39). For a divergent interpretation of Toltec history, see Chadwick (1971b:474).

59. This interpretation is supported by the abandonment first of Tollan's peripheries and the dumping of refuse in and around houses during occupation (Diehl 1983:160; Healan, Cobean, and Diehl 1989:247).

60. Armillas 1969.

61. Armillas 1969:697–701. Human-induced ecological changes probably owing to overpopulation, rather than climatic shifts, also caused depletion (Healan, Cobean, and Diehl 1989:248), but this happened later and was not a factor in Tollan's demise.

62. Diehl 1983:158–60. Pyramid B was destroyed during Tollan times, being abandoned, sacked, and burned (Diehl 1989b:20, 26; Healan, Cobean, and Diehl 1989:247).

63. Diehl (1974b:194–95) feels that Tollan's demise probably involved the Chichimecs or loss of control of its obsidian sources to the north and east, which were far enough away that small groups of invaders could have seized control of them if Tollan were already weakened internally.

64. The bow's arrival with the Chichimecs is fairly certain. Bows were used earlier in the north (by A.D. 900–950 at Casas Grandes [DiPeso 1974, 1:174]) and intimately associated with Chichimecs in the Mesoamerican mind. There are no depictions of bows and arrows at Tollan, nor any arrow points, but it is fairly securely dated as arriving in the Maya area by A.D. 1200, having been well absorbed into Mesoamerican tactics, suggesting an earlier arrival in central Mexico that must have predated the demise of Tollan. What is puzzling, however, is why the Toltecs had not adopted it earlier themselves. Because it was used in the north centuries before its introduction into Mesoamerica proper, their traders must have encountered it. I know of no extant examples of precolumbian Mesoamerican bows, with the possible exception of one in a museum in Brussels that is translated as Museo de Armas de Bruselas (perhaps the Musée Royal de l'Armée et d'Histoire Militaire?) (Peñafiel 1903:14–15, lam. 24). However, roughly contemporaneous bows have been discovered in the American Southwest. A cache of ninety-four bows (all but two intentionally broken) and some four thousand broken arrows were discovered in a cliff dwelling just south of the Gila Cliff Dwellings in New Mexico. The largest bow was just short of five feet and the smallest was just over three feet, with the average being around four and a half feet. Their strings were made of yucca fiber and the bow wood included black oak, pine, piñon, willow, mountain mahogany, and sycamore. The arrows were compound, made of sacaton reed, the shafts were augmented with gut bindings, and they were fletched with three feathers (Hibben 1938:36–38).

65. Quantitative data are lacking for Conquest-period Mesoamerican archers, but there is information concerning North American archery. The latter yielded arrow ranges of about 90 to 180 meters (Pope 1923:334–40), which made them very effective against massed targets. However, Ishi was able to hit a target four feet in diameter only two thirds of the time at distances up to 50 yards, dropping to a half to a third of the time at 60 yards (Heizer 1970:111).

66. Flannery and Marcus 1983d:185.

67. Marcus and Flannery 1983:218.

68. Caso 1966:145; Marcus and Flannery 1983:218; M. Smith 1963:277; 1966:151; Paddock 1966b:202. 8 Deer's career is recorded in six Mixtec codices: Bodley, Zouche-Nuttall, Selden II, Codex Vienna, Becker I, and Colombino (M. Smith 1963:276–77). Five are precolumbian, but Selden was written during the mid-sixteenth century (Glass 1975:11–13; Glass and Robertson 1975:95, 97, 111, 176, 196, 235).

69. Paddock 1966b:202.

70. Marcus and Flannery 1983:218; M. Smith 1963:277; 1966:151.

71. Paddock 1966b:202. M. Smith 1963:288; 1966:151. Codex Zouche-Nuttall is the Mixteca Alta version of this consolidation while Colombino is the south-coast version of the same story (M. Smith 1963:288; 1966:166). The political/military aspect of this consolidation is evidenced by the widespread practice of human sacrifice and the use of skullracks (e.g., Codex Zouche-Nuttall 1987:20, 81).

72. Flannery and Marcus 1983d:185; Paddock 1966b:202.

73. Caso 1966:128–29; Clark 1912:20–21; Flannery and Marcus 1983*d*: 185.

74. Flannery and Marcus 1983*d*:185; Marcus and Flannery 1983:218.

75. Recent analysis of the Mixtec codices indicated that the towns depicted are all relatively close and lie within the Mixtec area (Pohl and Byland 1990:123–27).

76. E.g., Codex Bodley 1960:10, 22, 25; Codex Colombino 1966:XXIV; Codex Selden 1964:6, 12, 16, 17; Codex Vienna 1963:III; Codex Zouche-Nuttall 1987:10, 75, 77. Caso (1966:144) puts Codices Colombino and Becker I in the thirteenth century, Codex Zouche-Nuttall at around 1330, Codex Bodley at the Spanish conquest, and Codex Selden dates to 1556. He does not venture an opinion about Codex Vienna, but it is considered to be precolumbian and Adelhofer (1963:9) notes that it ends in 1350, providing a minimum early date for its creation.

77. Shields with feather fringes are found in Codex Becker (1961:13), Codex Colombino (1966:VI, XXIV), and Codex Selden (1964:16), and examples without feather fringe are found in Codex Becker (1961:1, 2, 7, 9, 11), Codex Bodley (1960:22, 25), Codex Colombino (1966:III, VI, XVIII), Codex Selden (1964:12, 13), Codex Vienna (1963:20; 48, III), and Codex Zouche-Nuttall (1987:20).

78. Thrusting spears are depicted in Codex Becker (1961:1, 2, 4, 7, 11, 13), Codex Bodley (1960:22, 25, 28), Codex Colombino (1966:VI, XVIII, XXIV), Codex Selden (1964:6, 8, 12, 13, 16, 17), Codex Vienna (1963:9, 48, 50), and Codex Zouche-Nuttall (1987:52, 68, 70, 75, 76). Atlatls and darts are depicted in Codex Becker (1961:1, 2, 7, 9, 11), Codex Colombino (1966:I), Codex Selden (1964:1), Codex Vienna (1963:20, 26, 48, 50), and Codex Zouche-Nuttall (1987:3, 8, 29, 43, 77, 78, 80), and on carved bones (Caso 1969:202, 208).

79. Hafted knives are depicted in Codex Bodley (1960:31), Codex Colombino (1966:XVI), Codex Vienna (1963:8), and Codex Zouche-Nuttall (1987:4, 44, 69, 81). Unhafted examples are found in Codex Zouche-Nuttall (1987:3). Axes are depicted in Codex Becker (1961:2, 7), Codex Colombino (1966: XXIV), Codex Selden (1964:3, 16), and Codex Zouche-Nuttall (1987:20, 57). Although the depictions of axes suggest that they are used as weapons in combat, this is unlikely and they are probably execution tools.

80. Short swords are depicted in Codex Selden (1964:13, 17), Codex Vienna (1963:48), and Codex Zouche-Nuttall (1987:66, 68). These curved clubs are bladed (note the example in Codex Zouche-Nuttall [1987:66], which has blood pouring from the blades), but in most cases they are held with the curved portion forward which is the opposite of the way they are held by the Toltecs. Bows and arrows appear in Codex Bodley (1960:9, 10, 14, 24), Codex Colombino (1966:XVI), Codex Selden (1964:12), and Codex Zouche-Nuttall (1987:10, 11).

81. Although bows were used at the time all of these codices were painted, though not during the times represented in the codices themselves, they are not depicted in the earliest of these codices, the Becker I. This suggests that, at the

time it was executed in the thirteenth century, bows were still recognized as new and thus anachronistic for the period described in the codex. However, Colombino, which dates to about the same time, does include an image of a bow. Later codices include depictions of bows and arrows but they are relatively infrequent. All of the codices include images of atlatls, even though atlatls became relatively rare in the Late Postclassic Mixtec area, but none include representations of the broadsword that dominated warfare of that late period, which suggests that because of its relatively late introduction, the broadsword was recognized as anachronistic to the period recorded in the codices.

82. See, for example, the discussion of the Great Canterbury Psalter (Paris, B.N. MS lat. 8846) in Morgan (1982:47–49).

83. E.g., Codex Becker 1961:7, 11; Codex Vienna 1963:48, 50.

84. Morley, Brainerd, and Sharer 1983:150.

85. Andrews 1965:313; Andrews and Sabloff 1986:451; Culbert 1988:149; Morley, Brainerd, and Sharer 1983:157.

86. The notion that these intrusive peoples were Putun comes from Thompson (1970:3–47). He had generally accepted a Toltec intrusion, with some reservations (Thompson 1954:96–100), but subsequently shifted to the Putun, who were also called Chontal Maya.

87. Ball 1978:140; Culbert 1988:150; Morley, Brainerd, and Sharer 1983: 157, 160; Proskouriakoff 1970:466; Rands 1965:577; Robles C. and Andrews 1986:84; Willey 1984:12; Wren 1984:20. The Chol names of Nahua origin suggest that the dispossessed were among these factions, perhaps along with such groups as the Chontal and the Campeche Yucatec (Justeson, Norman, Campbell, and Kaufman 1985:70). The name Chontal is Nahuatl and means "foreigner" (Roys 1965:676).

88. Andrews 1965:317; Andrews and Sabloff 1986:434, 445–49; Pollock 1965:433; Proskouriakoff 1965:491, 496; Willey 1986:32–33. Among the numerous architectural innovations at Chichen Itza of Toltec origin were (1) colonnades, (2) round temples, (3) doorways with two columns in the form of a feathered serpent, (4) the general use of feathered serpents as ornament, (5) a battered basal zone on the exterior faces of most pyramids and building walls, (6) jaguar, Toltec, and vulture profiles, (7) skullrack, (8) atlantean figures, (9) warrior figures with characteristic clothing, ornaments, and insignia, (10) chac mools, and (11) standard bearers (Morley, Brainerd, and Sharer 1983:160–64). However, Andrews and Sabloff (1986:451) suggest that the presence of some architectural forms at Chichen Itza, such as the Castillo, that are not found at Tollan supports the theory that groups of nonclassic Mexicanized Mayas from the southern Gulf coast were in large part responsible for the new configuration. But while there is evidence of a Gulf coast influence at Chichen Itza in both ceramics (Andrews 1965:317; Willey 1986:33) and glyphs (Justeson, Norman, Campbell, and Kaufman 1985:70), these do not come from the Tabasco coastal zones (Willey 1986:31–32) but perhaps indicate the influence and possible presence of Gulf coast peoples as part of a multiethnic presence at Chichen. Some of the architectural forms, notably the prominent use of round columns, found at both Tollan and Chichen Itza, were present in northern Mexico well before their appearance at either of these Mesoamerican sites (Gamio 1971:62–63).

89. This remarkable similarity is further evidence of a Toltec intrusion. This similarity cannot be explained by the generality of the Toltec complex in central Mexico at that time since 8 Deer's Mixtec empire coexisted with the Toltecs yet did not adopt that military complex. Moreover, because of the close Mixtec ties with the Olmeca-Xicalanca, one would expect a similarity between these two, which makes the remarkable parallels between the Toltecs and the Itzas more easily explained by assuming they were the same group rather than that they were two different groups sharing a general tradition, when that general tradition was clearly not shared by groups much closer to the Toltecs both geographically and culturally.

90. Andrews 1965:314–15; Fowler 1989:41–42; Justeson, Norman, Campbell, and Kaufman 1985:70.

91. The Nahua interaction suggests a militaristic character to their presence among the lowland Maya since Nahuatl words such as "rule" and "shield" were borrowed (Justeson, Norman, Campbell, and Kaufman 1985:70). The arguments favoring the priority of Chichen Itza over Tollan almost always rest on finding potential predecessors for the Mexican elements at Chichen in earlier Maya sites. There are indeed predecessors at some sites, although these tend to be few and far between, were usually the result of Mexican intrusions during the Classic, and are never found to the extent they are at Chichen, nor in such clusters of Mexican traits. The argument rarely focuses on the evidence for the alleged Maya presence at Tollan. If that was the case, among other things, one would expect Maya glyphs, art, architecture, and language, yet there is no evidence for any of these. Moreover, there were no ceramic links between the two sites, indicating an absence of trade between Tollan and Chichen Itza, which is explained in Mexican traditions but there is no word of this unexpected result in the Maya area.

92. Available archaeological data from Chichen Itza are inadequate to date the Toltec era at that site precisely (Andrews and Sabloff 1986:445–46; Wren 1984:20). There are few carbon-14 dates from the "Old City" portion of the site, which contains the Maya architecture, and these indicate dates in the seventh century (Bolles 1977:195), although the dates in the hieroglyphic lintels are late ninth century (Bolles 1977:261). While it has been argued that the two sections of the city were contemporaneous, which would make Chichen earlier than Tollan and indicate the continued, simultaneous, importance of Maya rulers, there are no architectural connections between the two city sections. Nor does this possibility explain the distinctly different character of the Toltec portion of the site. There are Toltec military elements depicted in the murals of some of the rooms in the Old City (e.g., Bolles 1977:199, 202, 203, 205), but there is no way of knowing when these were painted. However, since murals were typically painted over repeatedly in Mesoamerica, they probably date from the later periods of Chichen Itza's occupation. The more plausible explanation is that the Old City was the original Maya city which the Itza invaders conquered and dominated, but they then erected their own political center for their new ethnically heterogeneous capital in the Mexican style.

93. Morley, Brainerd, and Sharer 1983:157, 159; Sabloff and Rathje 1975: 75–77.

94. For a discussion of these legends and their relation to Chichen Itza, see Tozzer (1957, 1:27–32).

95. Thompson (1942) interprets five warriors at Chichen Itza who are shown missing one leg as depicting the god Tezcatlipoca.

96. Willey 1986:27–30. The first Putun intrusion into Yucatan occurred as the Olmeca-Xicalanca presence in central Mexico ended, so the earlier Putun may have been Olmeca-Xicalancas who removed themselves to the Maya area. Scholes and Warren (1965:780) state that a group called the Popoloca (which means "foreigners," "barbarians," or "unintelligible" in Nahuatl) entered the Gulf coast lowlands following the collapse of Tollan. Most of the native historic traditions date from the diaspora following the collapse of Tollan (Carrasco 1971:463), but the Scholes and Warren thesis was proposed prior to the discovery of the Cacaxtla murals and could not take them into account. It is possible, even probable, that this group returned to the Gulf coast with the demise of Cacaxtla and may well have influenced northern Yucatan at a relatively early date.

97. Morley, Brainerd, and Sharer 1983:159–60. Andrews and Sabloff (1986:445) put Toltec influence at Chichen Itza at the end of the tenth cycle, possibly as early as A.D. 890. The Toltec connections are buttressed by the invading group's leader, Nacxit Xuchit, also carrying the Mexican title Quetzalcoatl (Morley, Brainerd, and Sharer 1983:159). See the discussion of dates in Tozzer (1957, 1:24–25). There appear to have been at least two incursions from the east coast of Yucatan (Roys 1966:162).

98. Andrews 1965:314–15; Schele and Friedel 1990:348; Willey 1986:33.

99. Morley, Brainerd, and Sharer 1983:160. Clearly, a major shift in political systems did take place (Andrews 1990:260).

100. Justeson, Norman, Campbell, and Kaufman 1985:70; Roys 1966:161.

101. Andrews 1965:318; Pollock 1965:433–34; Proskouriakoff 1965:496.

102. Andrews (1965:316–17) suggests that the absence of women helps account for the Itza's inability to establish themselves permanently. Much domestic pottery continued in use at Chichen Itza after the Itza intrusion (Ruz Lhuillier 1979:259), which indicates a continuation of Maya occupation, especially by Maya women. This is also supported by the general absence of comales for the preparation of tortillas, a staple in central Mexico (Taube 1989:33).

103. Robles C. and Andrews 1986:89.

104. Kristan-Graham (1989) asserts this pattern for both Tollan and Chichen Itza.

105. The Temple of the Chac Mool was built before the Temple of the Warriors (Morley, Brainerd, and Sharer 1983:158). In its outer chamber, four columns (one now missing) were originally carved with four Toltec warriors bearing weapons on each, oriented toward the center and front (Charlot 1931, 1:242; 2:plates 29–31). Another four columns (one now missing), similarly oriented, were in the inner chamber (Charlot 1931, 1:242; 2:plates 35–37). The two on the left (north) depicted priests with Toltec nose-bars, and the figure closest to the altar at the back of the chamber also carries a knife, presumably for ritual bloodletting, and is the only figure in the temple to be designated with a name glyph. The two columns on the right (south) depict god-impersonators

or elderly men dressed and equipped in Maya attire. Benches were located on each side of the inner chamber. Priests, god-impersonators, and dignitaries line the south bench whereas warriors and one old woman line the north bench (Morris 1931, 1:380).

A similar, though more elaborate, scene is depicted in the Temple of the Warriors. There, the outer chamber of the temple contains twelve columns, each with four figures oriented toward the center or front (Charlot 1931, 1:266; 2:plates 41–52). Those on the left (north) are Toltec warriors while those on the right (south) also include several Maya figures. The inner chamber contains eight columns with four figures each, oriented in the same fashion as those in the outer chamber, toward the center or front. The four on the left (north) are Toltec warriors and one old woman nearest the altar at the rear; those on the right (south) are a more eclectic mixture and include Maya figures (Charlot 1931, 1:266; 2:plates 55–62). Some of these figures have glyphs over their heads, probably denoting places or names. The painted bench depicts both Mayas and Toltecs on jaguar benches. The colonnade in front of the Temple of the Warriors continues this pattern on a grander scale with sixty-one columns of four figures each. Warriors are primarily depicted, but so too are priests and bound prisoners (Charlot 1931, 1:268; 2:plates 69–123).

The sculpture in the Lower Temple of the Jaguars (chamber E) of the Great Ball Court depicts a series of warriors that appears to represent the merger of Maya and Itza forces (reproduced in Maudslay [1889–1902, 3:plates 44–51], with additions in Cohodas [1978:figs. 16–18]). The carving shows five levels, separated by dividers composed of intertwined serpents, and each occupied primarily by soldiers. Level A holds twenty-four figures; B holds twenty-four plus an unnumbered central figure; C holds twenty-four figures; D holds sixteen plus an unnumbered central figure; and E holds twelve figures plus an unnumbered central figure. In each level, the figures on each side face the center, but the representations are not symmetrical. The depiction is one of a series of accession scenes at Chichen Itza, possibly the first, for this is the earliest temple in the Great Ball Court complex (Cohodas 1978:66–70; Wilson 1976:44, 52) which predates the Temple of the Warriors (Charlot 1931, 1:342). Cohodas (1978:220–24) interprets this scene as a solar cycle, but inter alia this demands construing the five levels as three and focuses almost exclusively on the central figures.

Of the twenty-four figures on level A, all but two carry thrusting spears. There are glyphs, which may be placeglyphs as well as offices, over all of the level A figures. James A. Fox (personal communication) identifies two of these glyphs as the Maya offices of nacom and batab. Not all are identifiable, but some are similar to central Mexican placenames found elsewhere (e.g., Xochicalco and Monte Alban), few are compound, and none are calendrical. These figures appear to represent the lords (mostly Maya) of various tributary towns. Those on the left carry harpoon-type spears with a series of barbs behind the point and may represent maritime areas, possibly the Laguna de Términos area (Roys 1966:157). Most of those on the right carry traditional Maya thrusting spears and may be lords of inland cities. Most carry Maya flexible rectangular shields, although two carry atlatls in addition to their spears, one carries a hafted knife (these three all wear noseplugs, like the other Toltecs), one carries an eccentric flint, two carry Maya celt-bladed clubs, and one carries a short staff decorated with two human skulls. All of these figures have speech scrolls of various ornamentation, indicating they are speaking or singing. This is particularly true of figure 13, a god-impersonator whose speech is very flowery. The central six figures all look upward toward the central scene in level B.

Level B holds the accession scene proper. This primarily involves the five central figures. The central figure is dressed as a god standing in front of a large feathered serpent who winds up into level C. On the left are two Toltec figures, but not soldiers. The first carries a staff and the second a sacrificial knife and bag, probably for a ritual bloodletting by the central figure. The two figures on the right are Maya priests. The rest of the figures on level B appear to be Toltec warriors, although figure 10 carries an ax, and there are glyphs above their heads, probably indicating the places over which they are lords. Everyone has speech scrolls, but the most elaborate are those of the priests, especially the first Maya priest whose glyph is exceptionally flowery. This flowery glyph is very similar to the glyph emanating from the neck of a decapitated ballplayer in a human sacrifice scene (Marquina 1964:858; Ruz Lhuillier 1979:242–43). The Toltec priests do not have glyphs above their heads; the Maya priests do, although they are in a style markedly different from those in the rest of the relief carving. These contextually anomalous glyphs may be Maya or central Mexican but are markedly different from the rest of the glyphs in this scene.

The right side of level C is filled with Toltec warriors, although some wear god masks. In addition to Toltec warriors, the left side has two figures carrying bowls, one of whom may be a woman. All of these figures have speech scrolls but no other glyphs. The center is dominated by the feathered serpent's head rising from the accession scene in the level below and the inner six figures have their heads tilted downward to focus on the serpent. The inner flanking two figures have the most elaborate speech scrolls, with the scroll on the right being in the form of a serpent head, suggesting that the newly accessioned king is now being addressed as Quetzalcoatl. The lack of possible placeglyphs in level C could denote a renewed political unity with the accession of the new king, but since they reappear in the next level, it seems likelier that these figures are lords of Chichen Itza and thus require no placeglyphs.

Level D is filled with Toltec warriors, all of whom have speech scrolls but only some have placeglyphs. The center is a jeweled serpent behind a Toltec warrior. This may be the newly accessioned king as the fully manifest Quetzalcoatl. However, he and the inner six figures are all looking downward toward the accession scene in level B and the feathered serpent in levels B and C.

The top level, E, contains a series of Toltec warriors, apparently without placeglyphs. Most of these figures have very small and simple speech scrolls that contrast markedly with those on the other levels, although the figures farthest away from the center have more elaborate examples. All of these figures are looking downward too, including the central figure who sits on a jaguar throne inside a sun disk. He is pointing down and his speech scroll is a serpent head. In all likelihood, he is the deceased, and now deified, predecessor of the king being crowned, and he is legitimizing the proceeding by also naming him as Quetzalcoatl. Schele (1976:14–15) has identified parallels to this interpretation on the tablets at the Temple of the Foliated Cross and the Temple of the Sun at Palenque, which show accession scenes and Palenque's rulers are depicted as gods at birth and after death.

In addition to its political significance, this investiture scene demonstrates the ethnic heterogeneity of Chichen society. Political legitimation required drawing the Maya into the ceremony. Maya priest are active participants, apparently bestowing the blessing on the king being installed, and thus giving the Itza rulers the de jure as well as the de facto right to rule. The sequence of central scenes also depict the varying social status of different groups in the Itza polity. Maya lords retained rule in tributary towns, as denoted at the bottom, but they also infiltrated Itza society at higher levels, though in smaller numbers. At or near the top, Toltecs dominated almost exclusively.

A similar scene is shown twice in the Upper Temple of the Jaguars and once in the North Temple (Maudslay 1889–1902, 3:plate 35; Seler 1960–61, 5:283; Tozzer 1957, 2:fig. 270). In each, a Toltec figure holding atlatls and darts and superimposed over a feathered serpent faces another figure in a sun disk. The latter figure is also Toltec and carries atlatls and darts, is seated on a jaguar throne, and has a stylized serpent-head speech scroll. As in the Lower Temple, these appear to be accession scenes in which the newly crowned king is designated Quetzalcoatl, and this is affirmed by his deceased and deified predecessor calling him by this title. The doorway is flanked by two stone columns, with armed Toltec warriors, variously holding atlatls, darts, and short swords (Maudslay 1889–1902, 3:plates 36–38). Although less reported, the North and South Temples of the Great Ball Court appear to contain similar scenes, strikingly so in the better documented North Temple. See the picture of the North Temple sculptures in Erosa Peniche (1951:following page 24) and Cohodas (1978:fig. 28). Cohodas's (1978:225–36) interpretation of these temples is in the same mold as his interpretation of the Lower Temple of the Jaguars.

106. In a minority opinion, Lincoln (1986:154) and Wren (1984:17) hold these to be personal names.

107. The vast bulk of the warriors depicted on the columns at Chichen Itza (Morris, Charlot, and Morris 1931, 2:plates 29–123) do not have associated glyphs, although a few do. At least fifty-seven of the 244 warriors depicted on the Northwest Colonnade had potential glyphs, although none with numerical modifiers (Morris, Charlot, and Morris 1931, 1:311; 2:plates 29–123). Some of the warriors on the door jambs of Temple A of the Great Ball Court have glyphs above their heads (Maudslay 1889–1902, 3:plate 38). Kristan-Graham (1989:198–99) suggests that these glyphs correspond to Yucatec patronyms. Of the very few examples that could be read as personal name glyphs, column 17, Temple of the Warriors, has the glyph for 10 Rabbit, using a Mexican rabbit but with a double bar for ten (Charlot 1931, 1:311; 2:plate 59) and one of the warriors on the door jambs of Temple A of the Great Ball Court has a glyph depicting a small creature and the number one (Maudslay 1889–1902, 3:plate 38).

108. Lincoln (1986:154), based on Proskouriakoff (1970:171).

109. Kelley 1976:240–42. Although the glyphs suggest that these events

occurred earlier—A.D. 869–881, according to the Thompson correlation—
Kelley's reconstruction puts them in the late twelfth and early thirteenth centuries. Part of the difficulty with these dated texts arises from the poor fit of the
northern Yucatan calendar with the standard correlations of those to the south.
See A. Chase (1986) for a discussion of the correlation problem.

110. Culbert 1988:150.

111. Miller 1977:197–200. For reproductions, see Coggins (1984:158–65)
or Miller (1977:201–208). However, because these murals were preserved in
watercolor copies rather than being photographed, many details may well be
wrong.

112. The Maya did use the atlatl, at least during the Itza phase (see the
examples at Kabah; Tozzer 1957, 2:fig. 603), so the battle murals may easily
reflect Toltec/Maya conflicts. *Mural 1 (north portion of west wall)*: blue figures
with round shields are attacking a peaceful village, presumably Maya. *Mural 2
(north wall)*: round-shielded warriors with atlatls and short swords are attacking
rectangular-shielded warriors in a Maya village. Above the scene are cartouches
with armed Toltec warriors and a sun disk with the center now missing. *Mural 3
(north portion of east wall)*: largely destroyed scene in red hills. Armed figure
with round shield and atlatl darts on left emerges from mouth of serpent. Lightly
clad combatants carry rectangular shields and atlatls. It is unclear whether the
people they are fighting remain in the surviving portions of the mural.

113. *Mural 4 (south portion of east wall)*: largely destroyed mural of Maya
village scene, apparently depicting the aftermath of a battle. No fighting continues but there are many soldiers, all armed with atlatls, darts, short swords, and
round shields. A Toltec commander at the bottom is giving orders. *Mural 5
(south wall)*: a siege scene in a Maya village in which both sides use atlatls and
round shields. Defenders are atop a pyramid and attackers are climbing it,
helped by suppressing fire from three siege towers. There is an armed figure in a
solar disk to the upper right and the mural is flanked by two armed men
standing in front of feathered serpents. *Mural 6 (south portion of west wall)*:
battle scene in a Maya village between two groups of similarly clad and armed
warriors; some wear shirts and back standards, others just shirts, and still others
no shirts; all carry round shields and atlatls. There is a sun disk with a seated,
armed figure at the bottom, and the entire scene is flanked by two armed men
backed by feathered serpents.

114. Miller (1977), followed by Coggins (1984), interprets these scenes cos-
mologically.

115. Morris 1931, 1:392; Morris, Charlot, and Morris 1931, 2:plate 139.

116. Lothrop 1952:42. See the lanceolet points recovered from the cenote at
Chichen Itza (Coggins 1984:37) and the rectangular shields in the mural on the
north wall of the Upper Temple of the Jaguars (Coggins 1984:161).

117. Willey 1972:37.

118. That atlatls were not significant Maya weapons is recognized by W.
Coe's (1965b:599) statement that this weapon was a new introduction at
Chichen Itza. However, slings were ancient in the Maya area (based on linguistic evidence), although Roys (1966:156) failed to find them at this time. They
were also widely reported at the time of the Spanish conquest.

119. Ruz Lhuillier 1979:236.

120. Note the examples of atlatls and darts depicted on the gold disks recovered from the cenote (Coggins 1964:47; Lothrop 1952:44–56). Atlatls and darts were recovered from the cenote at Chichen Itza (Coggins 1984:46–47, 103–104). See also the atlatl and darts depicted on a jadeite plaque recovered from the cenote (Coggins 1984:52), depictions in murals (Morris, Charlot, and Morris 1931, 2:passim), and the examples of barbed projectile points recovered from the cenote at Chichen Itza (Coggins 1984:47, 100).

121. The Toltec short swords were first identified at Chichen Itza (Charlot 1931, 1:252), albeit erroneously as "fending sticks" because they were thought to be defensive and, rather improbably, used to bat away incoming projectiles because in murals, their bearers are sometimes depicted in battle dress with shields and "fending sticks" but with no offensive arms in this interpretation (Morris, Charlot, and Morris 1931, 2:plate 139). Moreover, the "fending stick" is depicted elsewhere at Chichen Itza in a context that makes its offensive use obvious (Morris, Charlot, and Morris 1931, 2:passim). However, see the questionable example of one of the "fending sticks" recovered from the cenote at Chichen Itza (Coggins 1984:49). That short swords had obsidian blades is evidenced by a sacrifice scene in a bas relief carving at Chichen Itza in which the weapon is being used to cut the heart out of a sacrificial victim (Morris, Charlot, and Morris 1931, 2:plate 145).

122. Charlot 1931, 1:251–52; Morris, Charlot, and Morris 1931, 2:plate 167b; Proskouriakoff 1970:463–64. A knife is used in a sacrificial scene on gold disk H (Lothrop 1952:52–53). See also the somewhat more elaborate knife recovered from the cenote at Chichen Itza (Coggins 1984:51).

123. Tozzer 1957:40. What appears to be a wooden effigy of a thrusting spear was recovered from the cenote at Chichen Itza (Coggins 1984:108). See the thrusting spears on column 42 of the Northwest Colonnade and on columns 5 and 6 of the Temple of the Chac Mool (Morris, Charlot, and Morris 1931, 2:plates 36, 37, 42). Bows and arrows had not yet been introduced and none are depicted in any of the bas reliefs or frescoes at Chichen Itza (Tozzer 1957:40, 172).

124. Charlot 1931, 1:250. Some of the warriors armed with short swords, or atlatls and darts, and shields in the village raid mural in the Temple of the Warriors (Morris, Charlot, and Morris 1931, 2:plate 139) appear to be wearing jackets that may be armor that covers the torso but not the limbs. Lothrop (1952:40) disputes the interpretation that these left-arm sleeves are defensive armor on the grounds that they are assumed to be made of cloth wadded with cotton and hardened in brine, and any stiffening of the arm would put it out of action; others wear this on both arms (which he considers impossible) and still take active part in the battle. Moreover, he asserts that sleeves are not shown in battle scenes in any media. However, at least part of this interpretation appears to be based on an error. The widespread belief (e.g., Bray 1968:189; Hagen 1962:172; Vaillant 1966:219) that cotton was soaked in salt to strengthen it is based on de Landa (1973:52) but is not corroborated elsewhere. Gates (Landa 1978:16, footnote) believes this is a misinterpretation of *taab*, "to tie," for *tab*, "salt," and that the cotton was tied or quilted, not salted. This is clearly the case

in the Conquest era. Lothrop's assessment of the physical characteristics of the sleeve armor are most likely in error.

125. Morris, Charlot, and Morris 1931, 2:passim. However, a rectangular shield—probably flexible—does appear on column 5 of the Temple of the Chac Mool (Morris, Charlot, and Morris 1931, 2:plate 36) depicting a warrior who is also holding a thrusting spear. The shield grip is shown in the murals in Room 22 of Las Monjas at Chichen Itza (Bolles 1977:200) and the sculpture in chamber 27 of the Great Ball Court (Maudslay 1889–1902, 3:plate 46).

126. See examples of shields with and without feather fringes (Morris, Charlot, and Morris 1931, 2:plate 139) in the village raid mural in the Temple of the Warriors.

127. The atlatl has been considered the main technological difference between the Toltecs and the Maya (e.g., Roys 1966:155), probably because the short sword was misidentified as a fending stick, which led to its role being ignored.

128. Corroboration of this is offered in the Códice Borgia (1980, 3:13, 49, 63, 64, 70), where these weapons are also grouped together (and the curved club is studded with blades) and by a depiction of Tezcatlipoca wielding an atlatl in his right hand, with a shield, darts, *and* a curved bladed club in his left (Códice Borgia 1980, 3:17). The Codex Zouche-Nuttall also includes scenes of warriors holding shields, darts, and clubs (also shown are an atlatl and bow and arrows) in one hand and a variety of weapons in the other, including the atlatl, thrusting spear, and ax (Nuttall 1975:10, 20, 39, 52, 70, 75, 77).

129. See the primary retention of Maya thrusting spears as represented in carvings in the Lower Temple of the Jaguars in the Great Ball Court at Chichen Itza (Maudslay 1889–1902, 3:plates 44–48) and among the Late Postclassic Maya, at least in a supernatural context, in the Grolier Codex (Lee 1985:167–70).

130. Itza warriors are shown being paddled in oceangoing dugout canoes in a mural in the Temple of the Warriors (Morris, Charlot, and Morris 1931, 2:plate 159). An Itza warrior is shown in a dugout canoe apparently as part of an attack on a lake island temple in a mural in the Temple of the Warriors (Morris, Charlot, and Morris 1931, 2:plate 139). Another mural fragment also depicts Itza warriors in dugout canoes (Morris, Charlot, and Morris 1931, 2:plate 146). But most graphically, one of the metal disks (disk G) recovered from the cenote at Chichen Itza shows a scene of maritime conflict. Five men in a dugout canoe are pursuing two Maya swimmers and three rafts while the main figure casts darts at them. The pursuers are perhaps Maya allied with the Itza because they use Toltec weapons but are not wearing attire that is particularly Toltec in nature (Lothrop 1952:51–52, fig. 35). Canoes with soldiers armed with atlatls, darts, and round shields are also seen in a mural in Las Monjas at Chichen Itza (Willard 1926:facing 253).

131. Similar scenes of canoes bearing atlatlists are available for the Mixtec area during the reign of 8 Deer (e.g., Codex Zouche-Nuttall 1987:75, 80). However, the limited bodies of water in the area suggest a very small role for canoe-borne soldiers and the same may well have been true of Chichen Itza.

132. Schele and Friedel 1990:361.

133. The opening of Itza society to Maya penetration is seen in the various ascension scenes throughout Chichen Itza, in which Maya functionaries—primarily priests, but also warriors—participate. This is most graphically illustrated in the Lower Temple of the Jaguars, in which rulers of tributary towns are shown attending the crowning of an Itza ruler. The five-level depiction of this event also graphically displays the Itza social hierarchy. Although all the depicted warriors are among the elite (although not necessarily among the nobility), Maya rulers occupy most of the bottom register and decline in numbers going up, with the top two registers being exclusively Itza (Cohodas 1978:figs. 16–19; Maudslay 1889–1902, 3:plates 44–51). There is little direct evidence for the meritocratization of the Maya military during the Itza period, but by the time of the Spanish conquest, commoners made up a significant part of the armed forces, including its leadership. And, as noted by Proskouriakoff (1950: 170), there was a shift in Maya art from portrayals of individuals to groups, substantiating a shift from an aristocratic ideological tradition to a meritocratic one.

134. Robles C. and Andrews 1986:88. Teotihuacan covered at least twenty square kilometers (Millon 1981:199), but that site was enormously dense and had a population substantially larger than the much more dispersed Chichen Itza.

135. Kurjack in Andrews and Andrews (1980:16).

136. There were apparently military orders among the Maya of northern Yucatan, although the evidence postdates the Toltec intrusion and may reflect the emulation of that organization, albeit tailored to Maya social organization. Maya military orders are suggested by the representation of animal helmets and costumes worn by the Maya in the bas-relief sculpture in the Lower Temple of the Jaguars at Chichen Itza (Maudslay 1889–1902, 3:plates 44–45).

137. Tozzer 1957:84. Ruz Lhuillier (1951:332–35) argues for the fortification of Chichen Itza, but not convincingly.

138. The murals in Room 22 of Las Monjas at Chichen Itza depict the use of flaming atlatl darts thrown on the roofs of buildings (Bolles 1977:202–203, 211; McCurdy 1909:466; Willard 1926:facing 253). However, these straw-roofed structures appear to have been common houses and this tactic may have been less useful against the more substantial elite and civic buildings.

139. This mural is on the south wall of the Upper Temple of the Jaguars (Kubler 1984:316–18; Miller 1977:215; see also Coggins 1984:165).

140. Ball 1978:140.

141. Rainfall in the Yucatan Peninsula ranges from under 20 inches per year in the north to 80 inches in the south (Willey, Smith, Tourtellot, and Graham 1975:13). The Chichen Itza area averages only 20–30 inches per year (Culbert 1973b:11) whereas Mayapan just to the south averages about one meter (Pollard 1962:1).

142. Although based on studies in the Peten area and subject to various interpretations, the lowlands appear to have been largely jungle at this time (Cowgill, Goulden, Hutchinson, Patrick, Racek, and Tsukada 1966:123; Wiseman 1978:181).

143. Taube 1989:33.

144. Webster 1979:168.

145. Cuca is located near present-day Merida, Yucatan.

146. Kurjack and Andrews 1976:319–20; Webster 1976b:364; 1978:382–84; 1979:9, 59, 61.

147. Webster 1978:384–85; 1979:61, 62. However, a large amount of debris on the south side of the inner wall may cover a gateway (Kurjack and Andrews 1976:320).

148. Webster 1978:383.

149. Webster 1978:385; 1979:63.

150. Kurjack and Andrews 1976:320; Webster 1979:69, 71–72.

151. Webster 1976b:364; 1978:376–80; 1979:73, 100–101. Chacchob is fifteen kilometers southeast of present-day Teabo, Yucatan.

152. Webster 1978:378–80; 1979:103.

153. Webster 1979:104, 161–62.

154. Dzonot Ake was located near present-day Tizimin, Yucatan. Only a 560-meter segment of the wall remains today (Webster 1979:114, 146).

155. Webster 1976b:364; 1978:388; 1979:146, 158.

156. Kurjack and Andrews 1976:320; Webster 1978:380, 386; 1979:71, 163–64. However, Webster (1978:389) provisionally dates Dzonot Ake to the mid to late Postclassic.

157. Kurjack and Andrews 1976:324; Webster 1978:389; 1979:168. This assessment is based on the absence of Chichen Itza ceramics (Webster 1979:167).

158. Robles C. and Andrews 1986:84–85.

159. Kinz and Fletcher 1983:210; Robles C. and Andrews 1986:81, 84–85.

160. Morley, Brainerd, and Sharer 1983:154–56; Robles C. and Andrews 1986:81.

161. Benavides C. 1977:215–19; Robles C. and Andrews 1986:78.

162. The earliest known road of this type (sacbe, pl. sacbeob) in Yucatan is at Komchen (Morley, Brainerd, and Sharer 1983:333, 336). Causeways linking internal areas of sites and sometimes outlying dependencies were ancient in the Maya area. Internal causeways were present at El Mirador (Dahlin, Foss, and Chambers 1980:47–48; Matheny, Hansen, and Gurr 1980:1); at Uaxactun, groups A and B were connected by a 125-meter causeway, 30 meters wide at one end (A. L. Smith 1950:61), and there were two causeways at Becan (Thomas 1981:21–22). Although probably not constructed for this purpose, these roads could speed the movement of men and materiel to points of attack.

163. Folan 1983e:82; Littman 1958:173–76; Morley, Brainerd, and Sharer 1983:333–35; Rivet 1973:46; Thompson, Pollock, and Charlot 1932:19, 128. A roller presumably used in this process was found at Ekal, on the Coba-Yaxuna causeway. Requiring fifteen men to use, it was 13 feet wide, 2 feet in diameter, and weighed 5 tons (Morley, Brainerd, and Sharer 1983:335; Rivet 1973:46).

164. Folan 1983d:53; Morley, Brainerd, and Sharer 1983:333; Thompson, Pollock, and Charlot 1932:19–27.

165. Thompson, Pollock, and Charlot 1932:128.

166. Folan 1983e:83; Thompson, Pollock, and Charlot 1932:19–27, 129.

167. Falkenhausen 1985:117; Folan 1983*d*:53–54; Morley, Brainerd, and Sharer 1983:212; Robles C. and Andrews 1986:70.

168. Folan 1983*d*:53–54.

169. Andrews 1965:303; Andrews and Andrews 1975*b*:10; Folan 1983*a*:3; 1983*b*:13.

170. See Hassig 1991 for a fuller discussion of the economic and political roles of roads.

171. Andreski 1968:80; Creveld 1989:45.

172. Thompson, Pollock, and Charlot 1932:19.

173. Folan 1983*c*:40, 43.

174. Andrews 1975:102; Robles C. and Andrews 1986:89–90.

175. This date is based on the abandonment of the sites at the terminals of the Coba sacbe system around A.D. 1100 (Robles C. and Andrews 1986:90).

CHAPTER 9: THE AZTEC ERA

1. For example, Misantla (Acuña 1982–87, 5:190).

2. Except as noted, the discussion of the Aztecs is drawn from Hassig (1985, 1988) where the political and military significance of the Aztec empire is considered in greater detail.

3. The following is a list of major social divisions:

Upper nobles, *teteuctin*; sg., *teuctli*.

Kings, *tlatoqueh*; sg., *tlatoani*.

Lower nobles, *pipiltin*; sg., *pilli*.

Commoners, *macehualtin*; sg., *macehualli*.

Wards, *calpolli*.

Ward heads, *calpolehqueh*; sg., *calpoleh*.

Commoners attached to the land, *mayehqueh* or *tlalmaitin*; sg., *mayeh* or *tlalmaitl*.

Slaves, *tlatlacohtin*; sg., *tlacohtli*.

Meritocratic nobles, *cuauhpipiltin*; sg. *cuauhpilli*.

4. The three major exceptions are the Stone of Tizoc, depicting the king and fourteen semideified warriors taking captives (only one figure has Tizoc's name glyph) (Pasztory 1983:147–50); the carving of Moteuczomah Xocoyotl at Chapultepec (Nicholson 1961:402–403; Pasztory 1983:127–29); and the Dedication Stone, which depicts Kings Tizoc and Ahuitzotl (Pasztory 1983: 150–51).

5. Mesoamerica lacked the contagious person-to-person diseases that characterized the Old World (Burnet and White 1972:13; McNeill 1977:55). Some rudimentary chemical warfare may also have been employed in the form of smoke from burning food to entice besieged populations (Durán 1967, 2:93) and from fires in which chillis were burned (Durán 1967, 2:198). However, this was limited by its form of delivery to fixed targets and favorable winds. The

Quiche of highland Guatemala also threw gourds full of wasps among the enemy to disrupt them (Carmack 1968:79–80).

6. The following is a list of standard Aztec weapons:

Spearthrower, *atlatl*.

Dart, *tlacochtli*.

Sling, *tematlatl*.

Bow, *tlahuitolli*.

War arrow, *yaomitl*.

Quiver, *micomitl* or *mixiquipilli*.

Thrusting spear, *tepoztopilli*.

Bladed club, *huitzauhqui*.

Club with spherical knob, *cuauhololli*.

Club with four knobs, *macuahuitzoctli*.

Knife, *tecpatl* if of flint, or *itztli* if of obsidian.

Ax, *tlateconi*.

Broadsword, *macuahuitl*.

7. Maya warriors were reported to carry two quivers (López de Gómara 1965–66, 1:88); Byzantine quivers held forty arrows; those of the Turks held thirty to fifty (Jones 1987:96, 100); while late medieval English archers carried two quivers, each holding twenty-four arrows (Burne 1955:38).

8. Although there is no definitive evidence of the broadsword's first introduction, two Aztec conquest monuments—the Stone of Tizoc and a recently discovered similar monument—are instructive. The Stone of Tizoc is decorated with carvings depicting fifteen pairs of warriors. The warrior on the left is grasping the hair of the one on the right as a sign of conquest. The captured warrior is accompanied by a placeglyph naming the conquered town. Fourteen of the victorious warriors are attired in Toltec headdresses, pectorals, and aprons, and each has a smoking mirror in place of the left foot and another in his headdress, suggesting identification with both the Toltecs and Tezcatlipoca, god of war. The more elaborately attired fifteenth figure is identified by the glyph as Tizoc (ruled 1481–86). The weapons held by the various figures include shields, bows and arrows, and atlatls and darts.

A new monumental stone, a cuauhxicalli, was found in what was the ceremonial center of Tenochtitlan and bears marked similarities to the Stone of Tizoc, but depicts only eleven pairs of warriors and town glyphs. Although the carvings are remarkably similar in the two stones, the newly discovered dates to the late 1450s (Emily Umberger, personal communication). All of the depicted warriors are generic military leaders but some also hold Toltec short swords, which are totally absent on the Stone of Tizoc. When the newly discovered stone was carved, the Toltec short sword was either still in use or at least remembered as a functional weapon whereas on the Stone of Tizoc, while still seeking identification with the Toltecs, this weapon is not depicted, possibly because it was no longer in use nor remembered as a functional weapon, which further suggests that the broadsword had replaced it by this time. In addition to its recent introduction, the broadsword may not have been depicted because it lacked the ritual connotations of the short sword. At least at Chichen Itza, the short sword was used for ritual human sacrifice.

That broadswords were a central Mexican innovation is suggested by their absence in the desert north (Peckham 1965). However, at first Spanish contact, a weapon described as a broadsword was encountered in the West Indies and in Florida (Purdy 1977:264). It is uncertain whether the arms mentioned in the circum-Caribbean area were identical to the Aztec broadsword, especially because the Spaniards adopted the Taino word *macana* for this weapon and used it indiscriminately. I take this geographical distribution as reflecting a spread from Mexico into the Caribbean along with other Mesoamerican cultural artifacts and cultigens, rather than the reverse.

9. In earlier times, both ceramic and stone slingstones were made, but ceramic stones were apparently absent from the Aztec military inventory. This suggests that, perhaps as an economy measure in the face of severe logistical constraints, the Aztecs were concerned with reusing these projectiles and therefore used only stone, which was significantly less fragile than ceramic.

10. Jones 1987:7. However, Ferrill (1985:25) contests the necessity of this, pointing to a Roman depiction of densely packed slingers.

11. A pre-Aztec spindle whorl showing arrows in combat suggests they were integrated well before the rise of the Aztecs (Winning 1975:124–25).

12. Aztec armor included the following:

War shield, *yaochimalli*, not to be confused with the ornamental dance shield (*mahuizzoh chimalli*).

Wooden shield, *cuauhchimalli*.

War suit, *tlahuiztli* suit.

Kilt, *ehuatl*.

13. García Icazbalceta 1886–92, 3:48–49. Compare the role of archers in ancient Greek warfare (Jones 1987:6–7).

14. García Icazbalceta 1886–92, 3:48–51.

15. Creveld 1989:91–92; Jones 1987:33. Compare the six feet required between sword-wielding Roman soldiers (Dupuy 1984:17). See also Weller (1966:24). Closed formations were more typical in Europe during the late Middle Ages, primarily because massed formations could resist cavalry charges, a consideration that was irrelevant in prehispanic Mesoamerica.

16. Roman battles followed a similar sequence (Dupuy 1984:24; Weller 1966:23).

17. Compare this with the similar practice in ancient Greece (Ferrill 1985: 103).

18. Similarly, in the Old World, only the front ranks of a spearman formation typically fought (Jones 1987:2).

19. Envelopment was a typical tactic in symmetrical conflicts (Jones 1987: 45).

20. Calnek (1976:288; 1978:316), accepted by Sanders, Parsons, and Sant-ley (1979:154).

21. Estimates vary widely, but Sanders (1970:449) offers what I consider to be the low reasonable estimate, accepted in Sanders, Parsons, and Santley (1979:162, 184), while Cook and Borah (as reconstructed by Denevan 1976a: 81–82) offer the high reasonable estimate.

22. The nobles' school was called the *calmecac*, while the commoners' school was the *telpochcalli*.

23. The following are Aztec military ranks and orders:

Veteran warrior, *tequihuah*; pl., *tequihuahqueh*.

Captain, *cuauhyahcatl*.

General, *tlacateccatl*.

Commanding general, *tlacochcalcatl*.

Shorn one, *cuahchic* or *cuahchiqui*; pl., *cuahchicqueh*.

Otomí, *otomitl*; pl., *otontin*.

24. This unit is called a *xiquipilli*.

25. For a fuller discussion of the following points, see Hassig 1985:127–50.

26. These canoes integrated the valley both economically and militarily be-cause the Aztecs fought from them as well as used them for transport and supply.

27. *Xochiyaoyotl*.

28. Blanton and Kowalewski 1981:115.

29. This discussion of elite intermarriage is based on the seminal work of Pedro Carrasco (1984). See Hodge (1984:46–48, 70, 90, 95, 109, 111, 125–27, 138, 147–48) for specific examples within the Valley of Mexico.

30. Sons of tributary kings were educated as Aztecs in Tenochtitlan, where they may also have been hostages for their fathers' continued obedience to the Aztecs.

31. For example, the Matlatzincas in the Valley of Toluca to the west of Tenochtitlan were Aztec tributaries, often aided in their wars, and shared essen-tially the same social structure (Quezada Ramírez 1972:51–52).

32. Acuña 1982–87, 5:415. This appears to have been the case in the Tepeaca towns, where each had captains bearing the formal titles of tlacoch-calcatl and tlacateccatl (Acuña 1982–87, 5:245), positions which, among the Aztecs, were earned through military exploits.

33. Acuña 1982–87, 5:272; 6:146, 165, 173–74, 176, 188, 204, 218; 7:193, 237.

34. Acuña 1982–87, 6:204; 3:11.

35. E.g., Ichcateupan (Acuña 1982–87, 6:265) and Teloloapan (Acuña 1982–87, 6:325). The armies of other towns entered battle in an orderly, but unspecified way; e.g., Tetela (Acuña 1982–87, 6:311), and Cuezala (Acuña 1982–87, 6:317).

36. E.g., Alahuiztlan (Acuña 1982–87, 6:278).

37. The simple technology and utilitarian skills it demands makes the bow very difficult to control centrally (Goody 1971:43, 46).

38. Blanton and Kowalewski 1981:115; Marcus and Flannery 1983:217.

39. Spores 1983a:233.

40. Marcus and Flannery 1983:222; Spores 1983b:247–48.

41. Flannery 1983a:290; Flannery and Marcus 1983e:277; Marcus and Flannery 1983:221; Spores 1965:965; Whitecotton 1977:83–84.

42. Whitecotton 1977:94.

43. Bernal 1965a:810; Kowalewski, Feinman, Finsten, Blanton, and Nicholas 1989, 1:307, 317, 344, 513; Marcus and Flannery 1983:218; Spores 1965: 966; Spores and Flannery 1983:340.

44. Descent appears to have been traced ambilaterally, not lineally (White-cotton 1977:155). Zapotec social organization in the Postclassic continued to be defined primarily by descent, with the nobility occupying all the important civil, religious, and military positions (Whitecotton 1977:144, 146–48).

45. Kowalewski, Feinman, Finsten, Blanton, and Nicholas (1989, 1:307, 340, 364) suggest an economic basis to the political fragmentation because they maintain that the petty kingdoms each approximated a standard marketing area.

46. Acuña 1982–87, 2:67, 84, 90, 320–21, 349; 3:144; Flannery and Marcus 1983e:278.

47. Flannery 1983b:318; Flannery and Marcus 1983e:278; Spores 1965: 966; Whitecotton 1977:122–26.

48. Acuña 1982–87, 2:351. 1 braza = 1.67 meters; measure equivalents taken from Barnes, Naylor, and Polzer (1981:70–71).

49. The evidence for arms and armor is found in the following sources:
Bows and arrows: Zapotec (Acuña 1982–87, 2:63, 67, 77–78, 84, 148, 162, 181, 185, 257, 260, 351; 3:144, 172); Mixtec (Acuña 1982–87, 2:150, 216, 287, 295, 302, 308, 315, 321, 331, 367; 3:289; 5:37, 49, 58).
Broadswords: Zapotec (Acuña 1982–87, 2:67, 84, 90, 256, 351; 3:79, 95, 144, 148, 162, 172, 181, 185, 260); Mixtec (Acuña 1982–87, 2:144, 150, 216, 237, 287, 295, 302, 308, 315, 321, 367; 3:233, 239, 245; 5:37, 44–45, 53, 58). Flannery (1983b:319) reports the discovery of a tomb at Huitzo containing a man in his early twenties with backed and truncated obsidian blades that appear to be from a broadsword.
Spears: Zapotec (Acuña 1982–87, 2:78, 84, 90, 256; 3:181, 185); Mixtec (Acuña 1982–87, 2:331).
Slings: Zapotec (Acuña 1982–87, 3:144); Mixtec (Acuña 1982–87, 2:287, 295, 302; 5:53, 58).
Clubs: Zapotec (Acuña 1982–87, 2:256, 257); Mixtec (Acuña 1982–87, 2:331; 3:289).
Axes: Zapotec (Acuña 1982–87, 3:144); Mixtec (Acuña 1982–87, 3:233). Elsewhere, axes were used as execution tools rather than combat weapons and this is likely to be true here, or they may have been tools occasionally used as weapons by commoners.
Atlatls: Spores (1965:969) is correct in noting that there are no references to the atlatl in the Oaxaca region at this time, but there are a few references to darts (Zapotecs: Acuña 1982–87, 3:144, 148; Mixtecs: Acuña 1982–87, 3:233, 239), which I take to be atlatl darts, but not to atlatls themselves, just as there are sometimes references to either bows or arrows rather than the two together.

Spores' (1967:15) later reference to the atlatl among the Mixtecs may refer to examples shown in earlier codices.

Cotton armor: Zapotec (Acuña 1982–87, 2:67, 90, 256, 351; 3:79, 95, 144, 172, 260); Mixtec (Acuña 1982–87, 2:144, 150, 216, 287, 315, 331; 3:221, 233, 239, 245, 289; 5:37, 44–45, 49, 58).

Shields: Zapotec (Acuña 1982–87, 2:67, 78, 90, 256; 3:63, 79, 95, 144, 172, 181, 185, 260); Mixtec (Acuña 1982–87, 2:150, 216, 287, 295, 302, 308, 315, 321, 331; 3:30, 233, 239, 245, 289; 5:37, 44–45, 49, 58).

Helmets: Mixtec (Acuña 1982–87, 2:331). There are no reports of helmets for the Zapotecs.

50. Elam 1989:407. The Mixtecs were stratified into the hereditary ruling class, hereditary nobles, commoners, and an even lower landless group. Only the nobles practiced polygyny, and often did so to secure political alliances. But formal lineages were not a significant element of Mixtec social organization (Spores 1984:64–66, 69–70).

51. Flannery 1983*b*:318; Spores 1965:969. Zapotecs: Acuña 1982–87, 2:90, 351. Mixtecs: Acuña 1982–87, 2:52; 3:233.

52. Acuña 1982–87, 2:90; Flannery 1983*b*:318.

53. Acuña 1982–87, 2:52; 3:233; 5:37, 49.

54. The heavy use of atlatls and darts is apparent from their ubiquitous occurrence in the Codex Zouche-Nuttall (1987:3, 6–8, 10, 11, 13, 14, 17, 18–22, 26, 28–32, 34, 38, 42–54, 61, 63, 65–78, 80, 82–84).

55. Spores 1983*c*:259.

56. Gorenstein 1973:20–32, 63; Spores 1983*c*:259. Tepei el Viejo was conquered by the Aztecs in 1503.

57. Elam 1989:407; Flannery 1983*b*:319; Flannery and Marcus 1983*f*:300.

58. Flannery 1983*b*:320–22. See Peterson and MacDougall's (1974:10–37) discussion of the site center.

59. Peterson and MacDougall 1974:10.

60. Peterson and MacDougall 1974:40.

61. Marcus 1983*g*:316; Spores 1965:966–69. For a discussion of the nature of that alliance, see Hassig (1988:231–32).

62. Those Totonac towns claiming to have had no wars include Hueytlalpa, Juyupango, Matlatlan and Chila, Misantla, Xonotla, San Martin Tuzamapa, San Francisco, and Santiago (Acuña 1982–87, 5:155, 167, 172, 190, 385, 391, 395).

63. Governors were imposed by the Aztecs in Hueytlalpa, Juyupango, Matlatlan and Chila, and Papantla (Acuña 1982–87, 5:155, 167, 171, 176); all except Papantla were among those claiming to have no wars. Aztec garrisons were established at Cotaxtla (Acuña 1982–87, 5:315) and Acatlan (Acuña 1982–87, 5:358).

64. Acuña 1982–87, 5:162, 176, 385.

65. Stresser-Péan 1971:594–95. See also the example in Ekholm (1944:fig. 44*d*).

66. Ekholm 1944:461; Stresser-Péan 1971:594–95. See also Ekholm (1944: 461, fig. 44) for examples of animal masks that suggest military orders.

67. Gonzalez D'Avila 1904:164.

68. Gonzalez D'Avila 1904:167–68. In addition to full quivers, they also carried four or five arrows in their hands (Gonzalez D'Avila 1904:167).

69. Códice Tudela 1980:74v; Gomez de Orozco 1945:60; Sahagún 1950–82, 10:187.

70. Gomez de Orozco 1945:60; Paso y Troncoso 1939–42, 2:39.

71. Hassig 1988:169.

72. Acuña 1982–87, 7:67.

73. Acuña 1982–87, 4:186; 5:133; Muñoz Camargo 1947:29–30.

74. Muñoz Camargo 1947:31–32. For the feather standards of the four divisions of Tlaxcallan, see Acuña (1982–87, 4:276–77) and Muñoz Camargo (1947:114).

75. Muñoz Camargo 1947:29, 32.

76. Muñoz Camargo 1947:30, 115–17, 155.

77. Brand 1971:644–46; Gorenstein and Pollard 1983:1.

78. Chadwick 1971a:689; Gorenstein and Pollard 1983:23; Warren 1985:5. The capital had moved to Tzintzuntzan from the town of Patzcuaro shortly before the Spanish conquest.

79. Warren 1985:6. However, this population was probably the total of all the towns in and around the lake, rather than of Tzintzuntzan alone, as these towns were regarded as a single entity.

80. Brand 1971:636–37; Chadwick 1971a:677; Warren 1985:3–4, 9.

81. Gorenstein and Pollard 1983:101–104, 111–23; Warren 1985:9–10. The Tarascan king was called the *cazonci*.

82. Relación de Michoacán 1977:173.

83. Relación de Michoacán 1977:203, 208.

84. Relación de Michoacán 1977:224, 229–30. To consolidate his position, the king married all his predecessor's wives and then added as wives the daughters of the chiefs and lords (Relación de Michoacán 1977:230).

85. Acuña 1982–87, 9:166–67, 253, 266, 324, 343–44; Bernal 1952:221; Corona Núñez 1958, 1:52, 72; 2:22. 1 vara = .8359 meters; 1 palma = .20897 meters; measure equivalents taken from Barnes, Naylor, and Polzer (1981:70–71). Arms manufacture was overseen by hereditary officials who were also responsible for their storage, and other hereditary officials oversaw spies and wartime standard bearers (Relación de Michoacán 1977:177).

86. Acuña 1982–87, 9:200, 225; Corona Núñez 1958, 2:113; Relación de Michoacán 1977:192.

87. Relación de Michoacán 1977:192. The captain general is described as wearing large green feathers on his head, a silver shield, a tigerskin quiver, gold bracelets and earrings, cotton armor, a leather suit on his shoulders, and a bow in his hand. Commoners usually wore only loincloths (Acuña 1982–87, 9:148, 266, 324; Relación de Michoacán 1977:192; Vargas Rea 1944–46, 7/3:103).

88. Encyclopedia of Textiles 1972:71, 151, 555; Hochberg 1977:57–63.

89. There is no evidence that cotton was produced in the Patzcuaro area (Acuña 1982–87, 9:201).

90. These include Chichimecs, Otomies, Matlatzincas, Uetamaechas, Chontales, and the people of Tuspa, Tamazula, and Zapotlan (Relación de Michoacán 1977:191).

91. Relación de Michoacán 1977:186, 188–89. It is unclear when this feast took place. Caso (1967:252–53) suggests that the month of the same name ran from 18 July to 6 August, based on similarities between its feasts and those of the Aztec month of Tlaxochimaco. However, this is probably incorrect, for it is during the beginning of the rainy season when roads were at their worst and agricultural labor was in the greatest demand and thus all wrong for warfare.

92. Relación de Michoacán 1977:188, 191.

93. Relación de Michoacán 1977:188–89, 191–92, 194. Each unit commander was responsible for his soldiers and those who disobeyed were killed in the field (Relación de Michoacán 1977:194–95).

94. Relación de Michoacán 1977:196, 198.

95. Corona Núñez 1958, 2:21; Relación de Michoacán 1977:197.

96. Relación de Michoacán 1977:198.

97. Brand 1971:644–46.

98. E.g., Corona Núñez 1958, 1:49. Tarequato and Perivan, both ethnically Tarascan, were founded as new settlements by order of the Tarascan king (Barlow 1944:294, 299). The Tarascans resettled Chichimecs and Otomies at Celaya because it was on the frontier with the Mexicans (Corona Núñez 1958, 2:58). Xiquilpa was settled by people from Amula nine years before the Conquest (Barlow 1944:280). Necotlan and Taimeo were each settled by Otomies who fled the Valley of Toluca in the face of Aztec expansion, and they were given land by the Tarascan king (Vargas Rea 1944–46, 7/3:102, 109–10). One of Cuseo's dependent towns was settled by Matlatzincas who fled Toluca (Acuña 1982–87, 9:268).

99. Crónica mexicana 1975:400–401; Durán 1967, 2:267–69; Hassig 1988:183.

100. Brand 1971:644; Hassig 1988:183–87.

101. In an experiment assessing projectile point damage from use, Odell and Cowan (1986:204) note that all points were damaged to some extent, even when virtually all of them scored direct hits on animal carcasses.

102. Hassig 1988:186–87.

103. Brand 1971:637, 644; Gorenstein 1985:9; Hassig 1988:207–11. See Gorenstein's (1985) discussion of the Tarascan border fortification of Acambaro, and Armillas' (1944) discussion of the Aztec fortification at Oztuma.

104. Colección de . . . ultramar 1885–1932, 11:364; 13:221–22.

105. Morley, Brainerd, and Sharer 1983:167–68; Roys 1966:164–65; Willey 1986:37.

106. A. Andrews 1990:262–64; E. W. Andrews 1965:322; Morley, Brainerd, and Sharer 1983:169–71; Robles C. and Andrews 1986:91–93; Roys 1943:58. These Mexicans are often characterized as mercenaries, but this is probably inaccurate. Migrations into the Maya area from central Mexico continued for centuries and, based on the introduction of a new cooking pot, it appears that those who reached Mayapan were accompanied by women (Morley, Brainerd, and Sharer 1983:171). Numerous arrowheads were found at Mayapan: small points averaging three grams each were found and were unlike any points previously found at Maya sites. These points were not found at

Chichen Itza until after the city was reoccupied following its destruction (Proskouriakoff 1962:360).

107. The distance Mesoamerican arrows could achieve is unknown, but North American bows had ranges from 90 to 180 meters, varying with the size and pull of the bow and the weight of the arrows (Pope 1923:334–40). In fact, atlatl points, though numerous at Chichen Itza, are absent altogether at Mayapan, where arrow points are common (Proskouriakoff 1962:360–69).

108. Morley, Brainerd, and Sharer 1983:169.

109. E. W. Andrews 1965:322; Morley, Brainerd, and Sharer 1983:170–71; Robles C. and Andrews 1986:91–93; Roys 1943:58; 1966:167.

110. A. L. Smith (1962:211) puts Mayapan's population at 11,000–12,000, based on an estimate of 5.6 people per household and 2,100 houses; Sharer (Morley, Brainerd, and Sharer 1983:169) places its population at 15,000; and Willey (1986:37–38) follows Smith's estimate of 11,000–12,000 but adds another couple of thousand living outside the walls. Hardoy (1973:260–61) estimates Mayapan's population at 12,500 (erroneously printed as 17,500), based on 2,500 structures and an estimated five persons per structure.

111. G. Andrews 1975:411; Morley, Brainerd, and Sharer 1983:169; Shook 1952: A. L. Smith 1962:264; Webster 1976b:366; Willey 1986:37; Willey and Bullard 1965:368–69.

112. Because it was relatively low, Webster (1976b:366) likens this wall more to a breastwork than a defensive wall.

113. A. L. Smith 1962:209, 265.

114. Willey 1986:38.

115. E. W. Andrews 1965:324; Pollock 1965:437. The carving of the glyphs was crude, however.

116. During the Itza period, Maya art shifted its emphasis from individual to group portrayals (Proskouriakoff 1950:170) as would be expected with the introduction of a more egalitarian military form into the Maya area.

117. Colección de . . . ultramar 1885–1932, 11:96, 122, 149, 156, 176–77, 216, 227, 244, 271; 13:86, 104; Morley, Brainerd, and Sharer 1983:173; Roys 1943:58, 65; 1965:669, 671; 1966:169–70; A. L. Smith 1962:264; Tozzer 1957, 1:52–53. See also A. Andrews's (1984) modification of Roys's political divisions. The Xiu had strong connections with Mexico and appear to have migrated into Yucatan from there (Roys 1943:58–59). Internal wars within the same province were relatively infrequent, having been found only between Chauaca and Sinsimato in Chikinchel and between Ekbalam and some of its neighboring towns in Cupul.

118. Willey 1986:39; Willey and Bullard 1965:370.

119. Morley, Brainerd, and Sharer 1983:171, 357.

120. G. Andrews 1975:411; Lothrop 1924:65–66, 68, 70; Morley, Brainerd, and Sharer 1983:357; Webster 1976b:365.

121. G. Andrews 1975:425; Lothrop 1924:66, 68, 70, 74; Morley, Brainerd, and Sharer 1983:357.

122. Lothrop 1924:66, 68; Webster 1976b:365.

123. Lothrop 1924:69–70, 72.

124. G. Andrews 1975:425; Lothrop 1924:67, 115; Morley, Brainerd, and Sharer 1983:357.

125. G. Andrews 1975:425; Lothrop 1924:66, 68, 70–73, 74; Morley, Brainerd, and Sharer 1983:357.

126. Lothrop 1924:70–71. Perhaps gaps were left in Tulum's walls to enable large objects (e.g., boulders, trees, and so forth) to enter. Since the Maya did not, or could not, construct large entryways with defensible gates, leaving the ends open may have been their best alternative in the face of this, or some other, need for large-scale access to the enclosed city.

127. The peninsula on which Xelha is located is about two hundred yards long and wide and is joined to the mainland by a narrow tongue of land defended by a stone wall averaging eight feet high and eight to twenty-five feet thick (Lothrop 1924:134; Webster 1976b:365). The wall ends on the south end at a small cliff overlooking the water and, at the north end, extends into the shallow water so attackers could not wade around it. The only entrance to the peninsula was a narrow passage with a right-angle turn through the south end of the wall, defended by a parapet on the outer edge of the wall just to the north (Lothrop 1924:134).

128. Roys 1965:661–62.

129. Piña Chan 1978:44–46; Roys 1965:662; J. Thompson 1964:22–23.

130. Roys 1943:65; 1965:662.

131. Friedel 1983:382–83.

132. Andrews 1984:589–90; Roys 1965:669; 1966:172.

133. The Maya term for a local chief is *batab*.

134. Roys 1965:669. Ah Canul and Cupul were both ruled by their respective family groups. Government at Ah Canul seems to have been through consensus, whereas at Cupul whoever could seize power did so.

135. Roys 1965:669. This type of organization included the provinces of Chakan and Chikinchel.

136. Roys 1943:61–63; 1965:669.

137. Colección de . . . ultramar 1885–1932, 11:41, 80, 105, 122, 149, 157, 162, 178, 187, 202, 216, 227, 244, 256, 271, 289; 13:29, 45, 104, 113, 198, 208; Landa 1959:51; López de Gómara 1965–66, 1:88; Roys 1943:65; Villagutierre Soto-Mayor 1983:54, 68, 247. The bows were constructed of the wood of the *chulul*, or *Apoplanesia paniculata* (Colección de . . . ultramar 1885–1932, 11:55; Roys 1943:65; 1965:671), a flowering tree up to ten meters high found throughout southern Mesoamerica (Standley 1961:441–42). Follett (1932:380) claims that bows were poorly developed among the Maya and were restricted primarily to hunting.

138. Colección de . . . ultramar 1885–1932, 11:41, 80, 122, 157, 162, 178, 202, 216, 227, 244, 256, 271, 289; 13:29, 45, 113; Follett 1932:380–85; Landa 1959:52; Roys 1943:65–66; 1965:671. 1 braza = 1.67 meters; or a total of 3.34 meters; measure equivalents taken from Barnes, Naylor, and Polzer (1981:70–71).

139. Slings were called *yuumtun* in Maya. Colección de . . . ultramar 1885–1932, 11:41, 80, 256; Follett 1932:380; Roys 1943:66; 1965:671. The sword (or *hadzab* in Maya) used at Motul, Yucatan is described as being of chulul

wood and five palmas (1 palma =.20897 meters) long and three dedos wide (Colección de . . . ultramar 1885–1932, 11:80–81). Colección de . . . ultramar 1885–1932, 13:208; Follett 1932:380, 385–86; Landa 1959:52; Roys 1943: 66; 1965:671; Villagutierre Soto-Mayor 1983:54, 68. 1 dedo = .0174 meters; measure equivalents taken from Barnes, Naylor, and Polzer (1981:70–71).

140. Follett 1932:387–92; Landa 1959:52; Roys 1943:66; 1965:671. The knives at Motul, Yucatan, were made of stone and chulul wood; two-thirds of their length was handle and one-third was blade (Colección de . . . ultramar 1885–1932, 11:81).

141. Colección de . . . ultramar 1885–1932, 11:41, 105, 122, 157, 162, 178, 187, 202, 227, 244, 256, 271, 289; 13:29, 45, 113, 208; Follett 1932:399–400; Landa 1959:52; Roys 1943:66; 1965:671. Follett (1932:399–400) also mentions flexible shields, but he is generalizing from depictions that predate the Late Postclassic.

142. Colección de . . . ultramar 1885–1932, 11:41, 81, 257, 271; Follett 1932:394–99; Landa 1959:52; Roys 1943:66; 1965:671; Villagutierre Soto-Mayor 1983:54. Some of the soldiers of Teabo, Yucatan, wore a less elaborate form of cotton armor that consisted of wrapping cotton cloth around the body seven or eight times (Colección de . . . ultramar 1885–1932, 11:289).

143. Colección de . . . ultramar 1885–1932, 11:122, 149, 157, 179, 187, 216, 244, 271, 289; 13:46; Roys 1943:66; 1965:671–72; Villagutierre Soto-Mayor 1983:312.

144. War leader, nacom. Landa 1959:52; Morley, Brainerd, and Sharer 1983:216; Roys 1943:62; 1965:672.

145. A professional soldier was a holcan. Colección de . . . ultramar 1885–1932, 11:147–48, 215–16; 13:44. Dependencies owed war service to their cabeceras (Colección de . . . ultramar 1885–1932, 13:66).

146. Roys 1943:67.

147. Roys 1943:67; 1965:672.

148. Roys 1943:67.

149. Colección de . . . ultramar 1885–1932, 11:96; Roys 1943:67; Tozzer 1941:231.

150. Colección de . . . ultramar 1885–1932, 11:81.

151. Colección de . . . ultramar 1885–1932, 13:66; Roys 1943:65, 67; 1965:671.

152. Colección de . . . ultramar 1885–1932, 11:81, 105, 257; Roys 1943: 68–69. Motul, Yucatan, claimed to go to war over land, saltpans, and the ill treatment of vassals (Colección de . . . ultramar 1885–1932, 11:80). Access to salt was also an issue for the people of Tezoco (Colección de . . . ultramar 1885–1932, 13:90).

153. Roys 1965:672.

154. Roys 1943:67–68.

155. Borhegyi 1965a:42–43; 1965b:68, 71–73; Carmack 1968:62, 75–76; 1981:65; Morley, Brainerd, and Sharer 1983:222–23; Wauchope 1975:61. For example, Utatlan was fortified and was accessible by only two narrow entrances (Carmack 1981:196–98), and there was a fortress at Atitlan and stone walls at narrow places in the road (Acuña 1982–87, 1:96), but not at its dependencies of

San Bartolomé (Acuña 1982–87, 1:132) or San Andres (Acuña 1982–87, 1:134).

156. Borhegyi 1965a:43, 47; 1965b:71; Carmack 1968:59; Fowler 1989: 41–42, 46; Wauchope 1975:63–64. Most of this assessment is based on architectural and ceramic introductions, but it is also supported by the introduction of glyphs with Gulf coast connections (Justeson, Norman, Campbell, and Kaufman 1985:70).

157. Fowler 1989:41–42, 46; Fox 1977:82–83; 1978:270. Carmack 1977: 2; Fox 1978:2; 1987:143. The A.D. 1200 date is based on Carmack's calculations backward from the Conquest period, based on kings who ruled Utatlan, calculated at twenty-five years per generation (Carmack 1977:5; 1981:121–22). This date is fifty years earlier than his previous estimate (Carmack 1968:64). Fox (1978:275) suggests that the last migration resulted from the collapse of Chichen Itza.

158. Carmack 1977:2; 1981:44, 48–49; Fox 1978:2; 1987:3, 18–20.

159. Borhegyi 1965a:50; 1965b:71; Wauchope 1975:63. But contra Carmack 1968:59–61. Carmack (1981:37–38) questions some of Borhegyi's synthesis on the basis that he failed to clearly differentiate between Early and Late Postclassic, with the result that he placed the Quiche migration in the Early Postclassic.

160. Carmack 1968:72, 76–77; 1977:4; 1981:85–89; Fox 1977:83; 1987: 36–37. The political control over indigenous peoples is also attested by the massive infusion of Nahuatl (Carmack 1981:50; Fox 1978:2–3).

161. See Wauchope's (1948:19) characterization of Quiche armies.

162. Carmack 1968:72; 1977:4; 1981:48–49, 128; Fox 1978:2, 281. Quiche was the primary language at the Quiche capital of Utatlan, although Nahuatl was also spoken (Carmack 1981:3).

163. Carmack 1968:77; 1977:4; 1981:128; Fox 1978:3–4.

164. Acuña 1982–87, 1:88, 106, 129, 142. Their armor was so effective that no arrows, spears, or broadsword blades could penetrate it (Acuña 1982–87, 1:88, 129).

165. This assessment is based on surface surveys (Fox 1978:282). Carmack (1968:79–80; 1977:4; 1981:44) lists the Quiche arms and armor as including the ax, bow and arrows, spears, atlatls, broadswords, quilted cotton armor, and the round shield, without distinguishing temporal periods. Blowguns were used, but not as weapons (Dutton and Hobbs 1943:62–63).

166. Carmack 1977:6; 1981:148–49.

167. Carmack 1977:13; 1981:168.

168. Carmack 1977:6–7; 1981:124, 148–51, 155.

169. Carmack 1977:15; 1981:173. Fox (1989:672–73) discusses the symbolic nature of these divisions.

170. Carmack 1981:65–66.

171. Acuña 1982–87, 1:142; Carmack 1968:80.

172. Acuña 1982–87, 1:81, 100, 124, 138; Carmack 1981:93, 97.

173. Carmack 1968:80. This is doubtless a generalization because 8,000–16,000 men amount to two army units (two 8,000-man xiquipilli). Carmack (1981:91) uses this to estimate a sustaining population of 40,000 to 80,000.

Fox (1977:86) also suggests that the Quiche were successful because they could field larger armies than their opponents. Greater Utatlan, however, had no more than 10,000–20,000 inhabitants (Fox 1987:280).

174. Acuña 1982–87, 1:88, 129, 142.

175. Acuña 1982–87, 1:106; Carmack 1968:80–81.

176. Carmack 1977:4; 1981:61; Fox 1987:15, 17–18, 295; 1989:672. This military superiority is attributed to the way their lineage system allowed the Quiche to mass peoples (Fox 1987:22). However, Carmack (1968:78) also emphasized the role of training, equipment, and commitment in military success. Although the notion pioneered by Carmack and elaborated by Fox that the Quiche (and all the Postclassic Chontal Maya) were a segmentary lineage system and that this accounted for their expansion is intriguing, it does have some difficulties. This explanation demands that these migrants be strongly patrilineal, yet there is little evidence of this in most of Mesoamerica by Conquest times. It also ignores the marital ties that clearly occurred between ruling families, since such a connection would be primarily relevant in a bilateral kin system. And I see little difference between the social organization described for the Quiche and that of the Aztecs: both had lineages at the noble level, yet the Aztecs did not operate in the fashion Carmack and Fox suggest for the comparably organized Quiche.

177. Fox 1977:94; 1978:176, 224. Moreover, lineages were not stable. From the original three lineages, there were twenty-four major ones by the time of the Spanish conquest (Carmack 1977:10; 1981:157).

178. Carmack 1968:80; 1977:8; 1981:152–53. Members of this group were called *achij* (Carmack 1977:17; 1981:153, 177).

179. Carmack 1981:137–39; Fox 1977:94; 1978:176; 1987:31, 191; Guillemin 1959:23–24; 1965:11–18; 1967:23.

180. Carmack 1981:142–43; Fox 1978:176.

181. Fox 1978:176; Orellana 1984:57, 59–63, 77–88.

182. For a more detailed assessment of the Spanish conquest, see Hassig (1988:236–50).

CHAPTER 10: PATTERNS OF WARFARE IN MESOAMERICA

1. These two systems also partially reflect consensus and coercive theories of the state (e.g., Service 1978:21–34).

2. Price 1978:180.

3. See Raudzen 1990 for a consideration of the role of technological superiority in warfare.

4. Cultural choice appears to play a large role. For instance, crossbows dominated late medieval warfare in continental Europe whereas longbows dominated it in England; neither weapon made significant inroads against the other (Payne-Galloway 1986:32; Weller 1966:48). Archery was known but not used militarily in Anglo-Saxon armies (Weller 1966:30), nor did the Romans adopt it (Hogg 1968:31). See Basalla's (1988:79–88) discussion of military technology.

5. Stevenson 1897:98–101.

6. Stevenson 1897:295, 317, 328; see also Hassig (1988:116–17).

7. Jones (1987:623) suggests that medieval fortifications were so successful because of the low force-to-space ratio and lack of a centralized government.

8. Joseph Tainter (1988) offers an elegant theory of collapse. See also Hogg's (1968:142–43) discussion of the rise and fall of military systems. Arguments that see collapse resulting from moral decline rather than from material conditions are inherently judgmental and are not seriously considered here.

9. Kirchhoff 1952.

10. Galtung, Heistad, and Rudeng 1980:115–17.

11. Pasztory 1988a:75.

12. Hassig 1988:198–99.

References

Acosta, Jorge R.
    1961   "La Indumentaria de las cariátides de Tula." In Homenaje 1961.
    1974   "La pirámide de El Corral de Tula, Hgo." In Matos Moctezuma 1974*a*.

Acosta Saignes, Miguel
    1945   "Los Pochteca." *Acta Anthropológica* 1:9–54.

Acuña, René
    1982–87   *Relaciones Geográficas del Siglo XVI.* 9 vols. México: Universidad Nacional Autónoma de México.

Adams, Richard E. W.
    1973   "The Collapse of Maya Civilization: A Review of Previous Theories." In Culbert 1973*a*.
    1977*a*   *The Origins of Maya Civilization.* Albuquerque: University of New Mexico Press.
    1977*b*   *Prehistoric Mesoamerica.* Boston: Brown, Little and Company.

Adams, Richard E. W., and Richard C. Jones
    1981   "Spatial Patterns and Regional Growth Among Classic Maya Cities." *American Antiquity* 46:301–22.

Adelhofer, Otto
    1963   *Codex Vindobonensis Mexicanus 1: History and Description of the Manuscript.* Graz: Akademische Druck-u. Verlagsanstalt.

Agrinier, Pierre
    1970   *Mound 20, Mirador, Chiapas, Mexico.* Papers of the New World Archaeological Foundation, Number 28.
    1984   *The Early Olmec Horizon at Mirador, Chiapas, Mexico.* Papers of the New World Archaeological Foundation, Number 48.

Altman, Philip L., and Dorothy S. Dittmer
    1968   *Metabolism.* Bethesda, Maryland: Federation of American Societies for Experimental Biology.
Alvarado Tezozomoc, Hernando
    1975   *Crónica mexicana y Códice Ramírez.* México: Porrúa.
Anderson, Dana
    1978   "Monuments." In Sharer 1978*a.*
Andreski, Stanislav
    1968   *Military Organization and Society.* Berkeley and Los Angeles: University of California Press.
Andrews, Anthony P.
    1975   "Conclusions." In Andrews and Andrews 1975*a.*
    1984   "The Political Geography of the Sixteenth Century Yucatan Maya: Comments and Revisions." *Journal of Anthropological Research* 40:589–96.
    1990   "The Fall of Chichen Itza: A Preliminary Hypothesis." *Latin American Antiquity* 1:258–67. `
Andrews, E. Wyllys
    1965   "Archaeology and Prehistory in the Northern Maya Lowlands: An Introduction." In Willey 1965*a.*
Andrews, E. Wyllys IV, and Anthony P. Andrews
    1975*a*   *A Preliminary Study of the Ruins of Xcaret, Quintana Roo, Mexico: With Notes on Other Archaeological Remains on the Central East Coast of the Yucatan Peninsula.* Middle American Research Institute, Publication 40.
    1975*b*   "The Ruins of Xcaret, Quintana Roo, Mexico." In Andrews and Andrews 1975*a.*
Andrews, E. Wyllys IV, and E. Wyllys Andrews V
    1980   *Excavations at Dzibilchaltun, Yucatan, Mexico.* Middle American Research Institute, Publication 48.
Andrews, E. Wyllys IV, George E. Stuart, Irwin Rovner, Richard E. W. Adams, Michael P. Simmons, Elizabeth S. Wing, E. Wyllys Andrews V, Joann M. Andrews, T. Dale Stewart, and Joseph W. Ball
    1975   *Archaeological Investigations on the Yucatan Peninsula.* Middle American Research Institute, Publication 31.
Andrews, E. Wyllys V
    1981   "Dzibilchaltun." In Sabloff 1981.
    1986   *Research and Reflections in Archaeology and History: Essays in Honor of Doris Stone.* Middle American Research Institute, Publication 57.
Andrews, E. Wyllys V, and Jeremy A. Sabloff
    1986   "Classic to Postclassic: A Summary Discussion." In Sabloff and Andrews 1986.
Andrews, George
    1975   *Maya Cities: Placemaking and Urbanization.* Norman: University of Oklahoma Press.

Angulo V., Jorge
1987   "The Chalcatzingo Reliefs: An Iconographic Analysis." In Grove 1987a.

Arana, Raúl, and César Quijada
1984   "Tetícpac el Viejo, un Sitio con Tablero-Talud de Guerrero." *Cuadernos de Arquitectura Mesoamerica* 2:57–59.

Armillas, Pedro
1944   "Oztuma, Gro., Fortaleza de los Mexicanos en la Frontera de Michoacán." *Revista Mexicana de Estudios Antropologicos* 6:165–75.
1945   "Los Olmeca-Xicalanca y los Sitios Arqueologicos del Suroeste de Tlaxcala." *Revista Mexicana de Estudios Antropologicos* 8:137–45.
1948   "Fortalezas Mexicanas." *Cuadernos Americanos* 7:5:143–63.
1951   "Mesoamerican Fortifications." *Antiquity* 25:77–86.
1969   "The Arid Frontier of Mexican Civilization." *Transactions of the New York Academy of Sciences*, series II, 31:697–704.

Ashmore, Wendy
1979   *Quirigua Reports*. Vol. 1. Philadelphia: University Museum Monograph 37.

Aveni, Anthony F., and Gordon Brotherston
1983   *Calendars in Mesoamerica and Peru: Native American Computations of Time*. Oxford: BAR International Series 174.

Baird, Ellen T.
1989   "Stars and War at Cacaxtla." In Diehl and Berlo 1989.

Ball, Joseph W.
1975   "A Regional Ceramic Sequence for the Rio Bec Area." In Andrews, Stuart, Rovner, Adams, Simmons, Wing, Andrews, Andrews, Stewart, and Ball 1975.
1978   *Studies in the Archaeology of Coastal Yucatan and Campeche, Mexico: Archaeological Pottery of the Yucatan-Campeche Coast*. Middle American Research Institute, Publication 46.

Ball, Joseph W., and Jennifer T. Taschek
1989   "Teotihuacan's Fall and the Rise of the Itza: Realignments and Role Changes in the Terminal Classic Maya Lowlands." In Diehl and Berlo 1989.

Bandelier, Adolf F.
1880   "On the Art of War and Mode of Warfare of the Ancient Mexicans." *Reports of the Peabody Museum of American Archaeology and Ethnology* 2:95–161.

Barbour, Warren
1975   "The Figurines and Figurine Chronology of Ancient Teotihuacán, Mexico." Ph.D. diss., University of Rochester.

Barlow, Robert H.
1944   "Relación de Xiquilpan y su partido." *Tlalocan* 1/4:278–306.

Barnes, Thomas C., Thomas H. Naylor, and Charles W. Polzer
1981   *Northern New Spain: A Research Guide*. Tucson: University of
Arizona Press.

Barrera Rubio, Alfredo
1980   "Mural Paintings of the Puuc Region in Yucatán." In Robertson
1980.

Basalla, George
1988   *The Evolution of Technology*. Cambridge: Cambridge University Press.

Batres, Leopoldo
1912   "Las ruinas de Xochicalco." *XVII Congreso International de
Americanistas, 1910*, Mexico. Second session, 406–10.

Baudez, Claude F., and Peter Mathews
1978   "Capture and Sacrifice at Palenque." In Robertson and Jeffers
1978.

Bauer, Arnold J.
1990   "Millers and Grinders: Technology and Household Economy in
Meso-America." *Agricultural History* 64:1–17.

Baus de Czitrom, Carolyn
1986   "Appendice 3. Armas el las pinturas." In Lombardo de Ruiz, López de Molina, Molina Feal, Baus de Czitrom, and Polanco 1986.

Bell, Betty
1971   "Archaeology of Nayarit, Jalisco, and Colima." In Ekholm and
Bernal 1971*b*.

Benavides C., Antonio
1977   "Los caminos prehispánicos de Cobá." *XV Mesa Redonda*. Vol.
2. México: Sociedad Mexicana de Antropología.

Benfer, Alice N.
1974   "A Preliminary Analysis of the Obsidian Artifacts from Tula,
Hidalgo." In Diehl 1974*a*.

Benson, Elizabeth P.
1968   *Dumbarton Oaks Conference on the Olmec*. Washington, D.C.:
Dumbarton Oaks.
1971   "An Olmec Figure at Dumbarton Oaks." *Dumbarton Oaks
Studies in Pre-Columbian Art and Archaeology*, No. 8.
1981   *The Olmec and Their Neighbors: Essays in Memory of Matthew W. Stirling*. Washington, D.C.: Dumbarton Oaks.
1985   *Fourth Palenque Round Table, 1980*. San Francisco: The Pre-
Columbian Art Research Institute.
1986   *City-States of the Maya: Art and Architecture*. Denver: Rocky
Mountain Institute for Pre-Columbian Studies.

Bergesen, Albert
1980*a*   *Studies of the Modern World-System*. New York: Academic
Press.
1980*b*   "From Utilitarianism to Globology: The Shift from the Individual to the World as a Whole as the Primordial Unit of Analysis."
In Bergesen 1980*a*.

Bergesen, Albert, and Ronald Schoenberg
1980   "Long Waves of Colonial Expansion and Contraction, 1415-
            1969." In Bergeson 1980a.
Berlo, Janet Catherine
1983a   Text and Image in Pre-Columbian Art: Essays on the Interrela-
            tionship of the Verbal and Visual Arts. Oxford: BAR Interna-
            tional Series 180.
1983b   "The Warrior and the Butterfly: Central Mexican Ideologies of
            Sacred Warfare and Teotihuacan Iconography." In Berlo 1983a.
1989   "Early Writing in Central Mexico: In Tlilli, In Tlapalli Before
            A.D. 100." In Diehl and Berlo 1989.
Bernal, Ignacio
1952   "Relación de Tancítaro (Arimeo y Tepalcatepec)." Tlalocan 3/
            3:205–35.
1965a   "Archaeological Synthesis of Oaxaca." In Willey 1965b.
1965b   "Notas preliminares sobre el posible imperio teotihuacano."
            Estudios de Cultura Náhuatl 5:31–38.
1966   "Teotihuacán ¿Capital de imperio?" Revista Mexicana de Estu-
            dios Antropológicos 20:95–110.
1969   The Olmec World. Berkeley and Los Angeles: University of Cali-
            fornia Press.
Berrin, Kathleen
1988   Feathered Serpents and Flowering Trees: Reconstructing the Mu-
            rals of Teotihuacan. San Francisco: The Fine Arts Museums of
            San Francisco.
Bird, Junius B., and John Hyslop
1985   The Preceramic Excavations at the Huaca Prieta, Chicama Val-
            ley, Peru. Anthropological Papers of the American Museum of
            Natural History, Vol. 62, Part 1.
Blackiston, A. Hooton
1910   "Xochicalco." Records of the Past 9:299–308.
Blanton, Richard E.
1978   Monte Albán: Settlement Patterns at the Ancient Zapotec Capi-
            tal. New York: Academic Press.
1983a   "The Founding of Monte Albán." In Flannery and Marcus 1983a.
1983b   "The Urban Decline of Monte Albán." In Flannery and Marcus
            1983a.
Blanton, Richard E., and Stephen A. Kowalewski
1981   "Monte Alban and After in the Valley of Mexico." In Sabloff
            1981.
Boehm de Lameiras, Brigitte
1980   "La estrategia geopolítica de los estados del altiplano meosamer-
            icano: Teotihuacán, Tula, los Chichimecas y los Mexicas."
            Revista de la Universidad Complutense de Madrid 117:45–71.
1988   "Subsistence, Social Control of Resources and the Development
            of Complex Society in the Valley of Mexico." In Gledhill,
            Bender, and Larsen 1988.

Boksenbaum, Martin William, Paul Tolstoy, Garman Harbottle, Jerome Kimberlin, and Mary Neivens
1987   "Obsidian Industries and Cultural Evolution in the Basin of Mex-
           ico Before 500 B.C." *Journal of Field Archaeology* 14:65–75.
Boletín
1940   *Archivo General de la Nación, Boletín.* México: Archivo Gen-
           eral de la Nación.
Bolles, John S.
1977   *Las Monjas: A Major Pre-Mexican Architectural Complex at
           Chichén Itzá.* Norman: University of Oklahoma Press.
Bonampak
1955   *Ancient Maya Paintings of Bonampak Mexico.* Washington,
           D.C.: Carnegie Institution of Washington, Supplementary Publi-
           cation 46.
Boos, Frank H.
1966a   *The Ceramic Sculptures of Ancient Oaxaca.* New York: A. S.
           Barnes and Co., Inc.
1966b   *Corpus Antiquitatum Americanensium II, Colecciones Leigh y
           Museo Frissell de Arte Zapoteca.* México: Instituto Nacional de
           Antropología e Historia.
Borah, Woodrow, and Sherburne F. Cook
1963   *The Aboriginal Population of Central Mexico on the Eve of the
           Spanish Conquest.* Ibero-Americana 45.
Borhegyi, Stephan F.
1965a   "Archaeological Synthesis of the Guatemalan Highlands." In
           Willey 1965a.
1965b   "Settlement Patterns of the Guatemalan Highlands." In Willey
           1965a.
Boswell, Terry, Mike Sweat, and John Brueggemann
1989   "War in the Core of the World-System: Testing the Goldstein
           Thesis." In Schaeffer 1989a.
Brand, Donald D.
1971   "Ethnohistoric Synthesis of Western Mexico." In Ekholm and
           Bernal 1971b.
Bray, Warwick
1968   *Everyday Life of the Aztecs.* New York: G. P. Putnam's Sons.
Breton, Adele
1906   "Some Notes on Xochicalco." *Transactions of the Department
           of Archaeology, Free Museum of Science and Art* 2:1:51–67.
Browman, David L.
1978   *Cultural Continuity in Mesoamerica.* The Hague: Mouton Pub-
           lishers.
Brustein, William
1986   "Regional Social Orders in France and the French Revolution."
           Comparative Social Research 9:145–61.
Bullard, William R., Jr.
1970   *Monographs and Papers in Maya Archaeology.* Papers of the

Peabody Museum of Archaeology and Ethnology, Harvard University, Vol. 61.

Burland, C. A.
1952   "In the House of Flowers: Xochicalco and its Sculptures." *Ethnos* 17:119–29.

Burne, Alfred H.
1955   *The Crecy War: A Military History of the Hundred Years War from 1337 to the Peace of Bretigny, 1360.* New York: Oxford University Press.

Burnet, Macfarlane, and David O. White
1972   *Natural History of Infectious Disease.* Cambridge: Cambridge University Press.

Byers, Douglas S.
1967   *The Prehistory of the Tehuacan Valley.* Volume One, *Environment and Subsistence.* Austin: University of Texas Press.

Cacaxtla
1987   *Cacaxtla.* México: Citicorp.

Calloway, Colin
1987   *Crown and Calumet: British-Indian Relations, 1783–1815.* Norman: University of Oklahoma Press.

Calnek, Edward E.
1976   "The Internal Structure of Tenochtitlan." In Wolf 1976.
1978   "The Internal Structure of Cities in America: Pre-Columbian Cities; The Case of Tenochtitlan." In Schaedel, Hardoy, and Kinzer 1978.

Campbell, Lyle, and Terrence Kaufman
1976   "A Linguistic Look at the Olmecs." *American Antiquity* 41: 80–89.

Caporaso, James A.
1989   *The Elusive State: International and Comparative Perspectives.* Newbury Park, California: Sage Publications.

Carlson, John B.
1989   "Star Wars and Maya Merchants at Cacaxtla." College Park, Maryland: *Occasional Publications of the Center for Archaeoastronomy*, No. 7.

Carmack, Robert M.
1968   "Toltec Influence on the Postclassic Culture History of Highland Guatemala." Middle American Research Institute, Publication 26, Part 4.
1977   "Ethnohistory of the Central Quiche: The Community of Utatlan." In Wallace and Carmack 1977.
1981   *The Quiché Mayas of Utatlán: The Evolution of a Highland Guatemala Kingdom.* Norman: University of Oklahoma Press.

Carrasco, Pedro
1971   "The Peoples of Central Mexico and Their Historical Traditions." In Ekholm and Bernal 1971*b*.

1984   "Royal Marriages in Ancient Mexico." In Harvey and Prem
              1984.

Caso, Alfonso
1947   *Calendario y Escritura de las Antiguas Culturas de Monte
              Alban.* México: n.p.
1965*a*   "Sculpture and Mural Painting of Oaxaca." In Willey 1965*b*.
1965*b*   "Lapidary Work, Goldwork, and Copperwork from Oaxaca."
              In Willey 1965*b*.
1966   *Interpretation of the Codex Colombino.* México: Sociedad
              Mexicana de Antropología.
1967   *Los Calendarios Prehispánicos.* México: Universidad Nacional
              Autónoma de México.
1969   *El Tesoro de Monte Albán.* México: Instituto Nacional de
              Antropología e Historia.

Caso, Alfonso, and Ignacio Bernal
1965   "Ceramics of Oaxaca." In Willey 1965*b*.

Chadwick, Robert
1971*a*   "Archaeological Synthesis of Michoacan and Adjacent Re-
              gions." In Ekholm and Bernal 1971*b*.
1971*b*   "Native Pre-Aztec History of Central Mexico." In Ekholm and
              Bernal 1971*b*.

Charlot, Jean
1931   "Bas-Reliefs from Temple of the Warriors Cluster." In Morris,
              Charlot, and Morris 1931.

Charlton, Thomas H.
1977   "Teotihuacan: Trade Routes of a Multi-tiered Economy." *XV
              Mesa Redonda.* Vol. 2. México: Sociedad Mexicana de Antro-
              pología.

Charlton, Thomas, and Michael W. Spence
1982   "Obsidian Exploitation and Civilization in the Basin of Mex-
              ico." *Anthropology* 6:7–86.

Chase, Arlen F.
1986   "Time Depth or Vacuum: The 11.3.0.0.0 Correlation and the
              Lowland Maya Postclassic." In Sabloff and Andrews 1986.
1988   "Maya Warfare and the Classic Period Site of Caracol, Belize."
              Paper presented at the 87th annual convention of the American
              Anthropological Association, Phoeniz, Arizona.

Chase, Arlen F., and Diane Z. Chase
1987   *Glimmers of a Forgotten Realm: Maya Archaeology at Caracol,
              Belize.* Orlando, Florida: Orlando Museum of Art at Loch
              Haven.
n.d.*a*   "The Investigation of Classic Period Maya Warfare at Caracol,
              Belize." *Mayab,* in press.
n.d.*b*   "El Norte y el Sur: Politica, Dominios, y Evolución Cultural
              Maya (The North and the South: Politics, Polities, and Maya
              Cultural Evolution)." In Rivera and Jiménez n.d.

Chase, Diane Z.
1988   "The Cultural Dynamics of Prehistoric Maya Warfare." Paper presented at the 87th annual convention of the American Anthropological Association, Phoeniz, Arizona.
Chase-Dunn, Christopher
1989   *Global Formation: Structure of the World-Economy.* Cambridge, Massachusetts: Basil Blackwell.
Chaytor, Henry John
1941–42   "The Medieval Reader and Textual Criticism." *Bulletin of the John Rylands Library* 26:49–56.
Cheek, Charles D.
1976   "Teotihuacan Influence at Kaminaljuyu." *XIV Mesa Redonda.* Vol. 2. México: Sociedad Mexicana de Antropología.
1977   "Teotihuacan Influence at Kaminaljuyu." In Sanders and Michels 1977.
Cipolla, Carlo M.
1965   *Guns, Sails and Empires: Technological Innovation and the Early Phases of European Expansion 1440–1700.* New York: Minerva Press.
Clanchy, M. T.
1979   *From Memory to Written Record: England 1066–1307.* London: Edward Arnold.
Clancy, Flora S., and Peter D. Harrison
1990   *Vision and Revision in Maya Studies.* Albuquerque: University of New Mexico Press.
Clark, J. Cooper
1912   *The Story of "Eight Deer" in Codex Colombino.* London: Taylor and Francis.
Clark, John E.
1986   "From Mountains to Molehills: A Critical Review of Teotihuacan's Obsidian Industry." In Isaac 1986.
Clausewitz, Karl von
1943   *On War.* New York: Random House.
Cline, Howard F.
1975   *Handbook of Middle American Indians.* Vol. 14, *Guide to Ethnohistorical Sources*, Part 3. Austin: University of Texas Press.
Closs, Michael P.
1984   "The Dynastic History of Naranjo: The Early Period." *Estudios de Cultura Maya* 15:77–96.
Coale, Ansley J., and Paul Demeny
1966   *Regional Model Life Tables and Stable Populations.* Princeton: Princeton University Press.
Cobean, Robert H., Michael D. Coe, Edward A. Perry, Jr., Karl K. Turekian, and Dinker A. Kharker
1971   "Obsidian Trade at San Lorenzo Tenochtitlan, Mexico." *Science* 174:666–71.

Cobean, Robert H., and Alba Guadalupe Mastache
1989   "The Late Classic and Early Postclassic Chronology of the Tula
            Region." In Healan 1989*a*.
Codex Becker
1961   *Codices Becker I/II.* Graz: Akademische Druck-u. Verlags-
            anstalt.
Codex Bodley
1960   *Codex Bodley.* México: Sociedad Mexicana de Antropología.
Codex Colombino
1966   *Codex Colombino.* México: Sociedad Mexicana de Antropol-
            ogía.
Codex Selden
1964   *Codex Selden 3135 (A.2).* México: Sociedad Mexicana de
            Antropología.
Codex Vienna
1963   *Codex Vindobonensis Mexicanus 1.* Graz: Akademische Druck-
            u. Verlagsanstalt.
Codex Zouche-Nuttall
1987   *Codex Zouche-Nuttall.* Graz: Akademische Druck-u. Verlags-
            anstalt.
Códice Borgia
1980   *Códice Borgia.* 4 vols. México: Fondo de Cultura Económica.
Códice Tudela
1980   *Códice Tudela.* Madrid: Ediciones Cultura Hispanica del Insti-
            tuto de Cooperación Iberoamérica.
Coe, Michael D.
1961   *La Victoria: An Early Site on the Pacific Coast of Guatemala.*
            Papers of the Peabody Museum of Archaeology and Ethnology,
            Harvard University, Vol. 53.
1965*a*   "Archaeological Synthesis of Southern Veracruz and Tabasco."
            In Willey 1965*b*.
1965*b*   "The Olmec Style and its Distribution." In Willey 1965*b*.
1968   *America's First Civilization: Discovering the Olmec.* New York:
            American Heritage Publishing Co., Inc.
1978   *Lords of the Underworld: Masterpieces of Classic Maya Ceram-
            ics.* Princeton: The Art Museum, Princeton University.
1980   *The Maya.* New York: Thames and Hudson.
1981   "San Lorenzo Tenochtitlan." In Sabloff 1981.
1982   *Old Gods and Young Heroes: The Pearlman Collection of
            Maya Ceramics.* Jerusalem: The Israel Museum.
1989   "The Olmec Heartland: Evolution of Ideology." In Sharer and
            Grove 1989.
Coe, Michael D., and Richard A. Diehl
1980   *In the Land of the Olmecs.* 2 vols. Austin: University of Texas
            Press.

Coe, Michael D., and Kent V. Flannery
  1964   "The Pre-Columbian Obsidian Industry of El Chayal, Guate-
            mala." *American Antiquity* 30:43–49.
Coe, William R.
  1959   *Piedras Negras Archaeology: Artifacts, Caches, and Burials.*
            Philadelphia: Museum Monographs.
  1965*a*   "Tikal: Ten Years of Study of a Maya Ruin in the Lowlands of
            Guatemala." *Expedition* 8(1):5–56.
  1965*b*   "Artifacts of the Maya Lowlands." In Willey 1965*b*.
Coggins, Clemency Chase
  1975   "Painting and Drawing Styles At Tikal: An Historical and Icono-
            graphic Reconstruction." Ph.D. diss., Harvard University.
  1979   "Teotihuacan at Tikal in the Early Classic Period." *Actes du
            XLII Congrès International des Américanistes* 3:251–69.
  1984   "The Cenote of Sacrifice Catalogue." In Coggins and Shane
            1984.
Coggins, Clemency Chase, and Orrin C. Shane III
  1984   *Cenote of Sacrifice: Maya Treasures from the Sacred Well at
            Chichén Itzá.* Austin: University of Texas Press.
Cohen, Benjamin J.
  1973   *The Question of Imperialism: The Political Economy of Domi-
            nance and Dependence.* New York: Basic Books, Inc.
Cohen, Ronald, and Elman R. Service
  1978   *Origins of the State: The Anthropology of Political Evolution.*
            Philadelphia: Institute for the Study of Human Issues.
Cohodas, Marvin
  1978   *The Great Ball Court at Chichen Itza, Yucatan, Mexico.* New
            York: Garland Publishing, Inc.
Colección de . . . ultramar
  1885–   *Colección de documentos inéditos relativos al descubrimiento,*
  1932   *conquista y organización de las antiguas posesiones españoles
            de ultramar.* 25 vols. Madrid.
Contamine, Philippe
  1984   *War in the Middle Ages.* Oxford: Basil Blackwell.
Cook, Noble David
  1981   *Demographic Collapse: Indian Peru, 1520–1620.* New York:
            Cambridge University Press.
Cook, Sherburne F., and Lesley Byrd Simpson
  1948   *The Population of Central Mexico in the Sixteenth Century.*
            Ibero-Americana 31.
Cook de Leonard, Carmen
  1956   "Dos atlatl de la época Teotihuacana." In Estudios 1956.
  1967   "Sculptures and Rock Carvings at Chalcatzingo, Morelos." *Con-
            tributions of the University of California Archaeological Re-
            search Facility*, No. 3:57–84.

Corliss, David W.
1980   "Arrowpoint or Dart Point: An Uninteresting Answer to a Tire-
            some Question." *American Antiquity* 45:351–52.
Corona Núñez, José
1958   *Relaciones Geográficas de la diócesis de Michoacán, 1579–
            1580.* 2 vols. Guadalajara, México: Colección Siglo XVI.
Cosner, Aaron J.
1956   "Fire Hardening of Wood." *American Antiquity* 22:179–80.
Cowgill, George L.
1974   "Teotihuacan, Internal Militaristic Competition, and the Fall of
            the Classic Maya." In Hammond and Willey 1974.
1977   "Process of Growth and Decline at Teotihuacan: The City and
            the State." *XV Mesa Redonda.* Vol. 1. México: Sociedad Mexi-
            cana de Antropología.
1983   "Rulership and the Ciudadela: Political Inferences from Teoti-
            huacan Architecture." In Leventhal and Kolata 1983.
Cowgill, Ursula M., Clyde E. Goulden, G. Evelyn Hutchinson, Ruth Patrick, A.
A. Racek, and Matsuo Tsukada
1966   *The History of Laguna de Petenxil: A Small Lake in Northern
            Guatemala.* Memoirs of the Connecticut Academy of Arts and
            Sciences, Vol. 17.
Creveld, Martin van
1977   *Supplying War: Logistics from Wallenstein to Patton.* Cam-
            bridge: Cambridge University Press.
1985   *Command in War.* Cambridge, Massachusetts: Harvard Univer-
            sity Press.
1989   *Technology and War: From 2000 B.C. to the Present.* New
            York: The Free Press.
Croix, Horst de la
1972   *Military Considerations in City Planning: Fortifications.* New
            York: George Braziller.
Crónica mexicana
1975   *Crónica mexicana.* In Alvarado Tezozomoc 1975.
Cuevas, P. Mariano
1975   *Documentos inéditos del siglo XVI para la historia de México.*
            México: Porrúa.
Culbert, T. Patrick
1973a   *The Classic Maya Collapse.* Albuquerque: University of New
            Mexico Press.
1973b   "Introduction: A Prologue to Classic Maya Culture and the
            Problem of Its Collapse." In Culbert 1973a.
1988   "Political History and the Decipherment of Maya Glyphs." *An-
            tiquity* 62:135–52.
Dahlin, Bruce H.
1978   "Figurines." In Sharer 1978a.
Dahlin, Bruce H., John E. Foss, and Mary Elizabeth Chambers
1980   "Project Acalches." In Matheny 1980.

Davies, Nigel
1977   *The Toltecs: Until the Fall of Tula*. Norman: University of Oklahoma Press.

Davis, Byron L., Edward L. Kick, and David Kiefer
1989   "The World-System, Militarization, and National Development." In Schaeffer 1989*a*.

Delbrück, Hans
1982   *History of the Art of War Within the Framework of Political History*. Vol. III, *The Miadle Ages*. Westport, Connecticut: Greenwood Press.

Demarest, Arthur A.
1978   "Interregional Conflict and 'Situational Ethics' in Classic Maya Warfare." In Giardino, Edmonson, and Creamer 1978.

Denevan, William M.
1976*a*   "Mexico: Introduction." In Denevan 1976*b*.
1976*b*   *The Native Population of the Americas in 1492*. Madison: University of Wisconsin Press.

Díaz del Castillo, Bernal
1908–16   *The True History of the Conquest of New Spain*. 5 vols. London: Hakluyt Society.

Diehl, Richard A.
1974*a*   *Studies in Ancient Tollan: A Report of the University of Missouri Tula Archaeological Project*. University of Missouri Monographs in Anthropology, Number One.
1974*b*   "Summary and Conclusions." In Diehl 1974*a*.
1981   "Tula." In Sabloff 1981.
1983   *Tula: The Toltec Capital of Ancient Mexico*. New York: Thames and Hudson, Inc.
1989*a*   "The Physical Setting." In Healan 1989*a*.
1989*b*   "Previous Investigations at Tula." In Healan 1989*a*.
1989*c*   "A Shadow of Its Former Self: Teotihuacan during the Coyotlatelco Period." In Diehl and Berlo 1989.
1989*d*   "Olmec Archaeology: What We Know and What We Wish We Knew." In Sharer and Grove 1989.

Diehl, Richard A., and Janet Catherine Berlo
1989   *Mesoamerica After the Decline of Teotihuacan* A.D. 700–900. Washington, D.C.: Dumbarton Oaks.

Diehl, Richard A., and Lawrence H. Feldman
1974   "Relaciones entre la Huasteca y Tollan." In Matos Moctezuma 1974*a*.

DiPeso, Charles C.
1974   *Casas Grandes: A Fallen Trading Center of the Gran Chichimeca*. 8 vols. Flagstaff, Arizona: Northland Press.

Dobyns, Henry F.
1983   *Their Numbers Become Thinned: Native American Population Dynamics in Eastern North America*. Knoxville: University of Tennessee Press.

Doyle, Michael W.
1986   *Empires*. Ithaca: Cornell University Press.
Drennan, Robert D.
1979*a*   *Prehistoric Social, Political, and Economic Development in the Area of the Tehuacan Valley: Some Results of the Palo Blanco Project*. Museum of Anthropology, The University of Michigan, Technical Reports, Number 11.
1979*b*   "Excavations at Cuayucatepec (Ts281): A Preliminary Report." In Drennan 1979*a*.
1983*a*   "Ritual and Ceremonial Development at the Early Village Level." In Flannery and Marcus 1983*a*.
1983*b*   "The Tehuacán Valley at the End of the Palo Blanco Phase (A.D. 700)." In Flannery and Marcus 1983*a*.
1984   "Long-Distance Movement of Goods in the Mesoamerican Formative and Classic." *American Antiquity* 49:27–43.
1989   "The Mountains North of the Valley." In Kowalewski, Feinman, Finsten, Blanton, and Nicholas 1989.
Drucker, Philip
1943   *Ceramic Stratigraphy at Cerro de las Mesas, Veracruz, Mexico*. Bureau of American Ethnology, Bulletin 141.
1952   *La Venta, Tabasco: A Study of Olmec Ceramics and Art*. Bureau of American Ethnology, Bulletin 153.
1981   "On the Nature of Olmec Polity." In Benson 1981.
Drucker, Philip, Robert F. Heizer, and Robert J. Squier
1959   *Excavations at La Venta, Tabasco*. Bureau of American Ethnology, Bulletin 170.
Dumond, D. E., and Florencia Müller
1972   "Classic to Postclassic in Highland Central Mexico." *Science* 175:1208–15.
Dupuy, R. E., and T. N. Dupuy
1970   *Encyclopedia of Military History*. New York: Harper and Row.
Dupuy, Trevor N.
1979   *Numbers, Predictions and War: Using History to Evaluate Combat Factors and Predict the Outcome of Battles*. New York: The Bobbs-Merrill Co., Inc.
1984   *The Evolution of Weapons and Warfare*. Fairfax, Virginia: Hero Books.
1987   *Understanding War: History and Theory of Combat*. New York: Paragon House Publishers.
Durán, Diego
1967   *Historia de las Indias de Nueva España e islas de la tierra firme*. 2 vols. México: Porrúa.
Dutton, Bertha P., and Hulda R. Hobbs
1943   *Excavations at Tajumulco, Guatemala*. Santa Fe, New Mexico: Monographs of the School of American Research, No. 9.

Earle, T. K., and J. E. Ericson
1977   *Exchange Systems in Prehistory.* New York: Academic Press.

Edge, David, and John Miles Paddock
1988   *Arms and Armor of the Medieval Knight: An Illustrated History of Weaponry in the Middle Ages.* New York: Crescent Books.

Edmonson, Munro S.
1988   *The Book of the Year: Middle American Calendrical Systems.* Salt Lake City: University of Utah Press.

Ekholm, Gordon F., and Ignacio Bernal
1944   *Excavations at Tampico and Panuco in the Huasteca, Mexico.* Anthropology Papers of the American Museum of Natural History, Vol. 38, Part 5.

1971*a* *Handbook of Middle American Indians*, Vol. 10, *Archaeology of Northern Mesoamerica*, Part 1. Austin: University of Texas Press.

1971*b* *Handbook of Middle American Indians*, Vol. 11, *Archaeology of Northern Mesoamerica*, Part 2. Austin: University of Texas Press.

Ekholm-Miller, Susanna
1973   *The Olmec Rock Carving at Xoc, Chiapas, Mexico.* Papers of the New World Archaeological Foundation, Number 32.

Elam, J. Michael
1989   "Defensible and Fortified Sites." In Kowalewski, Feinman, Finsten, Blanton, and Nicholas 1989.

Eliade, Mircea
1974   *The Myth of the Eternal Return: or, Cosmos and History.* Princeton: Princeton University Press.

Encyclopedia of Textiles
1972   *AF Encyclopedia of Textiles.* Englewood Cliffs, New Jersey: Prentice-Hall, Inc.

Engels, Donald W.
1978   *Alexander the Great and the Logistics of the Macedonian Army.* Berkeley and Los Angeles: University of California Press.

Erosa Peniche, José A.
1951   *Guide to the Ruins of Chichen Itza.* Merida: Oriente.

Escalona Robles, Alberto
1953   "Xochicalco en la cronologia de la América media." *Revista Mexicana de Estudios Antropológicos* 13:351–69.

Estudios
1956   *Estudios antropologicos publicados en homenaje al doctor Manuel Gamio.* México: Dirección General de Publicaciones.

Evans, Oren F.
1958   "More on Wood Hardening by Fire." *American Antiquity* 23:312.

Falkenhausen, Lothar von
1985   "Architecture." In Willey and Mathews 1985.

Feldman, Lawrence H.
1974*a*   "Tollan in Hidalgo: Native Accounts of the Central Mexican Tolteca." In Diehl and Feldman 1974.
1974*b*   "Tollan in Central Mexico: The Geography of Economic Specialization." In Diehl 1974*a*.

Fenton, William N.
1968   *Parker on the Iroquois*. Syracuse, New York: Syracuse University Press.

Ferrill, Arther
1985   *The Origins of War: From the Stone Age to Alexander the Great*. New York: Thames and Hudson.

Fields, Virginia M.
1985   *Fifth Palenque Round Table, 1983*. San Francisco: The Pre-Columbian Art Research Institute.

Finer, Samuel E.
1975   "State- and Nation-Building in Europe: The Role of the Military." In Tilly 1975*a*.

Flannery, Kent V.
1968   "The Olmec and the Valley of Oaxaca: A Model for Inter-Regional Interaction in Formative Times." In Benson 1968.
1983*a*   "Major Monte Albán V Sites: Zaachila, Xoxocotlán, Cuilapan, Yagul, and Abasolo." In Flannery and Marcus 1983*a*.
1983*b*   "Zapotec Warfare: Archaeological Evidence for the Battles of Huitzo and Guiengola." In Flannery and Marcus 1983*a*.

Flannery, Kent V., and Joyce Marcus
1983*a*   *The Cloud People: Divergent Evolution of the Zapotec and Mixtec Civilization*. New York: Academic Press.
1983*b*   "The Earliest Public Buildings, Tombs, and Monuments at Monte Albán, with Notes on the Internal Chronology of Period I." In Flannery and Marcus 1983*a*.
1983*c*   "Monte Albán and Teotihuacán." In Flannery and Marcus 1983*a*.
1983*d*   "The Changing Politics of A.D. 600–900." In Flannery and Marcus 1983*a*.
1983*e*   "An Editorial Opinion on the Mixtec Impact." In Flannery and Marcus 1983*a*.
1983*f*   "Urban Mitla and Its Rural Hinterland." In Flannery and Marcus 1983*a*.

Flannery, Kent V., Joyce Marcus, and Stephen Kowalewski
1981   "The Preceramic and Formative of the Valley of Oaxaca." In Sabloff 1981.

Fleming, Patricia H.
1973   "The Politics of Marriage among Non-Catholic European Royalty." *Current Anthropology* 14:231–42.

Folan, William J.
1983*a*   "Archaeological Investigations of Coba: A Summary." In Folan, Kintz, and Fletcher 1983.

1983*b*   "The Importance of Coba in Maya History." In Folan, Kintz, and Fletcher 1983.

1983*c*   "Physical Geography of the Yucatan Peninsula." In Folan, Kintz, and Fletcher 1983.

1983*d*   "Urban Organization and Social Structure of Coba." In Folan, Kintz, and Fletcher 1983.

1983*e*   "The Ruins of Coba." In Folan, Kintz, and Fletcher 1983.

Folan, William J., Ellen R. Kintz, and Laraine A. Fletcher
1983   *Coba: A Classic Maya Metropolis*. New York: Academic Press.

Follett, Prescott H. F.
1932   "War and Weapons of the Maya." Middle American Research Series, Publication No. 4.

Foncerrada de Molina, Marta
1976   "La pintura mural de Cacaxtla, Tlaxcala." *Anales del Instituto de Investigaciones Estéticas* 46:5–20.

1980   "Mural Painting in Cacaxtla and Teotihuacán Cosmopolitism." In Robertson 1980.

1982   "Signos glíficos relacionados con Tláloc en los murales de la batalla en Cacaxtla." *Anales del Instituto de Investigaciones Estéticas* 50:1:23–33.

1987   "Un fragmento de pintura mural en Cacaxtla, Palenque, y el Popol Vuh." *Anales del Instituto de Investigaciones Estéticas* 58:29–33.

Fowler, William R., Jr.
1989   *The Cultural Evolution of Ancient Nahua Civilizations: The Pipil-Nicarao of Central America*. Norman: University of Oklahoma Press.

Fox, James A., and John S. Justeson
1986   "Classic Maya Dynastic Alliance and Succession." In Spores 1986.

Fox, John W.
1977   "Quiche Expansion Processes: Differential Ecological Growth Bases Within an Archaic State." In Wallace and Carmack 1977.

1978   *Quiche Conquest: Centralism and Regionalism in Highland Guatemalan State Development*. Albuquerque: University of New Mexico Press.

1987   *Maya Postclassic State Formation: Segmentary Lineage Migration in Advancing Frontiers*. Cambridge: Cambridge University Press.

1989   "On the Rise and Fall of *Tuláns* and Maya Segmentary States." *American Anthropologist* 91:656–81.

Fried, Morton H.
1967   *The Evolution of Political Society: An Essay in Political Anthropology*. New York: Random House.

Friedel, David A.
1983   "Political Systems in Lowland Yucatan: Dynamics and Structure in Maya Settlement." In Vogt and Leventhal 1983.

Friedel, David A., and Linda Schele
  1988   "Kingship in the Late Preclassic Maya Lowlands: The Instru-
              ments and Places of Ritual Power." *American Anthropologist*
              90:547–67.
Friedman, David
  1977   "A Theory of the Size and Shape of Nations." *Journal of Politi-
              cal Economy* 85:59–77.
Fuente, Beatriz de la, Silvio Trejo, and Nelly Gutiérrez Solana
  1988   *Escultura en Piedra de Tula*. México: Universidad Nacional
              Autónoma de México.
Gallagher, Jack
  1983   *Companions of the Dead: Ceramic Tomb Sculpture from An-
              cient West Mexico*. Los Angeles: Museum of Cultural History,
              UCLA.
Galtung, Johan, Tore Heistad, and Erik Rudeng
  1980   "On the Decline and Fall of Empires: The Roman Empire and
              Western Imperialism Compared." *Review* 4:91–153.
Gamio, Manuel
  1971   "The Chalchihuites Area, Zacatecas." In Hedrick, Kelley, and
              Riley 1971.
Gamble, Clive
  1986   "Hunter-Gatherers and the Origins of States." In Hall 1986.
García Cook, Angel
  1974   "Una secuencia cultural para Tlaxcala." *Comunicaciones Pro-
              yecto Puebla-Tlaxcala* 10:5–22.
  1978   "Tlaxcala: poblamiento prehispánico." *Comunicaciones Pro-
              yecto Puebla-Tlaxcala* 15:173–87.
  1981   "The Historical Importance of Tlaxcala in the Cultural Develop-
              ment of the Central Highlands." In Sabloff 1981.
García Cook, Angel, and Raziel Mora López
  1974   "Tetepetla: un sitio fortificado del 'Clásico' en Tlaxcala." *Comu-
              nicaciones Proyecto Puebla-Tlaxcala* 10:23–30.
García Cook, Angel, and Felipe Rodríguez
  1975   "Excavaciones arqueologicas en 'Gualupita las Dalias' Puebla."
              Comunicaciones Proyecto Puebla-Tlaxcala 12:1–8.
García Icazbalceta, Joaquín
  1886–92   *Nueva colección de documentos para la historia de México*. 5
              vols. México: Francisco Díaz de León.
García Payón, José
  1971   "Archaeology of Central Veracruz." In Ekholm and Bernal
              1971*b*.
Gay, Carlo T. E.
  1972   *Chalcacingo*. Portland, Oregon: International Scholarly Book
              Services, Inc.
Gendrop, Paul
  1987   *Compendio de Arte Prehispánico*. México: Editorial Trillas.

Giardino, Marco, Barbara Edmonson, and Winifred Creamer
1978   *Codex Wauchope: A Tribute Roll.* New Orleans: Bureau of
            Administrative Services, Tulane University.

Gibson, Eric C.
1985   "Inferred Sociopolitical Structure." In Willey and Mathews
            1985.

Giddens, Anthony
1984   *The Constitution of Society: Outline of the Theory of Struc-
            turation.* Berkeley and Los Angeles: University of California
            Press.
1987   *The Nation-State and Violence.* Volume Two of *A Contempo-
            rary Critique of Historical Materialism.* Berkeley and Los An-
            geles: University of California Press.

Glass, John B.
1975   "A Survey of Native Middle American Pictorial Manuscripts."
            In Cline 1975.

Glass, John B., and Donald Robertson
1975   "A Census of Native Middle American Pictorial Manuscripts."
            In Cline 1975.

Gledhill, John, Barbara Bender, and Mogens Trolle Larsen
1988   *State and Society: The Emergence and Development of Social
            Hierarchy and Political Centralization.* London: Unwin Hyman.

Goldstone, Jack A.
1982   "The Comparative and Historical Study of Revolutions." *An-
            nual Review of Sociology* 8:187–207.

Gomez de Orozco, Federico
1945   "Costumbres, Fiestas, Enterramientos y Diversas Formas de
            Proceder de Los Indios de Nueva España." *Tlalocan* 2:37–63.

Gonzales Ortega, José
1938   "El Cerro de Xochicalco." *Revista Geográfica Americana* 10:
            419–30.

Gonzalez D'Avila, Gil
1904   "Guerra de los Chichimecas." *Anales del Museo Nacional de
            México.* Segunda Epoca, Tomo 1:4:159–71.

Goody, Jack
1971   *Technology, Tradition, and the State in Africa.* London: Oxford
            University Press.

Gorenstein, Shirley
1973   *Tepexi el Viejo: A Postclassic Fortified Site in the Mixteca-
            Puebla Region of Mexico.* Transactions of the American Philo-
            sophical Society, Volume 63, Part 1.
1985   *Acambaro: Frontier Settlement on the Tarascan-Aztec Border.*
            Vanderbilt University Publications in Anthropology, No. 32.

Gorenstein, Shirley, and Helen Perstein Pollard
1983   *The Tarascan Civilization: A Late Prehispanic Cultural System.*
            Vanderbilt University Publications in Anthropology, No. 28.

Graham, Ian
  1967   *Archaeological Explorations in El Peten, Guatemala.* Middle
            American Research Institute, Publication 33.
  1978   *Corpus of Maya Hieroglyphic Inscriptions.* Vol. 2, Part 2,
            Naranjo, Chunhuitz, Xunantunich. Cambridge, Massachusetts:
            Peabody Museum of Archaeology and Ethnology.
  1979   *Corpus of Maya Hieroglyphic Inscriptions.* Vol. 3, Part 2,
            Yaxchilan. Cambridge, Massachusetts: Peabody Museum of Ar-
            chaeology and Ethnology.
  1980   *Corpus of Maya Hieroglyphic Inscriptions.* Vol. 2, Part 3,
            Ixkun, Ucanal, Ixtutz, Naranjo. Cambridge, Massachusetts:
            Peabody Museum of Archaeology and Ethnology.
  1982   *Corpus of Maya Hieroglyphic Inscriptions.* Vol. 3, Part 3,
            Yaxchilan. Cambridge, Massachusetts: Peabody Museum of Ar-
            chaeology and Ethnology.
  1986   *Corpus of Maya Hieroglyphic Inscriptions.* Vol. 5, Part 3,
            Uaxactun. Cambridge, Massachusetts: Peabody Museum of Ar-
            chaeology and Ethnology.
Graham, Ian, and Eric Von Euw
  1975   *Corpus of Maya Hieroglyphic Inscriptions.* Vol. 2, Part 1,
            Naranjo. Cambridge, Massachusetts: Peabody Museum of Ar-
            chaeology and Ethnology.
  1977   *Corpus of Maya Hieroglyphic Inscriptions.* Vol. 3, Part 1,
            Yaxchilan. Cambridge, Massachusetts: Peabody Museum of Ar-
            chaeology and Ethnology.
Graham, John
  1989   "Olmec Diffusion: A Sculptural View from Pacific Guatemala."
            In Sharer and Grove 1989.
Greene, Merle, Robert L. Rands, and John A. Graham
  1972   *Maya Sculpture from the Southern Lowlands, the Highlands
            and Pacific Piedmont: Guatemala, Mexico, Honduras.* Berke-
            ley: Lederer, Street and Zeus.
Gregg, Josiah
  1962   *Commerce of the Prairies.* 2 vols. Philadelphia: J. B. Lippincott
            Company.
Grove, David C.
  1968   "The Pre-Classic Olmec in Central Mexico: Site Distribution
            and Inferences." In Benson 1968.
  1970   "The Olmec Paintings of Oxtotitlan Cave, Guerrero, Mexico."
            *Dumbarton Oaks Studies in Pre-Columbian Art and Archaeol-
            ogy,* No. 6.
  1981a   "The Formative Period and the Evolution of Complex Culture."
            In Sabloff 1981.
  1981b   "Olmec Monuments: Mutilation as a Clue to Meaning." In
            Benson 1981.
  1984   *Chalcatzingo: Excavations on the Olmec Frontier.* New York:
            Thames and Hudson.

1987a   *Ancient Chalcatzingo.* Austin: University of Texas Press.
1987b   "Chalcatzingo in a Broader Perspective." In Grove 1987a.
1987c   "Other Ceramics and Miscellaneous Artifacts." In Grove 1987a.
1989a   "Olmec: What's in a Name." In Sharer and Grove 1989.
1989b   "Chalcatzingo and Its Olmec Connection." In Sharer and Grove 1989.

Grove, David C., Kenneth G. Hirth, David E. Bugé, and Ann M. Cyphers
1976   "Settlement and Cultural Development at Chalcatzingo." *Science* 192:1203–10.

Grove, David C., and Louise I. Paradis
1971   "An Olmec Stela from San Miguel Amuco, Guerrero." *American Antiquity* 36:95–102.

Guadalupe Mastache, Alba, and Robert H. Cobean
1989   "The Coyotlatelco Culture and the Origins of the Toltec State." In Diehl and Berlo 1989.

Guillemin, Jorge F.
1959   "Iximché." *Antropología e Historia de Guatemala* 11:2:22–64.
1965   *Iximché: Capital del Antiguo Reino Cakchiquel.* Guatemala: Instituto de Antropología e Historia de Guatemala.
1967   "The Ancient Cakchiquel Capital of Iximche." *Expedition* 9:2: 22–35.

Guillén, Ann Cyphers, and David C. Grove
1987   "Chronology and Cultural Phases at Chalcatzingo." In Grove 1987a.

Haas, Jonathan
1982   *The Evolution of the Prehistoric State.* New York: Columbia University Press.

Hagen, Victor W. von
1962   *The Aztec: Man and Tribe.* New York: Mentor Books.

Hall, John A.
1986   *States in History.* Oxford: Basil Blackwell, Ltd.

Hammond, Norman
1974   *Mesoamerican Archaeology: New Approaches.* Austin: University of Texas Press.
1977   *Social Process in Maya Prehistory: Studies in Honour of Sir Eric Thompson.* New York: Academic Press.
1982a   "The Prehistory of Belize." *Journal of Field Archaeology* 9: 349–62.
1982b   *Ancient Maya Civilization.* New Brunswick: Rutgers University Press.
1989   "Review of *Maya Postclassic State Formation: Segmentary Lineage Migration in Advancing Frontiers* by John W. Fox." *American Antiquity* 54:665–66.

Hammond, Norman, and Gordon R. Willey
1974   *Maya Archaeology and Ethnohistory.* Austin: University of Texas Press.

Hardoy, Jorge
    1973   *Pre-Columbian Cities.* New York: Walker and Co.
Harlan, Mark E.
    1979   "An Inquiry into the Development of Complex Society at Chalcatzingo, Morelos, Mexico: Methods and Results." *American Antiquity* 44:471–93.
Harrington, M. R.
    1908   "Some Seneca Corn-Foods and their Preparation." *American Anthropologist* 10:575–90.
Harrison, Peter D., and B. L. Turner II
    1978   *Pre-Hispanic Maya Agriculture.* Albuquerque: University of New Mexico Press.
Hart, Hornell
    1948   "The Logistical Growth of Political Areas." *Social Forces* 26: 396–408.
Harvey, H. R., and Hanns J. Prem
    1984   *Explorations in Ethnohistory: Indians of Central Mexico in the Sixteenth Century.* Albuquerque: University of New Mexico Press.
Hassig, Ross
    1985   *Trade, Tribute, and Transportation: The Sixteenth-Century Political Economy of the Valley of Mexico.* Norman: University of Oklahoma Press.
    1986   "One Hundred Years of Servitude: *Tlamemes* in Early New Spain." In Spores 1986.
    1988   *Aztec Warfare: Imperial Expansion and Political Control.* Norman: University of Oklahoma Press.
    1991   "Roads, Routes, and Ties That Bind." In Trombold 1991.
Haviland, William A.
    1969   "A New Population Estimate for Tikal, Guatemala." *American Antiquity* 34:429–33.
    1973   "Rules of Descent in Sixteenth Century Yucatan." *Estudios de Cultura Maya* 9:135–50.
    1977   "Dynastic Genealogies from Tikal, Guatemala: Implications for Descent and Political Organization." *American Antiquity* 42:61–67.
    1985   *Excavations in Small Residential Groups of Tikal: Groups 4F-1 and 4F-2.* Philadelphia: University Museum Monograph 58.
Headrick, Daniel R.
    1981   *The Tools of Empire: Technology and European Imperialism in the Nineteenth Century.* New York: Oxford University Press.
Healan, Dan M.
    1977   "Architectural Implications of Daily Life in Ancient Tollan, Hidalgo, Mexico." *World Archaeology* 9:140–56.
    1982   "Patrones Residenciales en la Antigua Ciudad de Tula." In Mastache, Crespo, Cobean, and Healan 1982.

1986   "Technological and Nontechnological Aspects of an Obsidian
            Workshop Excavated at Tula, Hidalgo." In Isaac 1986.

1989*a*   *Tula of the Toltecs: Excavations and Survey.* Iowa City: Univer-
            sity of Iowa Press.

1989*b*   "Tula, Tollan, and the Toltecs in Mesoamerican Prehistory." In
            Healan 1989*a*.

1989*c*   "Synopsis of Structural Remains in the Canal Locality." In
            Healan 1989*a*.

1989*d*   "The Central Group and West Group." In Healan 1989*a*.

Healan, Dan M., Robert H. Cobean, and Richard A. Diehl

1989   "Synthesis and Conclusions." In Healan 1989*a*.

Healan, Dan M., Janet M. Kerley, and George J. Bey III

1983   "Excavation and Preliminary Analysis of an Obsidian Work-
            shop in Tula, Hidalgo, Mexico." *Journal of Field Archaeology*
            10:127–45.

Healan, Dan M., and James W. Stoutamire

1989   "Surface Survey of the Tula Urban Zone." In Healan 1989*a*.

Healy, Paul F., and Nancy A. Prikker

1989   "Ancient Maya Warfare: Chronicles of Manifest Superiority."
            In Tkaczuk and Vivian 1989.

Hedrick, Basil C., J. Charles Kelley, and Carroll L. Riley

1971   *The North Mexican Frontier.* Carbondale: Southern Illinois Uni-
            versity Press.

Heizer, Robert F.

1967   "Analysis of Two Low Relief Sculptures from La Venta." *Contri-
            butions of the University of California Archaeological Research
            Facility,* No. 3:25–55.

1970   "How Accurate Were California Indians with the Bow and Ar-
            row?" *The Masterkey* 44:108–11.

1972   "An Unusual Olmec Figurine." *The Masterkey* 46:71–74.

Heizer, Robert F., and Irmgard W. Johnson

1952   "A Prehistoric Sling from Lovelock Cave, Nevada." *American
            Antiquity* 18:139–47.

Hellmuth, Nicholas

1975   "The Escuintla Hoards: Teotihuacan Art in Guatemala."
            F.L.A.A.R. Progress Reports 1:2:4–70.

1987   *Monster und Menschen in der Maya-Kunst.* Graz: Akademische
            Druck-u. Verlagsanstalt.

Henderson, John S.

1979   *Atopula, Guerrero, and Olmec Horizons in Mesoamerica.* Yale
            University Publications in Anthropology, Number 77.

Hester, T. R., M. P. Mildner, and L. Spencer

1974   *Great Basin Atlatl Studies.* Ramona, California: Ballena Press.

Hibben, Frank C.

1938   "A Cache of Wooden Bows from the Mogollon Mountains."
            American Antiquity 4:36–38.

Higbee, Edward
1948   "Agriculture in the Maya Homeland." *Geographical Review* 38:457–64.
Hirth, Kenneth G.
1976   "Teotihuacan Influence in the Eastern Valley of Morelos, Mexico." *XIV Mesa Redonda*. Vol. 2. México: Sociedad Mexicana de Antropología.
1977   "Toltec-Mazapan Influence in Eastern Morelos, Mexico." *Journal of New World Archaeology* 2:40–46.
1978a   "Interregional Trade and the Formation of Prehistoric Gateway Communities." *American Antiquity* 43:35–45.
1978b   "Teotihuacán Regional Population Administration in Eastern Morelos." *World Archaeology* 9:320–33.
1984a   "Xochicalco: Urban Growth and State Formation in Central Mexico." *Science* 225:579–86.
1984b   *Trade and Exchange in Early Mesoamerica*. Albuquerque: University of New Mexico Press.
1985   "Epiclassic Militarism and Social Organization at Xochicalco, Morelos." Paper presented at the 50th annual convention of the Society for American Archaeology, Denver, May 1–5, 1985.
1989   "Militarism and Social Organization at Xochicalco, Morelos." In Diehl and Berlo 1989.
Hirth, Kenneth, and Jorge Angulo Villaseñor
1981   "Early State Expansion in Central Mexico: Teotihuacan in Morelos." *Journal of Field Archaeology* 8:135–50.
Hirth, Kenneth G., and Ann Cyphers Guillén
1988   *Tiempo y Asenamiento en Xochicalco*. México: Universidad Nacional Autónoma de México.
Hirth, Kenneth G., and William Swezey
1976   "The Changing Nature of the Teotihuacan Classic: A Regional Perspective from Manzanilla, Puebla." *XIV Mesa Redonda*. Vol. 2. México: Sociedad Mexicana de Antropología.
Hochberg, Bette
1977   *Handspindles*. Santa Cruz, California: Bette and Bernard Hochberg.
Hodge, Mary G.
1984   *Aztec City-States*. Memoirs of the Museum of Anthropology, University of Michigan, Number 18.
Hogg, Ian
1981   *The History of Fortification*. New York: St. Martin's Press Inc.
Hogg, O. F. G.
1968   *Clubs to Cannons: Warfare and Weapons Before the Introduction of Gunpowder*. London: Gerald Duckworth and Co., Ltd.
Homenaje
1951   *Homenaje al doctor Alfonso Caso*. México: Imprenta Nuevo Mundo.

1961   *Homenaje a Pablo Martínez del Río en el vigésimoquinto aniversario de la primera edición de Los Orígenes Americanos.* México: Instituto Nacional de Antropología e Historia.

Hoopes, John W.
1985   "Trade and Exchange." In Willey and Mathews 1985.

Hopkins, Nicolas A.
1988   "Classic Mayan Kinship Systems: Epigraphic and Ethnographic Evidence for Patrilineality." *Estudios de Cultura Maya* 17:87–121.

Howard, Michael
1990   "Afterword: Tools of War: Concepts and Technology." In Lynn 1990.

Isaac, Barry L.
1986   *Research in Economic Anthropology: Economic Aspects of Prehispanic Highland Mexico.* Greenwich, Connecticut: JAI Press.

Ixtlilxóchitl, Fernando de Alva
1975–77   *Obras Históricas.* 2 vols. México: Universidad Nacional Autónoma de México.

Jiménez Moreno, Wigberto
1966   "Mesoamerica before the Toltecs." In Paddock 1966*a*.

Joesink-Mandeville, L. R. V., and Sylvia Meluzin
1976   "Olmec-Maya Relationships: Olmec Influence in Yucatan." In Nicholson 1976.

Johnston, Kevin
1985   "Maya Dynastic Territorial Expansion: Glyphic Evidence for Classic Centers of the Pasion River, Guatemala." In Fields 1985.

Jones, Archer
1987   *The Art of War in the Western World.* Urbana: University of Illinois Press.

Jones, Christopher, and Linton Satterthwaite
1982   *The Monuments and Inscriptions of Tikal: The Carved Monuments.* Philadelphia: University Museum Monograph 44.

Jubinal, Achille
1846   *La Armería real ou collection des principales pièces de la Galerie d'Armes Anciennes de Madrid. Supplement.* Paris: Dessins de M. Gaspard Sensi.

Justeson, John S., William M. Norman, Lyle Campbell, and Terrence Kaufman
1985   *The Foreign Impact on Lowland Mayan Language and Script.* Middle American Research Institute, Publication 53.

Kampen, Michael Edwin
1972   *The Sculptures of El Tajín, Veracruz, Mexico.* Gainesville: University of Florida Press.
1978   "Classical Veracruz Grotesques and Sacrificial Iconography." *Man* 13:116–26.
1979   "Classic Maya Elements in the Iconography of Rulership at El Tajín, Veracruz, Mexico." *Phoebus* 1:93–102.

Kan, Michael, Clement Meighan, and H. B. Nicholson
   1970   *Sculpture of Ancient West Mexico: Nayarit, Jalisco, Colima.
              The Proctor Stafford Collection.* Los Angeles: Los Angeles
              County Museum of Art.
Katz, Friedrich
   1972   *The Ancient American Civilizations.* New York: Praeger.
Kelley, David Humiston
   1976   *Deciphering the Maya Script.* Austin: University of Texas Press.
Kelley, J. Charles
   1971   "Archaeology of the Northern Frontier: Zacatecas and Du-
              rango." In Ekholm and Bernal 1971*b*.
Kennedy, Paul
   1987   *The Rise and Fall of the Great Powers.* New York: Random
              House, Inc.
Kerr, Justin
   1989–90   *The Maya Vase Book: A Corpus of Rollout Photographs of
              Maya Vases.* 2 vols. New York: Kerr Associates.
Kidder, Alfred V., Jesse D. Jennings, and Edwin M. Shook
   1946   *Excavations at Kaminaljuyu, Guatemala.* Washington, D.C.:
              Carnegie Institution of Washington, Publication 561.
Kidder, Tristam R.
   1985   "Artifacts." In Willey and Mathews 1985.
King, Mary Elizabeth
   1979   "The Prehistoric Textile Industry of Mesoamerica." In Rowe,
              Benson, and Schaffer 1979.
Kinz, Ellen R., and Laraine A. Fletcher
   1983   "A Reconstruction of the Prehistoric Population at Coba." In
              Folan, Kintz, and Fletcher 1983.
Kipp, Rita Smith, and Edward M. Schortman
   1989   "The Political Impact of Trade in Chiefdoms." *American An-
              thropologist* 91:370–85.
Kirchhoff, Paul
   1952   "Meso-America." In Tax 1952.
Kirchhoff, Paul, Lina Odena Güemes, and Luis Reyes Garcia
   1976   *Historia Tolteca-Chichimeca.* México: Instituto Nacional de
              Antropología e Historia.
Kirkby, Andrew
   1989   "State, Local State, Context, and Spatiality: A Reappraisal of
              State Theory." In Caporaso 1989.
Kiser, Edgar
   1989   "A Principal-Agent Analysis of the Initiation of War in Absolut-
              ist States." In Schaeffer 1989*a*.
Kolb, Charles C.
   1986   "Commercial Aspects of Classic Teotihuacan Period 'Thin
              Orange' Wares." In Isaac 1986.
Korfmann, Manfred
   1973   "The Sling as a Weapon." *Scientific American* 229:4:34–42.

Kowalewski, Stephen A., Gary M. Feinman, Laura Finsten, Richard E. Blanton, and Linda M. Nicholas
    1989   *Monte Albán's Hinterland, Part II: Prehispanic Settlement Patterns in Tlacolula, Etla, and Ocotlan, The Valley of Oaxaca, Mexico.* 2 vols. Memoirs of the Museum of Anthropology, University of Michigan, Number 23.

Kowalewski, Stephen A., and Laura Finsten
    1983   "The Economic Systems of Ancient Oaxaca: A Regional Perspective." *Current Anthropology* 24:413–41.

Krasner, Stephen D.
    1989   "Sovereignty: An Institutional Perspective." In Caporaso 1989.

Kristan-Graham, Cynthia Beth
    1989   "Art, Rulership and the Mesoamerican Body Politic at Tula and Chichen Itza." Ph.D. diss., University of California, Los Angeles.

Kubler, George
    1980   "Eclecticism at Cacaxtla." In Robertson 1980.
    1984   *The Art and Architecture of Ancient America.* New York: Penguin Books.

Kurbjuhn, Kornelia
    1977   "Fans in Maya Art." *The Masterkey* 51:140–46.

Kurjack, Edward B.
    1974   *Prehistoric Lowland Maya Community and Social Organization: A Case Study at Dzibilchaltun, Yucatan, Mexico.* Middle American Research Institute, Publication 38.

Kurjack, Edward B., and E. Wyllys Andrews V
    1976   "Early Boundary Maintenance in Northwest Yucatan, Mexico." *American Antiquity* 41:318–25.

Kurtz, Donald V.
    1987   "The Economics of Urbanization and State Formation at Teotihuacan." *Current Anthropology* 28:329–40.

Lagunas Rodríguez, Zaíd, Carlos Serrano Sánchez, and Sergio López Alonso
    1976   *Enterramientos Humanos de la Zona Arquelogica de Cholula, Puebla.* México: Instituto Nacional de Antropología e Historia.

Landa, Diego de
    1973   *Relación de las cosas de Yucatán.* México: Porrúa.
    1978   *Yucatan Before and After the Conquest.* William Gates, trans. New York: Dover.

Laporte, Juan Pedro, and Vilma Fialko C.
    1990   "New Perspectives on Old Problems: Dynastic References for the Early Classic at Tikal." In Clancy and Harrison 1990.

Larick, Roy
    1985   "Spears, Style, and Time among Maa-Speaking Pastoralists." *Journal of Anthropological Archaeology* 4:206–20.

Leclercq, Jean
    1982   *The Love of Learning and the Desire for God: A Study of Monastic Culture.* New York: Fordham University Press.

Lee, Thomas A., Jr.
1985   *Los Códices Mayas*. San Cristobal de las Casas: Universidad
            Autónoma de Chiapas.
Lee, Thomas A., Jr., and Carlos Navarrete
1978   *Mesoamerican Communication Routes and Cultural Contacts*. Pa-
            pers of the New World Archaeological Foundation, Number 40.
Leventhal, Richard M., and Alan L. Kolata
1983   *Civilization in the Ancient Americas: Essays in Honor of Gor-
            don R. Willey*. Albuquerque: University of New Mexico Press
            and Peabody Museum of Archaeology and Ethnology.
Lincoln, Charles E.
1986   "The Chronology of Chichen Itza: A Review of the Literature."
            In Sabloff and Andrews 1986.
Linné, S.
1934   *Archaeological Researches at Teotihuacan, Mexico*. Stockholm:
            Victor Pettersons Bokindustriaktiebolag.
1938   *Zapotecan Antiquities and the Paulson Collection in the Ethno-
            logical Museum of Sweden*. Stockholm: Bokförlags Aktiebola-
            get Thule.
1942   *Mexican Highland Cultures: Archaeological Researches at Teoti-
            huacan, Calpulalpan and Chalchicomula in 1934/35*. The Ethno-
            graphical Museum of Sweden, Stockholm, Publication No. 7.
1948   "Modern Blowguns in Oaxaca, Mexico." *Ethnos* 13:111–19.
Lister, Robert H.
1971   "Archaeological Synthesis of Guerrero." In Ekholm and Bernal
            1971*b*.
1978   "Mesoamerican Influence at Chaco Canyon, New Mexico." In
            Riley and Hedrick 1978.
Littmann, Edwin R.
1958   "Ancient Mesoamerican Mortars, Plasters, and Stuccos: The
            Composition and Origin of *Sascab*." *American Antiquity* 24:
            172–76.
Lombardo de Ruiz, Sonia
1986   "La Pintura." In Lombardo de Ruiz, López de Molina, Molina
            Feal, Baus de Czitrom, and Polanco 1986.
Lombardo de Ruiz, Sonia, Diana López de Molina, and Daniel Molina Feal
1986   "Comentarios Finales." In Lombardo de Ruiz, López de Mo-
            lina, Molina Feal, Baus de Czitrom, and Polanco 1986.
Lombardo de Ruiz, Sonia, Diana López de Molina, Daniel Molina Feal, Carolyn Baus de Czitrom, and Oscar J. Polanco
1986   *Cacaxtla: El Lugar donde Muere la Lluvia en la Tierra*. México:
            Instituto Tlaxcalteca de la Cultura.
López de Gómara, Francisco
1965–66   *Historia general de las Indias*. 2 vols. Barcelona: Obras Maestras.
López de Molina, Diana
1977*a*   "Los murales prehispánicos de Cacaxtla." *Antropología e Histo-
            ria* 20:2–8.

1977b "Cacaxtla y su relación con otras areas Mesoamericanas." *XV Mesa Redonda*. Vol. 2. México: Sociedad Mexicana de Antropología.

López de Molina, Diana, and Daniel Molina Feal
1986 "Arqueologia." In Lombardo de Ruiz, López de Molina, Molina Feal, Baus de Czitrom, and Polanco 1986.

Lothrop, Samuel Kirkland
1924 *Tulum: An Archaeological Study of the East Coast of Yucatan.* Washington, D.C.: Carnegie Institution of Washington, Publication 335.
1952 *Metals from the Cenote of Sacrifice, Chichen Itza, Yucatan.* Memoirs of the Peabody Museum of Archaeology and Ethnology, Vol. 10, No. 2.

Lowe, Gareth W.
1989 "The Heartland Olmec: Evolution of Material Culture." In Sharer and Grove 1989.

Lowe, Gareth W., Thomas A. Lee, Jr., and Eduardo Martinez Espinosa
1982 *Izapa: An Introduction to the Ruins and Monuments.* Papers of the New World Archaeological Foundation, Number 31.

Lowe, Gareth W., and J. Alden Mason
1965 "Archaeological Survey of the Chiapas Coast, Highlands, and Upper Grijalva Basin." In Willey 1965a.

Lowe, John W. G.
1985 *The Dynamics of Apocalypse: A Systems Simulation of the Classic Maya Collapse.* Albuquerque: University of New Mexico Press.

Luttwak, Edward
1976 *The Grand Strategy of the Roman Empire.* Baltimore, Maryland: The Johns Hopkins University Press.

Lynn, John A.
1990 *Tools of War: Instruments, Ideas, and Institutions of Warfare, 1445–1871.* Urbana: University of Illinois Press.

MacCurdy, George Grant
1909 "Anthropology at the Winnipeg Meeting of the British Association." *American Anthropologist* 11:456–77.

MacKinnon, J. Jefferson
1981 "The Nature of Residential Tikal: A Spatial Analysis." *Estudios de Cultura Maya* 13:223–49.

MacNeish, Richard S., Antoinette Nalken-Terner, and Irmgard W. Johnson
1967 *The Prehistory of the Tehuacan Valley.* Vol. 2, *Nonceramic Artifacts.* Austin: University of Texas Press.

MacNeish, Richard S., Frederick A. Peterson, and Kent V. Flannery
1970 *The Prehistory of the Tehuacan Valley.* Vol. 3, *Ceramics.* Austin: University of Texas Press.

Mahler, Joy
1965 "Garments and Textiles of the Maya Lowlands." In Willey 1965b.

Maler, Teobert
  1901   *Researches in the Central Portion of the Usumatsintla Valley.*
              Memoirs of the Peabody Museum of American Archaeology
              and Ethnology, Harvard University, Vol. 2, No. 1.
Mandeville, Margaret
  1974   "Chipped Stone Points from Tula." In Diehl 1974*a*.
Mann, Michael
  1987   *The Sources of Social Power.* Volume I, *A History of Power
              from the Beginning to* A.D. *1760.* Cambridge: Cambridge Uni-
              versity Press.
Marcus, Joyce
  1974   "The Iconography of Power Among the Classic Maya." *World
              Archaeology* 6:83–94.
  1976*a*   *Emblem and State in the Classic Maya Lowlands: An Epi-
              graphic Approach to Territorial Organization.* Washington,
              D.C.: Dumbarton Oaks.
  1976*b*   "The Iconography of Militarism at Monte Albán and Neighbor-
              ing Sites in the Valley of Oaxaca." In Nicholson 1976.
  1983*a*   "The Conquest Slabs of Building J, Monte Albán." In Flannery
              and Marcus 1983*a*.
  1983*b*   "Stone Monuments and Tomb Murals at Monte Albán IIIa." In
              Flannery and Marcus 1983*a*.
  1983*c*   "Teotihuacán Visitors on Monte Albán Monuments and Mu-
              rals." In Flannery and Marcus 1983*a*.
  1983*d*   "Changing Patterns of Stone Monuments after the Fall of
              Monte Albán, A.D. 600–900." In Flannery and Marcus 1983*a*.
  1983*e*   "Aztec Military Campaigns against the Zapotecs: The Documen-
              tary Evidence." In Flannery and Marcus 1983*a*.
  1983*f*   "A Synthesis of the Cultural Evolution of the Zapotec and
              Mixtec." In Flannery and Marcus 1983*a*.
  1987   *The Inscriptions of Calakmul: Royal Marriage at a Maya City in
              Campeche, Mexico.* University of Michigan Museum of Anthro-
              pology, Technical Report 21.
  1988   "Comment." In Sanders and Nichols 1988.
  1989   "Zapotec Chiefdoms and the Nature of Formative Religions."
              In Sharer and Grove 1989.
Marcus, Joyce, and Kent V. Flannery
  1983   "The Postclassic Balkanization of Oaxaca." In Flannery and
              Marcus 1983*a*.
Marquina, Ignacio
  1964   *Arquitectura Prehispánica.* México: Instituto Nacional de Antro-
              pología e Historia.
  1970*a*   *Proyecto Cholula.* México: Instituto Nacional de Antropología
              e Historia.
  1970*b*   "Pirámide de Cholula." In Marquina 1970*a*.
Mastache Flores, Alba Guadalupe, and Ana María Crespo Oviedo
  1982   "Analisís sobre la Traza General de Tula, Hgo." In Mastache,
              Crespo, Cobean, and Healan 1982.

Mastache, Alba Guadalupe, Ana María Crespo, Robert H. Cobean, and Dan M. Healan
1982   *Estudios Sobre la Antigua Ciudad de Tula*. México: Instituto Nacional de Antropología e Historia.
Matheny, Ray T.
1976   "Teotihuacan Influence in the Chenes and Rio Bec Areas of the Yucatan Peninsula, Mexico." *XIV Mesa Redonda*. Vol. 2. México: Sociedad Mexicana de Antropología.
1980   *El Mirador, Peten, Guatemala: An Interim Report*. Papers of the New World Archaeological Foundation, No. 45.
1986   "Early States in the Maya Lowlands during the Late Preclassic: Edzna and El Mirador." In Benson 1986.
Matheny, Ray T., Deanne L. Gurr, Donald W. Forsyth, and F. Richard Hauck
1983   *Investigations at Edzná, Campeche, Mexico*. Vol. 1, Part 1, *The Hydraulic System*. Papers of the New World Archaeological Foundation, Number 46.
Matheny, Ray T., Richard D. Hansen, and Deanne L. Gurr
1980   "Preliminary Field Report, El Mirador 1979 Season." In Matheny 1980.
Mathews, Peter
1980   "Notes on the Dynastic Sequence of Bonampak, Part 1." In Robertson 1980.
1983   *Corpus of Maya Hieroglyphic Inscriptions*. Vol. 6, Part 1, *Tonina*. Cambridge, Massachusetts: Peabody Museum of Archaeology and Ethnology.
1985   "Maya Early Classic Monuments and Inscriptions." In Willey and Mathews 1985.
Matos Moctezuma, Eduardo
1974a   *Proyecto Tula (1a Parte)*. México: Instituto Nacional de Antropología e Historia.
1974b   "Excavaciones en la Microarea: Tula Chico y la Plaza Charnay." In Matos Moctezuma 1974a.
1986   *Tula*. México: G. V. Editores.
Maudslay, A. P.
1889–   *Biologia Centrali-Americana; or, Contributions to the Knowl-
1902   edge of the Fauna and Flora of Mexico and Central America*. 6 vols. London: R. H. Porter and Dulau and Co.
Maurice, F.
1930   "The Size of the Army of Xerxes in the Invasion of Greece 480 B.C." *Journal of Hellenistic Studies* 50:210–35.
McNeill, William H.
1977   *Plagues and Peoples*. Garden City, New York: Anchor Books.
1982   *The Pursuit of Power: Technology, Armed Force, and Society Since A.D. 1000*. Chicago: University of Chicago Press.
McVicker, Donald
1985   "The 'Mayanized' Mexicans." *American Antiquity* 50:82–101.

Meighan, Clement W.
1974   "Prehistory of West Mexico." *Science* 184:1254–61.
Military Balance
1989   *The Military Balance 1989–1990*. London: The International
            Institute for Strategic Studies.
Miller, Arthur G.
1973   *The Mural Painting of Teotihuacán*. Washington, D.C.: Dum-
            barton Oaks.
1977   " 'Captains of the Itza': Unpublished Mural Evidence from
            Chichén Itzá." In Hammond 1977.
1978   "A Brief Outline of the Artistic Evidence for Classic Period Cul-
            tural Contact Between Maya Lowlands and Central Mexican
            Highlands." In Pasztory 1978a.
Miller, Mary Ellen
1986   *The Murals of Bonampak*. Princeton: Princeton University Press.
Millon, Clara
1973   "Painting, Writing, and Polity in Teotihuacan, Mexico." *Ameri-
            can Antiquity* 38:294–314.
1988a   "A Reexamination of the Teotihuacan Tassel Headdress Insig-
            nia." In Berrin 1988.
1988b   "Coyote with Sacrificial Knife." In Berrin 1988.
Millon, René
1973   *Urbanization at Teotihuacán, Mexico*. Vol. 1, *The Teotihuacán
            Map, Text*. Austin: University of Texas Press.
1976   "Social Relations in Ancient Teotihuacan." In Wolf 1976.
1981   "Teotihuacan: City, State, and Civilization." In Sabloff 1981.
1988a   "The Last Years of Teotihuacan Dominance." In Yoffee and
            Cowgill 1988.
1988b   "Where Do They All Come From? The Provenance of the Wag-
            ner Murals from Teotihuacan." In Berrin 1988.
Molina Feal, Daniel
1977   "Consideraciones sobre la cronología de Cacaxtla." *XV Mesa
            Redonda*. Vol. 2. México: Sociedad Mexicana de Antropología.
Mommsen, Wolfgang J.
1980   *Theories of Imperialism*. New York: Random House.
Moore, Charlotte B.
1974   *Reconstructing Complex Societies: An Archaeological Collo-
            quium*. Supplement to the Bulletin of the American Schools of
            Oriental Research No. 20.
Morgan, Nigel
1982   *Early Gothic Manuscripts (1): 1190–1250*. London: Harvey
            Miller.
Morley, Sylvanus G., George W. Brainerd, and Robert J. Sharer
1983   *The Ancient Maya*. Stanford: Stanford University Press.
Morris, Ann Axtell
1931   "Murals from the Temple of the Warriors and Adjacent Struc-
            tures." In Morris, Charlot, and Morris 1931.

Morris, Earl H., Jean Charlot, and Ann Axtell Morris
 1931   *The Temple of the Warriors at Chichen Itzá, Yucatan.* 2 vols.
           Washington, D.C.: Carnegie Institution of Washington, Publica-
           tion 406.
Moskos, Charles C., Jr.
 1976   "The Military." *Annual Review of Sociology* 2:55–77.
Müller, Florencia
 1970   "La Cerámica de Cholula." In Marquina 1970*a*.
Muñoz Camargo, Diego
 1947   *Historia de Tlaxcala.* México: n.p.
Nagao, Debra
 1989   "Public Proclamation in the Art of Cacaxtla and Xochicalco."
           In Diehl and Berlo 1989.
Navarrete, Carlos
 1974   *The Olmec Rock Carvings at Pijijiapan, Chiapas, Mexico and
           Other Olmec Pieces from Chiapas and Guatemala.* Papers of
           the New World Archaeological Foundation, Number 35.
Neff, Hector
 1989   "The Effect of Interregional Distribution on Plumbate Pottery
           Production." In Voorhies 1989.
Neumann, C.
 1971   "A Note on Alexander's March-rates." *Historia: Journal of An-
           cient History* 20:196–98.
Nicholson, H. B.
 1961   "The Chapultepec Cliff Sculpture of Motecuhzoma Xocoyo-
           tzin." *El México Antiguo* 9:379–444.
 1976   *Origins of Religious Art and Iconography in Preclassic Mesoamer-
           ica.* Los Angeles: UCLA Latin American Center Publications.
Noguera, Eduardo
 1945   "Exploraciones de Xochicalco." *Cuadernos Americanos* 4:
           119–57.
 1948–49   "Nuevos rasgos characteristicos encontrados en Xochicalco."
           Revista Mexicana de Estudios Antropológicos 10:115–19.
 1960   *Zonas Arqueologicas del Estado de Morelos.* México: Instituto
           Nacional de Antropología e Historia.
 1961   "Ultimos Descubrimientos en Xochicalco." *Revista Mexicana
           de Estudios Antropológicos* 17:33–37.
Norman, V. Gareth
 1973   *Izapa Sculpture, Part 1: Album.* Papers of the New World
           Archaeological Foundation, Number 30.
 1976   *Izapa Sculpture, Part 2: Text.* Papers of the New World Ar-
           chaeological Foundation, Number 30.
Nuttall, Zelia
 1975   *The Codex Nuttall.* New York: Dover.
Oakeshott, R. Ewart
 1960   *The Archaeology of Weapons: Arms and Armor from Prehistory
           to the Age of Chivalry.* New York: Frederick A. Praeger.

O'Connell, Robert L.
1989   *Of Arms and Men: A History of War, Weapons, and Aggression.* New York: Oxford University Press.
Odell, George H., and Frank Cowan
1986   "Experiments with Spears and Arrows on Animal Targets." *Journal of Field Archaeology* 13:195–212.
Oman, C. W. C.
1976   *The Art of War in the Middle Ages.* Ithaca: Cornell University Press.
Orellana, Sandra L.
1984   *The Tzutujil Mayas: Continuity and Change, 1250–1630.* Norman: University of Oklahoma Press.
Otterbein, Keith F.
1970   *The Evolution of War: A Cross-cultural Study.* New Haven: HRAF Press.
Paddock, John
1966a   *Ancient Oaxaca: Discoveries in Mexican Archaeology and History.* Stanford: Stanford University Press.
1966b   "Oaxaca in Ancient Mesoamerica." In Paddock 1966a.
1966c   "Monte Albán: ¿Sede de imperio?" *Revista Mexicana de Estudios Antropológicos* 20:117–46.
1978   "The Middle Classic Period in Oaxaca." In Pasztory 1978a.
1983a   "Yagul during Monte Albán I." In Flannery and Marcus 1983a.
1983b   "Some Thought on the Decline of Monte Albán." In Flannery and Marcus 1983a.
1983c   "The Rise of the Ñuiñe Centers in the Mixteca Baja." In Flannery and Marcus 1983a.
Palacios, Enrique Juan
1948   "La estimación del año natural en Xochicalco, acorde con la ciencia." *Actes du XXVIIIe Congrès International des Américanistes,* 461–66.
Palerm, Angel
1956   "Notas sobre las construcciones militares y la guerra en Mesoamérica." *Anales del Instituto Nacional de Antropología e Historia* 8:123–34.
Parker, Arthur C.
1968   "Iroquois Uses of Maize and Other Food Plants." In Fenton 1968.
Parker, Geoffrey
1988   *The Military Revolution: Military Innovation and the Rise of the West, 1500–1800.* Cambridge: Cambridge University Press.
Parsons, Lee A.
1978   "The Peripheral Coastal Lowlands and the Middle Classic Period." In Pasztory 1978a.

Parsons, Lee A., John B. Carlson, and Peter David Joralemon
1988   *The Face of Ancient America: The Wally and Brenda Zollman Collection of Precolumbian Art.* Indianapolis: Indianapolis Museum of Art.
Paso y Troncoso, Francisco del
1939–42   *Epistolario de Nueva España.* 16 vols. México: Antigua Librería Robredo, de José Porrúa e Hijos.
Pasztory, Esther
1974   "The Iconography of the Teotihuacan Tlaloc." *Dumbarton Oaks: Studies in Pre-Columbian Art and Archaeology,* No. 23.
1976   *The Murals of Tepantitla, Teotihuacan.* New York: Garland Publishing Co.
1978a   *Middle Classic Mesoamerica: A.D. 400–700.* New York: Columbia University Press.
1978b   "Historical Synthesis of the Middle Classic Period." In Pasztory 1978a.
1978c   "Artistic Traditions of the Middle Classic Period." In Pasztory 1978a.
1983   *Aztec Art.* New York: Harry N. Abrams, Inc.
1988a   "A Reinterpretation of Teotihuacan and its Mural Painting Tradition." In Berrin 1988.
1988b   "Feathered Serpents and Flowering Trees with Glyphs." In Berrin 1988.
1988c   "Small Birds with Shields and Spears and Other Fragments." In Berrin 1988.
Payne-Galloway, Ralph
1986   *The Crossbow: Mediaeval and Modern, Military and Sporting; Its Construction, History and Management.* London: The Holland Press.
Peckham, Stewart
1965   "Prehistoric Weapons in the Southwest." Santa Fe: Museum of New Mexico Press.
Peñafiel, Antonio
1890   *Monumentos del Arte Mexicano Antiguo.* 3 vols. Berlin: A. Ascher and Co.
1903   *Indumentaria Antigua: Vestidos Guerreros y Civiles de los Mexicanos.* México: Oficina Tip. de la Secretaría de Fomento.
Peterson, David A., and Thomas B. MacDougall
1974   *Guiengola: A Fortified Site in the Isthmus of Tehuantepec.* Vanderbilt University Publications in Anthropology, No. 10.
Piña Chán, Román
1962   "Informe Preliminar sobre Mul-Chic, Yucatán." *Anales del Instituto Nacional de Antropología e Historia* 15:99–118.
1972   *Teotenango: Primer Informe de Exploraciones Arqueologicas, Enero a Septiembre de 1971.* México: Gobierno del Estado de México.

1978   "Commerce in the Yucatan Peninsula: The Conquest and Colonial Period." In Lee and Navarrete 1978.

1982   *Exploraciones Arqueológicas en Tingambato, Michoacán.* México: Instituto Nacional de Antropología e Historia.

Pires-Ferreira, Jane W.

1975   *Formative Mesoamerican Exchange Networks with Special Reference to the Valley of Oaxaca.* Memoirs of the Museum of Anthropology, University of Michigan, No. 7.

1978   "Obsidian Exchange Networks: Inferences and Speculation on the Development of Social Organization in Formative Mesoamerica." In Browman 1978.

Pires-Ferreira, Jane Wheeler, and Billy Joe Evans

1978   "Mössbauer Spectral Analysis of Olmec Iron Ore Mirrors: New Evidence of Formative Period Exchange Networks in Mesoamerica." In Browman 1978.

Pohl, John M. D., and Bruce Byland

1990   "Mixtec Landscape Perception and Archaeological Settlement Patterns." *Ancient Mesoamerica* 1:113–31.

Pollard, H. E. D.

1962   "Introduction." In Pollock, Roys, Prouskouriakoff, and Smith 1962.

1965   "Architecture of the Maya Lowlands." In Willey 1965a.

1980   *The Puuc: An Architectural Survey of the Hill Country of Yucatan and Northern Campeche, Mexico.* Memoirs of the Peabody Museum of Archaeology and Ethnology, Vol. 19.

Pollock, H. E. D., Ralph L. Roys, T. Proskouriakoff, and A. Ledyard Smith

1962   *Mayapan, Yucatan, Mexico.* Washington, D.C.: Carnegie Institution of Washington, Publication 619.

Pope, Saxon T.

1923   "A Study of Bows and Arrows." *University of California Publications in American Archaeology and Ethnology* 13:9:329–414.

Porter, James B.

1989   "Olmec Colossal Heads as Recarved Thrones: Mutilation, Revolution, and Recarving." *Res* 17/18:22–29.

Price, Barbara J.

1978   "Secondary State Formation: An Explanatory Model." In Cohen and Service 1978.

Proskouriakoff, Tatiana

1950   *A Study of Classic Maya Sculpture.* Washington, D.C.: Carnegie Institution of Washington, Publication 593.

1962   "The Artifacts of Mayapan." In Pollock, Roys, Prouskouriakoff, and Smith 1962.

1963   "Historical Data in the Inscriptions of Yaxchilan." *Estudios de Cultura Maya* 3:149–67.

1964   "Historical Data in the Inscriptions of Yaxchilan (Part II)." *Estudios de Cultura Maya* 4:177–201.

1965   "Sculpture and Major Arts of the Maya Lowlands." In Willey
            1965a.
1970   "On Two Inscriptions at Chichen Itza." In Bullard 1970.
1971   "Classic Art of Central Veracruz." In Ekholm and Bernal
            1971b.
Puleston, Dennis E., and Donald W. Callender, Jr.
1967   "Defensive Earthworks at Tikal." *Expedition* 9(3):40–48.
Purdie, Francis Baillie
1912   "Ancient Temples and Cities of the New World." *Pan American Union Bulletin* 34:480–99.
Purdy, Barbara A.
1977   "Weapons, Strategies, and Tactics of the Europeans and the
            Indians in Sixteenth- and Seventeenth-Century Florida." *Florida Historical Quarterly* 55:259–76.
Quezada Ramírez, Maria Noemí
1972   *Los Matlatzincas: Epoca Prehispánica y Epoca Colonial hasta 1650.* México: Instituto Nacional de Antropología e Historia.
Rands, Robert L.
1952   "Some Evidence of Warfare in Classic Maya Art." Ph.D. diss.,
            Columbia University.
1965   "Jades of the Maya Lowlands." In Willey 1965b.
Rands, Robert L., and Barbara C. Rands
1965   "Pottery Figurines of the Maya Lowlands." In Willey 1965a.
Rattray, Evelyn Childs
1973   "The Teotihuacan Ceramic Chronology Early Tzacualli to
            Early-Tlamimilolpa Phases." Ph.D. diss., University of Missouri, Columbia.
Raudzens, George
1990   "War-Winning Weapons: The Measurement of Technological
            Determinism in Military History." *Journal of Military History* 54:403–33.
Redfield, Robert, and Alfonso Villa Rojas
1934   *Chan Kom: A Maya Village.* Washington, D.C.: Carnegie Institution of Washington, Publication 448.
Redmond, Elsa M.
1983   *A Fuego y Sangre: Early Zapotec Imperialism in the Cuicatlán Cañada, Oaxaca.* Memoirs of the Museum of Anthropology, University of Michigan, Number 16.
Redmond, Elsa M., and Charles S. Spencer
1983   "The Cuicatlán Cañada and the Period II Frontier of the
            Zapotec State." In Flannery and Marcus 1983a.
Relación de Michoacán
1977   *Relación de las ceremonias y ritos y población y gobierno de los indios de la provincia de Michoacán (1541).* Morelia, Michoacán, México: Balsal Editores, S.A.
Reyman, Jonathan E.
1978   "Pochteca Burials at Anasazi Sites?" In Riley and Hedrick 1978.

Rice, Don S., and Prudence M. Rice
1981 "Muralla de León: A Lowland Maya Fortification." *Journal of Field Archaeology* 8:271–88.
Ricketson, Edith Bayles
1937 "Part II: The Artifacts." In Ricketson and Ricketson 1937.
Ricketson, Oliver G., Jr.
1937 "Part I: The Excavations." In Ricketson and Ricketson 1937.
Ricketson, Oliver G., Jr., and Edith Bayles Ricketson
1937 *Uaxactun, Guatemala: Group E—1926–1931.* Washington, D.C.: Carnegie Institution of Washington, Publication 477.
Riley, Carroll L.
1952 "The Blowgun in the New World." *Southwestern Journal of Anthropology* 8:297–319.
Riley, C. L., and B. C. Hedrick
1978 *Across the Chichimec Sea: Papers in Honor of J. Charles Kelley.* Carbondale: Southern Illinois University Press.
Rivera, M., and F. Jiménez
n.d. *Los Mayas del Norte de Yucatán.* Madrid: Sociedad Española de Estudios Mayas y Instituto de Cooperación Iberoaméricana. In press.
Rivet, Paul
1973 *Maya Cities.* London: Elek Books Limited.
Robertson, Donald
1985 "The Cacaxtla Murals." In Benson 1985.
Robertson, Merle Greene
1976 *The Art, Iconography and Dynastic History of Palenque Part III.* Pebble Beach, California: Robert Louis Stevenson School.
1980 *Third Palenque Round Table, 1978, Part 2.* Austin: University of Texas Press.
Robertson, Merle Greene, and Donnan Call Jeffers
1978 *Tercera Mesa Redonda de Palenque.* Vol. IV. Monterey, California: Pre-Columbian Art Research.
Robicsek, Francis
1981 *The Maya Book of the Dead: The Ceramic Codex.* Charlottesville: The University of Virginia Art Museum.
Robles C., Fernando, and Anthony P. Andrews
1986 "A Review and Synthesis of Recent Postclassic Archaeology in Northern Yucatan." In Sabloff and Andrews 1986.
Rodgers, William Ledyard
1939 *Naval Warfare Under Oars, 4th to 16th Centuries: A Study of Strategy, Tactics and Ship Design.* Annapolis: United States Naval Institute.
Rosenau, James N.
1989 "The State in an Era of Cascading Politics: Wavering Concept, Widening Competence, Withering Colossus, or Weathering Change?" In Caporaso 1989.

Rowe, Ann Pollard, Elizabeth P. Benson, and Anne-Louise Schaffer
  1979   *The Junius B. Bird Pre-Columbian Textile Conference*. Washington, D.C.: The Textile Museum and Dumbarton Oaks.
Roys, Ralph L.
  1943   *The Indian Background of Colonial Yucatan*. Washington, D.C.: Carnegie Institution of Washington, Publication 548.
  1965   "Lowland Maya Native Society at Spanish Contact." In Willey 1965*b*.
  1966   "Native Empires in Yucatan: The Maya-Toltec Empire." *Revista Mexicana de Estudios Antropológicos* 20:153–77.
Ruppert, Karl, J. Eric S. Thompson, and Tatiana Proskouriakoff
  1955   *Bonampak, Chiapas, Mexico*. Washington, D.C.: Carnegie Institution of Washington, Publication 602.
Rust, William F., and Robert J. Sharer
  1988   "Olmec Settlement Data from La Venta, Tabasco, Mexico." *Science* 242:102–104.
Ruz Lhuillier, Alberto
  1951   "Chichen-Itza y Palenque, ciudades fortificadas." In Homenaje 1951.
  1979   *Chichén Itzá en la Historia y en el Arte*. México: Editora del Sureste.
Sabloff, Jeremy A.
  1981   *Handbook of Middle American Indians*. Supplement 1, *Archaeology*. Austin: University of Texas Press.
Sabloff, Jeremy A., and E. Wyllys Andrews V
  1986   *Late Lowland Maya Civilization: Classic to Postclassic*. Albuquerque: University of New Mexico Press.
Sabloff, Jeremy A., and William L. Rathje
  1975   "The Rise of a Maya Merchant Class." *Scientific American* 233:4:72–82.
Sáenz, César A.
  1961   "Tres Estelas en Xochicalco." *Revista Mexicana de Estudios Antropológicos* 17:39–65.
  1963   "Exploraciones en la Pirámide de las Serpientes Emplumadas, Xochicalco." *Revista Mexicana de Estudios Antropológicos* 19:7–25.
  1964*a*   "Las Estelas de Xochicalco." *XXXV Congreso International de Americanistas, 1962* 2:69–82.
  1964*b*   *Ultimos Descubrimientos en Xochicalco*. México: Instituto Nacional de Antropología e Historia.
  1967   *Nuevas Exploraciones y Hallazgos en Xochicalco: 1965- 1966*. México: Instituto Nacional de Antropología e Historia.
Sahagún, Bernardino de
  1950–82   *General History of the Things of New Spain: Florentine Codex*. Arthur J. O. Anderson and Charles E. Dibble, trans. 13 vols. Salt Lake City: University of Utah Press.

Sanders, William T.
1970   "The Population of the Teotihuacan Valley, the Basin of Mexico
          and the Central Mexican Symbiotic Region in the Sixteenth
          Century." In Sanders, Kovar, Charlton, and Diehl 1970.
1972   "Population, Agricultural History, and Societal Evolution in Me-
          soamerica." In Spooner 1972.
1974   "Chiefdom to State: Political Evolution at Kaminaljuyu, Guate-
          mala." In Moore 1974.
1978   "Ethnographic Analogy and the Teotihuacan Horizon Style." In
          Pasztory 1978a.
1981   "Ecological Adaptation in the Basin of Mexico: 23,000 B.C. to
          the Present." In Sabloff 1981.
1990   "Ranking and Stratification Among the Ancient Maya: A Per-
          spective from Copan." Public lecture given at Dumbarton Oaks,
          February 6.
Sanders, William T., Anton Kovar, Thomas Charlton, and Richard A. Diehl
1970   *The Natural Environment, Contemporary Occupation and 16th
          Century Population of the Valley. The Teotihuacan Valley Proj-
          ect. Final Report.* Vol. 1. Occasional Papers in Anthropology,
          No. 3. Department of Anthropology, Pennsylvania State Univer-
          sity.
Sanders, William T., and Joseph W. Michels
1977   *Teotihuacan and Kaminaljuyu: A Study in Prehistoric Culture
          Contact.* University Park: Pennsylvania State University Press.
Sanders, William T., and Deborah L. Nichols
1988   "Ecological Theory and Cultural Evolution in the Valley of
          Oaxaca." *Current Anthropology* 29:33–52.
Sanders, William T., Jeffery R. Parsons, and Robert S. Santley
1979   *The Basin of Mexico: Ecological Processes in the Evolution of a
          Civilization.* New York: Academic Press.
Sanders, William T., and Barbara J. Price
1968   *Mesoamerica: The Evolution of a Civilization.* New York: Ran-
          dom House.
Sanders, William T., and Robert S. Santley
1978   "Review of *Monte Albán: Settlement Patterns at the Ancient
          Zapotec Capital* by Richard Blanton." *Science* 202:303–304.
Santley, Robert S.
1984   "Chalcatzingo, the Olmec Heartland, and the Gateway Com-
          munity Hypothesis." *Journal of Anthropological Research* 40:
          603–607.
1989a   "Obsidian Working, Long-Distance Exchange, and the Teoti-
          huacan Presence on the South Gulf Coast." In Diehl and Berlo
          1989.
1989b   "Writing Systems, Political Power, and the Internal Structure of
          Early States in Precolumbian Mesoamerica." In Tkaczuk and
          Vivian 1989.

Santley, Robert S., Janet M. Kerley, and Ronald R. Kneebone
1986   "Obsidian Working, Long-Distance Exchange, and the Politico-
          Economic Organization of Early States in Central Mexico." In
          Isaac 1986.
Santley, Robert S., Thomas W. Killion, and Mark T. Lycett
1986   "On the Maya Collapse." *Journal of Anthropological Research*
          42:123–59.
Santley, Robert S., Ponciano Ortiz Ceballos, Thomas W. Killion, Philip J. Arnold, and Janet M. Kerley
1984   *Final Field Report of the Matacapan Archaeological Project:
          The 1982 Season.* Research Paper Series No. 15. Latin American
          Institute, The University of New Mexico.
Schaedel, Richard P., Jorge E. Hardoy, and Nora Scott Kinzer
1978   *Urbanization in the Americas from its Beginnings to the Present.*
          The Hague: Mouton Publishers.
Schaeffer, Robert K.
1989a   *War in the World-System.* New York: Greenwood Press.
1989b   "Introduction." In Schaeffer 1989a.
Schele, Linda
1976   "Accession Iconography of Chan-Bahlum in the Group of the
          Cross at Palenque." In Robertson 1976.
1986   "The Tlaloc Complex in the Classic Period: War and the Interac-
          tion between Lowland Maya and Teotihuacan." Paper pre-
          sented at the symposium, The New Dynamics, Kimbell Art Mu-
          seum, Fort Worth, Texas.
Schele, Linda, and David Friedel
1990   *A Forest of Kings: The Untold Story of the Ancient Maya.* New
          York: William Morrow and Company, Inc.
Schele, Linda, and Mary Ellen Miller
1986   *The Blood of Kings: Dynasty and Ritual in Maya Art.* New
          York: G. Braziller in association with the Kimbell Art Museum,
          Fort Worth.
Scholes, France V., and Dave Warren
1965   "The Olmec Region at Spanish Contact." In Willey 1965b.
Schortman, Edward M., and Patricia A. Urban
1983   *Quirigua Reports.* Vol. 2. Philadelphia: University Museum
          Monograph 49.
Seabury, Paul, and Angelo Codevilla
1989   *War: Ends and Means.* New York: Basic Books, Inc.
Séjourné, Laurette
1966a   *El lenguaje de las formas en Teotihuacán.* México: n.p.
1966b   *Arquitectura y pintura en Teotihuacán.* México: Siglo Veintiuno.
1966c   *Arqueología de Teotihuacán: la cerámica.* México: Fondo de
          Cultura Económica.
1969   *Teotihuacan: Métropole de l'Amérique.* Paris: François Mas-
          péro.

Sekunda, Nick
  1984   *The Army of Alexander the Great.* London: Osprey Publishing,
              Ltd.
Seler, Eduard
  1888   "Die Ruinen von Xochicalco." *Zeitschrift für Ethnologie* 20:
              94–111. (English translation in *Collected Works*, Vol. 2, Pt. 2,
              No. 2, pp. 80–97.)
  1960–61   *Gesammelte Abhandlungen zur Amerikanischen Sprach-und Al-
              tertumskunde.* 5 vols. Graz: Akademische Druck-u. Verlags-
              anstalt.
Service, Elman R.
  1975   *Origins of the State and Civilization: The Process of Cultural
              Evolution.* New York: W. W. Norton and Company.
  1978   "Classical and Modern Theories of the Origins of Govern-
              ment." In Cohen and Service 1978.
Sharer, Robert J.
  1974   "The Prehistory of the Southeastern Maya Periphery." *Current
              Anthropology* 15:165–76.
  1978*a*   *The Prehistory of Chalchuapa, El Salvador.* 3 vols. Philadel-
              phia: University of Pennsylvania Press.
  1978*b*   "Pottery." In Sharer 1978*a*.
  1978*c*   "Conclusions." In Sharer 1978*a*.
  1978*d*   "Archaeology and History at Quirigua, Guatemala." *Journal of
              Field Archaeology* 5:51–70.
  1989*a*   "Olmec Studies: A Status Report." In Sharer and Grove
              1989.
  1989*b*   "The Olmec and the Southeast Periphery of Mesoamerica." In
              Sharer and Grove 1989.
Sharer, Robert J., and David C. Grove
  1989   *Regional Perspectives on the Olmec.* Cambridge: Cambridge
              University Press.
Sheets, Payson
  1978   "Artifacts." In Sharer 1978*a*.
Shook, Edwin M.
  1946   "Blowguns in Guatemala." *Notes on Middle American Archae-
              ology and Ethnology, Carnegie Institution of Washington* 3:
              67:37–43.
  1952   "The Great Wall of Mayapan." *Current Reports, Carnegie Insti-
              tution of Washington* 1:2:7–35.
Siller, Juan Antonio
  1984   "Presencia de Elementos Architectónicos Teotihuacanoides en
              Occidente: Tingambato, Michoacán." *Cuadernos de Arquitec-
              tura Mesoamérica* 2:60–65.
Sinden, Peter G.
  1979   "Inequality and Political Conflict." *Comparative Studies in Soci-
              ety and History* 2:303–20.

Sivard, Ruth Leger
1986   *World Military and Social Expenditures 1986.* Washington, D.C.: World Priorities Inc.

Sjoberg, Gideon
1960   *The Preindustrial City: Past and Present.* New York: The Free Press.

Smith, A. Ledyard
1950   *Uaxactun, Guatemala: Excavations of 1931–1937.* Washington, D.C.: Carnegie Institution of Washington, Publication 588.
1962   "Residential and Associate Structures at Mayapan." In Pollock, Roys, Prouskouriakoff, and Smith 1962.

Smith, Bradley
1968   *Mexico: A History in Art.* Garden City, New York: Doubleday and Company, Inc.

Smith, C. Earle, Jr.
1983   "The Valleys of Oaxaca, Nochixtlán, and Tehuacán." In Flanner and Marcus 1983*a*.

Smith, Judith E.
1979   "Carbonized Botanical Remains from Quachilco, Cuayucatepec, and La Coyotera." In Drennan 1979*a*.

Smith, Mary Elizabeth
1963   "The Codex Colombino: A Document of the South Coast of Oaxaca." *Tlalocan* 4:276–88.
1966   *The Glosses of Codex Colombino.* México: Sociedad Mexicana de Antropología.

Sotheby's
1987   *Important Pre-Columbian Art,* November. New York: Sotheby-Parke Bernet.

Spence, Michael W.
1967   "The Obsidian Industry of Teotihuacán." *American Antiquity* 32:507–14.
1977   "Teotihuacán y el intercambio de obsidiana en Mesoamérica." *XV Mesa Redonda.* Vol. 2. México: Sociedad Mexicana de Antropología.
1981   "Obsidian Production and the State in Teotihuacan." *American Antiquity* 46:769–88.
1984   "Craft Production and Polity in Early Teotihuacan." In Hirth 1984*b*.
1986   "Locational Analysis of Craft Specialization Areas in Teotihuacan." In Isaac 1986.

Spencer, Charles S.
1979   "Irrigation, Administration, and Society in Formative Tehuacan." In Drennan 1979*a*.
1982   *The Cuicatlán Cañada and Monte Albán: A Study of Primary State Formation.* New York: Academic Press.

Spencer, Charles S., and Elsa M. Redmond
1979   "Formative and Classic Developments in the Cuicatlán Cañada:
          A Preliminary Report." In Drennan 1979*a*.
Spooner, Brian
1972   *Population Growth: Anthropological Implications*. Cambridge:
          MIT Press.
Spores, Ronald
1965   "The Zapotec and Mixtec at Spanish Contact." In Willey 1965*b*.
1967   *The Mixtec Kings and Their People*. Norman: University of
          Oklahoma Press.
1983*a*   "The Origin and Evolution of the Mixtec System of Social Strati-
          fication." In Flannery and Marcus 1983*a*.
1983*b*   "Postclassic Settlement Patterns in the Nochixtlán Valley." In
          Flannery and Marcus 1983*a*.
1983*c*   "Postclassic Mixtec Kingdoms: Ethnohistoric and Archaeologi-
          cal Evidence." In Flannery and Marcus 1983*a*.
1984   *The Mixtecs in Ancient and Modern Times*. Norman: University
          of Oklahoma Press.
1986   *Handbook of Middle American Indians*. Supplement 4, *Ethno-
          history*. Austin: University of Texas Press.
Spores, Ronald, and Kent V. Flannery
1983   "Sixteenth-Century Kinship and Social Organization." In Flan-
          nery and Marcus 1983*a*.
Standley, Paul C.
1961   *Trees and Shrubs of Mexico*. 2 vols. Washington, D.C.: Smithso-
          nian Institution Press.
Stark, Barbara
1981   "The Rise of Sedentary Life." In Sabloff 1981.
Stevenson, William Flack
1897   *Wounds in War: The Mechanics of Their Production and Their
          Treatment*. London: Longmans, Green.
Steward, T. D.
1956   "Skeletal Remains from Xochicalco, Mexico." *Estudios antro-
          pologicos publicados en homenaje al doctor Manuel Gamio*.
          México: Universidad Nacional Autónoma de México.
Stirling, Matthew W.
1943   *Stone Monuments of Southern Mexico*. Bureau of American
          Ethnology, Bulletin 138.
Stocker, Terrance
1974   "Mazapan Figurines from Tula." In Diehl 1974*a*.
1983   "Figurines from Tula, Hidalgo, Mexico." Ph.D. diss., University
          of Illinois.
Stoutamire, James
1974   "Archaeological Survey of the Tula Urban Zone." In Diehl
          1974*a*.
Stresser-Péan, Guy
1971   "Ancient Sources on the Huasteca." In Ekholm and Bernal 1971*b*.

Sugiyama, Saburo
  1989   "Burials Dedicated to the Old Temple of Quetzalcoatl at Teoti-
              huacan, Mexico." *American Antiquity* 54:85–106.

Summa
  1966   *Summa Anthropologica en homenaje a Roberto J. Weitlaner.*
              México: Instituto Nacional de Antropología e Historia.

Taagepera, Rein
  1968   "Growth Curves of Empires." *General Systems* 13:171–75.
  1978a   "Size and Duration of Empires: Systematics of Size." *Social Sci-
              ence Research* 7:108–27.
  1978b   "Size and Duration of Empires: Growth-Decline Curves, 3000
              to 600 B.C." *Social Science Research* 7:180–96.
  1979   "Size and Duration of Empires: Growth-Decline Curves, 600
              B.C. to 600 A.D." *Social Science History* 3:3/4:115–38.

Tainter, Joseph A.
  1988   *The Collapse of Complex Societies.* Cambridge: Cambridge Uni-
              versity Press.

Taube, Karl A.
  1989   "The Maize Tamale in Classic Maya Diet, Epigraphy, and Art."
              American Antiquity 54:31–51.

Tax, Sol
  1952   *Heritage of Conquest: The Ethnology of Middle America.*
              Glencoe, Illinois: The Free Press.

Thomas, David Hurst
  1978   "Arrowheads and Atlatl Darts: How the Stones Got the Shaft."
              American Antiquity 43:461–72.

Thomas, George M., and John W. Meyer
  1984   "The Expansion of the State." *Annual Review of Sociology*
              10:461–82.

Thomas, Prentice M., Jr.
  1981   *Prehistoric Maya Settlement Patterns at Becan, Campeche, Mex-
              ico.* Middle American Research Institute, Publication 45.

Thompson, Edward H.
  1904   *Archaeological Researches in Yucatan: Reports of Explorations
              for the Museum.* Memoirs of the Peabody Museum of American
              Archaeology and Ethnology, Harvard University, Vol. III, No. 1.

Thompson, J. Eric S.
  1930   *Ethnology of the Mayas of Southern and Central British Hondu-
              ras.* Field Museum of Natural History, Publication 274, Anthro-
              pological Series Vol. XVII, No. 2.
  1942   "Representations of Tezcatlipoca at Chichen Itza." *Notes on
              Middle American Archaeology and Ethnology, Carnegie Institu-
              tion of Washington* 1:12:48–50.
  1954   *The Rise and Fall of Maya Civilization.* Norman: University of
              Oklahoma Press.
  1955a   "The Subject Matter of the Murals." In Ruppert, Thompson,
              and Proskouriakoff 1955.

1955b   "Some Ethnological Notes on the Murals." In Ruppert, Thompson, and Proskouriakoff 1955.

1964   "Trade Relations Between the Maya Highlands and Lowlands." *Estudios de Cultura Maya* 4:13–49.

1965   "Archaeological Synthesis of the Southern Maya Lowlands." In Willey 1965a.

1966   "Merchant Gods of Middle America." In Summa 1966.

1970   *Maya History and Religion*. Norman: University of Oklahoma Press.

Thompson, J. Eric S., Harry E. D. Pollock, and Jean Charlot
1932   *A Preliminary Study of the Ruins of Cobá, Quintana Roo, Mexico*. Carnegie Institute of Washington, Publication 424.

Thompson, Philip C.
1982   "Dynastic Marriage and Succession at Tikal." *Estudios de Cultura Maya* 14:261–87.

Thomson, Charlotte W.
1987   "Chalcatzingo Jade and Fine Stone Objects." In Grove 1987a.

Tilly, Charles
1975a   *The Formation of National States in Western Europe*. Princeton: Princeton University Press.

1975b   "Reflections on the History of European State-Making." In Tilly 1975a.

Tkaczuk, Diana Claire, and Brian C. Vivian
1989   *Cultures in Conflict: Current Archaeological Perspectives*. Calgary: The University of Calgary Press.

Tolstoy, Paul
1971   "Utilitarian Artifacts of Central Mexico." In Ekholm and Bernal 1971a.

1989   "Coapexco and Tlatilco: Sites with Olmec Materials in the Basin of Mexico." In Sharer and Grove 1989.

Tourtellot, Gair, and Jeremy A. Sabloff
1972   "Exchange Systems Among the Ancient Maya." *American Antiquity* 37:126–35.

Toy, Sidney
1985   *Castles: Their Construction and History*. New York: Dover Publications, Inc.

Tozzer, Alfred M.
1941   *Landa's Relación de las Cosas de Yucatán*. Papers of the Peabody Museum of Archaeology and Ethnology, Harvard University, Vol. 18.

1957   *Chichen Itza and Its Cenote of Sacrifice: A Comparative Study of Contemporaneous Maya and Toltec*. Memoirs of the Peabody Museum of Archaeology and Ethnology, Vols. 11 and 12.

Trik, Helen, and Michael E. Kampen
1983   *The Graffiti of Tikal*. Philadelphia: University Museum Monograph 57.

Trombold, Charles D.
1991   *Ancient Road Networks and Settlement Hierarchies in the New World*. Cambridge: Cambridge University Press.

Tuggle, H. David
1968   "The Columns of El Tajín, Veracruz, Mexico." *Ethnos* 33:40–70.

Turner, B. L., II
1978   "Ancient Agricultural Land Use in the Central Maya Lowlands." In Harrison and Turner 1978.

Turney-High, Harry Holbert
1971   *Primitive War: Its Practice and Concepts*. Columbia: University of South Carolina Press.

1981   *The Military: The Theory of Land Warfare as Behavioral Science*. West Hanover, Massachusetts: The Christopher Publishing House.

United States Army
1971a   *Foot Marches. Field Manual No. 21–18*. Washington, D.C.: Department of the Army.

1971b   *The Infantry Battalions. Field Manual No. 7–20*. Washington, D.C.: Department of the Army.

1985   *Nutrition Allowances, Standards, and Education*. Army Regulation 40–25. Washington, D.C.: U.S. Government Printing Office.

Vaillant, George C.
1930   *Excavations at Zacatenco*. Anthropology Papers of the American Museum of Natural History, Vol. 32, Part 1.

1931   *Excavations at Ticoman*. Anthropology Papers of the American Museum of Natural History, Vol. 32, Part 2.

1935   *Excavations at El Arbolillo*. Anthropology Papers of the American Museum of Natural History, Vol. 35, Part 2.

1966   *Aztecs of Mexico: Origin, Rise, and Fall of the Aztec Nation*. Baltimore, Maryland: Penguin Books.

Vaillant, Suzannah B., and George C. Vaillant
1934   *Excavations at Gualupita*. Anthropology Papers of the American Museum of Natural History, Vol. 35, Part 1.

Valenzuela, Juan
1945a   "La segunda temporada de exploraciones en la región de los Tuxtlas, Estado de Veracruz." *Anales del Museo Nacional de Arqueología, Historia y Etnografía* 1:81–94.

1945b   "Las exploraciones efectuadas en los Tuxtlas, Veracruz." *Anales del Museo Nacional de Arqueología, Historia y Etnografía* 3:83–107.

Vargas Rea, Luis
1944–46   *Papeles de Nueva España colecionados por Francisco del Paso y Troncoso*. Vol. 7. México.

Vayrynen, Raimo
1989   "Economic Fluctuations, Military Expenditures, and Warfare in International Relations." In Schaeffer 1989a.

Vencl, Sl.
    1984   "War and Warfare in Archaeology." *Journal of Anthropological Archaeology* 3:116–32.
Villagutierre Soto-Mayor, Juan de
    1983   *History of the Conquest of the Province of the Itza*. Robert D. Woods, trans. Culver City, California: Labyrinthos.
Vivó Escoto, Jorge A.
    1964   "Weather and Climate of Mexico and Central America." In West 1964.
Vogt, Evon Z., and Richard M. Leventhal
    1983   *Prehistoric Settlement Patterns: Essays in Honor of Gordon R. Willey*. Albuquerque: University of New Mexico Press and Peabody Museum of Archaeology and Ethnology.
Von Euw, Eric
    1977   *Corpus of Maya Hieroglyphic Inscriptions*. Vol. 4, Part 1, *Itzimte, Pixoy, Tzum*. Cambridge, Massachusetts: Peabody Museum of Archaeology and Ethnology.
    1978   *Corpus of Maya Hieroglyphic Inscriptions*. Vol. 5, Part 1, *Xultun*. Cambridge, Massachusetts: Peabody Museum of Archaeology and Ethnology.
Von Euw, Eric, and Ian Graham
    1984   *Corpus of Maya Hieroglyphic Inscriptions*. Vol. 5, Part 2, *Xultun, La Honradez, Uaxactun*. Cambridge, Massachusetts: Peabody Museum of Archaeology and Ethnology.
Voorhies, Barbara
    1989   *Ancient Trade and Tribute: Economies of the Soconusco Region of Mesoamerica*. Salt Lake City: University of Utah Press.
Wallace, Dwight T., and Robert M. Carmack
    1977   *Archaeology and Ethnohistory of the Central Quiche*. Institute for Mesoamerican Studies, Publication No. 1.
Wallerstein, Immanuel
    1974   *The Modern World System I: Capitalist Agriculture and the Origins of the European World-Economy in the Sixteenth Century*. New York: Academic Press.
    1980   "Imperialism and Development." In Bergesen 1980a.
    1984   *The Politics of the World-Economy: The States, the Movements, and the Civilizations*. Cambridge: Cambridge University Press.
Walling, Stanley L., Jr.
    1982   "A Stylistic Analysis of the Cacaxtla Murals." *Estudios de Cultura Maya* 14:205–19.
Warren, J. Benedict
    1985   *The Conquest of Michoacán: The Spanish Domination of the Tarascan Kingdom in Western Mexico, 1521–1530*. Norman: University of Oklahoma Press.
Wauchope, Robert
    1948   *Excavations at Zacualpa, Guatemala*. Middle American Research Institute, Publication 14.

1975   *Zacualpa, El Quiche, Guatemala: An Ancient Provincial Center of the Highland Maya.* Middle American Research Institute, Publication 39.

Webster, David L.
1975   "The Fortifications of Becan, Campeche, Mexico." In Andrews, Stuart, Rovner, Adams, Simmons, Wing, Andrews, Andrews, Stewart, and Ball 1975.

1976a   *Defensive Earthworks at Becan, Campeche, Mexico: Implications for Maya Warfare.* Middle American Research Institute, Publication 41.

1976b   "Lowland Maya Fortifications." *Proceedings of the American Philosophical Society* 120:5:361–71.

1976c   "Warfare and the Evolution of the State: A Perspective from the Maya Lowlands." University of Northern Colorado, Museum of Anthropology, Miscellaneous Series, No. 19.

1976d   "On Theocracies." *American Anthropologist* 78:812–28.

1977   "Warfare and the Evolution of Maya Civilization." In Adams 1977a.

1978   "Three Walled Sites of the Northern Maya Lowlands." *Journal of Field Archaeology* 5:375–90.

1979   *Cuca, Chacchob, Dzonot Aké: Three Walled Northern Maya Centers.* Occasional Papers in Anthropology, No. 11. Department of Anthropology, The Pennsylvania State University.

Weiant, C. W.
1943   *An Introduction to the Ceramics of Tres Zapotes, Veracruz, Mexico.* Bureau of American Ethnology, Bulletin 139.

Weigand, Phil C.
1978   "The Prehistory of the State of Zacatecas: An Interpretation (Part I)." *Anthropology* 2:67–87.

1982   "Mining and Mineral Trade in Prehispanic Zacatecas." *Anthropology* 6:87–134.

Weigand, Phil C., Garman Harbottle, and Edward V. Sayre
1977   "Turquoise Sources and Source Analysis: Mesoamerica and the Southwestestern U.S.A." In Earle and Ericson 1977.

Weller, Jac
1966   *Weapons and Tactics: Hastings to Berlin.* New York: St. Martin's Press.

West, Robert C.
1964   *Handbook of Middle American Indians.* Vol. 1, *Natural Environment and Early Cultures.* Austin: University of Texas Press.

West, Robert C., and John P. Augelli
1976   *Middle America: Its Lands and Peoples.* Englewood Cliffs, New Jersey: Prentice-Hall, Inc.

Whalen, Michael E.
1988   "Small Community Organization During the Late Formative Period in Oaxaca, Mexico." *Journal of Field Archaeology* 15:291–306.

Whitecotton, Joseph W.
    1977   *The Zapotecs: Princes, Priests, and Peasants.* Norman: University of Oklahoma Press.
    1990   *Zapotec Elite Ethnohistory: Pictorial Genealogies from Eastern Oaxaca.* Vanderbilt University Publications in Anthropology, No. 39.

Whittaker, Gordon
    1980   "The Hieroglyphics of Monte Alban." Ph.D. diss., Yale University.
    1983   "The Structure of the Zapotec Calendar." In Aveni and Brotherston 1983.

Wilkinson, Richard G., and Richard J. Norelli
    1981   "A Biocultural Analysis of Social Organization at Monte Albán." *American Antiquity* 46:743–58.

Willard, T. A.
    1926   *The City of the Sacred Well.* London: William Heinemann, Ltd.

Willey, Gordon R.
    1965a   *Handbook of Middle American Indians.* Vol. 2, *Archaeology of Southern Mesoamerica*, Part One. Austin: University of Texas Press.
    1965b   *Handbook of Middle American Indians.* Vol. 3, *Archaeology of Southern Mesoamerica*, Part Two. Austin: University of Texas Press.
    1972   *The Artifacts of Altar de Sacrificios.* Papers of the Peabody Museum of Archaeology and Ethnology, Harvard University, Vol. 64, No. 1.
    1977   "The Rise of Maya Civilization: A Summary View." In Adams 1977a.
    1978   *Excavations at Seibal, Department of Peten, Guatemala. Artifacts.* Memoirs of the Peabody Museum of Archaeology and Ethnology, Harvard University, Vol. 14, No. 1.
    1979   "The Concept of the 'Disembedded Capital' in Comparative Perspective." *Journal of Anthropological Research* 35:123–37.
    1984   "Chichén Itzá and Maya Archaeology." In Coggins and Shane 1984.
    1985   "The Early Classic Period in the Maya Lowlands: An Overview." In Willey and Mathews 1985.
    1986   "The Postclassic of the Maya Lowlands: A Preliminary Overview." In Sabloff and Andrews 1986.

Willey, Gordon R., and William R. Bullard, Jr.
    1965   "Prehistoric Settlement Patterns in the Maya Lowlands." In Willey 1965a.

Willey, Gordon R., William R. Bullard, Jr., John B. Glass, and James C. Gifford
    1965   *Prehistoric Maya Settlements in the Belize Valley.* Papers of the Peabody Museum of Archaeology and Ethnology, Harvard University, Vol. 54.

Willey, Gordon R., William R. Bullard, Jr., John B. Glass, and Frank P. Saul
    1972   *The Human Skeletal Remains of Altar de Sacrificios: An Osteo-biographic Analysis*. Papers of the Peabody Museum of Archaeology and Ethnology, Harvard University, Vol. 63, No. 2.

Willey, Gordon R., and Peter Mathews
    1985   *A Consideration of the Early Classic Period in the Maya Lowlands*. Institute for Mesoamerican Studies, Publication 10.

Willey, Gordon R., and A. Ledyard Smith
    1969   *The Ruins of Altar de Sacrificios, Department of Peten, Guatemala: An Introduction*. Papers of the Peabody Museum of Archaeology and Ethnology, Harvard University, Vol. 62, No. 1.

Willey, Gordon R., A. Ledyard Smith, Gair Tourtellot III, and Ian Graham
    1975   *Excavations at Seibal, Department of Peten, Guatemala. Introduction: The Site and Its Settling*. Memoirs of the Peabody Museum of Archaeology and Ethnology, Harvard University, Vol. 13, No. 1.

Williams, Barbara J.
    1989   "Contact Period Rural Overpopulation in the Basin of Mexico: Carrying-Capacity Models Tested with Documentary Data." *American Antiquity* 54:715–32.

Wilson, Thomas H.
    1976   "The Architecture, Chronology and History of Chichen Itza, Yucatan." Ph.D. diss., University of California, Berkeley.

Winning, Hasso von
    1974*a*   *The Shaft Tomb Figures of West Mexico*. Los Angeles: Southwest Museum Papers, No. 24.
    1974*b*   "The Tumpline in Prehispanic Figures." *The Masterkey* 48: 109–14.
    1975   "A Victim of the Planet Venus?" *The Masterkey* 49:124–29.
    1980   "Ritual Cloth and Teotihuacan Warriors." *The Masterkey* 54: 17–23.

Winter, Marcus C.
    1977   "El impacto Teotihuacano y procesos de cambio en Oaxaca." *XV Mesa Redonda*. Vol. 2. México: Sociedad Mexicana de Antropología.

Wiseman, Frederick Matthew
    1978   "Agricultural and Historical Ecology of the Lake Region of Peten, Guatemala." Ph.D. diss., University of Arizona.

Wolf, Eric R.
    1976   *The Valley of Mexico*. Albuquerque: University of New Mexico Press.
    1982   *Europe and the People Without History*. Berkeley and Los Angeles: University of California Press.

Wren, Linnea H.
    1984   "Chichén Itzá: The Site and Its People." In Coggins and Shane 1984.

Wright, Henry T.
    1977   "Recent Research on the Origin of the State." *Annual Review of Anthropology* 6:379–97.
Yadin, Yigael
    1963   *The Art of Warfare in Biblical Lands in the Light of Archaeological Study.* 2 vols. New York: McGraw-Hill Book Company, Inc.
Yoffee, Norman
    1988   "Orienting Collapse." In Yoffee and Cowgill 1988.
Yoffee, Norman, and George L. Cowgill
    1988   *The Collapse of Ancient States and Civilizations.* Tucson: University of Arizona Press.
Zambrano, José Antonio
    1985   *La Zona Arqueológica de Tula.* México: Editorial del Magisterio "Benito Juárez."
Zeitlin, Robert N.
    1990   "The Isthmus and the Valley of Oaxaca: Questions about Zapotec Imperialism in Formative Period Mesoamerica." *American Antiquity* 55:250–61.

Index

Abaj Takalik, 27
Acamapichtli, 136
Acambaro, 254 n. 103
Acatlan, 252 n. 63
Acatucha, 209 n. 86
Accession scenes, 238 n. 104; Chichen
    Itza, 125, 238–41 n. 105; Tollan, 111
Achij, 259 n. 178
Acuña, René, 253 n. 74
Adams, Richard E. W., 222 n. 44
Adelhofer, Otto, 235 n. 76
Administered trade, 204 n. 38
Agricultural goods, 23, 59, 195 n. 60
Agricultural rites, 184 n. 29
Agricultural seasons, 19–21; Maya, 74,
    207 n. 61; Teotihuacan, 53
Agricultural surplus, 13, 190 n. 98
Agricultural tools, 184 n. 29
Aguas Calientes, 217–18 n. 27
Aguateca, 214 n. 7, 215–16 n. 17,
    216 nn. 18, 22, 216–17 n. 24; influ-
    ence on Cacaxtla, 224 n. 70
Ah Canul, 256 n. 134
Ah Xupan, 157
Ahuitzotl, 247 n. 4
Ajusco Mountains, 227 n. 100
Alahuiztlan, 250 n. 35
Alliances, 150, 252 n. 61
Altar 1 (Ucanal), 214 n. 7
Altar 3 (Ucanal), 214 n. 7
Altar 5 (Tikal), 218–19 n. 30
Altar 8 (Tikal), 214 n. 7
Altar 9 (Tikal), 214 n. 7

Altar 10 (Tikal), 214 n. 7
Altar de Sacrificios, 191 n. 7, 219–
    20 n. 35; armor, 126; ceramics,
    215 nn. 13, 15, 215–16 n. 17, 216–
    17 n. 24, 217–18 n. 27; slingstones,
    218–19 n. 30
Altars, 189 n. 85, 232 n. 37; depicting rul-
    ers, 14; destruction 183 n. 20
Altun Ha, 210 n. 102, 221–22 n. 37; influ-
    ence on Cacaxtla, 224 n. 70
Amatzinac region, 55
Amatzinac River Valley, 54
American Museum of Natural History,
    189–90 n. 89
American Southwest, 115, 188 n. 80,
    231 n. 26, 232 n. 44, 234 n. 64
Amethyst, 116
Amula, 254 n. 98
Anachronisms, 122–23
Anasazis, 232 n. 44
Ancestor worship, 64, 232 n. 37
Andrews, Anthony P., 255 n. 117
Andrews, E. Wyllys, 238 n. 102
Andrews, E. Wyllys V, 214 n. 3,
    236 n. 88, 238 n. 97
Andrews, E. Wyllys IV, 214 n. 3
Angers, château of, 32
Anglo-Saxon, 259 n. 4
Apartment compounds, 85, 198 n. 30,
    201 n. 94; fortified, 57; origins, 45
Apizaco, 54
Aristocratic societies, 51–53, 81, 88–90,
    98, 201 n. 97, 214 n. 7, 232 n. 37;

313

Designer: U.C. Press Staff
Compositor: Huron Valley Graphics
Text: 10/13 Sabon
Display: Sabon
Printer: Braun-Brumfield, Inc.
Binder: Braun-Brumfield, Inc.